Critical Service-Learning as Revolutionary Pedagogy

A Project of Student Agency in Action

Dedication of
LEF - Constitution: UN - Human Rights
include
Research Laboratory - Demonstration school
Ginsts quote.
- Lab, incubator school
workshop for the pursuit of knowledge! - Demo Ed - portion of
ED SJ & DE (Penny)
PEOP - Parents United
Demo Ed "Centurium Institute - etc
Yacovati

A volume In

Critical Constructions: Studies on Education and Society

Series Editor:

Curry Stephenson Malott, *Queens College/CUNY*

Critical Constructions: Studies on Education and Society

Curry Stephenson Malott, Series Editor

Parental Choice? (2010)
by P. L. Thomas

Critical Pedagogy in the Twenty-First Century: A New Generation of Scholars (2010)
edited by Curry Stephenson Malott and Bradley Porfilio

Critical Service-Learning as Revolutionary Pedagogy: A Project of Student Agency in Action (2011)
edited by Brad J. Porfilio and Heather Hickman

Critical Service-Learning as Revolutionary Pedagogy

A Project of Student Agency in Action

edited by

Brad J. Porfilio and Heather Hickman
Lewis University in Romeoville, IL

Information Age Publishing, Inc.
Charlotte, North Carolina • www.infoagepub.com

Library of Congress Cataloging-in-Publication Data

Critical service-learning as revolutionary pedagogy : a project of student agency in action / edited by Brad J. Porfilio and Heather Hickman.
p. cm. -- (Critical constructions: studies on education and society)
Includes bibliographical references.
ISBN 978-1-61735-432-8 (pbk.) -- ISBN 978-1-61735-433-5 (hardcover) -- ISBN 978-1-61735-434-2 (e-book)
1. Service learning. 2. Teachers--Training of. 3. Critical pedagogy. I. Porfilio, Bradley J. II. Hickman, Heather.
LC220.5.C755 2011
370.11'5--dc22
2011010597

Printed in the United States of America

DEDICATION

*We dedicate this volume to Adam Renner who passed away suddenly in late 2010. Adam was a key contributor to this volume and was an influential figure in the field of critical service-learning. He was an outstanding educator, a concerned citizen, musician, and a kind, honest man. An article in Substance News, for which Adam wrote, remarked that "his courage had taken remarkable forms—from being willing to sacrifice to help others, to always learning, and altering his views, on the path to discover what is true in order to make the world a little better. What could be a more powerful legacy?" (Gibson & Goslee, 2010).**

Adam left positive marks upon many, and we are honored to share his work in this volume and dedicate it to his legacy.

*Gibson, R., & Goslee, A., (2010, December 24). Adam Renner, of Rouge Forum and Substance, dies at the age of 40. *Substance News*. Retrieved from http://www.substancenews.net/articles.php?page=1862

CONTENTS

INTRODUCTION

Brad J. Porfilio and Heather Hickman

As corporate imperatives, ideologies, and practices have come to structure social relationships across the globe over the past decade, there has been increasing inequality, militarization, and human suffering in the "First World" and so-called "Third World" regions. The ruling elite's quest to consolidate its power, control labor power, and garner natural resources has resulted in the number of people undernourished in the world to cross "the one billion mark. Two billion people—one third of the world's population live on no more than a few dollars a day. A similar number have no access to proper sanitation or clean water" (Hearse, 2009, p. 19). The U.S.'s imperial armed forces' occupation of Iraq and their invasion of Afghanistan have led to over 1 million Iraqi's killed, ecological devastation, and thousands of U.S.'s coalition forces and Afghanistan soldiers killed or injured (http://www.justforeignpolicy.org/iraq). In First World regions, deindustrialization, the globalization of capital, the credit crisis, and the shrinking welfare state have collectively fuelled massive unemployment, underemployment, poverty, and homelessness. To take one example, more and more families with children in the U.S. are living out of their vehicles, in makeshift housing such as tents, boxes, caves, and boxcars, or are moving in and out of homeless shelters (National Coalition for the Homeless, 2008). The impact of neoliberal globalization on youth becomes even more telling when currently 1 in 50 U.S. children are homeless; about half of all school age children in the U.S who are "experiencing homelessness have problems with anxiety and depression, and 20% of homeless preschoolers have emotional problems that require professional care" (National Center on Family Homelessness, 2009).

The ability to teach students at all levels about how the social and economic structures across the globe are linked to the social conditions listed above as well as to other unjust institutional formations, such as racism, sexism, and homophobia has unfortunately been impeded by the corporate hijacking of schooling. The most blatant example of corporate and political leaders taking over schools to profit off of youths' bodies and minds and to block teachers from educating their students about the systemic nature of injustice in their schools, communities, and in the wider society exists in the United States. For instance, many urban schools across the United States, plagued by the state contracting its economic support of education, are unsafe, unsanitary, dilapidated, racially segregated and overcrowded institutions, where ill-equipped educators implement "drill and kill" methods of instruction. Urban schoolteachers often make students remain silent and passive in their classrooms, in the hope that they pass a battery of corporately-generated high-stakes examinations, forms of assessment that tie students' test scores to the amount of funding schools receive from the state and that determine whether schools are taken over by the state or by corporate entities. Moreover, these exams impact whether teachers and administrators lose their jobs or endure other sanctions, such as being ostracized by parents or other community members for not performing as well as "competing" (often well-funded and Whitewashed) academic institutions.

Despite the difficulty of teaching for personal and social transformation amid most educational contexts, there have been some scholar-practitioners over the past decade who have been able to implement critical service-learning projects inside of schools and within their surrounding communities to guide students to reflect upon the forces and structures responsible for injustice, to work collectively with disaffected communities to implement policies and practices to ameliorate suffering, and to teach others about how militarism, unemployment, homelessness, child-labor, racism, and sexism are tied to neoliberal globalization. Unlike traditional service-learning, which often promotes charity as a solution to social problems, establishes a hierarchy between academic communities and minoritized contexts, and is "deemed paternalistic" by some communities, (Mitchell, 2008, p. 51), critical service-learning is a political project, embedded with a social-justice orientation with a commitment to guiding students to develop the skills, ideas, and attributes necessary to foster equity and freedom in K–12 schools and other contexts (Mitchell, 2007). Therefore, if implemented correctly, critical service-learning is a revolutionary pedagogy, as it instills in students a sense of "freedom." That is, students develop the critical awareness in relation to what gives rise to the dark social realities of the present as well as gain the desire to remake the social world for the purposes of improving the lives of all people and to eliminate environmental derogation (Freire, 2005). For instance, teacher educators have documented how this form of pedagogy has pushed pre-service teachers to go beyond doing simple volunteer work and meeting school course requirements; they illustrate how service-learning can be transcendent when future teachers are asked to question the distribution of power in society as well as asked to reflect on "Why are conditions like this in the first place?" rather than "How can we help these people?" (Mitchell, 2007). Critical service-learning projects also ask in-service and preservice teachers to examine what gives rise to social inequalities and to analyze the persistence of "systemic barriers that thwart the achievement of students coming from marginalized backgrounds" (Brathwaite & Porfilio, 2004).They also attempt to forge authentic relationships between higher education institutions and the community served (Mitchell, 2007; Swaminathan, 2007; Wade, 2007).

Recent literature shows that there is much critical service-learning occurring in undergraduate programs (Daigre, 2000; Masucci & Renner, 2000; Mitchell, 2007). Daigre's work demonstrates an undergraduate critical service-learning experience at the University of Minnesota driven by the work of Freire and Giroux. Using their work, Daigre (2000) suggests that "by broadening our notion of education to include the production of subjectivities in public spheres outside of schooling," we can "develop a political and pedagogical discourse" that "extend[s] the imperatives of democracy in those public and private institutions that shape the quality of human life" (¶ 7). In this program students are challenged to first become critical students then become critical citizens both teaching and learning from their experience in local public schools. Similarly, Mitchell's (2007) work examines an extended program at the University of Massachusetts Amherst called the Citizen Scholars Program. This program is dedicated to attending to social change and challenging the distribution of power (p. 103). Like the example that Daigre provides, Mitchell's example demonstrates a clear classroom component that uses course readings to build knowledge of social justice. The work of Masucci and Renner (2000) is an account of their experience with critical service-learning in a graduate seminar at the University of Tennessee. Like the previous examples, the authors discuss the grounding of the work in the literature of social justice and the notion that "if we are to make a difference in the lives of the marginalized ... then we need to take their lives seriously and accept their agency" (¶ 50).

Each of the above examples demonstrates the benefit of critical service-learning on both the student and the community. Yet, examples of this work being done at the K–12 level are limited. Service-learning was an educational reform in the early 1990s (Hart, 2006) and examples in high schools can be found as far back as 1996 in the work of Wade and Saxe who discuss community service-learning in the K–12 social studies context. Terry (2006) takes a broader look at students' involvement and learning in service-learning activities. These studies show the evolution of service-learning in K–12 classrooms, but it is not until the work of Hart (2006) that critical service-learning is discussed in the K–12 environment.

Hart (2006) suggests that critical service-learning is a vehicle to "reverse the declining trends in civic engagement and narrow the inequality in academic achievement for marginalized student populations" (p. 17). As schools are challenged with educating students for democratic living, scholars debate what skills are needed to meet that challenge. Synthesizing the work of Dewey, Goodman, and others, he proposes that students need to have "responsibility for, participation in, and concern about society" (p. 19). Service-learning, however, does not achieve this, and in fact can become repressive rather than libratory. Instead, that work must be made critical by addressing the "larger social, economic and political factors" needed for social change rather than social service (p. 22). Hart shares the example of a seventh grade class dealing with issues of water quality in their community. This project demonstrates that critical service-learning is what Hart calls "us doing for us" rather than the "fortunate doing for the less fortunate" or "us doing for them" (p. 27). In another example, eighth grade students recognized that a cemetery for African American Civil War soldiers was in serious disrepair in comparison to a cemetery for white Civil War soldiers. From this critical consciousness, students restored the cemetery and developed a curriculum for younger students about the experience and histories of the soldiers in that cemetery. This work demonstrates the fusion of service-learning with a critical pedagogy.

Although there have been several scholarly texts produced on the topic of critical service-learning over the past several years (e.g., Butin, 2005; Calderón, 2007; O'Grady, 2000; Purmensky, 2009; Rhoads & Howard, 1999; Stoecker & Tyron, 2009), the academic literature is centered on projects conducted in Western contexts and in university settings. The literature also does not account for how neoliberal policies and practices have impacted educators' abilities to implement their political projects or document the challenges they face from students, administrators, or community members during the scope of the initiatives. Finally, scholars also pay little attention to whether their participants come to recognize how the "experiences, problems, languages, and histories that communities rely upon" work collectively to "construct a narrative of collective identity and possible transformation" (Johnson-Goodstar, Trinidate, & Tecle,

2010). The contributors in this volume will enrich the academic literature on critical service-learning in several important ways. First, several contributors will document the work of critical scholar-practitioners who have implemented critical service-learning projects in international contexts. Second, several contributors will highlight the transformative work implemented by schoolteachers in K-16. Third, the contributors will provide a critical analysis of how the larger power structures have generated specific social problems within the contexts of their given learning initiatives. Not only is this analysis necessary to help teachers, scholars, administrators, and citizens make sense of the social, political, and historical forces that perpetuate institutional forms of injustice against most global citizens, but it ensures that they recognize what accounts for specific social actors accruing unearned privileges inside and outside of their own lived worlds. Fourth, they will highlight how the neoliberal agenda has impacted life within their learning communities and how they were able to find fissures amid the status quo to implement and sustain their political projects. Finally, they will document how students' newfound understanding of social stratification and oppression led them to become to become agents of change in their schools and in their communities. Students will be portrayed as critical agents who hold the insight to engage in cultural work with their teachers, community groups, and other activists, where they conduct research projects to understand the interworking of their world, advocate for the implementation of policies, practices and initiatives to eliminate injustice, and teach others about what they have learned and why they have become civically engaged citizens.

Part I of this volume promotes sustainable learning that is different from traditional service-learning pedagogies or charity work, which swoops in and out without any learning occurring or sustainable change in how students view the nature of social stratification. The chapters here discuss challenging unjust policies and practices and asymmetrical relations of power and define how service is conceptualized among participants in critical service-learning projects. In the first chapter of this section, "Power and Service-Learning: Salience, Place and Practice," Clark and Nugent challenge the idea that service-learning has been opposed to critical approaches to education. In the first part of the chapter, the authors examine the extant service-learning literature for the purpose of illustrating that service-learning has never been disconnected from the world of critical theory. Indeed, critical scholars, such as Freire, McLaren, hooks, Shore, and Kinchloe, have impacted how some scholars and practitioners view the purpose of service-learning, how they view their relationships with students and participants, and how they engage with the Other to promote social transformation inside and outside of service-learning projects. Unfortunately, many burgeoning service-learning scholars are not aware of this connection because service-learning scholars have felt compelled to keep their connection to critical theory hidden. They generally fear reprisals from politicians, administrators and colleagues who oppose educational initiatives that might have "socialist" or any "political" overtones. Next, the authors pinpoint how the work of critical theory can be used to examine how power infuses the critical service-learning experience. Through their analysis of critical theoretical scholarship, they illustrate how six guiding principles have the power to eliminate social inequalities during the service-learning process as well as to position service-learning participants to recognize the urgency to challenge the status quo inside and outside of service-learning contexts. The authors conclude their chapter by illustrating how the six principals are put in action amid two underinvested high school learning communities, which are located in Chicago, Illinois and Los Angeles, California.

In the second chapter in this section, "Distant or Direct: Participant's Interactions With Service Recipients While Completing Ontario's Community Involvement Requirement," Schwarz provides a critical examination of Ontario, Canada's secondary schools' service-learning initiatives. Unlike most schools in the United States, students across the provenance of Ontario "must complete 40 hours of community involvement in order to graduate." Through quantitative surveys and qualitative focus groups, she found that her high income participants "spoke about overcoming stereotypes, reflecting on their own circumstances, and becoming 'aware' of social problems to varying extents," whereas their low-income counterparts "expressed having been already-prepared to encounter social problems through their own lived experiences." However, since secondary schools in Canada are neither required to have students be directly connected with participants during their mandated hours nor nudged to link service-learning to teaching students about the forces generating power dynamics in schools and in society, most of her participants did not have a deep understanding "of other people or wider social problems." The author concludes the chapter by suggesting how critical service-learning principles can be employed to strengthen "Ontario's community involvement requirement," making it a transformative rather than a mechanical educational practice.

In the third chapter in this section, "Critical Service-Learning and the Black Freedom Movement," Hayes pinpoints how several civic engagement activities, which have been historically generated by African American citizens in the United States, are exemplary examples of service-learning being grounded in the movement to radically transform schools and the wider society. In the first part of the chapter, the author illuminates how The Highlander Folk School, the Citizenship Schools of the Southern

Christian Leadership Conference (SCLC), and the Freedom Schools of the Student Nonviolent Coordinating Committee (SNCC), mobilized the Black community in the U.S. in their the ongoing pursuit to promote equity and social justice. In the final part of the chapter, Hayes connects us with the contemporary social context. Not only does she capture the salience of engaging disaffected, criminalized, and impoverished youth with the cultural work of the Black Freedom Movement, but she also argues, convincingly, that critical service-learning shows minoritized youth the value of engaging indigenous knowledge in the struggle to improve the conditions of their schools, communities, and other social contexts.

In the next chapter of this section, "Cognitive Dissonance in International Service-Learning: Possibilities and Challenges for Service-Learning Pedagogy," Doerr provides some practical elements involved in critical international service-learning through "a literature review of critical service-learning theory, critical educational theory," and her own reflexive narrative of a coordinator of a international service-learning program, Alternative Breaks, which is housed at the University of Maryland. Specifically, she illustrates how cogitative dissonance holds the power to help critical service-learning educators address some key unanswered questions: "Should we serve internationally when there are so many domestic communities that could benefit from this work? Can truly reciprocal and equitable relationships realistically be forged between universities and communities?" However, she warns us not to view her critical-learning initiatives in Guatemala or in Haiti, or for that matter, other critical scholars' pedagogical initiatives, as pedagogical blueprints that will necessarily provide participants' an ecumenical understanding of the world, eliminate social inequalities during the service-learning process, or lead participants to build collective movements to confront injustice. Rather, they should be used as entry-points to usher "social justice and advocacy" within international service-learning settings.

In the fifth chapter in this session, "To Build a Sustainable International Service-Learning Partnership: Pushing Service Learning the Beyond the Boundaries Toward a Revolutionary Project of Community and Consciousness in Jamaica," Renner traces the development of a critical service-learning project, which has, for the past 12 years, involved students, educators, and community members from the United States and similar constituents from Montego Bay, Jamaica. Through the participants' narratives and the history of the partnership, the author captures how this initiative, gradually, wrought "more criticality, more community, more consciousness." Although Renner cautions us not to view this sustained initiative "as a one-size fits all" approach to engaging in sustained international, critical-service projects, he recognizes the partnership forged in Jamaica should help other critical educators sustain similar initiatives as well as push them to guide their students to become insurgent educators who are capable of crossing "disciplined boundaries of service learning in order to work against neoliberal and alienating trends in schooling." The author concludes the chapter with conversations surrounding the revolutionary potential of sustaining critical service-learning projects in international and domestic contexts and the future of the Jamaican critical service-learning initiative.

In the sixth chapter of this section, "Service-Learning, Liberal Education, and the Public Schools," Mulcahy, Doromal, Journet, and Mulcahy set out to make the connection between critical service-learning and liberal education. To substantiate their contention, they, first, highlight two critical service-learning projects—one taking place in Timber Creek High School in Orlando, Florida and the other occurring in Hartford Magnet Middle School in Hartford, Connecticut. They unveil how educators and administrators in these settings are guiding students to learn the "importance of becoming both critically minded and civically engaged, how to oppose injustices, and how to communicate their thoughts and ideas to people in power." Next, the authors highlight several key texts and writings that have historically helped educators conceptualize how to challenge "the status quo whether in political ideology or educational structures and philosophies." They also use the above writings and texts to connect critical service-learning to fostering a "good education" in today's era of corporate accountability and standardization. The authors conclude the chapter by capturing how critical service-learning can resolve the tension of giving students practical skills and the ability to think critically about knowledge and power, self and Other and the functions of schooling. Educators can make this happen by ensuring action is a "duty vital to everyday living and personal fulfillment," while simultaneously showing "respect for societal needs and the autonomy and experience of the individual student."

In the final essay in this section, "Education, Critical Service-Learning, and Social Justice: The Australian Experience of Doing Thick Democracy in the Classroom," Zyngier details how neoliberal policies and practices are responsible for an "increase in economic and social divisions in and between schools in Australia." The growing lack of government support of public schooling in Australia, along with corporately-produced examinations and assessments, and restructuring schools through market principals, has lead to the creation of underfunded, test-polluted "sink schools" for impoverished and working-class students. To overcome the debilitating nature of neoliberal schooling in Australia, Zyngier highlights how a critical service-learning initiative, The ruMAD Program, is doing "schooling differently" with impoverished and minoritized students in over 200 schools. The program incorporates "values education into school curricula; and (b) encourages, educates, and empowers young people to enact social change and make a difference within their school and community and facilitate social change within their schools and local communities." The chapter concludes with a discussion on how educators can use critical service-learning and other pedagogical initiatives to empower minoritized students and convert "them from manipulated objects into active and critical subjects with critical agency."

Part II of this volume discusses the visions associated with critical service-learning in teacher education programs and other K–16 settings. None of these suggest a method for doing critical service-learning, which would be too reductive. Instead, each posits its own vision and demonstrates this with examples of critical work.

Part II begins with a chapter from Feige, Connolly and Furey. The authors of "The Humanity of Teaching and Learning: Scenarios of a Pedagogy of Compassion, Community, and Change" discuss the stagnation in school change. Following this, they suggest that critical service-learning has the potential to send ripples through that stagnation and change the landscape of schooling for students, teachers, and communities. To demonstrate this, the authors present three critical service-learning experiences carried out in three classrooms within the same high school. They show an experience connected to a local community, one to a regional community, and one to the international community. Each scenario includes both teacher and student reflection on the learning experience.

The second chapter in this section examines how preservice teachers are prepared with regard to inclusive and socially just practices. Additionally, it takes on this challenge in relation to the current practices in teacher education, which include shorter programs and more requirements. DeLuca, DeLagran, Ferguson, and Ho present The Equity Leadership Project as one approach to preparing educators mindful of inclusive and socially just pedagogies. This program includes critical service-learning, and therefore, shows how critical service-learning can be used in teacher education as a component of critical coursework. Student reflections on this work demonstrate the impact of critical service-learning on their philosophies of education and their overall sense of social responsibility.

Following this is a chapter from Hannah, Tinkler and Miller, which, in light of current standardizing practices in both PK–12 and higher education, argues for not only the presence of foundations courses for preservice teachers but also a critical perspective in those courses. To that end, critical service-learning in a Foundations of American Education course is examined for its impact on preservice teachers' understanding of educational equity and their own educational experiences. Both quantitative and qualitative methods are used to assess student achievement of critical service- learning goals (as defined by the authors).

Anders and Lester take a postcritical look at critical service-learning and the expectations associated with that work. The authors begin the chapter by situating themselves in the critical service work. Following this, there is detail about their work with narratives from their experiences that attempt to talk back to a neoliberal agenda that they suggests wants narratives of success. Finally, the authors discuss the predominant reactions of "decline and disinclination" they faced when inviting others to participate in their work. This narrative demonstrates critical service-learning while also being mindful of the people with whom the authors worked.

"Critical Openings and Possibilities: Navigating Challenges for Change" considers how teachers can work through oppressive structures to incorporate critical service-learning. In this chapter the author explores the barriers to such work and strategies employed by teachers in the field to overcome those barriers. To that end, the author describes principles of critical service-learning employed in various projects. The projects described are also closely linked to content area standards at a variety of grade levels. This demonstrates how standards based curricula and critical service-learning can work in conjunction with one another instead of in opposition. Of course, each project faced challenges, and those challenges along with how teachers faced them are at the heart of this chapter.

Hermann's chapter explores the lasing impact of critical service-learning on participants. Specifically, it examines how a life full of distraction can hold on to transformative experiences. Centered on the practice of radical social work, the author studies students who engaged in the State of New York Brockport's Vietnam Program. This program includes coursework as well as a global critical service-learning experience. Given the global nature of this work, the question of American hegemony is a central theme in the examination of students' experience and their reactions following reentry into U.S society. In conclusion, Herrmann poses the question of whether continued connection to critical service can help former students maintain their transformations achieved in the initial critical service-learning experience.

The final chapter in this section examines the path to critical service-learning. After exploring service learning, which was pursued to its fullest extent, Charest's chapter offers points on a continuum toward critical practice. This chapter includes analysis of service-learning experiences as they reflect moves away from traditional service-learning and toward critical service-learning. Charest shows that there are many entry points to service learning, which must be acknowledged. In so doing, he suggests radical pragmatism as a term to represent those points along the continuum to critical service-learning. Specifically, he suggests "that appropriating community organizing strategies and connecting them to school-based actions might allow educators to successfully challenge policies and develop ... notions of accountability that can alter current conceptions of power and control in schools."

Each part of this book includes a more direct introduction and guiding questions for consideration of the chapters together. In addition to this, each chapter author poses questions for the reader. These are meant to continue the process of critically reflecting upon and challenging the status quo for the purpose of creating a more just and equitable society through critically transformative experiences via critical service-learning.

REFERENCES

Brathwaite, F., & Porfilio, B. (2004). A school-based project: Increasing Ontario pre-service teacher candidates' experiences with cultural diversity. *Networks: Online Journal for Teacher Research* 7(2). Retrieved from http://journals.library.wisc.edu/index.php/networks/article/view/114/115.

Butin, D. W. (2005). (Ed.). *Service-learning in higher education: Critical issues and directions.* New York, NY: Palgrave

Calderón, J. Z. (2007). *Race, poverty, and social justice: Multidisciplinary perspectives through service learning,* Sterling, VA: Stylus.

Daigre, E (2000, December 22). Toward a critical service-learning pedagogy: A Freirean approach to civic literacy. *The Free Library.* Retrieved from http://www.thefreelibrary.com/Toward+a+Critical+Service-Learning+Pedagogy%3a+A+Freirean+Approach+to...-a068362994

Freire, P. (2005). *Pedagogy of indignation.* Boulder: Paradigm.

Hart, S. (2006). Breaking literacy boundaries through critical services learning: Education for the silenced and marginalized. *Mentoring & Tutoring: Partnership in Learning, 14*(1), 17–32. doi:10.1080/13611260500432236

Hearse, P. (2009). Decline and fall of neoliberal globalization. In T. Iltis, J. B. Foster, P. Hearse, A. Haneh, & D. Holmes's (Eds.), *Meltdown! A socialist view of the economic crisis* (pp. 19–28). Melbourne, Australia: Resistance Books.

Johnston-GoodStar, K., Trinidad, A., & A. Tecle, A. (2010). Critical pedagogy through the reinvention of place: Three cases of youth resistance. In B. Porfilio and P. Carr's (Eds.), *Youth culture, education and resistance: Subverting the commercial ordering of life* (pp. 197–218). Rotterdam, The Netherlands: Sense.

Masucci, M., & Renner, A. (2000). Reading the lives of others: The Winton Homes Library Project: A cultural studies analysis of critical service learning for education. *High School Journal, 84*(1), 36.

Mitchell, T. (2007). Critical service-learning as social justice education: A case study of the citizen scholars program. *Equity & Excellence in Education, 40*(2), 101–112. doi:10.1080/10665680701228797

Mitchell, T. D. (2008). Traditional vs. critical service learning: Engaging the literature to differentiate two models. *Michigan Journal of Community Service*

Learning, 14(2), 50–65. Retrieved from http://hdl.handle.net/2027/spo.3239521.0014.205

National Center on Family Homelessness. (2009). *State report card on child homelessness: America's youngest outcasts.* Retrieved from http://www.homelesschildrenamerica.org/pdf/rc_full_report.pdf

National Coalition for the Homeless. (2008, June). *Homeless Families with Children: NCH Fact Sheet.* Retrieved from http://www.nationalhomeless.org/publications/facts/families.html

O'Grady, C. R. (2000). (Ed.). *Integrating service learning and multicultural education in colleges and universities.* New York, NY: Routledge.

Purmensky, K. (2009). *Service-learning for diverse communities: Critical pedagogy and mentoring English language learners*. Charlotte, NC: Information Age.

Rhoads, R. A., & Howard, J. P. (1999). (Eds.). *Academic service learning: A pedagogy of action and reflection*. San Francisco, CA: Jossey-Bass.

Stoecker, R. and Elizabeth T. (2009) (Eds.). *The unheard voices: Community organizations and Service Learning*. Philadelphia, PA: Temple University Press.

Swaminathan, (2007). Educating for the "Real World": The hidden curriculum of community-service learning. *Equity & Excellence in Education, 40,* 134–43.

Terry, A. (2006). A K-12 Developmental service-learning typology. *International Journal of Learning, 12*(9), 321–330. Retrieved from Education Research Complete database.

Wade, R. C. (2007). Service-learning for social justice in the elementary classroom: Can we get there from here? *Equity and Excellence in Education, 40,* 156–165.

FOREWORD

Revolutionary Pedagogy and Twenty-First Century Socialism in the Bolivarian Republic of Venezuela

Mike Cole

According to the editors, the purpose of this book is:

> to understand how a Freirean critical pedagogy combined with service-learning, which we call critical service-learning, has the potential to resonate with those engaged in the learning to create a critical movement that challenges the boundaries of schooling and also empowers and transforms the societies in which we live through an examination of oppression.

It seems apposite in such a context to focus in this Foreword on revolutionary pedagogical processes in the Bolivarian Republic of Venezuela, where Freirean critical pedagogy combines with participatory democracy and community empowerment to promote education for twenty-first century socialism.[1]

A vision of twenty-first century socialism has been articulated by Hugo Rafael Chávez Frías, Venezuela's President. In 2010, he described knowledge and education as the first of three forms of power in the revolutionary process, the others being political power and economic power:

> When we talk about power, what are we talking about.... The first power that we all have is knowledge. So we've made efforts first in education, against illiteracy, for the development of thinking, studying, analysis. In a way, that has never happened before. Today, Venezuela is a giant school, it's all a school. From children of one year old until old age, all of us are studying and learning. And then political power, the capacity to make decisions, the community councils, communes, the people's power, the popular assemblies. And then there is the economic power. Transferring economic power to the people, the wealth of the people distributed throughout the nation. I believe that is the principal force that precisely guarantees that the Bolivarian revolution continues to be peaceful.[2] (as cited in Sheehan, 2010)

Elsewhere (Cole, 2011), I have differentiated schooling, an oppressive system using *institutions* to socialize young people into the norms and values of capitalism, from education which I view as a liberating and critical life-long process of human emancipation, both inside and outside of institutions. Venezuela as "a giant school" and "education for socialism" is exemplified by the Revolutionary Reading Plan launched by Chávez in 2009 (Pearson, 2009). "A change in spirit hasn't been achieved yet," Chávez suggested, and argued that the plan will be the "base for the injection of consciousness through reading, with which our revolution will be strengthened even more" (as cited in Pearson, 2009).

The plan involves the distribution by the government of 2.5 million books to develop the communal libraries. Chávez said that part of the plan was a "rescuing of our true history for our youth," explaining that many standard textbooks do not acknowledge the European imperialist genocide of the indigenous peoples and their resistance (Pearson, 2009). Chávez went on to recommend that people do collective reading and exchange knowledge, mainly through the communal councils and the popular libraries. He called on communal councils as well as "factory workers, farmers, and neighbors, to form revolutionary reading squadrons" one of whose tasks is to have discussions in order to "unmask the psychological war ... of the oligarchy" (as cited in Pearson, 2009). "Read, read and read, that is the task of every day. Reading to form conscious and minds," Chávez noted, "everyday we must inject the counter revolution a dose of liberation through reading" (as cited in MercoPress, 2009). Moreover, the revolutionary reading plan is intended to reaffirm values leading to "the consolidation of the new man and the new woman, as the foundations for the construction of a Socialist motherland, unravelling the capitalist imaginary" (as cited in MercoPress, 2009).

As far as more "formal" education is concerned, the Venezuelan Ministry of Culture stated on its website that the plan will help schoolchildren get rid of "capitalist thinking" and better understand the ideals and values 'necessary to build a Socialist country and society' (as cited in MercoPress,

2009). Education is increasingly put forward by the state as a social good, and a central factor in shaping the system of production (Griffiths & Williams, 2009, p. 37). In line with the Bolivarian Constitution, in addition to the urban and rural poor, access has been extended to traditionally disadvantaged or excluded groups, such as those of African descent and indigenous communities, though there is still much to do. Tom Griffiths and Jo Williams outline the essential factors in the Bolivarian Revolution's approach to education that make it truly counter-hegemonic. The Venezuelan approach, they argue, draws on concepts of critical and popular education within the framework of a participatory model of endogenous socialist development (Griffiths & Williams, 2009, p. 41). At the forefront, they note, is "the struggle to translate policy into practice in ways that are authentically democratic, that promote critical reflection and participation over formalistic and uncritical learning" (Griffiths & Williams, 2009, p. 41).

As in the United Kingdom and the United States, formal school education in Venezuela is based on an explicit, politicized conception of education and its role in society (Griffiths & Williams, 2009, pp. 41–42). However, whereas in the United Kingdom (e.g., Beckman, Cooper, & Hill, 2009) and the United States (e.g., Au, 2009), the capitalist state increasingly uses formal education merely as a vehicle to promote capitalism, in the Bolivarian Republic of Venezuela, "the political" in education is articulated *against* capitalism and imperialism and *for* socialism. In 2008 a draft national curriculum framework for the Bolivarian Republic was released. It stated that the system is "oriented toward the consolidation of a humanistic, democratic, protagonistic, participatory, multi-ethnic, pluri-cultural, pluri-lingual and intercultural society" (Ministerio del Poder Popular Para la Educación, 2007, p. 11, as cited in Griffiths & Williams, 2009, p. 42). It went on to critique the former system for reinforcing "the fundamental values of the capitalist system: individualism, egotism, intolerance, consumerism and ferocious competition ... [which also] promoted the privatisation of education" (Ministerio del Poder Popular Para la Educación, 2007, p. 12, as cited in Griffiths & Williams, 2009, p. 42).

One central message of the Bolivarian Revolution is that a fundamental counterhegemonic shift in the political economy towards socialism, including *universal* free access to education, with a high degree of equity in terms of opportunity and outcomes, can be achieved quite quickly (Griffiths & Williams, 2009, p. 34). As Griffiths and Williams conclude, the Bolivarian system consistently refers these back to the underlying project to promote the formation of new republicans, with creative and transformational autonomy, and with revolutionary ideas; and with a positive attitude towards learning in order to put into practice new and original solutions for the endogenous transformation of the country (Ministerio del Poder Popular Para la Educación 2007, p. 16, as cited in Griffiths & Williams, 2009, pp. 42–43).

THE THEORETICAL UNDERPINNINGS OF BOLIVARIAN EDUCATION

Venezuelan academic and political activist, Luis Bigott (2009) argues that Bolivarian education in Venezuela is based on the twentieth century Latin American critical/liberatory work of Orlando Fals Borda and Paolo Freire, both of whose work focused on the extension of education for the transformation of society (Griffiths & Williams, 2009, p. 43). I will deal with the contribution of each in turn.

Fals Borda

It is not surprising that Fals Borda, a Latin American socialist born in Columbia, an advocate of liberation theology, should figure prominently in Bolivarian education. He was one of the founders of participatory action research (PAR) that combines research and theory with political participation. Fals Borda's focus was the subordinated conditions of the Latin American societies. A sociologist, he outlined four guidelines for researchers:

- Do not monopolise your knowledge nor impose arrogantly your techniques, but respect and combine your skills with the knowledge of the researched or grassroots communities, taking them as full partners and co-researchers.
- Do not trust elitist versions of history and science which respond to dominant interests, but be receptive to counternarratives and try to recapture them.
- Do not depend solely on your culture to interpret facts, but recover local values, traits, beliefs, and arts for action by and with the research organizations.
- Do not impose your own ponderous scientific style for communicating results, but diffuse and share what you have learned together with the people, in a manner that is wholly understandable and even literary and pleasant, for science should not be necessarily a mystery nor a monopoly of experts and intellectuals (as cited in Gott, 2008).

As Griffiths and Williams (2009, p. 43) explain, a decidedly Venezuelan version of PAR is currently being put into practice by academics and teachers. They give the example of the Bolivarian University (UBV). Founded in 2003 as part of a major attempt to extend access to higher education, UBV is free to all students and "seeks to fundamentally challenge the elitism of many of the traditional universities." Social justice and equality are "at the core of all educational content and delivery," and all courses taken there use PAR methodology, "described as a multidisciplinary approach linking practice and theory." PAR methodology bases UBV students in their local communities, working alongside a mentor on a community project, which is a core part of their formal studies (Griffiths & Williams, 2009, p. 43). Griffiths and Williams (p. 43) give the examples of "Community Health students working with doctors within the *Barrio Adentro* health mission;"[3] and "Legal studies students establishing a community legal centre to advise and support families with civil law issues;" and education students working with a teacher/mentor in schools in their local community.

Classes are undertaken in the evenings, where all UBV students relate theory to their experiences in the project. As Griffiths and Williams (2009) explain:

> The approach is designed to place day-to-day decision-making and problem solving in the hands of local communities, as part of the broader societal reconstruction underway, with all participants gaining skills through the process. The intent is that the PAR methodology places researchers in positions of political leadership, but with the projects being democratically controlled and driven by the communities themselves and their own leaders, and aimed at realising the objectives of the community based organisations. (pp. 43–44)

Griffiths and Williams (2009, p. 44) conclude that while the evening discussions are interesting, what is most important is *who* is taking part in them. This is not only "social and economic inclusion" but *political* inclusion, with educational decision-making in the hands of staff, students, parents/carers *and the community at large*.

I had the privilege to teach a course at UBV for a week in 2006. The course I wrote and taught was titled "Introduction To World Systems: Global Imperial Capitalism or International Socialist Equality: Issues, and Implications for Education." Standards at UBV I found are very high—with seminar discussions and debate comparing more than favorably with universities in which I have taught in the UK and around the world. However, at UBV, as we have seen, advanced theory is very much linked to practice—that is, to improving the lives of people in the communities the students come from. Students are almost 100% working class at UBV.

While teaching there, I met a police officer who was studying for his second degree. He told me how the Chávez Government was humanizing the police force. He reckoned that Chávez has the support of about 75% of the Caracas police.

One thing that symbolizes the Bolivarian Revolution for me was the way in which, at the start of my last seminar at UBV, one of the caretakers arrived to unlock the seminar room, and then sat down, listened to and actively contributed to the seminar. His question was what percentage of the British working class did I think were revolutionary socialists. When I told him that the percentage was very very small indeed, he seemed somewhat bemused.

A focus on "community" is also apparent at the Indigenous University of Venezuela. Mecheduniya, who is Ye'kuana and writing an undergraduate thesis there on the cosmovision—traditional worldview—of his people, explains how students "analyze the situation in each of our communities and how we should be contributing to them as the Indigenous University because we are all part of our communities" (as cited in Martinez, Fox, & Farrell, 2010, p. 200). Everyone at the University learns "how to be responsible, disciplined, and to live in solidarity with one another." He also points out how students learn how to use modern technology, as well as traditional culture such as indigenous history, law, ethnology, ethnobotany and agroecology. After finishing at the University, Mecheduniya will return to his community "because that is the responsibility we have" (as cited in Martinez et al., 2010, p. 200).

Arguing in a similar vein, but about his work as a teacher and organizer for the community, rather than as a university student, and thus exemplifying Chávez's concept of Venezuela as "a giant school," Montiel, a member of the Wayúu community, stresses that everything he learns, he takes back into his community:

> It is the role of all of us to help with everything that is necessary for our community. Rather than talk about "I", we talk about "us." However, this is difficult because the habits of today have made us all more individualistic. So we are always learning how to share, how to be collective, and how to organize ourselves. (as cited in Martinez et al., 2010, pp. 208–209)

PAR principles of making "community" central to education are applicable to the whole of the education system. As we shall see shortly, it is pivotal in the work of the revolutionary teachers at the alternative school in Barrio Pueblo Neuvo.

Paulo Freire

Like Fals Borda, Paulo Freire is a Latin American socialist born in Brazil, and a liberation theologian. Exemplifying his beliefs, in an online video (Freire, 2007; Freire actually died in 1997) Freire makes reference to his belief in Marx with respect to the world and Christ as far as the "transcendental" is concerned. Freire is generally recognized as the founder of "critical pedagogy." As Peter McLaren (2000, p. 141) explains, Freire was able to link globally education and "a radical politics of historical struggle." He provided the illiterate with "both a language of critique and a language of hope" (McLaren, 2000, p. 155). For Freire, literacy was both a critique of capitalism and an introduction to a better way of life, a life of caring for others (McLaren, 2000, p. 155). Literacy programs for disempowered peasants devised by Freire and his colleagues are now used all over the world.

Freire was a keen advocate of "dialogic education," which entails a democratic learning environment and the *absence* of authoritarianism (as cited in Freire & Shor, 1987, p. 102). His work is axiomatic to *democratic* socialism, and like Chávez, Freire denied that Stalinist authoritarianism was intrinsic in socialism: As he once put it:

> I refuse to accept that the presence of authoritarianism within socialism is due to some ontological incompatibility between human beings and the essence of socialism. That would be the same as saying: "So averse is human nature to the fundamental virtues of socialism that only under coercion would it be possible to make it work." That which human ontology rejects, on the contrary, is authoritarianism, regardless of what attributes it may receive. (Freire, 1998, p. 49)

As McLaren (2000, p. 141) has argued, Freire "was one of the first internationally recognized educational thinkers who fully appreciated the relationship among education, politics, imperialism, and liberation," arguing that they "abut to one another as well as flash off each other."

Freire (1972) also formulated the concept of "banking education," where the teacher deposits information into an "empty account," and students are required to memorize the content and reproduce it. In this system the student who reproduces the information most accurately gets the highest grade. Freire urged teachers to detach themselves from capitalism where banking education is the norm, and to reinvent schools as democratic public spheres where meaningful *dialogue* can take place.

Another of Freire's (1970, 1972) concepts is that of conscientization, a developing consciousness by which, as knowing subjects, people achieve a deepening awareness of the sociocultural reality that shapes their lives. This also entails the consciousness that they have the capacity and the power to transform that reality. The relevance of this concept to the Bolivarian Revolution should, by now, be self-evident.

It should be stressed at this stage that, in terms of actual practice in the schools and universities, education based on the above revolutionary principles is by no means universal. Indeed, as Griffiths and Williams (2009, p. 44) point out, discussions with education academics and activists during fieldwork in Caracas in 2007, 2008, and 2009, repeatedly raised the challenge of the political and pedagogical conservatism of existing teachers, often in opposition to the government's Bolivarian socialist project (e.g., Griffiths, 2010).

REVOLUTIONARY EDUCATION IN AN ALTERNATIVE SCHOOL IN BARRIO PUEBLO NEUVO, MÉRIDA

Creating Space[4]

The school is a small project, started by committed socialist revolutionary residents and activists of Barrio Pueblo Nuevo, perhaps the poorest community in the city of Mérida in Western Venezuela. It caters for students aged between 8 and 15 years of age and since at the time of the fieldwork it had been operating for only 6 months, it was very much in its initiatory phase. The teachers want to create an alternative for young people that have been left behind in the public school system and re-engage them in participatory pedagogy consistent with socialist and democratic values. The school is currently linked to the Ministry of Education under the title of "alternative school" and receives some state funding.[5]

Reflecting on the overall context of his fieldwork at the school, Edward Ellis points out that the fact that the school is the exception rather than the rule as far as education in the country as a whole is concerned "need not be understood as distressing. It can be seen ... as a great opportunity to empower and encourage new forms of change." He underlines the spaces that the Chávez government has opened up for "independent and autonomous ... new projects to grow and develop." As Gerardo, a part-time collaborator at the school, a long-time community activist from the barrio, and an organic intellectual of the working class par excellence states: "ten years ago this wouldn't have been possible. This would have been called "terrorist" and would have to be underground." As he puts it, revolutionary teachers, unlike before, can advance faster, no longer having "to worry about being hunted down."

Gerardo points out that the school has opened many doors for people and that there are "a lot of expectations" from the Ministry of Education, which is hoping that the school might work as "a model for other schools."

Twenty-First Century Socialist Praxis

Gerardo is committed to socialist praxis, noting that "socialism is done, not decreed." Given that the words "revolution" and "socialism" are omnipresent in Venezuelan society, and can be used "without much thought," Gerardo is working on the *construction* of socialism in the school, being "a bit more responsible in this sense." As he explains, "here we practice socialism with concrete elements from everyday life ... sharing, working in a collective way, friendship, getting along, the fundamental bases of socialism with praxis." Having seen societies torn apart in a capitalist system based on consumption, and underlining Venezuela's stress on participatory democracy, Gerardo notes that the teachers are trying to teach the children to be "critical and proactive—not just criticism but how things can be changed," "we are trying to show that the children have a participatory role in society, and that this role can be transformative." Communication tools are crucial in this process—the radio, the television, the written word ... these things can lead to the transformation of society."

Lisbeida, a university student studying criminology and a dance instructor, working at the school and in the community as a volunteer, says of twenty-first century socialism, it "is being redefined, something that is flexible. I believe there are new understandings of what socialism is and how it can be implemented:

> But basically, the core concepts are the same: equality, social justice, elimination of class differences, more horizontal processes, all of this inside our school is an intrinsic part of what we are doing. It's our base.... So we are trying to transmit these values of equality, solidarity, cooperation, collective work

James Suggett, a writer for venezuelanalysis.com[6], who is also a community activist and a volunteer at the school, reflects Freireian analysis when he says he is critical of those teachers who view socialism as being authoritarian, those who believe they should be getting students into line. For Suggett, "socialism means creating a democratic space in the classroom," encouraging people "to recognize oppression and overcome it."

Communal, Cooperative and Democratic Living, and Learning

At the Alternative School in Barrio Pueblo Neuvo, each day starts with a communal breakfast, after which students are brought together to discuss what will take place that day. Sometimes communal cleaning of the community center where the classes are held ensues; sometimes the day starts with group activities, focused on reading, writing or mathematics, depending on what students wish to work on, or need to improve.

Addressing the socialist roots of Venezuela's indigenous communities, Gerardo illustrates Freire's process of conscientization as he points out that indigenous peoples have a tradition of companionship; solidarity, respect, and sharing; and that private property did not exist; and that teachers are trying to break the paradigms of Western society that value "capital more than people" and that prioritize individualism and competition. The school aims to provide the children with a point of departure so that they can all advance together toward socialism. Gerardo points to the use of a pedagogy that "involves the children in collective work and thinking" and includes cooperative games. When the teachers meet with the children, as Jeaneth (the main teacher of the school, a member of the community whose children are studying at the school) explains, the teachers try to emphasize "that we are a collective and if something happens to the group it affects us all."

Learning at the school is in line with Freire's advocacy of "dialogic education" which, as we have seen, entails a democratic learning environment and the *absence* of authoritarianism, "banking education" and grades. As Jeaneth puts it:

> we plan activities and then ask the children which they would like to work on. They choose the area. We have some basic parameters that they need to work in but they choose. Also, when we leave the school for a trip, we propose the idea to them and they take part in the discussion about how to plan the trip.

Tamara Pearson, like Suggett a writer for Venezuelanalysis.com and also a volunteer teacher of reading at the school, points out that:

> no one is forced to do anything and there are no punishments. If they don't want to participate in an activity, they can simply go somewhere else, or sit and watch. Hence, the weight is on the teacher to properly motivate the students and draw them in through the activity rather than discipline and threats of lower grades or whatever.

"There is no grading or competition," Pearson explains, "there's simply no sense of them competing with others." "The idea of the school" Pearson believes,

> is to teach using more creative and dynamic methods, without the usual competition and grades and failure and passing and who is first etc, with teachers who are very supportive and friendly, while also involving the community in school life, and vice versa.

Socialism and the Community

As Edward Ellis states, "there is a real emphasis on trying to increase students' participation in all activities." He gives the example of how "the students watched a movie and then discussed how to organize a screening of that same film in their community. A group conversation was held to identify what the steps necessary would be to put on this screening." As Ellis explains, "there is a lot of collaboration on the part of the community and different activities are led by different folks.... It is quite common for the students to leave the classroom to attend an event in the community." In addition, as Lisbeida points out, the school's "activities [are] open to the entire community so that the community is a protagonist in what happens in the school. In that way, the dance group which is part of the school is also part of the community." Emphasizing how PAR works in the community and school, Lisbeida explains:

> the idea is that the children have an impact in their community, carrying with them this experience to their homes and to their families so that their families also become integrated in the educational process that the school is trying to carry out. So there's a kind of feedback that we are trying to accomplish between the community and the school. And school-community means family, workers, etc. There is an important interaction which is very relevant to the educational process in the school.

This is not to glamorize the students' community. As Gerardo explains, some of the students come from homes where there are problems of violence, alcohol or drugs, or unemployment and its attendant problems. However, as Lisbeida believes, this can also be a strength for the students:

> As these students come from backgrounds that are very difficult, I think that this gives them the ability to see certain social realities with more clarity: justice, the marked differences between violence and love. I see this as a potential to create criticisms and questions with more meaning. Because they have experienced very difficult things, they are not going to be afraid and they are going to have a very strong base to be critical of things.

Gerardo points out that there is help from some government missions, such as Mission Barrio Adentro.

In addition, the teachers are trying to improve human relations, not only with cooperative games, from which the teachers are also learning, but there are physical spaces "with a community vision," such as a community library and a community radio station. As Lisbeida puts it:

> we've noticed that the children are arriving at their house with new attitudes and although we don't have a way to scientifically measure it, we can feel a difference in the attitude of the parents as well ... how they treat their children. Something very interesting is happening. Things are changing ... [the children] learn things based on what they already know and live. In this way, they can also learn that they have the potential to change the reality that surrounds them.

The students at the alternative school in Barrio Pueblo Neuvo are clearly being empowered, and already there are signs of progress. As Lisbeida enthuses,

> one of the things that we have seen with this process in the school is that the ones who were thought to be completely without potential or capacity to learn are making people turn their heads. They are doing some incredible things.

As Gerardo concludes:

> we've only had a short time operating but I have noticed a change in the way the children see things. Before, their world was just the barrio, but now they are looking a little bit beyond this. And I have seen that the children are speaking now, they are conversing.... Before everything was resolved through violence. Now there is more talking. There are still some very sharp words, but we are working on it. This has opened many doors for people. There are a lot of expectations.... And there are many things that we have learned about ourselves due to the students.

Thus, in launching the school and in teaching there, the teachers are learning too. Suggett concludes that this empowerment arises from the challenge of teaching the students in the school everyday. As he puts it, "the revolution is there in what they're doing and in their transformation process."

Racism

The comments on racism made by the teachers at the alternative school in Barrio Pueblo Neuvo underline observations made in Cole (2011), namely that like the rest of Latin America, Venezuela's history is scarred by colonialism's and imperialism's racist legacies. A few examples will suffice. Lisbeida talks of institutional racism in Venezuelan society, and relates it to social class:

> We can see very contradictory things. It seems that the problem has more to do with class. We see that the people from the barrios, the people in the countryside and in the coastal areas are more indigenous and black. Since colonization, the upper class has been composed of lighter skinned people. So when there are families from the upper and middle classes that have mestizo roots, there is a rejection of the people from the barrios and the lower classes and this has to do with their appearance, with indigenous or African traits.

Lisbeida believes that "within the poorer social groups, there is not much discrimination."

Gerardo explains how the school is attempting to challenge this institutional racism, which the students see in society in general, and in the movies:

> there are some problems with racism, especially in the Andean region. When the people see an Afro-Venezolano or an indigenous person, they think that they are inferior whereas someone blonde is seen as positive. These are concepts that have been handed down by the family and there is definitely racism present. But these ideas can't be erased in one day and we've tried to have the children recognize this and have them interpret these things. And little by little we have been dealing with this theme. The first thing to do is for us to recognize ourselves. We have a mixed group of children. Some are light skinned and others dark and we recognize that we are all equal, that we think the same, that we are the same.

Edward Ellis gives one example of the school's antiracist initiatives. In March 2010, the students attended a photo exhibit in a gallery in the city of Mérida. Here they were hosted by a professor of photography of the University of the Andes. The exhibit was called "Ancestral Wisdom" and touched upon the themes of local knowledge and native experiences, with photographs of elder community members who maintain local customs and traditions. During the visit, the professor of photography gave a short talk to the students emphasizing the need to recognize as Venezuelans the beauty within themselves—dark-skinned and native. He pointed out that Venezuelan people should not be looking to ideals of blonde haired, light-skinned Europeans as models for growth and development, but rather being proud as Latina/os and Venezuelans of different colors and backgrounds.

Finally, Lisbeida explains, the values the school is trying to promote have to do with respect, solidarity, cooperation, integration and understanding of differences. For her, antiracism is about respecting others. In

Venezuela, she believes, the theme of racism is different from the global North:

> Here when there exists a rejection of someone for their indigenous features, what is happening in reality is that we are rejecting ourselves. Because our way of being and our culture has these roots. So when this happens, the impact is different. It's like beating ourselves up. And this is the case even more in a community like the school where so many are dark-skinned and look a lot alike.

CONCLUSION

The Government of the Bolivarian Republic of Venezuela, led by Hugo Chávez, represents, I believe, the best currently existing model in the world for a future socialist society. However, as stressed by Gerardo, the part-time collaborator in the alternative school in Barrio Pueblo Neuvo, and by Chávez himself, the revolution will not be decreed from above. From a (neo-) Marxist perspective, it is important to stress the Chávez government's dialectic and symbiotic relationship with the Venezuelan working class.[7] However, as Martinez et al. (2010, p. 2) argue, President Chávez continues to be "the defining political factor" as revealed "by the typical political labels that … divide many Venezuelans between *Chavistas* and *anti-Chavistas.*" It is "precisely in the relationship and tension between the Venezuelan government and the social movements that the process of building a participatory democracy comes alive most vividly." Greg Wilpert (2010, pp. viii–ix) underlines this fact:

> To learn about … the movements that stand behind the Chávez phenomenon is … as important as learning about the Chávez government itself. One cannot truly make sense of one without the other. And making sense of and defending what is happening in Venezuela is perhaps one of the most important tasks for progressives around the world today, since Venezuela is at the forefront in the effort to find a real progressive alternative to capitalism, to representative democracy, and to U.S. imperialism.

The centrality to the Bolivarian Revolution of participatory democracy, in addition to representative democracy—elected individuals "representing" the people—has been a pillar of Chávez's philosophy since his first election victory in 1998.

While much remains to be done, particularly with respect to the full implementation of indigenous and Afro-Venezuelan rights (consistently acknowledged by Chávez, though not the whole of the Chávez government), there seems to be an abundance of hope for the future at the local and societal levels *despite* the forces opposing the revolution (see Cole, 2011).

With respect to education, we have witnessed that, viewed as a lifelong liberatory process, education is a key pillar of the revolution. I have noted how this is manifested in Chávez's concept of Venezuela as "a giant school." At the "formal" institutional level of education, the principles of the revolution have not been fully put into practice. Moreover, given the aforementioned conservatism of many teachers discovered by Griffiths and Williams, the challenge for Venezuelan revolutionary teachers to continue their counterhegemonic struggle against capitalism, racism and imperialism remains paramount.

It should be stressed that the overall societal reforms with respect to the "missions," a series of social justice, social welfare, antipoverty and educational programs that have massively reduced poverty and greatly increased educational opportunities along with the other ameliorative measures are precisely that—*reforms*. However, just as these societal reforms need to be seen in the context of the country having a revolutionary socialist president and millions of pro-Chávez workers, who are *or have the potential to become* revolutionary socialists, so do the reforms at the level of education in general and at the level of the alternative school in Barrio Pueblo Neuvo. In the same way that the societal reforms are reminiscent of those of the post-World War II Labour Governments in the United Kingdom, the educational reforms being carried out in Barrio Pueblo Neuvo recall those that took place, for example, in the Inner London Education Authority (ILEA) and other progressive authorities. Indeed, in some ways these U.K.-based educational reforms were more progressive, particularly with respect to equalities policies, as are equalities policies embedded in U.K. equalities legislation today (see Equality and Human Rights Commission, 2010).

In Mérida, there are, however, revolutionary teachers fostering, in Freire's terms, a deepening awareness of the sociocultural reality that shapes their students' lives. To reiterate, unlike the United Kingdom and the United States, either historically or contemporaneously, the promotion in future workers of the consciousness that they have the capacity and the power to transform that reality is supported in Venezuela by a revolutionary movement and a revolutionary president. It is for this reason that Chávez is so maligned by the U.S. and U.K. media, and labelled, against all the evidence, as a dictator (for a discussion, see Cole, 2011).

In the Bolivarian Republic of Venezuela, socialist education is promoted by and is pivotal to the revolutionary process. Whereas the liberation of the working class in the U.K. and the U.S. is, for the foreseeable future, forestalled, in Venezuela, for Chávez the epicenter of the revolution, socialism is unstoppable. Whatever the final outcome of twenty-first century socialism, in Venezuela's "giant school" conscientization is providing the working class, current and future, with the certainty that a different world is possible.

The practical implications of how U.K. and U.S. revolutionary teachers might move forward in promoting socialism of the twenty-first century, a socialism in which racism and *all* other equalities are consistently confronted, challenged, and overcome, is addressed in Chapter 6 of Cole (2011) where some fundamental underlying principles are established that I believe Marxist and other left radicals should adopt. These include efforts to promote the process of conscientization; a radical conception of pedagogy that centralizes dialogical education; Participatory Action Research; the replacement of the fixed ability paradigm with a commitment to learning without limits; and a structurally located sense of student empowerment. I also make suggestions for content, focusing on media education in order to resist processes of interpellation, and to be able to recognize and challenge hegemonic discourse; on multicultural antiracist education; and on political education.

In various ways, we all have much to learn from each other. The revolutionary teachers in the school in Mérida have expressed a desire for open collaboration with revolutionary pedagogical scholars and theorists outside of Venezuela (personal correspondence). The U.K. has a history of working class militancy, currently hindered by the ideological and repressive apparatuses of the British state, particularly since the advent of the Thatcher government, and accelerated under Tony Blair, and under the ConDem Government. Blair's mantra, "education, education, education," in essence creating a flexible workforce for capitalism, represents the antithesis of the forms of popular education advocated by Chávez. The U.K. also has an ongoing tradition of education for equality from which we can all learn (see Cole, 2009b; Hill & Helavaara Robertson, 2009).

With respect to the United States, San Juan (2010, p. xiv) has suggested that among other factors, the lack of a viable labor-union tradition has distorted historical materialist principles there. Hence, among many leftist academics, "there is no mention of the working class as a significant force for overthrowing capitalism, much less initiating a socialist revolution" (p. xiv). It is, in part, for this reason that a non-Marxist interpretation of critical race theory (CRT) is so preeminent among U.S. antiracist academics (for a Marxist critique of CRT, and a discussion of some of its strengths see Cole, 2009a). Recalling the centrality for Freire of popular literacy, San Juan (2010, p. xiv) shows awareness of how events in Venezuela may serve as a positive example to people in the United States, when he suggests that it is instructive to contrast the trend among those leftists in the U.S. who have abandoned the socialist cause with the revolutionary promotion of popular literacy in Venezuela, "a pedagogical experiment of historic significance for all anti-capitalist militants" (San Juan, 2010, p. xiv). Nevertheless, despite all this, as this volume demonstrates, revolutionary thought continues to exist among some key educationists in the United States.

As part of the more general process of conscientization for all workers, it is my hope that this Foreword will promote intercontinental collaboration between revolutionary teachers and revolutionary academics.

NOTES

1. The arguments in this Foreword are developed in greater depth in Chapter 5 of Cole (2011).
2. A common criticism levelled at Marxism is that it is inherently 'violent'. Engels, like Chávez, believed that a peaceful transition to socialism was desirable and possible, and that education could play a role in such a transition. For example, he stated: "we will have to concern ourselves above all with the measures by which we can avoid a violent and bloody overthrow of the social conditions" of capitalism (Engels, 1845/1975, p. 243). With respect to education, he wrote: "the calm and composure necessary for the peaceful transformation of society can ... be expected only from an *educated* working class" (p. 243). While Marxists recognize that violence has been perpetrated on a grand scale *in the name of Marxism* it is, in fact, neoliberal capitalism that is currently unleashing unabashedly an orgy of violence, hitherto unprecedented, causing masses of avoidable deaths from world poverty and imperialist conquest (for a discussion of Marxism, social revolution and violence, see Chapter 10 of Cole, 2008.
3. Mission Barrio Adentro which means literally "Mission inside the Barrio" provides comprehensive publicly-funded health care, and sports training to poor and marginalized communities. Barrio Adentro delivers de facto universal healthcare from cradle to grave.
4. The fieldwork at this school was carried out on my behalf by Edward Ellis. I am most grateful to him for this. The subheadings in this section of the chapter reflect the main issues and concerns that arose in Ellis's interviews.
5. For an update on developments at the school (see Motta & Cole, 2012).
6. Venezuelanalysis.com, in its own words:

   > is an independent website produced by individuals who are dedicated to disseminating news and analysis about the current political situation in Venezuela. The site's aim is to provide on-going news about developments in Venezuela, as well as to contextualize this news with in-depth analysis and background information. The site is targeted towards academics, journalists, intellectuals, policy makers from different countries, and the general public.

7. The Venezuelan working class should not be viewed as constituting a traditional industrial proletariat. Some 60% of Venezuelan workers are involved in the informal economy (street vendors and so on), primarily in the barrios from where Chávez draws his support (Dominguez, 2010).

REFERENCES

Au, W. (2009). *Unequal By design: High-Stakes Testing and the standardization of inequality*. New York, NY: Routledge.

Beckman, A., Cooper, C., & Hill, D. (2009). Neoliberalization and managerialization of "education" in England and Wales: A case for reconstructing education. *Journal for Critical Education Policy Studies, 7*(2), Retrieved from http://www.jceps.com/PDFs/07-2-12.pdf

Bigott, L. (2009, January). *Popular education in Venezuela and Latin America*. Presentation to a delegation of visiting education academics to Venezuela, coordinated by Tom Griffiths and JoWilliams, Caracas, National Assembly Building

Cole, M. (2008) *Marxism and educational theory: Origins and issues*. New York, NY: Routledge.

Cole, M. (2009a) *Critical race theory and education: A Marxist response*. New York, NY: Palgrave Macmillan.

Cole, M. (2009b) *Equality in the secondary school: Promoting good practice across the curriculum*. London: Continuum.

Cole, M. (2011) *Racism in the UK and the US: Towards a socialist alternative*. New York, NY: Palgrave Macmillan.

Dominguez, F. (2010, July). *Education for the creation of a New Venezuela*. Paper delivered at *Latin America and Education*, Marxism And Education: Renewing Dialogues Xiii, Institute of Education, University of London.

Engels, F. (1845). Speeches in Elberfeld. *Marx and Engels, Collected Works, Volume 4*. Retrieved from www.marxists.org/archive/marx/works/1845/02/15.htm (Original work published 1975)

Equality and Human Rights Commission. (2010). Retrieved from http://www.equalityhumanrights.com/

Freire, P. (1970) *Cultural action for freedom*. Harmondsworth, England: Penguin.

Freire, P. (1972) *Pedagogy of the oppressed*, Harmondsworth, England: Penguin.

Freire, P. (1998) *Pedagogy of the Heart*, New York, NY: Continuum.

Freire, P. (2007). *Paulo Freire-Karl Marx* (subtitled) [Video]. Retrieved from http://www.youtube.com/watch?v=pSyaZAWIr1I&feature=related

Freire, P., & Shor, I. (1987) *A pedagogy for liberation: Dialogues on transforming education*. London: Macmillan Education.

Gott, R. (2008). Orlando Fals Borda: Sociologist and activist who defined peasant politics in Colombia. *The Guardian*. Retrieved from http://www.guardian.co.uk/world/2008/aug/26/colombia.sociology

Griffiths, Tom G. 2010. Schooling for twenty-first century socialism: Venezuela's Bolivarian project. *Compare: A Journal of Comparative and International Education, 40*(5), 607-622.

Griffiths, T. G., & Williams, J. (2009). Mass schooling for socialist transformation in Cuba and Venezuela *Journal for Critical Education Policy Studies,* 7(2), 30–50. Retrieved from http://www.jceps.com/index.php?pageID=article &articleID=160

Hill, D., & Helavaara Robertson, L. (2009). *Equality in the primary school: Promoting good practice across the curriculum.* New York, NY: Routledge.

Martinez, C., Fox, M., & J. Farrell, J. (2010). *Venezuela speaks: Voices from the Grassroots.* Oakland, CA: PM Press.

McLaren, P. (2000). *Che Guevara, Paulo Freire, and the pedagogy of revolution.* Lanham, MD: Rowman and Littlefield.

MercoPress. (2009, May 17). To school for reading classes with Karl Marx and Che Guevara. Merco Press. Retrieved from http://en.mercopress.com/2009/05/17/to-school-for-reading-classes-with-karl-marx-and-che-guevara

Motta, S. C., & Cole, M. (2012). *Constructing twenty-first century socialism in Latin America: The role of radical education* New York, NY: Palgrave Macmillan.

Pearson, T. (2009). Venezuela opens national art gallery and launches National Reading Plan. *venezuelanalysis.com.* Retrieved from http://venezuelanalysis.com/news/4402

San Juan, E., Jr. (2010). Foreword. In D. Kelsh, D. Hill, & S. Macrine (Eds.), *Class in education: Knowledge, pedagogy, subjectivity* (pp. xi–xviii). New York, NY: Routledge.

Sheehan, C. (2010). Transcript of Cindy Sheehan's interview with Hugo Chavez, *March 30.* Retrieved from http://venezuelanalysis.com/analysis/5233

Wilpert, G. (2010). Prologue. In C. Martinez, M. Fox, & J. Farrell (Eds.), *Venezuela speaks: Voices from the grassroots* (pp. v–ix). Oakland, CA: PM Press

PART I

The purpose of this part of the volume is to understand how a Freirean critical pedagogy combined with service learning, which we call critical service-learning, has the potential to resonate with those engaged in the learning to create a critical movement that challenges the boundaries of schooling and also empowers and transforms the societies in which we live through an examination of oppression.

This section begins with a chapter that considers how service learning can be made critical, why it is imperative, and what it can look like. Following this, a chapter will be presented that considers a required community involvement component in a school system and what making such a component critical might mean for social transformation. Two other chapters will examine the sustainability of critical service-learning. One looks at how critical service-learning can empower alienated youth in communities of color to engage in a movement and the other considers how to maintain the transformative experiences of the learning that occurs through critical service. The final chapters will look at how critical service-learning can expand the boundaries of schooling. They discuss the dangers of traditional service learning in international contexts and suggest the need for a critical orientation in order to challenge the power of the status quo over time. Following each author's presentation, there will be time for questions.

Readers will develop a deeper understanding of how service learning has the potency to become a transformative pedagogical device in the Freirean sense of linking educational practices to personal awareness and social transformation. Specifically, the critical service-learning projects embedded in these chapters capture how students and teachers across the globe have developed socially-just personas through engaging in sustained learning partnerships, which are characterized with the servers and the served working in solidarity to understand what forces give rise to oppression in their communities, to engage in sustained cultural work to eliminate social inequalities, and to remake themselves as democratic agents of change who engage in praxis across national, racial, and class borders in order to understand the social and historical contractions mediating our lives.

Guiding Questions:

- What ought to be the key principals that guide the development, implementation, and evaluation of critical service-learning projects? Are there different guidelines to consult when establishing critical service-learning projects in international contexts?
- What impact has critical theory played in the development of service-learning scholarship and initiatives for the past 40 years?
- Do the cultural manifestations of social groups historically marginalized across the globe have the power to nudge teachers and their students to become critically aware and active in the struggle to transform schools and the wider society?
- How can K–12 schoolteachers use critical service-learning projects to promote a liberal and practical form of education amid structures that promote conformity, corporatism, and injustice?
- What role does a student's social class status play in their perception of the value of critical service-learning projects, in their receptivity to examining the factors responsible for imbalanced power relationships inside and outside of service-learning initiatives, and in their desire to engage in additional social-justice initiatives?

CHAPTER 1

POWER AND SERVICE-LEARNING

Salience, Place, and Practice

Andrea Yoder Clark and Maura Nugent

Critical theorists examine power relationships within society to document how power is shared and transferred among social groups (Darder, Baltadano & Torres, 2003). This discussion of power in service-learning is informed by critical theorists Foucault (1977) and Gramsci (1971), and is contextualized using Freire's (1970) critical insight. Gramsci's (1971) social reproduction theory is used to demonstrate that when service-learning is enacted without attention to imbalances of power, service-learning can perpetuate the dominant group's monopoly on power within society. Alternatively, Foucault's (1977) conception of power as a dynamic process, resisting linear interpretations of the powerful imposing on the powerless, provides a fresh perspective on how service-learning can be used as a tool to break through systems of social reproduction when multiple dimensions and directions of power are attended to within service-learning practice. Finally, Freire's (1970) conscientization helps us understand the importance of developing an explicit awareness of one's per-

Critical Service Learning as a Revolutionary Pedagogy: A Project of Student Agency in Action, pp. 3–27

sonal power through service-learning. Service-learning can be a vehicle in which the manifestation of Freire's (1970) conscientization is possible through praxis, or the synthesis of reflection in action. This can be enacted through the service-learning process when the development of specific skills and knowledge are used to empower students to work with others to accomplish meaningful change in their world.

In this chapter, we challenge the notion that service-learning is opposed to critical theoretical approaches to education. We demonstrate six principles that can help guide service-learning practitioners to address power imbalances that appear in service-learning practice. These six principles are developed through a synthesis of critical theoretical influences in the service-learning literature. The chapter will further demonstrate these principles in action through two critical service-learning experiences. It is argued that service-learning can become a truly transformational pedagogy when implemented with attention to power dynamics within the service experience (Yoder Clark, 2009).

METHODOLOGY

In this chapter, attention to power in service learning is explored through synthesizing critically influenced service-learning research found in the *Michigan Journal of Community Service Learning* from 1994–2007. Additionally, critical ethnographic interviews were used to explore service-learning leaders' understanding of power. Seven interviews were conducted from each group of service-learning leaders. The pioneers were identified in the Stanton, Giles, and Cruz (1999) seminal publication, *Service-Learning: A Movement's Pioneers Reflect on its Origins, Practice and Future*. The 2007 emerging leaders were chosen by the National Youth Leadership Council and the National Service-Learning Partnership. Each subject interviewed was selected for the social justice focus of their service-learning work. Each interview began by asking how power should be defined within the context of the service-learning experience. These definitions were added to an initial definition of power formulated from the insights of critical theorists Foucault (1977), Gramsci (1971), and Freire (1970). Those definitions of power were synthesized into the definition of power[1] utilized for this study (Yoder Clark, 2009).

Finally, those interviewed were asked to identify how they addressed imbalances of power that emerged during their service-learning practice. These insights were triangulated with data obtained from the service-learning literature to identify best practices for attending to imbalances of power in critical service-learning experiences.

Critical Theory: A Critique of Service-Learning or a Tool for Change in Service-Learning Practice?

The critical theory of education and the practice of service-learning have not traditionally been associated. In fact, each approach has been perceived as inhabiting very different ends of the educational spectrum. Service-learning is a teaching and learning strategy employed across education demographics from parochial schools to general comprehensive public high schools. As of February 2004, 28% of all K–12 institutions were involved in some type of service-learning (Levine, 2008). While service-learning can be a highly effective transformative pedagogy, not all service-learning is equal. Service-learning that does not adhere to quality standards, while often well meaning, does not consistently produce positive results (Levine, 2008). Levine reports that multiple studies (Billig, 2000; Center for Human Resources, 1999) have struggled to identify service-learning programs that adhere to current quality standards. These same studies have demonstrated inconsistent and often negligible results from programs that do not adhere to quality standards. In fact, the 1999 study reported by Melchior, Bailis, and colleagues of the Center for Human Resources sought to evaluate 210 randomly selected service-learning programs funded by the federal Learn and Serve America Program. This study was limited to programs that adhered to current quality standards. When the 210 selected programs were edited for adherence to quality standards, the number of eligible programs fell from 210 to 17 (8% of original total). This failure to fully implement the existing quality standards, even among federally selected and funded initiatives, adds to the lack of positive results attributed to service-learning (Levine, 2008).

This chapter contends programs that fail to produce high quality service-learning will more than likely add to the social reproduction of inequality through the service-learning process. However, when service-learning is implemented in accordance with current standards of quality within the service-learning field, (Levine, 2008) and with consideration to the expression of power in service-learning practice, service-learning can support transformational educational objectives as evidenced by the two programs outlined later in chapter. As we illustrate below, despite the dramatic differences in popular perception of the two educational approaches, critical theory and high quality service-learning can work together to promote personal and social transformation in schools and in the wider society.

Roots in Critical Theory

Service-learning pioneers have identified founders of the service-learning field who informed their pedagogy, at least in part, from the critical theoretical tradition. Founders of the service-learning movement such as Dwight Giles, Nadinne Cruz, Timothy Stanton, and Ken Reardon identified in Stanton, Giles, and Cruz's (1999) seminal publication *Service-Learning: A Movements Pioneers Reflect on its Origins, Practice and Future*, cited Paulo Freire as one important influence on their work in their early years. The origin of service-learning during the 1960s and 1970s coincided with the publication of Paulo Freire's (1970) initial work, *Pedagogy of the Oppressed*. This work has been integral in shaping critical education theory for the past 40 years (Darder, Baltodano, & Torres, 2003). Not coincidently, a recent review of the service-learning field's primary academic journal, *Michigan Journal of Community Service Learning*, revealed that Paulo Freire's (1970) *Pedagogy of the Oppressed* has been cited in 24% of all articles published from the journals inception in 1994 through the 2007 edition (Yoder Clark, 2009). While the popularity of Paulo Freire's (1970) work in service-learning's primary journal is noteworthy, Table 1.1 cites references to over 19 authors commonly associated with critical theory in the *Michigan Journal of Community Service Learning* from 1994–2007, providing additional evidence for a persistent link between the two fields (Yoder Clark, 2009).

This consistent influence of critical theory on service-learning is often overlooked. In fact, Nadinne Cruz, a field pioneer, mentions a conscious strategic decision by service-learning founders to distance the field from critical theorists when developing the field's first theoretical model in 1979. This was due to the highly conservative political climate of the time when critical theory was demonized by many politicians, scholars, and practitioners. Critical theory was characterized as being part of the "communist agenda," which was allegedly predicated on taking over the West intellectually, economically, and militarily (Yoder, 2008). Additionally, Pineros-Shields (1996) documents similar strategic moves in the first national service-learning programs established by Clinton's legislation in the 1990s. The National and Community Service Act of 1990 began the call for youth civic action and culminated in Clinton's National Service Trust Act of 1993. The National and Community Service Trust Act began the federal institutionalization of service-learning with the creation of Ameri-Corps and similar programs administered by the newly created Corporation for National Service (Kahne & Westheimer, 1996; Melchior, 2000). The 1993 National and Community Service Trust Act was instrumental in the expansion of service-learning research and practice through the establishment of the federally funded Learn and Serve America Program (Billig, 2000; Melchior, 2000).

Despite the establishment of political support for service-learning during the Clinton's presidency, the push to divorce service-learning from liberal activist activity that "politicized education" was still present.

Table 1.1. Critical Authors Informing Service-Learning Work in Michigan Journal of Community Service-Learning From 1994–2007

Author Referenced	%
Freire	63%
Giroux	22%
Shor	12%
Foucault	10%
Habermas	10%
Fine	10%
Borda	8%
hooks	8%
Aronowitz	6%
Bordieau	6%
McLaren	6%
Brofenbreener	4%
Gramsci	4%
Marcuse	4%
Apple	2%
Althusser	2%
Bahktin	2%
Kincheloe	2%

Pineros-Shields (1996) reports explicit directives within Americ-Corps to move away from "overtly political" educational objectives and decisions when implementing programs. Both Cruz (as cited in Yoder, 2008) and Pineros-Shields (1996) cited a fear of conservative political backlash and systematic elimination of funding. People spearheading these initiatives were cognizant that the federal government had previously withheld support and funds for the activist-oriented, service-learning VISTA program under the Nixon administration.

Despite the resistance to openly support critical theory, the service-learning field continues to reach out to critical scholars in order to make service-learning a transformative endeavor. For instance, Service-Learning Investment Prospectus published by the Academy for Educational Development in 2005 identified the need within the service-learning field to broaden its pedagogy, practice and theoretical models to include strategies that have been proven to bring about civic engagement and critical consciousnesses in urban communities. This call to broaden the field to address the needs of more diverse audiences has manifested in other ways. In 2007, the National Youth Leadership Council and the National Service Learning Partnership joined forces to identify 22 Service-Learning Emerging Leaders working with diverse communities. In 2007, the National Youth Leadership Council created the Service-Learning Urban Institute to highlight best practices in service-learning within urban communities. This institute identifies a Bernard Gill Fellow each year in order to recognize the work of exceptional urban service-learning practitioners. In 2010, the Bernard Gill Fellowship was awarded to Dr. Jeff Andrade-Duncan, a prominent author and practitioner in the field of critical educational theory, civic engagement, and youth culture, again increasing the connections between the two fields. Finally, the publication of this volume attests to a growing awareness of the potential of service-learning to become a vehicle towards truly transformational pedagogy.

SERVICE-LEARNING THROUGH A CRITICAL LENS

Critical theorists examine power relationships within society to document how power is shared and transferred among social groups (Darder, Baltadano, & Torres, 2003). Social reproduction (Gramsci, 1971) is a process in which the social institutions and positions of power within society are protected and upheld by the dominant culture at the expense of marginalized communities. From this perspective, service-learning programs that use groups with more social power to enact service-learning in order "to help" a group with less power, can often lead to feelings of patronization and alienation (Weah, Simmons, & Hall, 2003). Service-learning enacted within the context of unbalanced power relationships can also lead to greater feelings of difference and intolerance rather than moving towards cultural understanding and cross cultural relationships (Weah, Simmons, & Hall, 2003). Often, in service-learning characterized by unbalanced power relationships, the dominant group uses their social status to create change *for* an underserved group, instead of working *with* a marginalized community to help themselves (Yoder, 2008; Weah, Simmons, & Hall, 2003). When this occurs, the service act is perceived as "a hand out," or charity, resulting in feelings of shame or embarrassment around positions of need (Weah, Simmons, & Hall, 2003). Moreover, some minoritized groups internalize the myth that they are socially and culturally inferior to participants giving a "hand out" during the service-learning process, creating additional psychological obstacles for underserved groups to utilize their personal power (Fereire, 1970). When this pattern persists, the dominant groups' monopoly on power is upheld (Gramsci, 1971).

Identifying the Service-Learning Leaders: The Pioneers and the Emerging Leaders

It is interesting to note differences between the two groups of service-learning leaders (see Appendix A). Most pioneers began their careers in service-learning as the field developed in the 1960s and 1970s. The emerging leaders are just beginning their careers with an average of eight years experience in the field. It is also worth noting that most of the original service-learning pioneers trained undergraduate students in a university setting who then performed service within underserved communities. In contrast, 86% of the emerging leaders are employed in nonprofit community based organizations where service-learning is used to accomplish community goals. Additionally, the emerging leaders often work with populations they would themselves affiliate with in urban centers.

POWER AND CRITICAL THEORY

Classic critical theory developed an understanding of the relationship between culture and power and how it is used in the domination of oppressed groups (Giroux, 2003; Held, 1980; Kellner, 1989). Gramsci (1971) and Foucault (1977) are emphasized in this chapter due to their specific contributions around the mediation of power through societal institutions and relationships, as well as how power manifests in the construction of knowledge (Darder, Baltadano, & Torres, 2003). This emphasis on social relationships and the role of social institutions on learning is of particular importance to service-learning. Service-learning that is enacted within the larger social institution of schooling is susceptible to the processes of social reproduction occurring within this system.

POWER AND THE SERVICE-LEARNING LITERATURE

While power is only beginning to be explored in relation to service-learning practice within the literature, the following authors offer great insight into best practices for addressing power in service-learning.

Varlotta (1996) provides insight around how to address power dynamics within service-learning experiences Varlotta (1996) suggests that service-learning practitioners begin by engaging participants through their past experiences or their historicity. This enables the service-learning facilitator to situate the service experience where participants are. She then asks practitioners to question the general perception that power dynamics within the service experience are linear, from server to served. Drawing on Foucault's (1977) perception of non-linear power relationships that describe the fluidity of power, Varlotta (1996) asks us to consider that power dynamics within the service experience are alterable and constantly changing. Varlotta reminds practitioners that everyone in the service experience has power, allowing the reader to better envision the back and forth exchange of power between the server and the served. This insight allows us to step outside of the image of "server" and "served" to consider a mutual relationship between partners, each bringing something of value to the table and each equally engaging in the process of learning from their own position of power.

Further, Varlotta (1996) draws on Freire's (1970) "dialogic process" of "co-investigation" to demonstrate how power can be shared between all parties in the service-experience including professors, students, and the community served. The process of co-investigation allows each stakeholder in the service-learning experience to work together, each bringing valuable knowledge and expertise to the experience. Varlotta's (1996) model allows us to begin to imagine what service-learning informed by critical theory's conception of power might look like. The following authors begin to wrestle with these ideas.

Madsen-Camacho (2004) explicitly explores the process of implementing service-learning informed by critical pedagogy. Madsen-Camacho (2004) validates the point of view raised in this chapter, the idea that service-learning inherently creates imbalances of power between the server and served, stating, "I argue that while community service learning is ideally designed to be rooted in mutuality and reciprocity between servers and served, issues of power and privilege can create an asymmetrical relationship between both" (p. 31). Madsen-Camacho (2004) calls on the field to reflexively examine itself in its practice and implementation. Madsen-Camacho (2004) points out the possibility for service-learning experiences to reproduce and enforce unequal social relationships without conscious attention to power issues. This author emphasizes that reflexivity, or the process of experiencing what it means to have been denied power as well as empowerment, must be experienced not just intellectualized in service-learning.

In conclusion, Madsen-Camacho (2004) highlights the need for identity formation during the service- learning process through sustained contact with "the Other" in a reciprocal service immersion experience. The experience must focus on relationship building first before service begins.

Green (2001) explores the role race and class play in creating imbalances of power in service-learning. This author reminds us that the process of openly naming power imbalances is a required first step in recognizing the inequity within the world. Green (2001) discusses how she makes the connection between race and class differences and power in the service-learning experience, when she states:

> It meant considering how race and class affect the service-learning situation. When working toward a true consensus it is important to acknowledge the power differentials and differences in resources, methods and values [reference to differences in the African American service site relative to the university]. (p. 19)

Green (2001) also discusses how she navigates these power relationships when participants enter at different levels of power in the service-learning experience. From the perspective of the university, she talks about the honesty necessary to truly acknowledge imbalances in resources and power, as well as differences in methods and values, that often exist between the university and the partnering community organization. Green (2001) emphasizes including the community and their expertise when designing service-learning courses. Additionally, Green (2001) points out that it is necessary for the university to adjust to the community, just as often as the community concedes to the university, with the ultimate goal of a long-term sustainable partnership between both groups. Finally, as a professor, Green (2001) asks students to examine the issues of race and White privilege through readings, discussions, and journal entries. She focuses on students' experiences as White members of the dominant society working with a diverse and nondominant community.

Dunlap, Scoggin, Green, and Davi (2007) explore the process of White students' development of racial awareness during service-learning experiences. The authors have developed a model to guide professors through helping students navigate the identity formation process. Dunlap et al. (2007) are consistent with both Madsen-Camacho (2004) and Green (2001) because they suggest that identity formation should be an ongoing process in the service-learning, as it helps those from the dominant community understand and address power imbalances within the service experience. The following recommendations are provided in the Dunlap, et al. (2007, p. 27) for mediating reflection around power in service-learning:

1. Provide students grappling with racial identity formation issues regular and consistent opportunities for reflection that include appropriate freedom, opportunities and boundaries for self-expression around identity formation issues.

2. Provide curriculum resources that name, explain and support this process for students, including opportunities to support their accommodation of new ideas and experiences into a new understanding of racial groups and differences, rather than the assimilation of these new experiences into more narrow explanations.
3. Articulate the breadth and depth of the support systems that exists for students to help them through this process.

Kiely (2005) explores the cognitive dissonance incurred from new and uncomfortable situations that challenge our previous perceptions, in addition to the importance of emotions, mental processing and connection to those in the service environment. Keily employed a longitudinal case study design in which multiple data sources (document analysis, observation, semi-structured and structured interviews) were triangulated to identify emergent themes that unfolded during the research process. Keily (2005) found that more intense cognitive dissonance is created when those providing the service are confronted with extreme differences in resources and power (such as extreme poverty) for the first time, and that these extreme forms of dissonance have a long lasting effect on students. Keily (2005) did emphasize that building relationships with those served is one way to help deal with dissonant experiences. Kiely also found that this extreme exposure to dissonance created long lasting change in students and often profoundly altered the course of their motivations throughout their careers and into their lives in the future. Keily (2005) also found that the intense effects of the service experience were not the same when less extreme forms of dissonance were created. Finally, he demonstrated that these intense dissonant experiences led students to go through the process of identity formation. In this study, Keily (2005) found that the identity formation process was best supported through regular conversational support, journaling and other forms of instruction.

Further insights are provided by Pompa (2002), who explored a case study investigating the transformative potential of a service-learning class on the criminal justice system. The study took place inside a prison, where both university students and prison inmates took a criminal study class together. In this model, Pompa (2002) begins by acknowledging the potential for reproduction of unequal social relationships when power is not acknowledged and addressed.

To mediate the effects of power within this service experience, Pompa suggests the participants engage in a "mutual immersion" experience. Through team building exercises in the initial class sessions, the two groups quickly become one. The students and inmates were positioned to undergo the process of identity formation together, simultaneously sharing their lives and building relationships. The immersion model of this program allowed both students and inmates to begin to understand each other as people; they got beyond stereotypical labels associated with "youth" and "prisoners."

Pompa (2002) also challenge traditional teacher student power dynamics, asking the teacher to share power with students through creating a safe context for learning. A safe learning context occurs when teacher and students have the power to engage in dialogues, which are characterized by suspended judgment, honesty and respect. Additionally, chairs are arranged in a circle in order to create a visible safe space. Arranging the seats in a circle also facilitates the power sharing process as there is no front, back, good or bad area of the class. This emphasis on how context shapes teaching and learning is consistent with critical theory.

Finally, all students are encouraged to "find their voice" through public reading of their class work. This allows students to express their ideas and give them the platform to build up their esteem (Pompa, 2002). In the end, the students submitted a report to the prison staff recommending changes within the prison culture. This final step in the process allowed students to feel that their work has value and is usable within the world.

Pompa's (2002) work is inspiring in that it covers the entire process of critical service-learning from identity formation through personal transformation, albeit in a nonlinear fashion. Identity formation occurs when students are required to interact with the "Other," are given opportunities to share their lives, and then led through reflective processing of their initial assumptions of why people are oppressed or are afforded unearned privileges in society. Personal transformation occurs when students come to an understanding of how power mediates their lives and the lives of the Other. Additionally, authentic meaningful end products give the students work value outside the classroom. Here, this occurred when the students' work was read and considered by the prison staff. Their work has altered prison procedures and practices so as to provide more resources and power to the imprisoned. When leading students along the path of implementing their work in the world, it is essential to provide students with the requisite skills and knowledge that will produce progress toward real community level change. Critical theory demonstrates that in order for work to be truly transformational, opportunities for real community level change need to be presented (Freire, 1970).

The existing literature on power in service-learning highlights a few similarities across studies, demonstrated in Table 1.2. The majority of studies highlighted the role of long-term immersion to help break down barriers to power, to facilitate relationship building among service participants and to trigger identity formation through prolonged experiences with the "Other." The process of relationship building is essential to identity formation, facilitating the re-evaluation of our assumptions in relation to the "Other."

Strategies for addressing power dynamics in the service-learning process were also identified in two groups of interviews with service-learning pioneers and emerging leaders. These insights are synthesized in Figure 1.1 and are listed alongside the contributions from the service-learning literature. Principles commonly explored in the field of critical theory are also included to provide additional evidence for the connection between the two fields. The insights of both interview groups are well aligned with critical theory principles and the existing service-learning literature; yet, in most areas practice fell short of truly conceptualizing critical theory principles. This demonstrates the need to approach service-learning with an explicit critical theoretical lens. The limited attention to critical theory themes within the service-learning literature demonstrates that there is room for expansion and growth toward critical theoretical principles. This will help ensure the service-learning field addresses themes of injustice, inequity and power. Combining the insights of the pioneers and emerging leaders with those of the literature, this study has identified six principles for addressing power in service-learning practice as seen in Table 1.3. These principles and accompanying strategies offer a good starting point for further investigation into quality critical service-learning that addresses issues of power.

In the next section, two models implementing these principles are explored. Both models are implemented by service-learning practitioners representing the dominant culture within under invested communities. Kelvyn Park High School's Social Justice Academy is an in school model

Table 1.2. Emergent Themes in the Literature Indicating Best Practices for Service-Learning Practice With Attention to Power

	Principle	*Authors*
1.	Include identity formation experiences/ mutual immersion in service experience or in prepare for service	Madsen-Camacho (2004); Green (2001); Dunlap et al. (2007); Kiely (2005); Pompa (2002)
2.	Explicitly name and ID imbalances of power within the service experience	Varlotta (1996); Green (2001); Pompa (2002)
3.	Engage in coinvestigation/dialogic process	Varlotta (1996); Pompa (2002)
4.	Emphasize relationship building	Madsen-Camacho (2004); Kiely (2005); Pompa (2002)
5.	Involve community in design and implementation of service	Green (2001); Pompa (2002)

in Chicago, Illinois. Additionally, the Elementary Institute of Science, is an after school service-learning program in San Diego, California, providing an example of critical service-learning implemented within a community based organization.

THE SOCIAL JUSTICE ACADEMY MODEL: KELVYN PARK HIGH SCHOOL

Kelvyn Park is a Chicago public high school on the northwest side of the city. In the 2008–2009 school year Kelvyn Park enrolled 1,563 students.

Table 1.3. Six Principles of Best Practice for Addressing Power in Service-learning

Principle for Addressing Power	*Strategies From Critical Theory*	*Strategies From Pioneers*	*Strategies From SL Literature*	*Strategies From Emerging Leaders*
1. Developmentof Individuals Personal Power	– Personal Transformation Through Ideological Clarity – Acknowledge Subjectivity	– Leading through facilitation - Employ emergent leaders in community	– Identity formation – Provide opportunities to develop the skills for success	– Engaging Indigenous Leadership – Acknowledging and using student experience
2. Create Space for True Partnership with all Stakeholders	– Acknowledge Subjectivity	– Simultaneous development of community power and assets – Employ Emergent Leaders in the community	– Identity formation	– Allow youth voice – Train in necessary skills and personal development
3. Situate Learning in Authentic Real World Contexts	– Situating Learning in Social Context	– Role of Context in all work – Culturally Reflective Mentorship	– Mutual immersion model – Mentorship in prison writing program and reading tutoring	– Relevant curriculum that builds off life experiences – Peer to peer mentors matched by socio-economics, culture and age

Table 1.3. Six Principles of Best Practice for Addressing Power in Service-learning

Principle for Addressing Power	*Strategies from Critical Theory*	*Strategies From Pioneers*	*Strategies From SL Literature*	*Strategies From Emerging Leaders*
4. Long-Term Relationship Building Across Stakeholders	– Building connections through establishing community	– Long term organizational partnerships – Becoming a member of the community – Building community – Acting as advocates for Community Members	– Relationship Development – Long-Term Sustainable Projects	– Building Trust – Partnering with Outside Groups to Work with Youth – Collaborative, Cooperative Relationships – Open Communication
5. Explicitly Name Power Relationships	– Naming and engaging manifestations of power	– Explicitly addressing and naming power	– need to address power in SL	– implicitly addressed through program elements
6. Produce Meaningful Action Toward Transformational Change	– Transformational change in the world	– Meaningful positive roles for youth	– Action toward change	– Meaningful opportunities for youth to create change – High Standards – Curriculum connected to purpose and action – Creating opportunities for success

Of those 89.2% were Latino(a), 8.2% Black and 2.2% White. The Latino(a) population includes large populations of students from Mexico and Puerto Rico in addition to a variety of Central American, South American and Carribbean Island countries. 15.6% of the students are labeled as Limited English Proficient. 90.3% of the students are designated Low Income. The attendance rate for 2009 was 76.3%. The graduation rate was 73.8%.

The Social Justice Academy (SJA) was started by two Kelvyn Park High School English teachers, Jesse Senechal and Maura Nugent, who had an interest in social justice education. As they worked on curriculum together, they also began discussing larger issues in the school—such as the high dropout rate and the lack of academic engagement from many students. The creation of SJA began with a discussion among the teachers about the school's JROTC program. They observed that in informal conversations with their classes many students identified JROTC as their favorite subject. It became clear that JROTC fulfilled many students' desire to take on leadership roles and to exercise power. In addition, unlike most classes at Kelvyn Park, there was an appeal in JROTC's clear tie to a viable post secondary option—enlistment in the military. These observations around the success of JROTC led to a series of questions. Did a successful program for student leadership at Kelvyn Park have to be tied to the JROTC model? Could Kelvyn Park High School have a program based in community service and community leadership, rather than military service and military leadership? From these questions, the Social Justice Academy was born.

The original goals of the SJA were: (1) to provide a rigorous curricula integrated with service-learning projects and themes of social justice; (2) to actively train students for leadership in school and in the community; and (3) to serve as an advisory model to help support students academically, emotionally, and socially. It began as a small program in the English Department for 55 randomly selected freshmen. The decision to randomly select students was a purposeful one: The intent was to understand how a program such as the SJA could best serve the "typical" Kevlyn Park student. In the following year the SJA expanded, so that students took a social justice section of their English class as a blocked class during freshmen and sophomore years.

The curricula were integrated with multiple service-learning projects throughout the year. From the start Mr. Senechal and Ms. Nugent envisioned the curricula as the service-learning projects, and the service-learning projects as the curricula. This was a reflection of Freire's (1970) concept of praxis: the synthesis of reflection and action. Service-learning is a good pedagogical tool to enact praxis with its emphasis on reflection and authentic applications of learning. The SJA's model of service learning is different than traditional service-learning models because the SJA students were serving their own community as well as breaking down the notion of service as actions done by members of advantaged groups to members of disadvantaged groups. Although the service-learning projects were facilitated by two teachers whose race and class afforded them societal power, the students themselves directed the projects.

As students progressed to their junior and senior year, they remained in the *SJA* homerooms and were provided with additional leadership opportunities in the community. This, as well as the multiple service-learning projects, led to the development of a key partnership for the SJA, the Logan Square Neighborhood Association (LSNA). In 2009, the *SJA* expanded to become a "Small Learning Community" within Kelvyn Park High School. In the "small learning community" model, the students are taught through social justice themes expressed through service-learning projects from teachers who identify themselves as social justice educators in all of their core academic classes from their sophomore through senior years.

As the Social Justice Academy developed and grew, two elements emerged as being key to its success. The first was a grounding in critical theory. Even before the proposal for the SJA was approved by their principal, Mr. Senechal and Ms. Nugent began reading and discussing critical education theory together. They formed a partnership with DePaul University that grew into a research group, which included professors, graduate students, SJA teachers, and high school students. For almost a year prior to the beginning of the social justice academy, as well as during the SJA's first year, Mr. Senechal and Ms. Nugent engaged in intensive study groups with the guidance and participation of a DePaul professor and two graduate students. In addition, when the Social Justice Academy had the opportunity to expand in 2009, the focus on theory continued. The veteran SJA teachers formed a social justice education reading group, reaching out to teachers in other subject areas who might be a good fit. The year of monthly reading and discussions served as an induction to social justice teaching for the new Science, Math, and History teachers. In these ways, thoughtful reflection using critical education theory has always been a core part of the Social Justice Academy's development.

The use of critical education theory to understand the realities of their classroom practice allowed the teachers to understand both their successes and areas for growth in their work. In turn, they honed their identities as social justice educators. For example, it was through the initial study group that Mr. Senechal and Ms. Nugent realized one of the flaws of their program the first year: The lack of opportunity to "practice hope." In *Teachers as Cultural Workers: Letter to Those Who Dare to Teach*, Paulo Freire (1994) writes "hope needs practice in order to become historical concreteness ... without the struggle, hope ... dissipates ... loses its bearings, and turns into hopelessness" (p. 7). Through the first year study group, the SJA team came to understand how crucial the "concrete practice of hope" was to the work they were trying to do. The existing curriculum was heavy on critical social analysis, which often left students feeling defeated by a heightened awareness of social inequities. For example, a unit on race designed to empower students resulted in bringing out the students' own prejudices and stereotypes as well as highlighting their lack of power in society as working class youth of color.

The SJA teachers studied tapes of classroom discussions and noticed slumped bodies, heads laid listlessly on the desk, and audible groans when it came time to move the chairs into a circle for discussion. Given the fact that the discussion matter was relevant to the students' real lives outside of the classroom, and the format itself was highly interactive—these defeated postures and resistance could not be explained away as typical student boredom. In one classroom discussion a particularly perceptive and outspoken student expressed her frustration in a heated outburst, effectively saying that she would rather not have her eyes "opened" to these inequities because now she was left with the knowledge and no outlet to eliminate the inequalities.

Furthermore, these expressions of apathy and resistance were in sharp contrast to the students' behaviors and comments during the one significant community project the class undertook that year—an oral history project with adult community mentors. Students became alive in this work: Interacting in a lively and connected way with the adult mentors, demonstrating real engagement in the interviewing, writing, revising, as well as demonstrating true pride in the finished project and final public sharing of the work. Studying their own classroom practice, with the aid of critical theory and informed reflection, the teachers understood that their curriculum which emphasized analysis of power inequities did not give students enough opportunities to experience the ways they did have power—such as through collective organizing and community action. The *SJA* teachers began to understand that students needed to be consistently involved in community action to balance the critical social analysis.

This led to the second key element of Social Justice Academy's development and growth: The partnership with a local community based organization, Logan Square Neighborhood Association (LSNA), a nonprofit, multi-issue, grassroots community organization that works on issues ranging from affordable housing, to school reform, to neighborhood safety.

The SJA's partnership with LSNA began the first year of the program. The most significant community project of the first year—the oral history project—was done in partnership with LSNA. LSNA and Kelvyn Park were then awarded a grant from the Local Initiatives Support Corporation, which would fund a continuing partnership.

Because this grant allocated more resources to the cultural work, it allowed more room to solidify and expand the relationship. LSNA and the SJA have continued to partner on long term, significant projects. This is a key best practice (as outlined above) for addressing imbalances of power in critical service-learning initiatives.

One example of such a project was a semester of work that culminated in students creating an original documentary on the issue of affordable housing and gentrification. Students worked with LSNA to use their documentary, *Shelter: One Community's Struggle,* to educate the community about the need for affordable housing in their rapidly gentrifying neighborhood. The "*Shelter*" project was a dynamic one that involved several steps. The first step was to identify an issue of injustice in their community. Students spent several weeks identifying possible topics, interviewing LSNA staff and community residents, and participating in consensus building discussions facilitated by LSNA staff. Through this process, the students chose the topic of gentrification. They then researched the issue through intensive reading, interviews, surveys, and multimedia documentation. During their research and filmmaking, SJA teachers were meeting frequently with LSNA staff to plan the next steps of the project. Affordable housing is one of LSNA's areas of work; therefore, multiple opportunities arose for students to participate in direct action, such as door knocking, attending protests and community meetings, and speaking with the local alderman.

The *Shelter* project is a classic example of how SJA's partnership with LSNA worked. It also illustrates the importance of relationship building as a best practice for addressing power in critical service-learning. In the case of the SJA, relationship building resulted in partnerships that made the practice of hope concrete through the authentic application of learning. Students were actively involved in real work: They addressed inequities and injustices in their community. Incorporating the practice of hope was transformative. Before students felt apathetic, hopeless, powerless—commenting often that "things will never change," or that "no one will listen to us." Working with LSNA inevitably changed the way students talked about their ability to affect change. They began to see themselves as agents of change. The authentic opportunities to apply learning that came from this partnership also demonstrate the importance of contextualizing students' work in the real world. This is, indeed, another best practice for addressing power in critical service-learning. Finally, because students were able to contribute to real community change, the work was transformative demonstrating the final step in addressing power in service-learning. The student comment below indicates the transformative effect of the community work on *SJA* students:

> It makes me look at many different things and many different situations. Like, when I think about and when I see other people present or when I present.... I think of everything and how it connects. And how it is important as women and especially minorities to stick together and try our best because I think that's our power and we just don't realize that. (*SJA* Student, Class of 2008)

The partnership with LSNA also allowed SJA teachers to mitigate power imbalances realized during their own process of identity formation informed by reading critical theory. It is important to note, that while identity formation is listed as a best practice for addressing power in service-learning with students, it is also a crucial practice for teachers as well. Mr. Senechal and Ms. Nugent recognized that as middle-class White teachers, originally from outside the neighborhood, their perspective was inherently limited. This was compounded by the imbalance of power inherent in the teacher-student relationship. This realization helped Mr. Senechal and Ms. Nugent work to privilege student voice in the classroom and in the curriculum. While this was the goal, in practice, this was very difficult because students often lacked the critical knowledge that could inform their point of view. Consequently, they often fell back on mainstream, hegemonic explanations for the unjust societal conditions they were exploring in the curriculum and service learning. Mr. Senechal and Ms. Nugent struggled to find a balance between teacher voice and student voice, as well as negotiating the inherent problems of power and perspective created by their own racial and class privilege.

The partnership with LSNA was integral in addressing issues of power. Through working with LSNA, students began to have close contact and real relationships with the community organizers and community leaders who shared the same background them. This example of culturally reflective mentorship demonstrates another best practice for addressing power in service-learning. The contact with critical community activists gave students a much broader base of knowledge. In addition, the perspective that *SJA* teachers lacked was brought in through the work with LSNA.

THE ELEMENTARY INSTITUTE OF SCIENCE COMMISSION ON SCIENCE THAT MATTERS

The Elementary Institute of Science (EIS) is a science education nonprofit organization in San Diego, California that provides affordable hands-on after school and summer science classes in the under invested area of south east San Diego. EIS serves students from all areas of San Diego; however, a majority of students come from the immediate neighborhood. In 2009, EIS served a total of 650 students from 250 different schools in San Diego.

The Commission On Science That Matters (COSTM) program grew out of community requests to extend the existing elementary science program. This program is designed for students ages 14–17; it allows them to work with a mentor in a science field, applying science learned at EIS to produce a tangible useful product for the mentor's company that also benefits the students' community. The COSTM program is a year-long commitment that begins in the summer.

During the program's 6 week summer component, students attend daily classes on the science topic addressed as well as attend classes to develop the necessary skills to complete service projects and explore related social and environmental justice issues. All projects are presented around an annual science theme such as health, energy or water. Each student takes part in daily public speaking and leadership classes during the summer to refine their skills. Students who attend multiple years of the program act as leaders, mentoring incoming students. Student leaders assist in the identification and solicitation of mentors, deciding on program projects, in addition to putting on occasional classes for new incoming students. This emphasis on building and utilizing student leadership is purposeful, allowing the program facilitator to mediate the inherent power imbalances between students and their adult teachers and mentors.

As the summer draws to a close, students choose a specific project they would like to work on for the remainder of the school year. Once the students have chosen their topic, they meet as a group to create a plan of action to complete their project. The document outlines goals, objectives and deadlines. This is formally written up and presented by the student team to mentors at a working lunch sponsored by EIS.

For the remainder of the school year, students meet as a group at EIS once per week after school to accomplish their goals. Mentors meet with student project groups monthly to ensure they are meeting their deadlines and working toward their goals. Finally, in the Spring, student teams present their work to the mentoring organization, families and other relevant professionals in the community. The strong emphasis on culturally reflective mentoring relationships helps broaden students' exposure to professionals and experts that share a similar worldview. This also allows the program facilitator, a member of white middle class culture, to utilize the expertise of others to complement her inherently limited perspective and experience as it relates to being socially marginalized in North America's unjust society.

One example of a past project includes examining a proposed California law addressing controls on greenhouse gas emissions. The students worked with the California Center for Sustainable Energy and their policy experts to understand how this proposed law would impact their families and their community. Students also examined different compliance levels with existing laws in parts of the city with different socioeconomic demographics. They found less compliance with existing laws and more health hazards in the community within which EIS was housed. Students explored issues of environmental justice around this topic through discussions facilitated by the author.

Based on this information, they proposed solutions presented in the new state law to the San Diego City Council and asked the council members why the discrepancy among neighborhoods was so great. The San Diego City Council was very impressed with their presentation and asked them to come back in order to add their newfound expertise to the city's revision of the general plan. Students' projects have also addressed: The disproportionate rise in type 2 diabetes in young adults of color through the creation of new marketing materials with the San Diego Chapter of the American Diabetes Association, how to keep families healthy and healthy through the creation of cookbooks, and improving students well-being through the development of a heath fair for local Grade 5 students.

This program's grounding in principles of critical theory helped ensure its success. The program developer and director, Andrea Yoder Clark was enrolled in a social-justice focused PhD program during the program design and development. As a part of this program, she was regularly exploring critical theoretical approaches to education and utilized this program model to satisfy program requirements, including the completion of her qualifying exams and portion of her final dissertation. The regular support from professors and other graduate students at the university allowed her to consistently review, modify and inform her practice from a critical theoretical perspective.

Additionally, the inclusion of partners from mentoring organizations was a key element allowing students to connect with culturally responsive mentors within the sciences. This program was also well funded, allowing students to take advantage of state of the art computer and curriculum resources. Also important was the large programmatic emphasis on skill building. Students developed the public speaking, leadership and practical skills necessary to complete all projects. Finally, the authentic nature of the projects gave students tasks that required the application of learning within a real world environment. Students were often recognized for their work by various local government bodies, including a local city council member and the National Youth Leadership Council (NYLC). Outside funding also allowed students to attend national conferences on service learning and education. This also enabled them to present their work to professional audiences. Students presented at the NYLC Annual Conference in 2007 and 2008, as well as at the American Educational Research Association (AERA) Annual Conference in 2009. The authentic nature of students work as well as the regular venues for public presentation infused their work around environmental and social justice with hope and possibility, allowing students to impact their larger communities.

SIMILARITIES ACROSS PROGRAM EXAMPLES

While all critical service-learning programs differ according to the needs of their populations, some principles and strategies can be applied across programs. In both of the critical service-learning initiatives outlined above, heavy emphasis was made to support practitioners in the application of critical theory to examine and revise their practice. Programs partnered with universities and other critically-minded practitioners for the purpose of providing the necessary intellectual and social support for their work. Both programs emphasized the importance of culturally reflective mentorship, either from one strategic community partner or several, as in the EIS example. This was especially important for these specific programs as the program leaders were representatives of dominant culture and unable to fully relate to the experiences of marginalization experienced by their students.

The six principles for enacting critical service-learning outlined earlier in this chapter were enacted in both programs. Identity formation experiences, along with skill building and learning activities, ensured that students were able to use their personal power to build long-term sustainable relationships with culturally reflective mentors in partnering institutions. The relationships resulted in personal and community transformation. The emphasis on authentic application of learning serving real needs generated hope and possibility among the participants in both programs.

Implications for the Field

A discussion of power dynamics in service-learning will add to the critical service-learning literature. The service-learning field has asked for greater attention to diversity as well as the need to identify more critical service-learning strategies that work well with diverse students (Gasang, 2003; Weah, Simmons, & Hall, 2003). This chapter contends that long-term change in service-learning can only be accomplished through explicit attention to power at all stages of the service-learning process. Imbalances of power are often experienced directly in the lives of marginalized communities. Increased attention to imbalances of power in service-learning with diverse students can make service-learning experiences more relevant to the lives of these students. The dearth of research in the service-learning field around power leaves much room for future study.

QUESTIONS FOR REFLECTION

1. What additional best practices can help mediate differences in power that emerge in the the service-learning experience?
2. What additional insights can be gleaned from the critical theory literature to informattention to power in service-learning?
3. Where do imbalances of power most impact the service-learning experience?
4. How do experiences from different positions of power affect participation in service-learning?
5. What are other successful models of service-learning practice that attend to issues of power?

NOTE

1. Power-access, knowledge of how, and the ability to effect change outside of oneself through explicit recognition of the role of societal institutions and systems; the sociocultural context and the role of relationships in shaping one's experience of being powerful or powerless.

Appendix A

Participant Characteristics

	SL Emerging Leaders		*SL Pioneers*	
	n=7		*n*=7	
Ethnicity	*n*	%	*n*	%
White	1	14%	5	72%
African American	3	43%	1	14%
Hispanic/Latino	3	43%	–	–
Asian/Pacific Islander	–	–	1	14%
Ethnicity	*n*	%	*n*	%
Female	5	71%	2	29%
Male	2	29%	5	71%

REFERENCES

Billig, S. (2000). The effects of service-learning. *The School Administrator, 57*(7), 12–19.

Darder, A., Baltadano, M., & Torres, R. (2003). Critical pedagogy: An introduction. In A. Darder, M. Baltadano, & R. Torres (Eds.), *The Critical Pedagogy Reader* (pp. 1–21) New York, NY: Routledge-Falmer.

Dunlap, M., Scoggin, J., Green, P., & Davi, A. (2007). White students' experiences of privilege and socioeconomic disparities: Toward a theoretical model. *Michigan Journal of Community Service Learning, 13*(2), 19–30.

Fine, M., & Weiss, L. (2003). *Silenced voices and extraordinary conversations: Re-imagining public schools*. New York, NY: Teacher College Press.

Foucault, M. (1977). *Knowledge and power.* New York, NY: The Harvester Press.

Freire, P. (1970). *Pedagogy of the oppressed.* New York, NY: Continuum.

Friere, P. (1994) *Teachers as cultural workers: Letters to those who dare to teach*. New York, NY: Continuum.

Gasang, J. (2003). Bringing diversity and service-learning center stage. In M. Duckenfield, C. Klopp, B. Donnelly, M. Ogden (Eds.), *The generator* (pp. 33–43), Minneapolis, MN: National Youth Leadership Council.

Giroux, H. (2003). Critical theory and educational practice. In A. Darder, M. Baltadano, & R. Torres (Eds.), *The critical pedagogy reader* (pp. 27–56). New York, NY: Routledge-Falmer.

Gramsci, A. (1971). *Selections from the prison notebooks*. London: Lawrence & Wishart.

Green, A. (2001). "But you aren't white?" Racial perceptions and service-learning. *Michigan Journal of Community Service Learning, 8*(1), 18–26.

Held, D. (1980). *Introduction to critical theory: Horkheimer to Habermas*. Berkeley, CA: University of California Press

Kahne, J., & Westheimer, J. (1996). In the service of what? The politics of service-learning. *Phi Delta Kappan*, 77(9), 592–599.

Kellner, D. (1989). *Critical theory, Marxism and modernity.* Baltimore, MD: John Hopkins University Press.

Kiely, R. (2005). A transformational learning model for service-learning: A longitudinal case study. M*ichigan Journal of Community Service-Learning, 12*(1), 5–22.

Kincheloe, J. (2008). *Critical pedagogy primer.* New York, NY: Peter Lang.

Levine, P. (2008) Service-learning and the national education debate. *The Generator.* Minneappolis, MN: National Youth Leadership Council

Madsen-Camacho, M. (2004). Power and privilege: Community service learning in Tijuana. *Michigan Journal of Community Service Learning, 10*(3), 31–42.

Melchior, A. (2000) Costs and benefits of service-learning. *The School Administrator, 57*(7), 25–32.

Pompa, L. (2002). Service-learning as crucible: Reflections on immersion, context, power and transformation. *Michigan Journal of Community Service Learning, 9*(1), 67–76.

Pineros-Shields, T. (1996) *History and debate: Political advocacy in national service*. Boston, MA: Tufts University.

Stanton, T., Giles, D., & Cruz, N. (1999). *Service-learning: A movements pioneers reflect on its origins, practice and future.* San Francisco, CA: Jossey-Bass.
Shor, I. (1992) Empowering *education: Critical teaching for social change.* Chicago, IL: University of Chicago Press.
Varlotta, L. (1996). Service-learning to transform communities. *Michigan Journal of Community Service learning, 3*(1), 22–30.
Weah, W., Simmons, V. C., & Hall, M. (2003). Service-learning and multi-cultural/multiethnic perspectives: From diversity to equity. *Phi Delta Kappan, 81*(9), 673–680.
Yoder, A. (2008, March) *The forgotten legacy: Calling on service-learning's history with critical theory to create praxis in underserved urban environments.* Paper presented at the American ducational Research Association Annual Conference, New York, NY.
Yoder Clark, A. (2009). *Power and service-learning: Implications in service-learning for social justice.* Claremont, CA: Claremont Graduate University.

CHAPTER 2

DISTANT OR DIRECT

Students' Interactions With Service Recipients While Completing Ontario's Community Involvement Requirement

Kaylan C. Schwarz

Community involvement activities can be partly distinguished according to the extent of opportunity they offer servers to directly interact with service recipients. By direct interaction, I am referring to face-to-face exchanges between the providers and beneficiaries of community involvement assistance. Existing literature tends to advocate community involvement activities involving sustained contact with marginalized social groups. For example, Billig (2002) reviewed dozens of studies from the 1990s and concluded that servers' positive personal gains were likely to be maximized with increased in-person interaction among community members. More recently, Reinders and Youniss' (2006) longitudinal survey of 620 middle-upper class secondary school students in Washington, DC revealed that servers' ongoing exchanges with people in obvious need was positively associated with servers' self-awareness, helpfulness, anticipated future civic engagement and intent to volunteer in the future. Thus, community

Critical Service Learning as a Revolutionary Pedagogy:
A Project of Student Agency in Action, pp. 29–46

involvement experiences that involve opportunities to build personal relationships over time may play an important role in fostering the development of the server's civic-related outcomes.

When servers have the opportunity to directly interact with service recipients, Yates and Youniss (1996b) describe servers' potential to be "transformed" as a progression along three linear levels of "transcendence." In level 1—the least transformative outcome—servers begin to replace simplistic and sweeping categorizations of "others" (often construed as minority and marginalized social groups) with the understanding that individuals possess unique biographies that are shaped by their distinct contexts. At level 2, servers inventory and compare their observations of service recipients' lives to their own lived experiences, and respond to observed discrepancies by developing a heightened awareness of, and appreciation for, their own privilege. Finally, in level 3—the most transformative outcome—servers' direct interactions with formally distant "others" inspire them to search for the underlying causes of encountered social problems. Thus, directly interacting with service recipients is not an immediate pathway to profound personal transformation: there are a number of ways (of varying criticality) that servers might "transcend" in response to their encounters with other people.

I find Yates and Youniss' (1996) "transcendence levels" useful for organizing a discussion of the potential implications of student servers' direct interaction with service recipients. However, one caution is that Yates and Youniss appear to assume that servers are largely unaware of social problems before completing their community involvement activities. This suggests to me that the authors envision servers as economically privileged, and thus, begin their community involvement journeys a considerable distance apart from the contexts of service recipients. Thus, this chapter considers whether low-income participants reflect upon their interactions with service recipients differently than high-income participants. Indeed, while high income participants in this study spoke about overcoming stereotypes, reflecting on their own circumstances, and becoming "aware" of social problems to varying extents, low-income youth expressed having been already prepared to encounter social problems through their own lived experiences.

This chapter will explore Ontario secondary school students' reflections of their distant and direct interactions with service recipients during the completion of mandatory community involvement hours. In September 1999, the Government of Ontario instituted this community involvement requirement—whereby all secondary school students must complete 40 hours of community involvement in order to graduate—in an effort to "encourage students to develop awareness and understanding of civic responsibility and the role they can play in supporting and strengthening their communities" (Ministry of Education and Training, 1999, p. 6). However, while Ontario's community involvement requirement is a mandatory program for all secondary school students, procedures for its completion are loosely regulated by the Ministry of Education. Students are provided the autonomy to choose where, when and how they will complete their community involvement hours. Furthermore, these activities are performed outside of school hours and without teacher supervision. In this context, students across the province participate in a wide and diverse range of community involvement activities, the selection of which is largely dependent on the personal contexts and desires of the server. Furthermore, unlike many service-learning programs in the United States, Ontario's community involvement requirement allots no avenue for formal preparation or structured reflection in a classroom setting. When students reach their minimum hours, they simply fill out their school board's prescribed completion form and provide verifying signatures from on-location supervisors. Given these parameters, students' differential access to time, resources and social networks may markedly influence the types of community involvement activities in which they participate, and therefore, the extent of their interaction with service recipients.

This study employed a mixed-methods approach involving quantitative surveys and qualitative focus groups among a sample of 50 current and recently graduated secondary school students of widely contrasting socioeconomic statuses from a large, urban city in Southern Ontario. All participants had taken part in Ontario's community involvement requirement as a condition of their graduation. In addition, the sample was closely balanced for socioeconomic background, gender distribution and presence of visible minorities. Participants were not explicitly asked to disclose their socioeconomic background; however, inferences were made based on known demographics of participants' geographic location as well as the typical populations served by the schools and organizations to which the participants were affiliated.

	Number of Participants	*Gender Distribution*	*Number of Visible Minorities*
Total	50	26 Female, 24 Male	19
Total High Income	26	17 Female, 9 Male	11
Total Low Income	24	9 Female, 15 Male	8

To locate my sample, I targeted independent (private) secondary schools, alternative secondary schools in priority neighborhoods, and youth-oriented community organizations, whose catchment populations included the disparate socioeconomic demographics of interest. Using a snowball sampling method, "gatekeepers" were extended a written invitation to participate in the study via e-mail and requested to forward the study information to their professional contacts and organizational LISTSERV.

Qualitative focus groups and quantitative surveys were conducted across ten data collection sessions, each involving between one and nine participants. Upon arrival, participants were asked to individually complete an anonymous quantitative survey. The survey primarily sought to learn about (1) participant demographics, (2) the types of community involvement activities that participants completed to fulfill their 40-hour requirement, and (3) whether participants had encountered opportunities to directly interact with service recipients during their community involvement experiences. The purpose of the focus groups was to learn about (1) participants' interpretations of their distant or direct interactions with service recipients, (2) participants' sense of their own civic agency, and (3) participants' perceptions of the wider social problems they may (or may not) have encountered during their community involvement activities. Pseudonyms are used for all quotations. The use of both quantitative surveys and qualitative focus groups allowed me to compare multiple perspectives and gain insight into participants' perceptions of their experiences.

In this study, high and low income participants' opportunities to forge relationships with service recipients varied considerably: some (mostly high-income) participants heralded their newfound bonds as the chief benefit and main positive memory of their community involvement experience, while other (mostly low-income) participants reported seldom having had exposure to anyone outside of their project supervisors or other volunteers. In this chapter, I will focus on participants' experiences of both distant and direct interaction with service recipients, although the latter will be highlighted. Using Yates and Youniss' (1996) proposed levels of transcendence as organizational markers, I will discuss the variety of ways that participants in this study reflected on their personal learning in relation to their interactions with service recipients.

DISTANT INTERACTION WITH SERVICE RECIPIENTS

One criticism of school-based community service activities is that student projects are too often undertaken in the comfortable confines of the classroom, involving no direct interaction with marginalized groups (Schmidt, Shumow, & Kackar, 2007). For example, collecting canned goods during a local food drive may provide an important contribution to organizations working to alleviate poverty and hunger; however, such activities do not take place in settings where student servers could directly interact with the individuals who rely on such subsistence. Without opportunities to develop relationships through direct interaction with service recipients, student servers may be less likely to develop the qualities that are desirable for democratic citizenship, namely, an appreciation for diversity and an understanding of personal and sociohistorical contexts.

When secondary schools provide on-campus opportunities for students to complete their community involvement hours, these initiatives may inadvertently cloister students by offering little exposure to the "outside world." In this study, over three-quarters (20/26) of the high-income participants reported on the survey that they had completed a portion of their community involvement activities on their school campus, detached from in-person contact with service recipients. About half of these school-based activities were one-time events and an additional one-fifth involved on-campus fundraising initiatives. This further suggests a transient and abstract connection to service recipients. Kielsmeier, Scales, Roehlkepartain, and Neal (2004) similarly found that school-based service activities were often fleeting in nature: 80% of the service activities reported in their study were one-time events. Drawing on one typical example from this study, Jamie worked with his school staff to organize a fundraiser for a well-known international charity:

> We organized a canvassing around the neighbourhood, raised over $1,000, which we donated to that charity [to] help kids and families around Third World countries.... After we completed that, we had everyone stand up for a minute of silence [to support an anti-poverty campaign].... [Then we] made a recording and posted it online so people around the world could see our initiative.

Jamie evaluated this particular experience very positively, and he appeared to take pride in having helped generate a collective effort toward an issue of importance. However, Jamie's commendable pursuits to raise awareness and resources involved no direct contact with any impoverished people and did not appear to provoke an understanding of (or yearning to discover) why people are impoverished in the first place.

Detachment from service recipients may be exacerbated among independent school students who live in residential halls during the school year. These students may have few opportunities to leave their campuses outside of the structured excursions that are facilitated and supervised by school staff, perhaps making it difficult for students to forge a connection with, or develop an understanding of, their wider community. For example, Jamie seemed momentarily puzzled when I asked him how the community had benefitted from his community involvement hours: "as a boarded student, I haven't seen much of the outside, except during the holidays. So in terms of how I benefited the community, I don't exactly know how." In this study, at least five other high-income participants were known to live on-campus during the school year. If these boarded students encounter few opportunities to physically depart from their campuses, it seems unlikely that they will significantly heighten their understanding of community involvement's impact on individual people, the wider community, or society-at-large. Thus, while high income schools may provide ample opportunity for their students to complete community involvement hours on-campus, students' resulting distance from the actual communities being served may inadvertently hinder opportunities to develop an understanding of marginalized groups of people and the social problems that affect their lives.

Low-income youth do not often have the luxury to choose whether or not to be (at least physically) embedded in their communities. In this study, no low-income participant described being isolated from their community during the completion of their community involvement hours. Instead, Samantha explained that there was no partition available to separate her from community life: "I have been involved in the community because of my life; being around certain people and certain things that I honestly never thought that I'd be around." Samantha's comment suggests that there is a certain intractability between low-income participants and their communities. Still, low-income participants did not necessarily have opportunities to directly interact with service recipients during their community involvement activities. On the survey, one-third (8/24) of low-income participants reported having *no* interaction with people beyond their minimal encounters with project supervisors or other volunteers. For example, during Focus Group 8 (low income), the participants collectively recounted that no one in the group had come into contact with a single service recipient during their community involvement hours:

Anthony: I didn't work with anybody. When I worked for the church, they just put me in the basement cleaning chairs.... The only person that I worked with was one of my classmates that I went with.

Arden: Ultimately, I didn't really have much contact with anybody ... the closest I would have had [to direct interaction] would be the server position at the Seniors Dinner, and even there it's like less of a relationship than they'd have with a waiter.

Shane: I actually didn't see the faces of the people I helped. I didn't see one of them ...

Trevor: ... I never got to actually meet any patrons of the Food Bank ... [so] it's not like I got to know any of any of these people or understand where they are coming from.

In the days following Focus Group 8, I received follow-up correspondence from Shane, who informed me that he and his coparticipants had continued discussing their community involvement activities long into the evening, and that these conversations centred on their shared absence of direct interaction with service recipients. Shane divulged that the focus group session had prompted them to question whether community involvement activities could serve the public in a meaningful way if they entailed no involvement with the intended beneficiaries of such service. The group had also considered whether a student server could harness the personal benefits of "being engaged" without actually interacting among the community or building relationships with people outside of their existing social circles. Thus, when "the community" is omitted from community involvement activities, student servers may question the legitimacy or value of such experiences as they pertain to their own development and understanding the social dynamics that impact community development.

During this second conversation with Shane, as well as in most of my discussions with low-income participants, I got the sense that participants had *wanted* to develop impactful relationships with other people during their community involvement activities. For example, all of the members of Focus Group 8 (Shane, Anthony, Arden, and Trevor) expressed regret that more meaningful social interaction had not taken place between themselves and service recipients. They attributed their lack of direct interaction to the nature of the community involvement activities they had completed rather than a lack of desire to interact meaningfully with service recipients. On the survey, the eight low-income participants who reported having no interactions with service recipients all completed either administrative tasks or physical labour to fulfil their community involvement requirement. These activities—which included inventorying sports equipment, constructing a backyard deck, canvassing for donations, filing paperwork and shovelling a driveway—provided few opportunities to interact with service recipients or the wider community by virtue of their design. However, low-income participants' "choice" to complete these activities over more meaningfully engaging ventures may have been linked to the placement options that low-income participants believed were available to them. Thus, while low-income participants may have desired to complete community involvement activities that allowed them to forge relationships with service recipients, they did not appear to know how to access the placements that would allow such interactions to happen.

Thus, in this study, participants' lack of direct interaction with service recipients during community involvement activities appeared to be the result of both too much *and* too little opportunity. While the abundance of on-campus opportunities appeared to keep some high-income (particularly independent school) participants physically sectioned away from the community, low income participants' physical embedding within their communities seemed irrelevant when participants reported not knowing how to access opportunities for meaningful contact with others.

DIRECT INTERACTION WITH SERVICE RECIPIENTS

On the survey, all but two high-income participants reported having had some level of direct interaction with service recipients during their community involvement placements. High-income participants most commonly interacted with children (21 mentions), the elderly (5 mentions), people with special needs (6 mentions), and people of low-income background (3 mentions). Just over one-third of high income participants noted that they had worked with more than one category of service recipients. Furthermore, when high-income participants were asked to recall their most significant memory from their community involvement experiences, over three-quarters described situations which highlighted the relationships they had built with people in their community. Also, when I asked high-income participants how they had benefited personally from their community involvement experiences, over half spoke of skills related to relationship building, such as knowing how to interact with a diverse group of people. Thus, the majority of high-income participants in this study had some opportunity to directly interact with service recipients, and when they did, the resulting relationships featured prominently as positive memories and perceived catalysts for personal development.

In comparison, fewer low-income participants (about half) reported having had some level of direct interaction with service recipients. Low-income participants reported interacting with children (nine mentions), the elderly (five mentions), and people of low-income background (three mentions), however, none of these participants worked with more than one category of service recipients. This is presumably related to the fact that low-income participants reported less variety in the types of community involvement experiences they completed. When I asked low-income participants to recall their most significant memory from their experiences completing community involvement hours, under one-third described situations that mentioned a relationship they had forged with service recipients. Furthermore, when I asked how these participants benefited personally from their community involvement experiences, only one-fifth spoke of skills related to relationship building. Thus, the extent to which high and low income participants' comments emphasized their relationships with other people appeared commensurate with whether or not they had had opportunities to directly interact with service recipients.

OVERCOMING STEREOTYPES

In this study, high-income participants who had had opportunities to directly interact with service recipients reported a diminished sense of "otherness" between themselves and people from less advantaged social groups. About one-third of high-income participants spoke about having had to confront and dismantle their own negative stereotypes regarding the population they were serving. For example, remembering his community involvement placement at a local soup kitchen, Jeremy recalled having to "check his baggage" upon arrival:

> I admit, I was 14 years old and I was scared ... and I was, I confess, kind of ignorant. But as the process went along.... I definitely saw the homeless population differently. Many of the times I thought they must be escaped criminals or whatever ... [but the homeless] are not people that we should be afraid of; they are people that we should be trying to help.

This quote was very similar to other reflections from high-income participants who worked among the homeless population. Through his direct interaction with a marginalized population, Jeremy appeared to tackle a previously held assumption and reported being able to reframe his understandings as a result of this experience. Thus, community involvement activities that include direct interaction with other social groups may provide high-income servers with face-to-face models who challenge them to replace sweeping stereotypes with qualified understandings of individual contexts.

However, I was not entirely convinced that the high-income participants in this study had set aside their stereotypes in response to their brief encounters with the "Other." After all, socially desirable answers may be common in research where both the researcher and the participants' peers are present. It also seems unlikely that 40 hours of community involvement could eradicate all traces of high-income participants' former understandings of other social groups. Furthermore, rarely did a high-income participant speak about the potential commonalities between themselves and the people they had encountered during their community involvement activities. This is consistent with what Battistoni's (1997) called the "philanthropic view" and what Kahne and Westheimer (1996) called "charity," which both posit that affluent servers feel obligated to help the less advantaged, but do not conceive of those served as being part of their own communities. Thus, even when high-income participants claimed to overcome their stereotypes, they also appeared to maintain a comfortable distance between themselves and the people they sought to help. This finding lends support to Melchior's (1998) study of Learn and Serve America programs, in which participants reported high levels of satisfaction with the personal relationships they forged with service recipients, however, shifts in participants' civic attitudes were quite small (3–5%). Thus, while a few of the high-income participants may have come to recognize that their stereotypes could not be applied to all members of a marginalized group, I did not get the sense that any high-income participant did (or could have) entirely reframed their attitudes toward other people as a result of their brief community involvement experiences.

In this study, high-income participants did not automatically overcome their stereotypes of other social groups simply by directly interacting with members of those populations. When I asked whether any of the high-income participants had changed their attitudes or opinions as a result of their community involvement experiences, about one-fifth definitively answered "no." In fact, in one instance, a high-income participant's direct interaction with service recipients had appeared to reinforce her stereotypes of the homeless population. When Lily reflected on her experiences distributing sandwiches during a school-organized anti-poverty campaign, she reflected on her shifting perceptions as follows: "I kind of thought homeless people are [on the street] because they don't have money, [but when you meet them] you see that a lot of them choose to be there." During her brief encounters with members of the homeless population, Lily apparently strengthened her sense that poverty is the result of personal deficiency rather than stemming from systemic inequities. Lily's comment is reminiscent of Hondagneu-Sotelo and Raskoff's (1994) study of undergraduate students at the University of Southern California who, after completing voluntary semester-long service project in low-income schools, judged social problems to be the result of individual character deficits. Similarly, when Hollis (2002) collected reflection papers from her undergraduate sociology class after students had completed 20 hours of service at various neighborhood sites, she found that their written responses tended to objectify community residents and blame them for their own problems. Thus, while Lily's comment was an exception among both high and low income participants, it is nonetheless an important example of how community involvement can serve to fortify students' preconceptions or engender new misconceptions, especially if divorced from guided critical reflection.

Low-income participants tended to reflect quite differently from high-income students on their positioning in relation to service recipients: rarely did a participant in the low-income group make a comment that implied a division between themselves and the service recipients they encountered. On the contrary, low income participants' comments tended to imply closeness between themselves and service recipients. For example, low-income participants referred to service recipients using the descriptors "friend" or "family" on nine occasions, terms which were not utilized in any of the high-income focus groups. Furthermore, about one-quarter of the low-income participants explicitly stressed the similarities and shared personal histories between themselves and service recipients. For example, Andrea explained her reason for completing her community involvement hours in a youth program designed to empower at-risk girls: "I want to help [these young women] out because [they] are going through the same thing that I've been through." Here, Andrea spoke about the community involvement requirement as an opportunity to better the lives of those with a shared history rather than impacting the lives of distant "Others." Thus, low-income participants may locate service recipients more proximally if they envision themselves to be members of the same community or social group.

Low-income participants rarely spoke of having had personally struggled to overcome preconceived notions of other social groups. On the contrary, low-income participants seemed to have implicitly "known" to view service recipients as individuals with unique contexts rather than relying on stereotypes. For example, on three occasions, low-income participants made reference to the importance of learning about personal narratives as the foundation for relationship-building between student servers and service recipients. For example, Andrea voiced her opinion that community involvement is largely ineffective in eliminating wider social problems because student servers pay little attention to "what [the recipient's] story is, about their history, what they go home to.... Everyone has a different story [and] a different past ... it's all different when they go home and the door is closed." Here, Andrea went on to describe the act of listening to, and sharing in, personal narrative as a fundamental element of "successful" community involvement activities. Throughout my focus groups with low-income participants, I got the sense that this propensity to seek explanations in individual contexts may have stemmed from participants' own experiences feeling categorized by negative stereotypes. Thus, if adolescents are already familiar with the consequences of judgements based on preconceived notions, as the low-income participants in this study appeared to be, then their capacity to "overcome stereotypes" may be deeply ingrained through personal experience rather than the result of direct interaction with others during community involvement activities.

REFLECTING ON ONE'S OWN CIRCUMSTANCES

When high-income participants reported having had interacted with people from other social groups during their community involvement experiences, they typically spoke about the transformative benefits of, in Victor's words, seeing beyond their own "comfortable lifestyle." For example, in separate focus groups, five high-income participants used the term "bubble" to describe the cocooning nature of their affluent upbringings. Jeremy reflected that, having been raised in a resource-rich household, it was all-too-easy for him to "forget" about the circumstances affecting other people: "you don't really see [social problems] and you kind of start living in a little bubble, and the important thing about giving back is that it opens you up to that world." Additionally, about one-third of high income participants reflected that their community involvement experiences had encouraged them to widen their orbits of concern beyond their inner circle of friends and family. For example, when I asked Natalie how she had benefited from her community involvement hours, she explained: "I guess my experience allowed me to broaden my horizons past my immediate sort of social network and to recognize different parts of my community that were in need." Thus, direct interaction with service recipients appeared to provide an avenue for some high-income participants to become more familiar with previously unchartered territory.

Outside of their self-described "bubbles," high-income participants who experienced direct interaction with service recipients described being confronted with realities that were far removed from both their expectations and personal norms. For example, prior to working with a local ministry focused on poverty alleviation, Madeline noted that she had assumed that her lived experience had been reasonably representative of the wider citizen population, however: "giving out food to the poor and stuff, [you] kind of learn [that their] world isn't actually like what we're used to living, like nice houses and everything." Here, Madeline apparently came to recognize a disparity between her own life and the lives of less-advantaged communities. Thus, direct interaction with service recipients may urge high-income participants to readjust their understanding of the workings of the social world.

About half of high-income participants spoke about how direct interaction with service recipients had encouraged them to recognize their unusually privileged upbringings. For example, Michelle reported that a March Break volunteer excursion to the Dominican Republic had illuminated the stark contrast between the living conditions she had been accustomed to and those experienced daily by the service recipients she encountered:

> We couldn't drink the water that came out of our taps. We didn't have water heaters, and we lived in a building that looked like a prison for two weeks, and we ate rice and beans. And it's like, I come from this amazing place ...

> it's like incredibly wealthy, Whole Foods is down the street, you can buy whatever you want from anywhere around the world. We have these great beds. We have hot water, safe water, and just having that all go away, it's like "wow, this is happening to so many people."

Here, Michelle compared her own lifestyle with the shortage of accoutrements in the community she served, and responded to this discrepancy by expressing gratitude for her own fortunate status. This finding echoes King's (2004) case study of four students during a week-long service trip to Tijuana, Mexico who, despite the shortness of the program, reported that they came to reevaluate the taken-for-granted elements of their lifestyles and recognize facets of their privilege, which were previously unbeknownst to them. Thus, when high-income participants had the opportunity to directly interact with service recipients during their community involvement hours, some came to recognize the various manifestations of their own privilege, and furthermore, appeared to deepen their sense of appreciation toward these advantages.

In contrast, low-income participants did not speak about crossing into unfamiliar territory in order to complete their community involvement activities. They also did not speak about needing to widen their concern beyond their traditional social networks. Instead, low-income participants typically reported working with service recipients that were located *within* their own social groups. For example, five low-income participants mentioned completing their community involvement hours within a community program that they had been formally enrolled in themselves and that had played a large supporting role in their own childhoods. These participants described such organizations as second homes, the staff members as surrogate parents, and the service recipients as extended family members. In addition, low-income participants seemed to have a shared awareness of the circumstances that affect lives of others. For example, Veronica described feeling compelled to reach out to her former community program in order to share her experience with new members:

> I've grown and I've actually done it, been there myself, in terms of what young women and youth go through and all the issues they face. I've been through that myself. And now, being on top and being the person who can educate, [I feel I can] enlighten youth with my knowledge.

Here, Veronica's direct interaction with service recipients did not appear to stimulate any novel revelations regarding the lives of others, perhaps because she had navigated similar situations throughout her own life.

Low-income participants did not speak about developing an appreciation of their own lifestyles in relation to their interactions with service recipients. This may be partly attributed to the fact that this group of participants were not privileged, and by extension, did not appear to witness a large disparity between their own lives and the lives of service recipients. In fact, Jeffery mentioned that, in drawing parallels between himself and the service recipients he encountered, he had grown more cognizant of his own income-related struggles. Furthermore, Jeffery shared that he had originally resented having to provide community involvement to other community members when he had not been the recipient of similar aid: "I felt that I was helping others when I felt that perhaps I should have been helped." While Jeffery's comment was not typical of all low-income participants, it is nonetheless an example of how low-income participants may reflect on their own circumstances during their encounters with service recipients.

BECOMING "AWARE" OF SOCIAL PROBLEMS

All of the high-income focus groups I conducted spoke about becoming more "aware" of social problems as a result of their direct interaction with service recipients: the term "eye-opening" was peppered throughout almost all of the high-income focus group transcriptions. About one-third of high income participants made specific reference to how, prior to their community involvement experiences, they had not recognized the extent of need in their communities. For example, Miranda expressed feeling surprised upon discovering the severity of social problems within an international context:

> I think that all of us *kind of* know about social issues ... but I don't think any of us sort of knew the extent of it.... We've had [school assemblies] on the Dominican and Africa and the state that things are in, but I don't think any of us ... were as aware as we probably should have been.

This process of becoming "exposed" to the reality of social problems (beyond the understandings gleaned from in-school presentations) was perceived as a strong positive take-away in every focus group I conducted with high income participants. Thus, high-income participants' direct interaction with service recipients appeared to provide a window to the magnitude of some entrenched social problems.

When high-income participants asserted that their direct interaction with marginalized social groups had "opened their eyes" to the plethora of social problems impacting contemporary society, I got the sense that the depth of these understandings remained relatively shallow. With few exceptions, high-income participants either made observational comments about the specific ways social problems were evidenced in service recipients' lives, or, used ambiguous phrasing to describe a general understanding of the existence of social problems. For example, when Jessica described her experiences working with less-advantaged children at a summer camp, she reflected that: "I did a lot of learning about [social problems] like inequality and depression and poverty and stuff." Here, as was typical within almost all of my conversations with high-income participants, Jessica did not verbalize concerns about the contributing forces that underlie the inequality, depression and poverty she had encountered during her interactions. This finding lends support to Einfeld and Collins' (2008) study of 10 Americorps volunteers, where the more privileged study participants had become "conscious" of existing social inequalities, but did not appear to have integrated any deep interpretations of justice into their personal understandings of civic engagement. Thus, while it would be naive to expect student servers to grasp the full complexity of social problems after only 40 hours of community involvement, high-income participants in this study only noted the symptoms of social problems rather than questioning the possible causes.

Low-income participants did not typically speak about becoming more "aware" of social problems during their community involvement experiences. Instead, five low-income participants asserted that they had entered their community involvement activities already equipped with a lived understanding of social problems. For example, when I asked Tom whether any of his opinions or attitudes had changed as a result of his community involvement experiences, he maintained that: "My perception didn't change from community service. It changed from life." Presumably, if low-income youth are exposed daily to the effects of social problems, these students may interpret their personal history as more educative than their experiences completing community involvement hours. Thus, just as Einfeld and Collins (2008) found that Americorps volunteers who had previously experienced injustice communicated a more sophisticated awareness of how hardship moulds the day-to-day lives of other people, none of the low-income participants in this study suggested that community involvement had been at the helm of profound realizations regarding the workings of the social world.

CONCLUDING THOUGHTS

When completing mandated community involvement activities, secondary school students may or may not directly interact with people from diverse social groups. In this study, students' opportunities to encounter service recipients appeared to be related, in part, to their socioeconomic status: low-income participants reported having had less access to the types of community involvement activities that would have brought them into sustained contact with others. However, while servers' direct interaction with service recipients is presumed to be one catalyst for the development of civic-related outcomes, the results of this study question whether briefly interacting with service recipients serve to deepen students' understanding of other people or wider social problems.

In this study, Yates and Youniss' (1996) proposed "transcendence levels" seemed inadequate for describing low-income participants' community involvement experiences: members of this group did not tend to report having had to dismantle preexisting stereotypes, overcome stark contrasts between themselves and service recipients, or increase their awareness of social problems. Thus, while Yates and Youniss provide worthwhile learning benchmarks for student servers, their framework must be reconceptualized to acknowledge diverse students' pre-existing and lived understanding of social problems.

This study did not examine potential "best practices" or "better practices" for strengthening Ontario's community involvement requirement, however, a programmatic shift toward critical service-learning could be explored as one response to the results presented in this chapter. For example, critical service-learning departs from traditional and hierarchical notions of service, in which privileged servers attend to the needs of less fortunate others. Because student servers in Ontario come from a wide range of social backgrounds, this characteristic may serve to accommodate a wider conception of "who" servers are.

Critical service-learning could also help students pursue aspects of "transcendence" from a critical stance. In a critical service-learning model, when servers directly interact with service recipients, they do not simply "encounter" others in an effort to "humanize" them. Instead, the goal of critical service-learning is to create equitable partnerships rooted in respect and a sense of shared humanity. Thus, in recognizing others' strengths and resources, students could learn to challenge deficit interpretations of social problems and avoid reliance on sweeping stereotypes. Also, because critical service-learning is attuned to the situating of (and power dynamics between) servers and recipients, students could begin to reflect critically on their own location and positioning. Finally, critical service-learning explores the various social, historical and political contexts of inequities; potentially probing students to heighten their reflexive insight into the intersecting causes of social problems, and how they might work to dismantle them.

I believe Ontario's community involvement requirement could be implemented in a manner that better prepares students for their interactions with service recipients, and to navigate these experiences in a critical manner. Thus, future research should explore how critical service-learning might serve to enrich the experiences of diverse students completing community involvement in the Canadian context.

QUESTIONS FOR REFLECTION

1. In what other ways are less privileged students' experiences of community involvement different from high-income participants? How could theoretical models of community involvement be more encompassing of these potentially diverse experiences?
2. Does "community involvement" necessitate servers' direct interaction with service recipients? Can "distant" community involvement activities still serve the public in a meaningful way?
3. What *could* students in Ontario realistically learn about other community members and wider social problems within 40 hours of community involvement?
4. When students complete mandatory community involvement hours, how do the *service recipients* view their distant or direct interactions with student servers?
5. Are community involvement activities an adequate method for the dual-role of responding to social problems and educating youth for democratic citizenry? What other models might be available to educators?

REFERENCES

Battistoni, R. M. (1997). Service learning and democratic citizenship. *Theory into Practice, 36*(3), 150–156.

Billig, S. H. (2002). Support for K–12 service-learning practice: A brief review of the research. *Educational Horizons, 80*(4), 184–189.

Einfeld, A., & Collins, D. (2008). The relationships between service-learning, social justice, multicultural competence, and civic engagement. *Journal of College Student Development, 49*(2), 95–109.

Hollis, S. A. (2002). Capturing the experience: Transforming community service into service learning. *Teaching Sociology, 30*(2), 200–213.

Hondagneu-Sotelo, P., & Raskoff, S. (1994). Community service-learning: Promises and problems. *Teaching Sociology, 22*(3), 248–254.

Kahne, J., & Westheimer, J. (1996). In the service of what? The politics of service learning. *Phi Delta Kappan, 77*(9), 592–599.

Kielsmeier, J.C., Scales, P. C., Roehlkepartain, E. C., & Neal, M. (2004). Community service and service-learning in public schools: Reclaiming children and youth. *The Journal of Strength-Based Interventions, 13*(3), 138–143.

King, J. T. (2004). Service-learning as a site for critical pedagogy: A case of collaboration, caring, and defamiliarization across borders. *The Journal of Experiential Education, 26*(3), 121–137.

Melchior, A. (1998). *National evaluation of Learn and Serve America school and community based programs: Final report.* Waltham, MA: Center for Human Resources, Brandeis University.

Ministry of Education and Training. (1999). *Ontario secondary schools, grades 9-12: Program and diploma requirements.* Retrieved from http://www.edu.gov.on.ca/eng/document/curricul/secondary/oss/oss.pdf

Reinders, H., & Youniss, J. (2006). School-based required community service and civic development in adolescents. *Applied Developmental Science, 10,* 2– 12.

Schmidt, J. A., Shumow, L., & Kackar, H. (2007). Adolescents' participation in service activities and its impact on academic, behavioral, and civic outcomes. *Journal of Youth and Adolescence, 36*(2), 127–140.

Yates, M., & Youniss, J. (1996b). Community service and identity development in adolescents. *Journal of Research on Adolescence, 6,* 271–284.

CHAPTER 3

CRITICAL SERVICE-LEARNING AND THE BLACK FREEDOM MOVEMENT

Kecia Hayes

According to Mitchell (2008), Robert Rhoads initially introduced the concept of *critical community service* into the service-learning literature in 1997. In so doing, he provided a framework through which a substantive distinction could be made between community service that privileged a transformative social justice orientation and those that do not. Mitchell (2008) leverages the work of Ginwright and Cammarota (2002) to illustrate the point. She notes that a traditional service-learning project around homelessness might engage students in a food drive for the homeless; whereas a critical service-learning approach would engage students in an inquiry process to understand the root causes of the social inequality of homelessness and the social institutions as well as policies that contribute to the problem. The students would also learn how to devise a strategic plan to challenge the institutions and policies causing oppression, so that they become more responsive to the needs of the homeless.

Since the introduction of the concept, there have been various definitions proffered, but critical service-learning can be broadly understood as

Critical Service Learning as a Revolutionary Pedagogy: A Project of Student Agency in Action, pp. 47–69

experiential learning that empowers people to recognize, expose, and eradicate the social injustices that structure their lives within a hegemonic social order. In essence, it is a process that transforms individuals into counterhegemonic social agents to effectively dismantle the master's house and establish social structures that are more egalitarian. As indicated by Mitchell (2008), critical service-learning more specifically "embraces the political nature of service and seeks social justice over more traditional views of citizenship. This progressive pedagogical orientation requires educators to focus on social responsibility and critical community issues. Service-learning, then, becomes 'a problem-solving instrument of social and political reform' " (Mitchell, 2008, p. 51). Within the context of this definition of critical service-learning, some of the civic engagement strategies historically embraced by African Americans in their quest for social equality emerge as viable examples.

Young people's participation within the Black Freedom Movement was shaped to develop their organic intellectualism and sociopolitical agency; to remap their understandings of social identity, capital, and networks; and to create sustainable social transformation, as opposed to episodic initiatives that fail to develop and strengthen marginalized communities. This idea is well-reflected in the words of Ella J. Baker, a pivotal leader within the Black Freedom Movement,

> In order for us as poor and oppressed people to become a part of a society that is meaningful, the system under which we now exist has to be radically changed. This means that we are going to have to learn to think in radical terms. I use the term radical in its original meaning – getting down to and understanding the root cause. It means facing a system that does not lend itself to your needs and devising means by which you change that system. (Ransby, 2003, p. 1)

While the explicit focus of the work was the sociopolitical transformation of an unjust society, the means to this end implicitly developed participants' *conscientização*, which can be understood as "learning to perceive social, political, and economic contradictions, and to take action against the oppressive elements of reality" (Freire, 1996, p.17).

Today, many of our most vulnerable youth exist in communities that reflect not only an absence of resources to meet their basic needs, but also a concentrated and persistent presence of conditions that facilitate the hegemonic reproduction of social inequality and marginalization. According to the National Center for Children in Poverty (NCCP), there are fourteen million children living below the federal poverty level of $22,050 a year for a family of four. This represents a 21% increase for the period of 2000 to 2008. Black, Hispanic, and Native American children are disproportionately represented in the number of American youth living in poverty and extreme poverty. These youth are more likely to experience overcrowded housing, food insecurity and unmet medical needs. The Children's Defense Fund reports that they also are more likely to have a head of household who is not a high school graduate. Typically, they attend high poverty schools wherein teachers tend to have less experience, less training and fewer advanced degrees than teachers in low poverty schools and they have educational outcomes (i.e., low rates of high school and college graduation) that make them more likely to have significantly lower lifetime earnings. They are more likely to have contact with the foster care and/or justice systems. All of which positions them as *at-risk* for civic death, which ensure they are unable to effectively participate in the economic, social and political domains of society.

In consideration of this circumstance as well as the transformative potential of critical service-learning at the level of the individual and the community, it is appropriate that we work to deepen our understanding of critical service-learning. This chapter seeks to do so from the perspective of the African American community's socioculturally indigenous knowledge and efforts to struggle against racialized social injustice. It will first explore critical service-learning through the sociocultural lens of particular efforts within the Black Freedom Movement to identify intersecting principles of practice—those places where the efforts of initiatives within the Black Freedom Movement coincide with components of the critical service-learning construct. This part of the discussion will focus on three initiatives within the Black Freedom Movement to mobilize and organize the masses to civically engage in the struggle for social equality and justice for the racially marginalized. The three initiatives include: The Highlander Folk School, the Citizenship Schools of the Southern Christian Leadership Conference (SCLC), and the Freedom Schools of the Student Nonviolent Coordinating Committee (SNCC). While not herein discussed due to limited space, the Black Panther Party is another initiative of the Black Freedom Movement that utilized strategies similar to those of the Highlander Folk School, the Citizenship Schools and the Freedom Schools to mobilize the community for racialized social justice. Second, the chapter will focus on the relevance of critical service-learning to contemporary urban communities of color, specifically in terms of empowering educationally and civically alienated young people to effectively engage in the work necessary to transform their lives and their communities.

Three Key Initiatives Within the Black Freedom Movement

In 1932, Myles Horton established the Tennessee Highlander Folk School with the goal of engaging people in a learning process that would enlighten and empower them to make decisions for themselves about how to effectively engage civil society. They would also learn the how to transform it, so that it better reflected the democratic ideal. Within this context, there were several ideas that framed the development of Highlander. First, the work would best be achieved through a focus on small groups of people. These would be individuals who already were connected to an organization dedicated to the democratic ideal such as a labor union, commune, cooperative, or community-based organization; and who, subsequent to their own training and transformation, would return to their communities to grow the work among their neighbors. Second, the educational program, while unambiguously political, fundamentally would be shaped by the learning needs of the students. Their experiences would be the point of entry for phenomenological and critical inquiry. Third, the learning could not be relegated to a cognitive domain but had to be experienced. In the first instance, Highlander sought to be the democratic ideal towards which students should work. This manifested, for instance, in racial integration during a time when the societal norm was racial segregation. In the second instance, Highlander had a program of community work that led to the creation of a residential program. These ideas are evident in Horton's (1998) reflection that

> a majority of the students were sent by a union or cooperative, and they were expected to return better prepared to deal with the problems of their organizations. Usually they were poorly equipped to study, but eager to learn. Education almost inevitably meant academic training to them, so we made the courses somewhat formal, partly to meet their expectations. Yet most of our program was designed to encourage students to become involved in the community and to relate themselves to situations similar to the ones they would encounter after returning home. As part of their preparation they attended union meetings in neighboring towns and assisted in organizing campaigns in industrial communities. (p. 78)

While Highlander's work during the 1930s and 1940s was primarily focused on the labor movement, it shifted during the 1950s and 1960s to support the growing Civil Rights movement. Additionally, Highlander created a specific program for young people, the Annual Highlander Folk School College Workshops, in 1953 to respond to the requests of parents and interests of young Blacks who wanted to be politicized and mobilized for the Movement. Throughout the years, many notable leaders of the Civil Rights movement, including Martin Luther King Jr., attended workshops at Highlander. Interestingly, Highlander's approach was consistent with W.E.B. DuBois's belief that education within the African American community had to be used for the social uplift of the community. The value of an education is evident in its service to community.

It is important to understand that while the Citizenship Schools and the Freedom Schools were distinctly different initiatives within the Black Freedom Movement, they were influenced, in different ways, by the work of the Highlander Folk School. The Citizenship Schools began in 1958 as an adult education program under the auspices of Highlander, and the educational program was primarily shaped by four key individuals—Myles Horton, Esau Jenkins, Septima Clark, and Bernice Robinson. Jenkins, Clark, and Robinson were from Charleston, South Carolina and had attended workshops at Highlander prior to the inception of the adult education program that evolved into the Citizenship Schools. Jenkins was a businessman and community leader on Johns Island, South Carolina. He also was a leader of two important community-based organizations: the Progressive Club and the Citizens Club. They had the mission of promoting voter registration and civic involvement. Jenkins wanted Highlander to help him develop the literacy skills of members of his community, so that they could pass voter registration tests. Clark was a public elementary schoolteacher in Charleston, South Carolina and had worked on Johns Island for several years. In 1955, she was hired as a part-time employee by Horton to assist with efforts to develop a civic empowerment campaign in the Charleston area. When she refused to renounce her NAACP membership, Clark was dismissed from her position as a public elementary school teacher in 1956. She then became a full-time employee of Highlander. Robinson was a beautician within the community, and ultimately was convinced by Clark and Horton to teach the first Citizenship School class, which was established on Johns Island, South Carolina. In many ways, Robinson was the chief architect of the educational program of the Citizenship Schools as she, the pioneering teacher, developed the curricular framework.

As an overarching goal, the Citizenship Schools sought to bring the masses into the Black Freedom Movement by cultivating local leaders who could mobilize their communities for civic and political engagement, especially in terms of voter registration. The development and evolution of the schools were guided by three fundamental principles: overcoming illiteracy as a means to strengthen the electoral power of Blacks, utilization of an interactive pedagogy that privileges the experiences and culture of the students as the point of entry for learning, and integration of an explicitly political approach to education that inextricably linked knowledge acquisition with collective social action to overcome racism (Levine, 2004, p. 389). Over time, voter registration was understood to be a benchmark in the process and not the ultimate goal of the education acquired by students of the Citizenship Schools. Voting was the first step, and the second step was geared towards helping people understand the meaning of the ballot as well as how to strategically use a range of sociopolitical tools to challenge the system of oppression. "With no organization to guide you your vote will be scattered thin or sold out to some politician who decides to be good overnight and only for one night" (Levine, 2004, p. 410). According to Levine, this second phase generated significant activism and community improvement projects across the South Carolina islands. In 1961, the Citizenship Schools were transferred to the Southern Christian Leadership Conference. By 1970, when the initiative ended, nearly 2,500 African Americans taught basic literacy and political education to tens of thousands of their neighbors across South Carolina, including many of the island communities.

The third initiative is the Freedom Schools, which were developed in 1964 by the Student Nonviolent Coordinating Committee as part of their Mississippi Summer Voter Registration Project. SNCC developed with the explicit support and facilitation of Ella J. Baker who organized a meeting of activist youth, some of whom had attended workshops at Highlander with their parents, at Shaw University. During that historic meeting, the young people decided to establish their own organization as opposed to having their efforts subsumed under the banner of the SCLC or the NAACP. According to Baker, whose influence over SNCC had significant permanence, "one of the major emphases of SNCC, from the beginning, was that of working with indigenous people, not working for them, but trying to develop their capacity for leadership" (Ransby, 2003, p. 273). Charlie Cobb, who developed the proposal for the Freedom Schools as part of SNCC's 1964 Mississippi Summer Project, elaborates on Baker's point, "the core of our efforts was the belief that Black people had to make decisions about and take charge of the things controlling their lives.... Stated another way, people would have to redefine themselves" (Perlstein, 2002, p. 252). Within the context of this fundamental ideal, the Freedom Schools sought to provide young people with an educational program that focused on literacy, practical skills for daily life, and political awareness. The intent of the Freedom Schools was to "utilize African American culture to broaden the political message of, and include heretofore alienated members of the Black community in, the freedom movement" (Street, 2004, p. 276).

In a fundamental way, the Freedom Schools sought to politicize the masses as was the mission of the Highlander Folk School but in so doing, the leaders of the Freedom Schools would explicitly leverage not only the contemporary experiences and local culture of participants as a point of entry, but also the sociocultural history of the African American community as a means to anchor and organize the masses in a tradition of social struggle and change. The Freedom Schools utilized a pedagogical approach that privileged the use of students' experiences as a point of entry for discussion and learning, collaborative inquiry and questioning, and case study methodology wherein students would learn to draw out the economic, social, and political implications of the phenomena that shaped their lives. The vision for the Freedom Schools was for it "to become the foundation for a state-wide youth movement which would eventually take over SNCC's role in the community and produce a new generation of community leaders" (Street, 2004, p. 278). While the Freedom Schools were conceived by Cobb, the implementation was achieved with significant assistance from Bob Moses and Staughton Lynd. According to Hale (2009), the immediate legacy of the Freedom Schools was that the initiative successfully achieved its educational mission such that students organized boycotts to protest unequal resourcing of their public schools and were vigilant watchdogs of civil rights violations. The enduring legacy of the Freedom Schools is evident in the sustained civic engagement of its students and teachers as well as the establishment of the Children's Defense Fund Freedom School program.

INTERSECTIONS BETWEEN CRITICAL SERVICE-LEARNING AND THE BLACK FREEDOM MOVEMENT

In various ways, these three different initiatives within the Black Freedom Movement incorporated particular components of critical service-learning into their work to politicize and mobilize the masses in the struggle against racial injustice within our society. Mitchell (2008) delineates four essential components of the critical service-learning model and they provide an effective framework to anchor an examination of the ways in which critical service-learning intersects with the activities of the three initiatives of the Black Freedom Movement.

REIMAGINING THE ROLES OF PARTICIPANTS

The first essential component is the idea that critical service-learning "reimagines the roles of community members, students, and faculty in the service-learning experience" (Mitchell, 2008, p. 50). As participants engage with each other and in the work of service-learning, they are forced to rethink their identity formations in terms of the extent to which they understand themselves and others to possess important civic capital and to be effective agents of social change.

Marable (2002) reminds us that, "You become a social actor in the real world not on the basis of any objective criteria, but by the stereotypes imposed on you externally by others" (p. 3). The three different initiatives designed to politicize and mobilize the masses within the Black Freedom

Movement as well as the critical service-learning paradigm recognize the significance of Marable's idea. They capture the extent to which participants' acceptance of the stereotypes and socially imposed role assignments circumscribe their ability to transform society through their civic engagements. As Mitchell (2008) suggests, there is a need for the work to allow participants to fluidly move between different roles, and for the work to help participants develop a sense of efficacy across the different roles in order to facilitate their reimagining of roles. The overarching work of Highlander, the Citizenship Schools, and the Freedom Schools, explicitly aimed to help students not only understand their ability to be change agents within the political sphere and to act accordingly, but also to develop a sense of individual and collective efficacy around their newfound political agency.

While Mitchell (2008) primarily focuses on the re-imagining of roles in terms of who is teacher and who is learner, whether in the classroom or community context, the Citizenship Schools, the Freedom Schools, and Highlander not only attended to the dynamics of stereotyped roles of teacher and learner, but also focused on other role configurations. In the first instance, the work within each of the initiatives challenged the traditional definitions or stereotypes of the roles of teacher and learner through the utilization of pedagogical approaches that privileged the idea that students shape their learning. Teachers had to facilitate a process of collaborative inquiry to elicit students' experiences as the point of entry for the group to begin to identify and analyze the social inequities within society. This approach stood in contrast to the more commonplace practice of banking knowledge, as defined by John Dewey, wherein teachers selected the content and inculcated students with particular understandings around the content. The culturally indigenous knowledge and phenomenological understandings of students were engaged as instructional assets to expand the knowledge production. Students ascended to the position of partner with the teacher to coconstruct knowledge and new understandings. In so doing, the work of the participants within the different initiatives disrupted culturally dominant ideas of who is socially and intellectually deficient as well as redefined expectations and valuations of the knowledges that each role—teacher and learner—brings to the educational dynamic.

Not only did participants experience new types of role configurations in terms of the production of knowledge—teachers are not the only ones who produce and students do not simply consume, but they also experienced the application of their knowledge production to socially problematic situations. According to Horton,

> It was education for action.... Now, how are you going to act on this? Let's just plan what you're going to do when you go back. Let's start talking about how you're going to use this new insight and understanding you've got.... So they begin to formulate their actions so when they leave, they're geared to action.... Then we say, now when are you going to do this? (Morris, 1984, p. 145)

The impact of this explicit connection of learning and doing was significant in three ways: first, it strengthened participants' sense of efficacy around their capacity to produce knowledge, even if they occupied the role of student or learner, that can be used to solve social problems; second, students' formulation and implementation of social action plans helps them to experience efficacy around their capacity to be social change agents within civil society despite occupying a position or role that is socially oppressed; and third, it exposed members of the community to a politicized *possible self*, as they witness individuals who occupy similar roles and social positionalities successfully engaging in social change efforts. The concept of possible self suggests that an individual can transform her identity formation to achieve the vision of who she wants to become.

> An individual is free to create any variety of possible selves, yet the pool of possible selves derives from the categories made salient by the individual's particular sociocultural and historical context and from the models, images, and symbols provided by the media and by the individual's immediate social experiences. (Markus & Nurius, 1996, p. 954)

This point regarding the reimagining of roles is well-illustrated in several key aspects of the Citizenship Schools. First, Horton and Clark intentionally identified someone, Bernice Robinson, whose professional role assignment was beautician to be the teacher of the first Citizenship School. They believed "the first people you want to avoid are certified teachers, because people with teaching experience would likely impose their schooling methodology on the students" (Horton, 1998, p. 101). The intentionality of Horton and Clark's selection of teachers from a pool of people who did not occupy the traditionally defined role of teacher directly and effectively challenged people's preconceived notions of different roles. Second, Robinson began her class by informing students that "I am not a teacher, we are here to learn together" (Horton, 1998, p. 103). She effectively equalizes the power differential within the learning dynamic by repositioning everyone in the role of knowledge producer. Furthermore, she serves as an example to the community that a beautician, someone who is not a socially sanctioned teacher, evidenced by certification, can fulfill the responsibility of helping to educate her neighbors.

In this way, she becomes a representation of a possible self for others within the community, which helps the teacher recruitment efforts of Horton and Clark.

REDISTRIBUTION OF POWER

The second component is the notion that critical service-learning intentionally "not only acknowledges the imbalance of power in the service relationship, but seeks to challenge the imbalance and redistribute power through the ways that service-learning experiences are both planned and implemented" (Mitchell, 2008, p. 57). In so doing, participants in the critical service-learning project must not only become cognizant of the power differentials that exist across the various stakeholders, but also of the complex historical dynamics of our society that have structured and continue to perpetuate such differentials.

Mitchell (2008) notes, the pedagogy of the paradigm "names the differential access to power experienced by students, faculty, and community members, and encourages analysis, dialogue, and discussion of those power dynamics" (p. 56). Within this context, the historical dynamics that structured the power differentials are just as important to explore as the contemporary dynamics that perpetuate and reinforce the power imbalance. Any examination of the articulated mission, vision, and goals of the three initiatives within the Black Freedom Movement reveals a strong commitment to the work of dissecting the power dynamics of the society and to establishing more balanced power dynamics within their organizations. However, it is important to more specifically examine three issues that emerge from the consideration of the redistribution of power and the efforts of the different initiatives. The first is the extent to which literacy acquisition was foundational to address the power imbalance; the second is the ways in which the racialized power imbalance was historically and globally contextualized; and the third is the tension that was created when the Freedom Schools intentionally recruited people outside of the community to serve as teachers.

Levine (2004) notes that Clark and Horton initially differed in their opinions of the extent to which literacy should be privileged with the educational program. Clark vigorously argued that African Americans had to experience an educational program that developed their literacy skills, whereas Horton believed that the emphasis should be placed upon the development of people's ability to mobilize for sociopolitical action, especially voter registration, which did not necessarily require more than a certain degree of functional literacy. Clark, perhaps because of her experience of being an educator in South Carolina, deeply understood that

African Americans had to become literate to not only pass the voter registration tests, but to overcome the other ways in which they were disempowered in civic life. She embraced a much more comprehensive approach to the idea of social uplift and civic engagement for African Americans through her explicit recognition that literacy was the means by which people would understand what to do with the ballot or the vote as well as how to strategically navigate through the social and economic domains of society. An example of how Clark and Robinson effectively privileged literacy development and connected it to sociopolitical action that would help to empower their students is evident in the instructional text, *My Reading Booklet*, which evolved into the *Southern Christian Leadership Conference Citizenship Workbook* that they developed. The *Citizenship Workbook* contained activities to support students' vocabulary-building, narrative composition, letter writing, and phonics. In addition, the Workbook contained a community organizing section with guides and materials for planning voter registration campaigns and canvassing as well as lyrics for freedom songs.

The extent to which students used their newly developed literacy skills to civically engage different domains of society from an empowered perspective is evident in the reports of several Citizenship Schools. In one instance, students used their literacy skills to initiate a local campaign to win more paved streets for their neighborhood. Moreover, at another Citizenship School, Mr. Mack, a student who learned to read and write at the Citizenship School, achieved a new degree of confidence and efficacy that helped him to become a supervisor at his job and a respected community leader (Levine, 2004). Ultimately, Clark clearly understood that the community's historically poor access or exclusion from appropriate educational opportunities fundamentally shackled it to a social position of perpetual powerlessness. She believed that "literacy further represented an agency for responding to these conditions [historical conditions of subjugation and a racialized power imbalance], and potentially transforming them" (Schneider, 2007, p. 247). The idea of literacy as a political act wherein power is redistributed to those who learn to critically read and write—as they are more readily able to interpret and assess the world that comes to them through a text as well as to use the written word to express their interpretations of their lived experiences—was not only readily embraced and privileged by the Citizenship Schools, but also similarly by the Freedom Schools.

Both the Citizenship Schools and the Freedom Schools made explicit efforts to immerse students in a historical and global contextualization of the racialized power imbalance. Robinson, engaged students in the Universal Declaration of Human Rights of the United Nations as a means to help them understand their position within the global context, which helped to illuminate how their local experiences reflected a power imbalance that was not consonant with a global understanding of humanity and citizenship. In Clark and Robinson's *Citizenship Workbook*, they included materials to introduce students to the work of Gandhi as well as individuals such as Martin Luther King Jr., Crispus Attucks, Sojourner Truth, and Harriet Tubman to expose them not only to the fact that the phenomenon of power imbalance and oppression is a global circumstance, but also to the idea that people, some of whom were of their racially marginalized community, historically and contemporarily had been working to challenge oppression.

The Freedom Schools' efforts included considerations of the experiences of the African Diaspora, and a historical contextualization of the Civil Rights/Black Freedom Movement within the African American tradition of opposition and resistance to oppression.

> The task of the freedom schools, therefore, was not only to explore black history in itself but also to desegregate the history of nations by emphasizing multiracial and international history.... Thus African history would not focus exclusively on the impact of white settlers and colonialism, but would encompass tribal society and African culture. The negative experience of slavery would not be separated from the concept that slavery inadvertently led to the development of a unique African American culture and the contribution of whites would not be written out of the history of the civil rights movement. (Street, 2004, p. 283)

The Freedom Schools seemed to take a more comprehensive approach to their efforts to expose students to the historical and global contextualization of the experiences of racialized peoples, which was a powerful tool to illustrate how power inequities are differently structured, reinforced, and reproduced as well as to provide students with clear examples of how oppressed people across to the world and throughout time have resisted the imposition of such inequities. This degree of contextualization provided students with a framework to more deeply explore the meanings of a redistribution of power.

Interestingly, SNCC's efforts to staff the Freedom Schools included the intentional recruitment of approximately 1,000 individuals from outside of the community, primarily from college campuses, to serve as volunteers. This created concerns within the organization. Some members argued that the use of external volunteers, who were overwhelmingly White, would heighten the profile of the struggle as the media better attended to the Movement; whereas others argued that local leaders, overwhelmingly Black, would be relegated to a subjugated position with the influx of the volunteers. This would, in turn, undermine the core values of the organization and its work. To further make their point, members cautioned that external volunteers were likely to feel entitled to leadership positions because of their formal skills and training, believe the unfounded stereotypes of White superiority and Black inferiority, harbor patronizing and paternalistic attitudes, be inexperienced and naïve about life in Mississippi, and stifle the development of locally indigenous Black leadership. In what seems to be a compromise, a SNCC affiliate in Greenville decided that no White person could serve as a project director or generally hold leadership positions.

SNCC's use of White volunteers from outside of Mississippi communities illustrates a substantive challenge to the idea of a redistribution of power. On the one hand, the goal to create bridges across racialized and classed social networks should be a component of critical service-learning work because it can help to leverage current forms of capital and generate new forms of capital to transform social conditions that unjustly hobble some and privilege others. However, on the other hand, there must be concern about the collateral damage that occurs when another layer of subjugation is created with the unintentional messaging of the idea that work is made more valid or legitimate by virtue of the inclusion of people who occupy positions of power and privilege. The point herein isn't to avoid the circumstance or create layers of interventions to superficially address symptoms of the uneven distribution of power, but to understand that the bridging of social networks requires significant work to engage all participants in an explicit and deep analysis of the complex power differentials. As Mitchell (2008) cautions, individuals must have an explicit analysis, dialogue, and discussion of the power dynamics. This idea is further developed by Lopez and Stack's (2001) discussion of bridging social networks. They advise that such work must acknowledge and map the racialized and sociocultural pathways of social policies and practices, including those that are seemingly neutral, that disconnect the marginalized from society. They also suggest establishing a safe space wherein participants can decode and translate the culture of power to subsequently plan a strategy effectively challenge it, providing participants with opportunities to learn unfamiliar codes of culture of power so they can practice how to enact those codes in order to achieve their goals, and nurturing an inclusive cultural citizenship that privileges the right to be culturally different from the dominant community without compromising the right to belong to and participate in all domains of civil society.

AUTHENTIC RELATIONSHIPS

The third component emphasizes "developing authentic relationships in the classroom and in the community" (Mitchell, 2008, p. 50). While this is primarily understood in terms of relationships between individuals, it must be recognized that critical service-learning can generate a more authentic relationship between the production and utilization of knowledge and the participants. Ultimately, the relevance and purposefulness of knowledge is made more substantive for all participants in the critical service-learning project as education becomes inextricably and meaningfully linked to community development and renewal.

There must be an explicit effort to develop an authentic relationship that "challenges the self-other binary and emphasizes reciprocity and interdependence" (Mitchell, 2008, p. 58). This part of the work is deeply connected to reimagining roles and redistribution of power. It further requires participants to actively avoid failing into the false belief that *everyone is the same* because this ideation ignores the reality of power imbalances that are inherent across our hegemonic society, and undermines the urgent need for sociopolitical transformation of our civil society. Furthermore, this approach significantly obscures the substance of people's phenomenological understandings of their lived experiences of privilege and subjugation, which enriches the knowledge that a group can produce around the social issues that must be confronted.

Participants also must establish common goals for the work, shared understandings of the work to be done, respect, and relational trust. As this work is done, participants can address the issue of power, as it undoubtedly will impact how people approach the development of connection. Mitchell (2008) recognizes that such work will support an analysis of power as well as facilitate the development of coalitions or bridges between different social networks. Whether working with the labor movement or the Civil Rights movement, Highlander was cognizant of these nuances around the creation of authentic relationships. They consequently were very thoughtful and intentional about the ways in which they worked to establish relationships with their collaborators in the overall effort to achieve social change.

For instance, as Horton and Clark planned the development of Citizenship Schools, they worked to deepen their relationships with the communities in which they sought to embed a school. They would engage with community residents in their daily chores in order to learn the local language of the community, to converse with them about what they understood as the needs of the community as well as to ascertain what residents considered to be community assets in terms of work towards political engagement. They were able to achieve a comprehensive understanding of the context of the lives of the community members by doing chores along with people as well as by listening to how people made meaning of their lives and defined social change. In 1955, they sponsored an all-day conference of meetings and panel discussions to better understand how local community leaders perceived the organizing and mobilization needs.

Alternatively, SNCC encountered problems with their efforts in 1965 to create a Residential Freedom School in Chicago for African American youth that likely stemmed, in large part, from their failure to attend to the notion of building authentic relationships.

> We went into the southside talking about "freedom," which to the southern kid meant the vote, education, eating where you wanted to, etc.,... But "freedom" to the southside kids meant getting out of the ghetto and they couldn't really see how this fit into what the southern kids were talking about. (Perlstein, 2002, p. 257)

This disconnect represents an attempt to overlay a phenomenological understanding of issues of oppression from one community at a particular point in time onto another that also is experiencing oppression but in different ways or at least arriving at different interpretations of their experience. In so doing, SNCC did not afford the Chicago participants, students and teachers, with the opportunity to collectively engage in a critically reflective learning process to substantively define the work through an identification of the pertinent issues, construction of goals for their collaboration, and establishment of shared understandings about how the work would get done.

Within the context of authentic relationships, there is a need to also recognize it as a dynamic that envelopes the knowledge production process. In each of the initiatives, it is clear that the work privileged the use of students' experiences and indigenous knowledges as viable points of entry to engage in collaborative inquiry of social injustice and to develop action plans that connected their new understandings to the exercise of civic agency. Just as there needs to be a connection between individuals, there also needs to be a connection between participants and the knowledge that gets produced and leveraged for social action. This circumstance must be emphasized within the space of the classroom as well as the space of community such that community members' indigenous knowledge is made relevant as an acknowledged asset to the academic work that occurs in the classroom as well as in the community development and social change work that occurs in the field. It is within this context that SNCC's work with the Chicago participants seems to have been problematic.

SOCIAL CHANGE PERSPECTIVE

The fourth component positions critical service-learning as "working from a social change perspective" (Mitchell, 2008, p. 50). In articulating an orientation of social change as a guiding principle of critical service-learning, the change should be evident at the individual, community, and societal levels. The goal, in part, is to transform and evolve how participants make sense of the world around them and others as well as to transform the structural inequities that hobble communities and their members. In discussing the importance of a social change orientation for the work, Mitchell (2008) reminds us that societies tend not to invite change. As such, it requires people to agitate the society into transformation and in so doing people are changed just as the society is changed. It is undeniable that the work of the Highlander Folk School, the Citizenship Schools, and the Freedom Schools was specifically shaped by a deep orientation towards societal transformation for justice and equality for racialized communities; and that these initiatives of the Black Freedom Movement were successful in their efforts towards such social change, especially at the societal level. As essential elements of the Black Freedom Movement, the Highlander Folk School, the Citizenship Schools, and the Freedom Schools helped to transform American society in several ways. Through the work, America's social institutions, particularly the public school systems, underwent racial desegregation. Additionally, there was passage of the Civil Rights Act of 1964 and the Voting Rights Act of 1965, which led to a significant increase in the number of African Americans who were registered to vote and the election of more than 1,000 African American officials in 1969. The hegemony within the social and political domains of American society had been effectively pierced.

It equally is important to examine the impact at the individual and community levels, particularly the various ways in which students who participated in the different initiatives enacted new understandings of their citizenship role. For instance, Levine (2004) shares a recollection by Robinson of a story wherein a Citizenship School student, who also is employed at an oyster factory, is arrested on false charges of illegally selling a jar of oysters without a permit. Upon hearing of the arrest, the local SCLC organization secures a lawyer for the student and on the day of the trial, members of the community flood the courtroom. The all-White jury returns with a not guilty verdict, which was uncommon as evidenced by other legal cases involving members of the African American community during that time. The African Americans within the community stepped out of the citizenship role of civic compliance that was thrust upon them by virtue of their racialized positionality of subjugation within an unjust social system, and into the citizenship role of civic watchdog to bear witness to the legal process as well as to ensure that the civil rights of their sister were not violated. They fundamentally changed their racialized role definitions around citizenship that had been crafted by a dominant culture that rendered them inferior. Not only did they internalize this new understanding of their role as citizen, but they enacted it and consequently challenged the thinking and actions of some of their White neighbors.

The students of the Freedom Schools were also transformed. At the school in Hattiesburg, students drafted their own Declaration of Independence, which acknowledged the need for African Americans to actively reject the American customs that have disadvantaged them within the economic, sociocultural, and political domains of society. The Declaration reflected an evolution of students' meaning making of their experiences as racially subjugated citizens within American society. They rejected the inevitability of racial marginalization, began to explicitly problematize the ways in which the practices of the dominant culture were problematic for the community's social uplift and advancement, and articulated a vision of themselves as empowered change agents. "Although a political document, its mere production suggests much about the creation of an oppositional culture within the freedom schools and how the students were beginning to translate this culture into their own lives" (Street, 2004, p. 286).

Eventually, the Hattiesburg Declaration of Independence led to students organizing a youth conference to discuss and draft a political platform for the Mississippi Freedom Democratic Party (MFDP). The students' platform addressed their concerns around housing, health programs, and education. Young people benefited from the work not only in terms of being exposed to the pedagogical practice of the Socratic method and critical inquiry, which framed the way which instruction occurred across the three initiatives, but also in terms of a re-imagining of what it means to be a young person who has no formal power within the social domain. They were made aware of their informal power and sociocultural capital as well as the tools to maximize the potency of such elements within the social sphere. They effectively challenged the racialized and generational role definitions that were imposed upon them.

RELEVANCE TO CONTEMPORARY URBAN COMMUNITIES OF COLOR

According to the Corporation for National & Community Service (2008), there has been an increase to 68% of the number of K–12 public schools that provide students with service opportunities. Less than 24% of the schools offer service-learning opportunities wherein the service is linked to academic instruction. There is a service-learning gap that mirrors the achievement gap. Only 20% of schools in low-income neighborhoods have such programs whereas 27 percent of schools outside of low-income communities have service-learning programs. Hart (2006) argues that the potential that service-learning participation can accrue to young people in terms of their academic achievement, civic engagement, and sociopersonal development is not being realized. The lack of sufficient service-learning opportunities within schools in low-income communities is especially problematic when one considers the civic engagement barriers confronting our most vulnerable urban youth. Insofar as civic engagement, particularly voting, tends to be a communal activity, young people who reside in communities where there has been a significant loss of voting eligibility due to felon disenfranchisement laws fail to be exposed to effective models of civic engagement, including valuation of the right, privilege, and responsibility to vote. Furthermore, in their longitudinal survey of 1,000 young adults, Manza and Uggen found that those who had contact with the criminal justice system demonstrated significantly lower levels of political efficacy than those who had not been arrested or incarcerated. Responding to the statement "people like me have no say in what the government does," 57% of the former inmates agreed whereas only 39 percent of those who had not been incarcerated were in agreement with the statement (Uggen, 2002). These circumstances, along with other debilitating social conditions previously outlined in this discussion, envelope the lives of vulnerable urban youth and their communities; and demonstrate an erosion of the civic engagement gains made during the Black Freedom Movement. However, critical service-learning offers a framework whereby we might begin to stem the tide by empowering vulnerable youth to be social change agents for themselves, their communities, and civil society. To do so, we must attend not only to the important programmatic design considerations that emerge from the critical service-learning literature, but also to essential themes arising from the work of the different initiatives of the Black Freedom Movement.

In the first instance, Mitchell (2007) in her case study of the Citizen Scholars Program (pps. 109–110) delineates some essential considerations for developing a critical service learning program. She specifically recognizes the need to:

- Bring intentional focus to issues of justice through readings and dialogue
- Writing opportunities need to focus learners on self, service, and the broader social context
- Encourage prolonged experiences in service that move toward progressively deeper action
- Support student-directed learning through opportunities for shared teaching

- Provide exposure to issues of exclusion, marginalization, and oppression to encourage action beyond service
- Support students where they are and affirm the commitments they are able and willing to make

Relatedly, Smyth, Angus, Down, and McInerney (2009), in their discussion of school and community renewal, seem to expand upon the perspective of Mitchell (2007) by providing additional key considerations. They specifically advise that critical service-learning projects for urban youth and communities must attend to the following (Smyth, Angus, Down, & McInerney, 2009, pps. 131–135):

- Building a different kind of politics
- Fostering people-centered capacity building
- Investing in indigenous leadership
- Deconstructing stereotypes and pathologizing practices
- Linking the local and the global

When we consider these design recommendations within the context of the work and outcomes of the Highlander Folk School, the Citizenship Schools and the Freedom Schools, there are two additional features that emerge as fundamentally essential for a critical service-learning project seeking to be a catalyst to transform our vulnerable youth into social change agents.

First, there is the need for a contemporary critical service-learning project to primarily position the phenomenological understandings of the lived experiences of our vulnerable youth as an educational asset. It must intentionally and explicitly engage them in a process whereby their phenomenological understandings of their lived experiences as well as their cultural and knowledge artifacts are surfaced and leveraged as points of entry for subsequent knowledge production. They need routinized opportunities to critically reflect upon their evolving understandings and actions as emergent change agents. This emphasis on the phenomenological is evident in the work of the herein discussed initiatives of the Black Freedom Movement. It allowed the disempowered to indigenously and meaningfully define the issues, goals, and strategic plans to address the injustices that shaped their lives. Participants consequently were able to re-imagine externally imposed roles and stereotyped identity formations as they began to recognize themselves as knowledge producers. Today's vulnerable youth, at best, are positioned only as passive consumers of knowledge. In order to begin the metamorphosis to social change agent, they need to have a similar pedagogical experience that values their phenomenological understandings as intellectual assets to create new knowledge; and that empowers them with the efficacy to imagine and construct a new possible self. It would help them to substantively disrupt the script that positions them as intellectually deficient and as predatory social menaces.

Second, while Smyth and his colleagues appropriately stress the need to link the local with the global, a feature attended to by those who developed and participated in the initiatives of the Black Freedom Movement (i.e., the utilization of the Universal Declaration of Human Rights of the United Nations), there is also a need to anchor participants in the sociocultural history of the subjugated community. Today's vulnerable youth, particularly those within the African American community, are disconnected from the historical context of their lives and need to be deeply tethered to the sociocultural history of their community in more authentic and meaningful ways. They need to understand not only the injustices endured by their ancestors but also their ancestors' communal struggle for societal change and justice. This focus represents another nuance of the authentic relationship building that must occur as part of the critical service-learning dynamic, and that is evident in the initiatives of the Black Freedom Movement. Just as the focus on the community's sociocultural history (i.e., workbooks that included information on Crispus Attucks, Harriet Tubman and Sojourner Truth) helped participants within the initiatives to more deeply understand the evolution of the conditions that shaped their lives and experiences and to understand their connections to a historically persistent struggle for justice and equality, it can similarly help vulnerable youth of color. Additionally, an immersion into the sociocultural history of the community can provide a basis for vulnerable youth of color and their communities to develop new insights about their interdependence, generational and intergenerational, as well as the need to create durable bridges across the different social networks within their communities.

Unfortunately, much of the community interdependence evident during the period of the Black Freedom Movement has eroded as communities have had to weather negative social conditions such as mass incarceration and persistent poverty. In order for our vulnerable youth of color to understand what it means to be a racialized change agent in pursuit of a more just society and to become one, they must comprehend the racialized historical context of the work. This focus not only would have the impact of strengthening the young people's ability and efficacy to re-imagine themselves as social change agents, but also to position or anchor their utilization of knowledge for community uplift and development within the historical context of their community.

Unquestionably, the critical service-learning paradigm, coupled with or nuanced by the frameworks evident in the work of the Highlander Folk School, the Citizenship Schools, and the Freedom Schools, provides an effective means for us to engage our most vulnerable youth within an educational endeavor that meaningfully empowers them to utilize their indigenous knowledges as a point of entry to critically participate within civil society in ways that stimulate and nurture the development of their communities. It also provides them with the experiences to substantively interrupt the mediated social images and narratives within the public sphere that problematize and marginalize them so that they can imagine and achieve a possible self that is more authentic. The work to realize a reimagined sociopolitical self is an essential feature of the critical service-learning paradigm as well as the work of the Highlander Folk School, the Citizenship Schools, and the Freedom Schools because it is the foundation from which individuals begin to transform into social change agents who substantively alter their lives and their communities in the quest for a more egalitarian and socially just society.

QUESTIONS FOR REFLECTION

1. An important construct of the critical service-learning paradigm is the idea that it will engage people in an examination of the social institutions and policies that reproduce and reinforce the root causes of the social inequities. Schools are an important social institution within our society and when we specifically think about the experiences of the African American community, schools often have been implicated as a root cause of persistent racial inequalities. In consideration of this circumstance, where should the work of critical service-learning be primarily embedded or from what types of organizations should the work emerge in order to preserve its conceptual authenticity and maximize its potential for social transformation?
2. By reaching out to White college students to obtain volunteers for the Freedom Schools, SNCC strategically sought to leverage the cultural, economic, and political capital of the social networks to which the students belonged. However, in so doing, they explicitly and intentionally had to establish practices to mitigate the power imbalance between volunteers and participants. What strategies can be embedded within critical service-learning initiatives to effectively manage the tension between the creation of sustainable bridges across high-resourced and low-resourced social networks or

communities and the redistribution power across the two social networks?

3. Two of the issues that plagued the Black Freedom Movement's work around the politicization and mobilization of the masses were sustainability and transferability. In the development and implementation of critical service-learning initiatives, how can we intentionally address the challenge of sustainability and transferability?
4. An important element across the different initiatives within the Black Freedom Movement, particularly the Highlander Folk School and the Citizenship Schools, was the identification of assets within the community that could be leveraged through a politicized and critical education to build the capacity of others and to grow the Movement. To what extent do our critical service-learning paradigms engage in community asset mapping from an indigenous, as opposed to a dominant culture, perspective?
5. To what considerations must school-based and out-of-school educators attend in order to collaboratively develop sustainable critical service-learning projects for society's vulnerable youth populations?

REFERENCES

Children's Defense Fund. (2010). *The State of America's Children 2010*. Retrieved from http://www.childrensdefense.org/child-research-data-publications/data/state-of-americas-children-2010-report.html

Corporation for National & Community Service. (2008, November). *Issue brief: Community service and service-learning in America's schools.* Retrieved from http://www.nationalservice.gov/pdf/08_1112_lsa_prevalence_factsheet.pdf

Freire, P. (1996). *Pedagogy of the oppressed*. New York, NY: Continuum.

Ginwright, S., & Cammarota, J. (2002). New terrain in youth development: The promise of a social justice approach. *Social Justice, 29*(4), 82–95.

Hale, J. (2009). A history of the Mississippi Freedom Schools, 1954–1965 (Doctoral dissertation, University of Illinois at Urbana-Champaign).

Hart, S. (2006). Breaking literacy boundaries through critical service-learning: education for the silenced and marginalized. *Mentoring & Tutoring, 14*(1), 17–32.

Horton, A. (1998). *The Highlander Folk School: A history of its major programs, 1932-1961*. Brooklyn, NY: Carlson.

Horton, M. (1998). *The long haul: An autobiography.* New York, NY: Teachers College Press.

King, M. L., Jr. (1968). *Where do we go from here: Chaos or community?* Boston, MA: Beacon Press.

Levine, D. (2004). The birth of the Citizenship Schools: Entwining the struggles for literacy and freedom. *History of Education Quarterly, 44*(3), 388–414.

Lopez, M., & Stack, C. (2001). Social capital and the culture of power: Lessons from the Field. In S. Saegert, J. Thompson, & M. Warren (Eds.), *Social capital and poor communities* (pp. 31–59). New York, NY: Russell Sage Foundation.

Marable, M. (2002). *The great wells of democracy: The meaning of race in American life*. New York, NY: BasicCivitas Books.

Markus, H., & Nurius, P. (1996). Possible selves. *American Psychologist, 41*(9), 954–969.

Mitchell, T. (2007). Critical service-learning as social justice education: A case study of the Citizen Scholars Program. *Equity & Excellence in Education, 40*(2), 101-112.

Mitchell, T. (2008). Traditional vs. critical service-learning: Engaging the literature to differentiate two models. *Michigan Journal of Community Service Learning*, 50–65.

Morris, A. (1984). *The origins of the Civil Rights Movement: Black communities organizing for change*. New York, NY: The Free Press.

Perlstein, D. (2002). Minds stayed on freedom: Politics and pedagogy in the African-American Freedom Struggle. *American Educational Research Journal, 39*(2), 249–277.

Ransby, B. (2003). *Ella Baker & the Black Freedom Movement: A radical democratic vision*. Chapel Hill, NC: The University of North Carolina Press.

Schneider, S. (2007). Organic classrooms: Rhetorical education at the Highlander Folk School, 1932–1961 (Doctoral dissertation, Pennsylvania State University).

Smyth, J., Angus, L., Down, B., & McInerney, P.. (2009). *Activist and socially critical school and community renewal: Social justice in exploitative times*. Rotterdam, The Netherlands: Sense.

Street, J. (2004). Reconstructing education from the bottom up: SNCC's 1964 Mississippi summer project and African American culture. *Journal of American Studies, 38*(2), 273–296.

Uggen, C. (2002). Prisoner reentry and the institutions of civil society: Bridges and barriers to successful reintegration—BARRIERS TO DEMOCRATIC PARTICIPATION. *A Report of the Reentry Roundtable, The Urban Institute*. Retrieved from http://www.urban.org/publications/410801.html

CHAPTER 4

COGNITIVE DISSONANCE IN INTERNATIONAL SERVICE-LEARNING

Possibilities and Challenges for Service-Learning Pedagogy

Elizabeth Doerr

INTRODUCTION

Dissonance is the word that best describes my current view of service-learning. I refer to dissonance from two perspectives—one is a personal conflict I feel with the field of service-learning and the other is the transformational experience students involved in service-learning gain through confronting the complexity of the issue at hand. Service-learning educators must have a sense of personal conflict with service-learning in order to be critical and effective. The personal conflict is not meant to be discouraging—although at times it may feel that way—rather it should be there in order to ask the tough and critical questions about the effective-

Critical Service Learning as a Revolutionary Pedagogy: A Project of Student Agency in Action, pp. 71–93

ness of service-learning. Service-learning involves many risks that should be acknowledged, such as the potential to perpetuate negative stereotypes and reinforce the misconception that "help" must come from outside the community. Various scholars of critical service-learning (Crabtree, 2008; Rosenberger, 2000; Mitchell, 2008) also grapple with the potential risks associated with the structure of service-learning programs. Rosenberger (2000) says that she "became concerned that service learning easily carries connotations of 'doing good,' of the 'haves' giving to the 'have-nots,' of 'we' serving 'them'—perspectives that reproduce power" (p. 24). The service-learner is almost always in a position of privilege going into the community. Thus, she posits whether service-learning perpetuates the power relationships in the oppressive social structure. Specifically with international service-learning, Crabtree (2008) highlights several observations that could involve risk:

- Local children become enamored with the foreign students and the material possessions they take for granted.
- Students and other visitors leave piles of used clothing and other "gifts" after project/trip completion.
- Community members fight about project ownership as development activities exacerbate internal political and interpersonal divisions.
- Members of neighboring communities wonder why no one has come to help them.
- Projects reinforce for communities that development requires external benefactors; national governments rely on NGOs to respond to the needs in their community.
- Many students return to pursue courses of study and careers with little apparent divergence from the path of/toward privilege. (pp. 18–19)

These observations suggest the potential barriers to successful community development due to student involvement in a particular community. The critical service-learning approach is a method by which to mitigate these risks through implementing reciprocal structures and strong education about social change and social justice. Despite the conscious attempt to mitigate the risks to the various participants in these projects, it is integral to engage dissonance in service-learning projects to usher personal and social transformation. Doubt and frustration are challenges both educators and students alike must overcome so the experience can be transformational. Moreover, addressing potential pitfalls and critiques of service-learning both through research and critical service-learning pedagogy has the power to "redistribute power among all participants in the service-learning relationship, developing authentic relationships in the classroom and in the community, and working from a social change perspective" (Mitchell, 2008, p. 50). Especially in an international setting, the assumptions students often make about the culture and the people they are serving represent a manifestation of paternalism, erroneous suppositions about the community's problems and a misguided concept of how change can be made. Finally, to create dissonance within service-learning projects, educators and institutions must examine the (generally unjust) power relationships already in place through student-community relationships.

This chapter will highlight the practical pedagogical elements of an international critical service-learning experience supported by a literature review of critical service-learning theory, critical educational theory, and personal reflection on my experience as a service-learning educator. The examples I use are not meant to demonstrate the perfect critical service-learning scenario—as no such example currently exists—rather they provide an illustration of real-world elements of service-learning designed to foster social justice. This discussion will focus on how critical education in service-learning can combat the potential problems that arise in an international context where students might make harmful assumptions about the people, the culture and the politics of the community they are serving. This chapter addresses the previously mentioned challenges showing that critical service-learning serves as a way to avoid these potential problems, while concomitantly holding the power to promote transformational learning experiences as well as fostering a deep, reciprocal relationship with the community through a focus on reflection and dialogue about cross-cultural elements and the root causes of systemic inequalities.

THE PERSPECTIVE OF A CRITICAL-SERVICE SCHOLAR AND EDUCATOR

To provide some context I believe it is important to discuss my perspective as an educator. I coordinate a program at the University of Maryland called Alternative Breaks, which sends hundreds of students on 7- to 10-day service-learning immersions. Although a great variety of service-learning examples exist, my specific experience is related to the immersion experiences that focus on targeted social issues. Short-term immersion experiences such as Alternative Breaks have become a popular movement on college campuses (Kezar, 2002; Kiesa et al., 2007; Lange, 2002; Pritchard, 2001), where students are engaged in service and activities educating about specific social issues. Despite the limited amount of time students spend on service activities, program design can facilitate students' experience, so they are engaged in a critical exploration of social issues. A program such as this provides an entry-point for students to reflect on their work more critically and begin to think from a social justice lens.

Each Alternative Break trip at the University of Maryland is organized and led by two student trip leaders, usually undergraduate students. They research the community organizations and design the itinerary. Prior to the trips, the trip leaders participate in a comprehensive training focusing on skills and knowledge, so that students learn to work well with community organizations and learn how to be educators for their participants during the experience. The conceptual items of training include: Reflection on power and privilege, theories of "good service," the reality of social change, and the practical components of creating an effective and educational experience. This chapter reflects on what I have found useful and important as an educator to improve our practices in the program.

I am constantly questioning the role of service in social change. I often question whether the service relationship is creating more harm than good, or if this work perpetuates structural inequalities. Furthermore, I struggle to find a way not to let the logistical coordination get in the way of the educational components and the intentionality of programming. Although occasionally these questions discourage me, they are what drive me to seek better practices. I am learning that the field of service-learning is messy. There are neither magic pedagogies nor learning activities that necessarily ensure we can overcome all the risks involved. But through my experiences, I have come to see that the many successes in engaging students in critical questions about our social positionality and our view of service are worth the effort. These risks drive me to work towards developing a curriculum and pedagogical method that transform perspectives and people. It is a constant journey of grappling with the personal dissonance as well as creating an experience of dissonance for the students.

This chapter is part of that journey in which I will specifically focus on the example of international service-learning and confront the questions and critiques related to sending privileged students to work in developing communities worldwide. The example which I will primarily use is a trip to Guatemala during the Winter of 2010. During this experience, there were two student trip leaders, nine student participants, and two staff advisors, including me, where the target issue was sustainable development. I will utilize the example to explore dissonance as the key to critical pedagogy in service-learning. The following section will give an overview of cognitive dissonance theory and how it applies to a critical service-learning experience.

DISSONANCE AND CRITICAL SERVICE-LEARNING

Morton and Campbell (2007, p. 12) describe "cognitive dissonance" as "the temporary gap that exists between what we think we already know and a contradictory experience or piece of evidence." It is this moment of dissonance that drives the service-learner to question the way in which she or he previously viewed the world. This might be expressed through frustration with one's service or through feeling overwhelmed by the magnitude of the problem. Morton and Campbell describe this as the critical moment for the educator to engage the service-learner in a process of transformative learning. This section will provide a foundation of cognitive dissonance in order to place it in the context of critical service-learning.

In his 1957 work *A Theory of Cognitive Dissonance*, Leon Festinger introduces the concept: An individual strives towards consistency within oneself where her or his beliefs are consistent with her or his actions. Festinger replaces the words "consistency" with *consonance* and "inconsistency" with *dissonance* (p. 2) and bases his theories on two general hypotheses:

1. The existence of dissonance, being psychologically uncomfortable, will motivate the person to try to reduce the dissonance and achieve consonance.
2. When dissonance is present, in addition to trying to reduce it, the person will actively avoid situations and information which would likely increase the dissonance. (p. 3)

In service-learning, the point at which the individual wants to make change—represented by discomfort—is where the opportunity for transformational learning lies. Festinger said that dissonance typically occurs when there is an introduction of new events or information that does not correspond to the mental map of the individual's perception of reality. He further states that dissonance is more or less an everyday occurrence and that "very few situations are clear-cut enough so that opinions or behaviors are not to some extent a mixture of contradictions" (p. 5). Thus, people are in a constant state of attempting to reduce that dissonance: "if the hypotheses stated above are correct, then as soon as dissonance occurs there will be pressures to reduce it" (p. 5). These are mental pressures to find some consonance with the situation at hand.

Festinger (1957) suggests to reduce dissonance an individual might do several things to change the elements that create the inconsistency. A person can change her or his behavior to fit the environmental situation (p. 19), a frequent occurrence in reducing dissonance when a person purely modifies her or his actions to the environment. Second, a person could change the environmental elements, or the situation (pp. 19–20). I might also add that a change in environment is not necessarily permanent, so the person is likely to revisit the dissonance at another time. Last, Festinger states, "in order to eliminate a dissonance completely, some cognitive element must be changed" (p. 21). This happens when a person seeks out new information which may end in a change in the perception of the magnitude of the dissonance or a change in belief altogether.

In critical service-learning pedagogy, these methods are important in informing how to mediate the internal tension one feels when confronted with a notion that challenges one's view of reality. Aronson's (1997) description of dissonance theory aptly explains an effective approach educators can use in service-learning. He states,

> Dissonance theory is more than simply a theory about consistency. It is essentially a theory about sense-making: how people try to make sense out of their beliefs, their environment, and their behavior—and thus try to lead lives that are (at least in their own minds) reasonable, sensible, and meaningful. (p. 129)

Dissonance is an opportunity for service-learners to make sense of the world in a context that is wholly unfamiliar to them. Educators must utilize these moments as ways to push service-learners to be critical about their existing beliefs about service-learning and the attendant social issues. Elliot and Devine (1994) also see cognitive dissonance as "arousal" of one's beliefs that lead to motivation for an "attitude change process" (p. 383). Therefore, the response to this dissonance is important because as the individual is engaging in the unconscious "dissonance-reduction strategy" (p. 383), an intervention by the educator must take place in order to provide a means of processing the newfound knowledge. What we seek is not necessarily to have students change their environments, but rather to change their actions and behaviors because of what they are learning. Service-learning should push students out of their comfort zones to confront challenging issues. But that experience cannot go unmediated, an educator must be present to help facilitate that change.

Critical service-learning pedagogy is what creates a mechanism for controlled dissonance through the presentation of challenging questions. There is a difference between dissonance by default where the individual must grapple with inconsistencies by nature of the experience and dissonance by design where the dissonance is the intended intermediate outcome. Thus, to create successful controlled dissonance, an educator must consider various elements. The selection of the community or the organization with which to work is the first consideration. In the case of the Guatemala example, we decided to work with the community because it modeled an important values system. Because the nature reserve and coffee plantation on which we worked displayed a non-hierarchical and egalitarian governing system, there was the possibility of working directly *with* the community on the design of the exchange rather than just coming into do work *for* the community. Second, the intentional structure of the program is intended to create reciprocity and mutuality with the community. Third, the dissonance must also be mediated through dialogue and reflection by the service-learners. Reflection is a mechanism for processing the dissonance encountered through the experience and is essential to a critical focus on service-learning.

This introduction of cognitive dissonance theory serves to lay the groundwork for a discussion about critical service-learning and how to create situations both where dissonance takes place as well as to facilitate the attitude change process through critical service-learning pedagogy. The discussion following will address not only why the dissonance is important, but also how to create that dissonance through the structure of such a program. Critical service-learning is rooted in a basis of education for social justice. The following section will highlight the importance of a social justice lens in service-learning and how it is involved in critical service-learning pedagogy.

SERVICE-LEARNING FOR SOCIAL JUSTICE AND CRITICAL SERVICE-LEARNING

Not all service-learning programs promote social justice. Westheimer and Kahne (2004) focus on two programs as a part of a 2-year study, "one program aimed to advance participatory citizens and the other justice-oriented citizens" (p. 238). I advocate through this discussion for "justice-oriented" service-learning, which is often characterized as critical service-learning. Mitchell (2007) describes critical service-learning as an approach towards education about social change and "its questioning of the distribution of power in society, and its focus on developing authentic relationships between higher education institutions and the community served" (p. 101). Mitchell touches on the way in which this approach occurs, however, it is important to begin with why service-learning should have a social justice focus and how critical service-learning lends itself to the redistribution of power in society.

Schulz (2007) states that critical service-learning has the capacity to remind "students of the *social* (or human) component of social justice [... which] assists in delineating projects that are both doable and faithful to the concept" (p. 30). When detached from the issue, social justice work or social change might seem uncomplicated and simple to the students. But to be engaged in social justice work firsthand, one is introduced to the complexities of creating change and is awakened to that through a dissonant experience. Schulz proposes one definition: "Social justice is an ongoing process that requires communicative engagement particularly in the diagnosis of social injustice, assessing prevailing rationales for such injustice, and devising communicative strategies for equitable redress" (p. 31). Active experience in this process will assist in teaching about social change, issues of power and privilege and the root causes of social issues. Bell (1997, p. 13) asserts that people from the dominant group have great potential to affect change by exposing the "social, moral, and personal costs of maintaining privilege so as to develop an investment in changing the system by which they benefit, but for which they also pay a price." But in order for those people to make change, a moment of transformation has to take place whereby they can gain a greater understanding of their privilege, be motivated to create change and to learn how to effectively do so. I propose that change to come about through the dissonance that occurs during a social justice-oriented, critical service-learning experience.

By challenging standard lecture-style education practices in higher education, service-learning pedagogy is a unique opportunity to confront important questions about the relationship between higher education and the community; thus, providing a focus on social justice. Butin (2005) states that the dominant mode of teaching tends to:

> suppress ... fundamental questions of higher education pedagogy: How is knowledge created and by whom? What is the "usefulness," if any, of disciplinary knowledge? What is the role of higher education in a liberal democracy? What is the role, moreover, of students, faculty, and institutions in their local and global communities? (p. viii)

With critical service-learning pedagogy, the positionality of students, faculty, and community are critically examined. As Butin asserts, when service-learning is "deeply done," it "subverts some of our most foundational assumptions of our sense of identity as higher education faculty" (p. ix). Furthermore, the exchange also calls us to question all roles involved in the partnerships between higher education representatives and the community. Butin continues, "service-learning is politically contested in that it is fundamentally an attempt to reframe relations of power" (p. x). Not all service-learning programs are created through a social justice lens, thus, when I write of the potential of service-learning, I refer to service-learning pedagogy with a critical focus.

Another important factor in critical service-learning is that experiential pedagogy must be supported by complete and correct information about the sociopolitical history of that context in which the learning is taking place. Gruenewald (2008) discusses the need to combine critical and place-based pedagogies stating, "the two most significant intersections between these traditions are place-based education's call for localized social action and critical pedagogy's recognition that experience, or Freire's (1970) 'situationality,' has a geographical dimension" (p. 317). Furthermore, critical place-based education serves to "explicitly examine the place-specific nexus between environment, culture, and education" (p. 320). Although Gruenewald speaks more specifically about the education among community members, this concept can also be applied to critical service-learning where service-learners engage in an exploration of the intersection between the community, culture and environment throughout their engagement with the community.

Critical service-learning engages in what well-known Brazilian educator and activist, Paulo Freire (1974) describes as education for critical consciousness:

> The special contribution of the educator to the birth of the new society would have to be a critical education which could help to form critical attitudes, for the naïve consciousness with which the people had emerged into the historical process left them an easy prey to irrationality. Only an education facilitating the passage from naïve to critical transitivity, increasing men's ability to perceive the challenges of their time, could prepare the people to resist the emotional power of the transition. (p. 29)

Furthermore, the educator's role depends on the service-learning objective. Rosenberger (2000) says that in service-learning, the critical consciousness is gained primarily by students of privileged standpoint, whereas Freire refers mostly to consciousness-raising among the traditionally underprivileged. The practices, however, can be transferable and can be engaged in among both parties in the service-learning experience. Thus, Rosenberger brings up an interesting contrast in the use of Freirian pedagogy in critical service-learning. She explains that a contrast "is between a revolutionary program aimed at bringing down the dominant elite and a service program operating within existing democratic structures" (p. 29). The democratic structures, she argues, might even be the cause of some of the structural problems that the service communities face; thus it is an interesting contradiction that one must be aware of when employing such pedagogical methods.

This is precisely the reason that critical service-learning educators must be conscious of the potential problems that stem from this contradiction. Rosenberger further asks,

> is service-learning willing to participate in the unveiling and problematizing of the present reality of our society and to respond to the difficult, complex issues of inequity, oppression and domination? Is service-learning willing to make less-privileged people subjects and not objects. (p. 32)

The remainder of this chapter examines major components to consider for a critical service-learning program structure, reciprocity, mutuality and reflection. All of these components involve a level of dissonance that facilitates a change in mindset among the service-learners.

RECIPROCITY AND MUTUALITY

The structure of a critical service-learning program must create an environment where cognitive dissonance can take place through the establishment of a reciprocal and mutual relationship with the community partner. This can often be a difficult process, but it is important for practitioners to be intentional about the relationship being forged between the students and the community. As discussed previously, Rosenberger (2000) grapples with the inherent power relations: "I became concerned that service learning easily carries connotations of 'doing good,' of the 'haves' giving to the 'have-nots,' of 'we' serving 'them'—perspectives that reproduce positions of power" (p. 24). Crabtree (2008) further calls upon the language and values expressed by the international development community which perpetuates phenomena of "blaming the victim" and the "development of internal colonialism in postcolonial states" (p. 23). The attitudes perpetuated by the Western tendency to believe that "we" have the right answer to the problems of the "underdeveloped" countries, increases the potential of perpetuating a paternalistic attitude among students and faculty.

Crabtree (2008) further states that "participation [by service-learners] is seen largely as a means to improve the effectiveness of externally determined projects rather than as an end in itself, as a means to challenge the root causes of underdevelopment" (p. 23). Thus, there is often little or no focus of understanding the root causes of social inequalities during the service-learning experience. Especially in international service-learning projects, surface-level involvement of the community mirrors the problems developing communities experienced from colonialism to the imperialism of outside aid and assistance.

Butin (2010) echoes these sentiments that service-learning has the potential to perpetuate inequalities: "there is little empirical evidence that service-learning provides substantive, meaningful and long-term solutions for the communities it is supposedly helping" (p. 12). Service-learning, he states, "may simply reinforce students' deficit notions that blames the individual or so-called culture of poverty for the ills that allowed those students to engage in such service in the first place" (p. 13). If students and faculty go into a project with a deficit-based view of the community, they will have an arduous time increasing community members' capacity to solve problems. It further limits the community's own sense of its place in the solution to local problems and simply might create frustration between the community and the service-learners.

Crabtree's (2008) and others' observations are that this outlook might negatively affect the community. For example, other communities may be jealous of such outside assistance, community service projects might exacerbate internal politics of ownership and, just as with service-learning students, the community may get the idea that only outside help can solve problems (p. 19). This last point is important because service-learning projects have the potential to disempower a community. As Freire (1974) and others (Crabtree, 2008; Rosenberger 2000) assert, change cannot just come about from the outside; it needs to come from the members of the community in order for it to be viable and sustainable. To overcome these risks, critical service-learning must be based on reciprocity and mutuality with the community.

Rosenberger (2000) states, "In service-learning literature, the terms reciprocity and mutuality convey the notion that both parties benefit from the interaction, both are teachers and learners and both are involved in developing and structuring the service project" (p. 34). It can be difficult for practitioners of critical service-learning to create reciprocity with community partners, but the example from a recent experience as the staff advisor for the trip to Guatemala serves as an example of how a community and a university can work together to move in the direction of a reciprocal and mutual structure to a transformative experience.

In Guatemala, the situation would have it that the community in which we worked was an incredible example of sustainable development—both in the environmental and the social aspects of the issue. A nonhierarchical relationship exists between the managers of the reserve and the community members. A system of leadership among community members was put in place in order to ensure that the community was involved in its own successes. Therefore, we went into an ideal situation to have a reciprocal relationship with the community. Although the Guatemalan community lives in an ideal setting, elements of underdevelopment that might be apparent in other rural areas in Guatemala do exist there, and the additional assistance from our university students was welcome.

The community's input was central to the decision-making of the project from the very beginning of our discussions about this project. As the coordinator, I visited Guatemala several months prior to the service-learning trip to meet community members, learn about the community and help identify the possibility of sending in a student program. During that visit, we met extensively with community leaders to discuss potential projects. In the end, the community decided on a project to build a playground for the kindergartners at the local school. They observed that the older children had a place to play, but the younger children were often pushed around or hurt when playing with the older kids. Thus, the community leaders came to a consensus.

Neither the student trip leaders nor I were involved much in the planning of the actual activities during the students' visit. We communicated regularly with our local contacts, but our input was limited. Upon arrival, we found that the community had been preparing for the project for several weeks. The carpentry instructor at the recently-established school of carpentry, along with the general manager, worked together to plan the building of the playground. They selected five carpentry students who would then lead a team of two to three university participants on various aspects of the project. This set the stage for the exchange between the carpentry students and the university participants. Considerable challenges with the language barrier dissipated as students learned more about their Guatemalan carpentry team leaders and vice versa. A beautiful playground was built, and a strong relationship was created. Furthermore, the carpentry students had a great learning experience. This happened to be their first major project after being in the carpentry program. Not only were they working on their first major project, but were able to teach carpentry to others.

Reciprocity was created first by enabling community-identified needs. The community, as the major implementer of the project plans, guided the students' physical labor and assistance. The university students, who did not generate the ideas, were able to see the input from the community. This example seems like a manifestation of Crabtree's (2008) assertion:

> At the end of the day, [international service-learning] projects are not about providing material support to our partners in developing countries and communities—after all, how much can we really do in the face of such extreme poverty and structural inequality? [International service-learning] is about producing global awareness among all participants, providing opportunities to develop mutual understanding, and creating shared aspirations for social justice and the skills to produce it. (pp. 29–30)

Students may enter the service experience with a sense that they can create change, but their hope often fades when they learn that social change is much more complex. The reciprocal structure can provide discussion and enlightenment for service-learners who can also note the capabilities of the community members.

During the 6 days we spent in the community, many students reflected on the skills and abilities of the community members and were impressed by the amount of work that had gone into the project prior to our arrival. This step was the first in being able to create the dissonance, which in this sense was not a result of frustration but of a sense of awe about how much a community can do to improve its own situation without the help of someone from the outside. The students were able to lend a hand, but it was very evident that the community was likely able to make these changes on its own. It was the relationships built along the way that became the most important part. This experience was structured to create that moment of dissonance in which the participants became somewhat disoriented with the confrontation of what they thought they believed about the community compared to the reality. The students were able to see that they were not necessarily there to "help" or create major change, but to forge relationships. This can be somewhat perplexing when the student thinks her or his original intent was to help make a change. The educator must "meet" the students in order to channel the thoughts of doubt or frustration into something transformative.

REFLECTION

In critical service-learning, the dissonance an individual experiences must be met with a means to process it. Reflection is that response where educators can meet their students where they are at in order for the cognitive transformation to take place. Morton and Campbell (2007) describe reflection as "the process of balancing cognitive dissonance so that it becomes a motivating perplexity, rather than an emotional or psychological threat that results in withdrawal or a retreat to over-simple dualisms" (p. 13). Educators can never predict the exact responses of the students to the experience, but we can provide a way to help them process the thoughts. Crabtree (2008) states that "hoped-for changes include moving students from a charity orientation towards more of a social justice orientation on issues such as global awareness, service, development, and the roles of individuals as change agents" (p. 26). Dialogue and discussion help students become open to ways to individually respond. Reflecting together with others is the first step to that change. It is important, first, to focus on the various areas on which the reflection should be directed and the risks that are involved if the issues of power and privilege and root causes do not surface. Three components that should be central to critical service-learning reflection are power and privilege, identification of the root causes of the social issues and action or "praxis" as Freire (1974) puts it.

POWER AND PRIVILEGE

Power and privilege in the service relationship need to be addressed. Rosenberger (2000) discusses her concerns about the power relationship already in place with university students coming in to "help" a community. The structure of a reciprocal and mutual exchange is necessary to facilitate this realization, but dialogue about why a non-hierarchical relationship is important as well as encouraging students to reflect on their own privilege. Mitchell (2008) states, "an aspect of the service-learning experience that practitioners cannot escape or diminish is that students engaged in service-learning will undoubtedly have greater societal privilege than those whom they encounter at their service placements" (p. 56). Many students, I have noticed, have not thought about their own privilege from this perspective. Experiential learning can help students reexamine their privilege and ask the difficult questions, as Rosenberger posits: To what extent does our presence in a community perpetuate inequality in society? It is not an easy question, but that is what reflection is about—thinking critically not only on the issues in society, but on our own presence in the activities themselves. Without reflecting on our positionality, we risk students coming away from the experience with the belief that the "underdeveloped" communities cannot change without outside help.

During the Guatemala experience, the trip leaders conducted two reflection activities that focused on privilege. Each activity was designed to get us to think critically about our own privilege as well as experiences that have caused us to feel marginalized. During one activity called "Privilege Walk" or "Cross the Line," the facilitator gave participants a statement asking them to go to one side of the line if the statement described them. An example statement is, "If there have been times in your life when you skipped a meal because there was no food in the house cross the line" or "If you attended private school cross the line" (University of Albany, 2009). Each participant was instructed to take a look around at who was on what side of the line and to avoid talking or reacting.

Afterwards, we sat in the circle and each person stated their first reactions to the activity without a response from anyone else in the group. The discussion continued with a series of questions that addressed the feelings of each participant while each one connected the activity to the context in which we were working. Questions might include: *What are your initial observations or feelings from the experience? How did it feel to be where you were when the questions were asked? How does your experience in the activity relate to the community in which we are working?* This gave students a clear context in which they could relate and direct their thoughts about privilege in relation to the community.

A common discussion was about the acknowledgement that despite the variation of privileges as well as feelings of marginalization by the members of the group, there was a very clear divide between our group's privileges in relation to the Guatemalan community's. This led to a dialogue about power and privilege in society. Although very little exploration of the structural inequalities in Guatemalan society took place during this first discussion, it was an issue that we addressed throughout the course of the week as we worked in the community and engaged in educational sessions with various community members. This demonstrates the importance of establishing a context in which the participants can examine power and privilege.

An interesting theme in our discussions came out of students' challenges with language. They were able to relate their experience to that of immigrants in the United States. The University of Maryland is located near a large Salvadorian and Guatemalan immigrant community. Many students have come across people from these communities struggling with English. Because of the challenges that students themselves faced with language, they began to relate more closely with those communities back home. However, the discussion of power and privilege helped them recognize their position of privilege when coming to Guatemala made it much easier to gain acceptance and feel confident in unfamiliar social world, as compared with Spanish-speaking immigrants coming to the United States.

It was an eye-opening experience that helped them identify the inequalities in society and begin to think about how to address them. In this group's case, we brainstormed how to not only be more sensitive to those who face challenges with language in the United States, but also how to get involved in nonprofit organzations that focus on immigrant rights and advocacy. Activities such as these are excellent tools to begin discussions about social justice issues in society. The discussion should lead to identifying and addressing the root causes of the social inequality at hand and should be realistic and achievable for students to engage in. For example, we discussed whether we could realistically get involved in creating social change in the community in Guatemala. It was decided that we could not do it from the outside, but that change needed to come from within the community, something that was already being done by the community. In the final blog post, a student writes:

> [Sustainable Development], when seen in the context of community service, requires that the human component be realized and respected. Meaning, service should only be done in a way which completely involves the community being served and community members' particular needs (as defined by community members). If service is not done in this way, and is instead the projection of what some people (namely, outsiders) think a community needs, it risks being viewed as paternalistic and may not be sustainable. Why not sustainable? Because the objective of social change in a community is to have the PEOPLE in a community have the power to execute the change. If change is performed entirely with thoughts and resources (material and otherwise) from the outside, the locus of power does not exist within the community itself. This creates dependencies that are counter-intuitive to any change being able to be ethically sustained for a long period of time. (Anonymous, 2010)

This passage eloquently summarizes the points that we came to in our discussion about the unequal service partnership. Here, we recognized the need for a shift in power through grassroots development. This discussion, therefore, leads into the identification of root causes to the social issues we are exploring.

ROOT CAUSES

Examining structural inequalities in society is the key to addressing the root causes of social issues. Ginwright and Cammarotta (2002) say creating a sense of social awareness "places an emphasis on community problem solving through critical thinking that raises questions about the roots of social inequality" (p. 90). This can be difficult because typical service activities often involve solutions to surface-level problems. For example, serving visitors at a soup kitchen may provide a warm, nutritious meal for a number of homeless individuals for one day, but it does not target the structural cause to hunger or homelessness. The root cause of the problem could be related to various structural problems, such as lack of employment opportunities, lack of government assistance for the unemployed, health care, housing policies, or inequalities in education. Without a discussion about these possibilities, we run the risk of a service-learner leaving the experience with an uninformed and narrow view of the situation. As Crabtree (2008) asserts, it could lead to a case of "blaming the victim" (p. 23). In international service-learning, without reflecting on root causes, the stakes may be, arguably, higher. We risk perpetuating the cycle of narrow-minded approaches to development, which Crabtree describes as "legacies of colonialism, failures to use indigenous knowledge, ongoing inequitable global trade arrangements, corruption of southern governments along with persistent tribalism, the devastating outcomes of structural adjustment on third world debt, and failure of NGOs alike" (p. 24). As with the exploration of power and privilege, providing a relatable context for service-learners to approach the discussion allows for a way to process that dissonance experienced from that knowledge.

ACTION

Possibly the most challenging aspect of reflection is the action component. Freire (1970) describes this as "praxis," which involves reflection and action linked together. Rosenberger (2000, p. 31) calls upon Freire's description of "praxis as cultural action for freedom" by stating that it "assumes characteristics of a cultural revolution; a utopian vision of reality, an unveiling and problematizing of present reality, and an action conceived and enacted with the people." Throughout the course of the experience, it is desirable that students realize they are not going to make the change in the community, but the community itself must do so. Once this is realized, educators must facilitate a discussion on how to create action related to this new perspective. The dissonance is what inspires that desire for action.

One aspect of dissonance is whether the student believes they can be a part of any change if they are not a part of the community. Dissonance might also be the feeling that the problems are much bigger than originally realized. "Praxis"—reflection and action—must be used at this point to keep the participant from abandoning the social justice mindset.

No one clear way exists for encouraging action among service-learners. But the encouragement must be practical and feasible. I always see critical service-learning experiences such as that in Guatemala as an entry-point to social justice and advocacy. But, it cannot be left there. A practical tool kit must be in place for individual follow up. Immersions have one advantage over long-term individual service-learning: Being immersed in a foreign environment with several like-minded peers manages to facilitate the creation of a community of social justice seekers. That community is much more able to act together and encourage action than if a service-learner feels alone.

As Mitchell (2008) states, "without the exercise of care and consciousness, drawing attention to root causes of social problems, and involving students in actions and initiatives addressing root causes, service-learning may have no impact beyond students' good feelings" (p. 51). If we come away from the experience thinking that we had "done good work," then we have not created that appropriate dissonance so students can become critical thinkers. Throughout our time in Guatemala, the student trip leaders guided our group through a number of reflective activities. One discussion pushed the group to think more concretely about how they can get involved in the social issues they explore through the experience. Once we spoke with the owner of a nature reserve several hours from the community in which we worked. He spoke for over an hour about "sustainable development," which we had seen from a more community-based perspective with the previous community. We noticed that sustainable development involved elements of community, environment, and production as it was conducted by the organization there.

With this speaker, we gained a more macrolevel perspective of sustainable development. He said that sustainable development was a contradictory term. Throughout the course of the hour, he discussed how he grapples with this issue, but at the same time, still feels comfortable in utilizing the term for the means of creating a better world. The views expressed during the subsequent reflection activity demonstrated the immense amount of dissonance we were all feeling with this newfound concept. The students began to question whether sustainable development in itself was good. If so, then how do we make the best out of it? We did not come up with any concrete answers, but we developed a list of activities regarding sustainable development and cross-cultural engagement. This brainstorming session gave all of us a sense of empowerment. We learned of several activities in which we can get involved to help bring about social change. The reflection made action palatable and conceivable for each of us.

I admit that the greatest pedagogical challenge I face is how to create a mechanism for action for each student on the trip. Our program requires a local service component for all of the trip leaders to organize both before and after the trip. However, we have not found a strong formula in engaging in these issues locally, aside from linking service-learners to local community organizations. This can be particularly challenging with international service-learning trips because the communities in which we work are so far removed from students' home environment. Engagement in international service-learning programs, therefore, is an entry-point and not the end. Thus, there must be options available for students to engage in activities that are both local and global.

FACILITATOR'S ROLE IN REFLECTION

Although the process of reflection is intended to redistribute the power, there still must be a person in a role that facilitates and guides discussion. Freire (1970) notes that the reflection and action cannot go unmediated; rather there must be some kind of instruction or structure in place in order to create an environment for dialogue. Brockbank and McGill (1998) acknowledge that there is still a power dynamic between the learners and the teacher, but that "to be reflective the dialogue should make explicit the social power relations between the parties" (p. 60). What is important is how the teacher or instructor uses her or his authority. They state, "there is virtue in making that power explicit because it enables the learner to recognize the teacher's authority bounded by qualities that can enhance learning or inhibit learning, in the exercise of power" (p. 60). The expertise that a teacher can bring to the dialogical process can be utilized to highlight important aspects of an experience or push forward critical questions that might otherwise graze the surface of the conversation.

As Freire (1970) might see it, the facilitator assists in posing the problem to the group with the experience of critical service-learning as the context. This certainly does not mean that the facilitator is not also learning from the experience. Freire states, "the teacher is no longer merely the-one-who-teaches, but one who is himself taught in dialogue with the students, who in turn while being taught also teach" (p. 80). Thus, the process of reflection is an opportunity to engage in nonhierarchical learning where students and teachers alike are teachers and learners.

The facilitator has the role of placing dissonant questions and simulations in an interactive process. The learning should progress throughout the experience to build up to a culmination of realizations that come from the dissonance. The following quote from one of the Guatemala blog posts illustrates how the reflection activities facilitated by the trip leaders pushed the learning process along:

> Our creative reflection activity involved us writing our own haiku, summarizing the activities and emotions of the day. The restrictive process of writing a haiku paralleled the struggles of communicating with a limited Spanish vocabulary. It was comforting to know many of the other [group members] felt the same way. We were able to relate to each other and discuss our struggles in communicating with our team leaders. By the end of our discussion, it was agreed that without the patience of our [Guatemalan] team leaders, our relationships, growing daily, would not be a possibility. (Anonymous, 2010)

The insights that came out of this discussion enabled us all to look closely at our experiences with people of different cultures and challenged us to think more critically about our positions of privilege. The reflection activity presented an opportunity for us to channel these thoughts we were having that day into a productive discussion that challenged our social positionality.

CONCLUSION

In coordinating a program such as Alternative Breaks, there is no concrete, clear-cut way to implement critical service-learning. It is messy business and that should be acknowledged on a daily basis. Hui (2009) offers the insight,

> Just as we risk students feeling unable to take action because they are overwhelmed by the weight of uncovering new complexities about the world, educators risk rendering themselves useless if they do not embrace that which they do not know and admit and commit to learning with and from students. (p. 26)

As educators, there is a responsibility to understand and acknowledge what we do not know and what we need to know and to be honest and open about that in the work that we do. Dissonance is inherently a part of being a critical service-learning educator and it cannot be ignored. Through our work, we can hopefully begin to address some of the unanswered questions: *Should we serve internationally when there are so many domestic communities that could benefit from this work? Can truly reciprocal and equitable relationships realistically be forged between universities and communities?* The questions are not easy to ask, and certainly not easy to answer, but they are imperative to keep present in our thoughts to maintain a critical approach to service-learning.

Ivan Illich's 1968 speech to the Conference on Inter-American Student Projects (CIASP), *To Hell with Good Intentions*, calls for the eradication of all volunteer programs that bring people from the United States to other poverty-stricken countries to "help" them. Every time I read it, I experience that moment of dissonance that makes me cringe with defensiveness about the work I have chosen, but also brings a nod of agreement. This is a cognitive place where all educators should find themselves and should continue to revisit. It can make the work difficult because one is constantly questioning whether we are engaging in something effective or destructive, but as Hui (2009) asserts, it is important for educators to be honest about that uncertainty and frustration and to explore that frustration alongside students. It is easy to feel the ego burn in those moments, but I believe this sense of dissonance drives educators to be critical of their work and therefore to be committed to improving practices and recognizing the importance of doing away with or avoiding harmful ones. Certainly not all harm will be eradicated through this self-critical process, but the process will begin to open our eyes to better ways of carrying out critical service-learning programs. This does not happen alone—it happens through partnerships, relationships, listening, and learning. These elements include the important parties in the service relationship: The educator, the community, the student and all the stakeholders in between.

By listening and learning, educators and practitioners can also engage in comprehensive assessment processes that shed light on the strengths and the gaps within programs. I believe strongly in the utilization of theory to inform practice. The combination of assessment and theory assists educators and coordinators to identify a way forward through service-learning practice. Critical service-learning involves a process of investigating prior practices and other programs' practices as well as interrogating current practices in order to implement the lessons learned throughout the process. This process is not something that ever ceases. There are always means by which practices can be improved. Certainly this can also be a point of dissonance among educators because it requires a great deal of work and analysis and often overlaps with the immediate programmatic needs. But as difficult and complex as it may be, it is imperative to engage in this investigative work in order to do the work that we set out to do. Another point of dissonance is the lack of community voice in service-learning literature. I recognize that my discussion throughout this paper clearly lacks discussion about the community, even with the section about reciprocity and mutuality. This is an important omission to note in the realm of service-learning literature. Very little research has been conducted on the impact on the community in service-learning and there is a need to learn more about the community's experiences with the service-learning partnership. I hope that as critical service-learning becomes of greater focus, the community voice will be heard more strongly.

One organization that is leading the way with this critical approach is the national alternative breaks organization, Break Away. Their work is driven by the Active Citizen Continuum (Break Away, n.d.) and most recently, they have been working on means by which to take alternative breaks to a more complex and critical level through the forming of an "action-compact" to respond to the January 2010 earthquake in Haiti. Break Away invited four universities, including the University of Maryland, to participate in this Haiti Compact which included a site visit and will involve a forthcoming report that demonstrates the work done to identify best practices for work in Haiti. What has come of this Compact is not just a view of what universities can do in Haiti, but it gave us all a greater sense of practical implementation of critical service-learning practices. Much of this work has come about through the shared dissonance felt by all members of the Compact and that desire to identify the weaknesses in our programs and move forward more effectively and critically.

The term dissonance resonates with me as an educator as I grapple with the challenges of critical service-learning and become energized about the possibilities. This acknowledgement of dissonance among educators has the potential to strengthen service-learning programs by asking the difficult questions. It is difficult to say what lies ahead for the field of service-learning, but with educators dedicated to critical service-learning through a social justice lens, there is great potential for creating a community of critically-minded students, educators and community members.

QUESTIONS FOR REFLECTION

1. Considering international service-learning programs involve an inherent power dynamic between the service-learners and the community, what are the potential harms to the students and the community if that power relationship goes unaddressed? Further-

more, what pedagogical methods can be used in order to address that power dynamic?

2. As an educator, reflect on your own potential dissonance with service-learning. What do you believe has potential and what do you find as a challenge to service-learning practice?
3. Regarding Ivan Illich's speech, *To Hell with Good Intentions* (http://www.swaraj.org/illich_hell.htm), what are the real challenges that you might see in the service-learning partnerships and how can you reconcile the work of service-learning with the challenges he poses?
4. What is the difference between traditional service-learning and service-learning for social justice? What practices model service-learning for social justice?
5. What barriers does the dominant higher education (and general education) structure pose to service-learning for social justice? How can those barriers be overcome?

REFERENCES

Anonymous. (2010, January 25). *Our last day: Panajachel, and reflections on sustainability*. Retrieved from http://www.awbguatemalatrip.blogspot.com/

Aronson, E. (1997, Spring). Back to the future: Retrospective review of Leon Festinger's "A theory of cognitive dissonance." *The American Journal of Psychology, 110*(1), 127–137.

Bell, L. A. (1997). Theoretical foundations for social justice education. In M. Adams, L. A. Bell, & P. Griffin, (Eds.), *Teaching for diversity and social justice*. London: Routledge.

Break Away (n.d.). *The active citizen continuum*. Retrieved from www.alternativebreaks.org/Active%20Citizen%20Continuum.pdf

Brockbank, A., & McGill, I. (1998). *Facilitating reflective learning in higher education*. Buckingham, England: Society for Research in Higher Education.

Butin, D. W. (2010). *Service-learning in theory and practice: The future of community engagement in higher education*. New York, NY: Pelgrave Macmillan.

Butin, D. W. (2005). Preface: Disturbing normalizations of service-learning. In D. W. Butin (Ed.), *Service-learning in higher education* (pp. 3–24). New York, NY: Pelgrave Macmillan.

Crabtree, R.D. (2008, Fall). Theoretical foundations for international service-learning. *Michigan Journal of Community Service Learning*, 18–36

Elliot, A. J., & Devine, P. G. (1994). On the motivational nature of cognitive dissonance: Dissonance as psychological discomfort. *Journal of Personality and Social Psychology, 67*(3), 382–394.

Festinger, L. (1957). *A theory of cognitive dissonance*. Stanford, CA: Stanford University Press.

Freire, P. (1970). *Pedagogy of the oppressed.* New York, NY: Continuum.

Freire, P. (1974). *Education for critical consciousness.* New York, NY: Continuum.

Ginwright, S., & Cammarota, J. (2002). New terrain in youth development: The promise of a social justice approach. *Social Justice, 29*(4), 82–95.

Gruenewald, D. (2008, June). The best of both worlds: A critical pedagogy of place. *Environmental Education Research, 14*(3), 308–324.

Hui, S. M. (2009, December). Difficult dialogues about service learning: Embrace the messiness. *About Campus, 14*(5), 22–26.

Illich, I. (1968, April 20). *To hell with good intentions.* Presented at the Conference on Inter-American Students Projects, Cuernavaca, Mexico. Retrieved from http://www.swaraj.org/illich_hell.htm

Kezar, A. (2002, May/June). Assessing community service learning: Are we identifying the right outcomes? *About Campus,* 7(2), 14–21.

Kiesa, A., Orlowski, A. P. Levine, P., Both, D., Kirby, E. H., Lopez, M. H., & Marcelo, K. B. (2007). *Millennials talk politics: A study of college student political engagement.* College Park, MD: CIRCLE: The Center for Information & Research on Civic Learning & Engagement.

Lange, N. (2002, May/June). How did September 11th affect students? *About Campus,* 7(2), 21–24.

Mitchell, T. D. (2008, Spring). Traditional vs. critical service-learning: Engaging the literature to differentiate two models. *Michigan Journal of Community Service-Learning,* 50–65.

Mitchell, T. D. (2007). Critical service-learning as social justice education: A case study of the Citizen Scholars Program. *Equity & Excellence in Education, 40*(2), 101–112.

Morton, K. & Campbell, J. (2007). Reflection. In J. Campbell & J. Hamerlink (Eds.), *Civic engagement in higher education: Reflections on power, evaluation, risk management* (pp. 7–38). Upper Midwest Campus Compact Consortium.

Pritchard, I.A. (2001, September/October). Raising standards in community service learning. *About Campus, 6*(4), 18–24.

Rosenberger, C. (2000). Beyond empathy: Developing critical consciousness through service learning. In C. R. O'Grady (Ed.), *Integrating service learning and multicultural education in colleges and universities* (pp. 23–43). Mahwah, NJ: Erlbaum.

Schulz, D. (2007). Stimulating social justice theory for service-learning practice. In J. Z. Calderón (Ed.), *Race, poverty and social justice* (pp. 23–35). Sterling, VA: Stylus.

University of Albany, School of Social Welfare. (2009). *Module 5: Privilege walk activity.* Retrieved from http://www.albany.edu/ssw/efc/pdf/Module%205_1_Privilege%20Walk%20Activity.pdf

Westheimer, J., & Kahne, J. (2004, Summer). What kind of a citizen? The politics of educating for democracy. *American Educational Research Journal, 41*(2), 237–269.

CHAPTER 5

TO BUILD A SUSTAINABLE INTERNATIONAL SERVICE-LEARNING PARTNERSHIP

Pushing Service-Learning Beyond the Boundaries Toward a Revolutionary Project of Community and Consciousness in Jamaica

Adam Renner

INTO THE UNKNOWN

I really have been searching inside myself to figure out
who I am since we've returned. While I have not come to a conclusion,
I hope that I never completely do.
I hope that I continually grow, change, and question who I really am....
Challenging myself to become more knowledgeable,
to use critical literacy in the classroom,
and to start taking action for the community
is what evolved from this trip.
(Student reflection from 2009)

Critical Service Learning as a Revolutionary Pedagogy: A Project of Student Agency in Action, pp. 95–113

Perhaps we had no business making the first trip to begin with. Hubris? Naiveté? Adventure? Now, looking back 13 years and reflecting on as many trips, we hope we have ameliorated any actions performed out of hubris. We are still a bit naïve. And, adventure has turned to partnership. We hope. Like the student reflection cited above we continue the long process of introspection. We engage praxis to the fullest extent we can. We challenge ourselves to be better, to do more, and to build community (toward solidarity, toward sustainability) across complicated national/racial/class borders. The journey is not perfect, so, necessarily, the partnership revealed in the following pages is less a model and more a lesson in process—one that, hopefully, illuminates an evolutionary trajectory of more criticality, more community, more consciousness.

Service-learning work is uneven. It is shot through with contradictions, inconsistencies, and imperfections. Service cannot (in fact, must not) adhere neatly to a one-size-fits-all criterion. It is the giving of one's self. It is the connection of human beings dialectically related to the structures/systems within which we live. It must be process. To that end, the following pages illustrate such a process in praxis, which juxtaposes developing work with our partners (action) with constantly new understandings of theory that further enhanced the developing work (reflection).

So, the work here is twofold. On one hand, this chapter illuminates a particular partnership, what has been learned along the way, and how the partnership can be sustained. On the other hand, it formulates an argument regarding the importance of creating and the need to support a type of insurgent educator who is prepared to push the disciplined boundaries of service-learning in order to work against neoliberal and alienating trends in schooling.

Permit me one more introductory remark. When treating the action portion of this evolutionary trajectory, the first person plural is preferred since the developing work secured contributions from many people from both the United States and Jamaica, particularly my partner, who has joined me in this work from its inception in 1998. Plus, the work is intimate and cannot be captured with a distant third person narrative. How else shall we narrate our lives? As well, perhaps I seek to assuage embittered notions of our (that is, United States) position of power in an undoubtedly hierarchical partnership. We went there. Our partners did not come here. Our partners *could not* come here. So, the story begins with stratified positions. The work involves closing our social distance. The chapter concludes with final comments on where we are now in terms of that social distance and suggests the degree to which service-learning may or may not have revolutionary potential.

Taking Service to the Next Level: The Addition of Reflection

Our trips to Jamaica began in 1998 when I was teaching at a high school in Cincinnati, OH. Our itinerary the first year had been arranged by an organization that sponsored a friend's mission trip, so we relied heavily on *its* guidance to specify sites for our "service." Since we did not have a firmly articulated plan as to what our "project" was, we characterized our trip as one of wanting to go and help in any way we could in schools and orphanages. Help, we found, was something most of these places were looking for—along with exhaustive lists of supplies. During that first year, which was a trip of 11 days, traveling with several high school students, we visited a few orphanages and two schools.

Unfortunately, most of the places we visited did not expect our arrival since our liaison who had designed the itinerary did not bother to inform any of these locations we were coming—much to the chagrin of those administrators. We soon recognized the pattern and reconfigured our itinerary based on a limited experience in the few places we had been. During that first trip, then, we focused our attention on three orphanages and a church where we attended an evening youth service. As a result of this first experience, though chaotic, we wanted to return.

Plans for the second trip took place shortly after our return to the United States as thoughts of what we had seen and experienced remained near. Preparations for this second trip, which we problematically termed "Mission 99," were much more involved. We planned our own itinerary with the organizations we had visited the previous year and engaged in fund-raising activities to help offset our expenses and to raise money and supplies for the needs of the orphanages and one school (affiliated with the church we visited). We successfully secured a good sum of money and awareness regarding the trip and 29 people went to Jamaica. In the orphanages, like the first year, we encountered rooms full of children with little support staff to handle the overwhelming needs of the children. In the school/church we discovered a building covered with a tin roof, supported by concrete block walls, and filled to the brim with homemade desks, 50 children, and 1 teacher.

These first 2 years, heavily influenced by that spirit of hubris, naiveté, and adventurousness, were at best informed by a pamphlet I read, produced by the National Association of Secondary School Principals (1997), entitled, "Taking service to the next level." During my tenure as a high school teacher, I had more than 200 students involved in community service projects in the local community. After review of the pamphlet, I understood that service could be connected to the classroom through this concept of "service-learning." Simultaneous to developing a service-learning course for the school's curriculum, a student asked if it was possible to create an international service experience. Jamaica is what emerged. And, we were able to use the National Association of Secondary School Principals (NASSP) framework of *preparation*, *action*, *reflection*, and *demonstration* as a foundation for our preparatory work in Jamaica. Reflection, then, became an important addition and enhancement to the service work. To that end we incorporated more deliberative opportunities to *think* about what we were *doing*. This reflective turn would open up new vistas of consideration.

Evangelism Versus Missionizing Versus Social Justice: Differentiating the Reasons Why We Engage in Service

Noting the problematic "mission" theme and our meeting with a Christian group outside a church during the second year (who tried to "save" us), plans for additional years did not include any hint of mission (though we understand with increasing clarity the difficulty of extricating ourselves from such a connotation). During the third year, we framed the trip as one of "building bridges." As I had left the high school to start working on my doctorate full time, a smaller group of eight of us went that third year—six of whom had been previously—and we stayed for 28 days, working in two of the orphanages (the two where it was clear that a reciprocal relationship may begin to bud) and the church/school. I also completed a pilot study on Jamaican social service providers' impressions of mission groups traveling from the United States. For this trip, we again brought supplies to the orphanages and taught a week's worth of lessons at the school. A similar fourth trip unfolded in 2001 lasting two weeks. On this trip we had an opportunity to meet with a sociologist from the University of the West Indies in Kingston, Jamaica. Speaking in hushed tones in a tightly drawn circle in the main campus quad of the university, we understood how differently academics in the Global South perhaps needed to talk about their social justice work.

Bolstered by my own burgeoning academic work, in a comparatively more democratic location, I applied theories of cultural studies to this service-learning work with the help of a fellow graduate student, Matt Masucci, and a compelling instructor in this doctoral program, Handel Wright. In fact, Masucci and I completed a small study in Knoxville, TN regarding our service-learning work in a local housing project. From our analysis, we formulated a differentiated approach to service-learning for which "servers" might become aware: evangelistic versus missionary versus social justice methods. We used more religious terminology in framing this differentiation since the service project in which we engaged was enacted by a local, mainline, Protestant church. Evidently, the church had not consulted the community regarding what was needed (if anything).

During an interview, one of the pastors of the church let me know that they were there to "be the body of Christ" for these children by creating a library for their use. Turns out, the community did not need a library. A public library existed within walking distance. Masucci and I quickly understood that, at least from the perspective of this pastor, the church, through its *evangelism*, was there to serve itself—perhaps reserving their spots for a presumed afterlife.

The church members sent to work in the "library" were a kind collection of women with good intentions who genuinely wanted to serve. They perceived a library was needed, sublimating an analysis that had to do with the fact that these children were both poor *and* Black. Church literature suggested that 90% of the housing project was African American. Actually, the housing project was 90% White. But, it was decidedly poor. Indeed, in their mind, it seems the church equated poverty with Blackness. In any event, Masuccci and I termed this a *missionary* approach in which 'servers' attempt to meet the "perceived" needs of the served.

Launching from our cultural studies readings on the social construction of difference and service-learning literature—especially Stephen Fisher's (1997) conception of "service-learning for social justice," and his call to move service-learning beyond "therapeutic exercises," Masucci and I pointed to ways in which service-learning frameworks might arc in the direction of social justice. In 2000, we developed a "critical service-learning" framework of *preaction reflection* (moments that seek a Freirean notion of "political clarity"), *theory* (mostly sociocultural theory that would help inform the actions performed), *action*, and *reflection*, evolving the earlier framework I used from the NASSP.

In a later essay, Masucci and I (2001) attempted to more closely analyze our framework and theory by posing a few problematics that needed reconciliation: what role teacher education can play toward such a critical service-learning framework: the (im)possibility of launching such programs, imminently, and the social distance between "server" and "served." (These problematics, of course, continue to inform the development of my analysis of service-learning.) Related, my interviews with our Jamaican partners from 2000 elicited interesting themes that would provide a fount of additional recycling themes and problematics for the next decade to come. For example, my informal discussions with administrators at children's homes in 1998 and 1999, which elicited negative feelings toward many of the U.S. groups coming to Jamaica, did not bear out in more formalized interviews. Once I turned on the tape recorder, our Jamaican partners were more guarded and measured in their critique, if that critique existed at all. For instance, Mr. James (a pseudonym), administrator of one of the orphanages which houses children with physical disabilities and with whom we continue to partner, was quite critical of and frustrated with U.S. mission groups in my discussions with him over our first couple of visits. When asked, more formally in an interview, what things U.S. mission groups might keep in mind when visiting Jamaica, Mr. James responded, "Nothing, really." Continuing later in the interview, "We really appreciate all the help our U.S. friends bring to us."

My naiveté, of course, had gotten the best of me. I was still a relative outsider who may or may not be able to be trusted with such critique. I was accessing differing levels of a revelatory script. Over time these scripts would augment and become more transparent (though, even 13 years later, I recognize that I do not have full access to the script, nor, do I suppose, conversely, have I revealed all of my script).

In any event, these interviews illuminated how two of our partners were interested in exploring the long term nature of a partnership. One, Ms. Matthews (a pseudonym), a teacher with whom we continue work today at her current school, suggested that we should work toward "grasping the most valued things"—that is, learning the best of what both the U.S. teachers/students and Jamaican teachers/students have to offer. Similarly, in the spirit of working together, Mr. James submitted: "What is in a grain of sand? Nothing. But, you put a whole lot of them together and you have a desert. What is in a raindrop? Nothing. But, you put a whole lot of them together and you have a flood."

Accessing a little more from Fisher's (1997) work, we also began to understand that we should participate more in the "public life of the community" rather than just the "private lives of the inhabitants" (p. 4). This take on involvement, then, advances a reconceptualized notion of a "citizen politics" focused on ameliorating structural issues of injustice. As an example, at the behest of Mr. James, our work the following year would connect us with the broader community surrounding the orphanage. Revealing results of a survey of young men in the community, Mr. James suggested he could use help starting a club football team. Beginning that following year, we outfitted a men's football team to compete in the Montego Bay league and arranged for an annual U.S./Jamaica football match on our trips. Connected to this concept of the public life of the community, we would later be influenced by the work of Paul Kivel (2000), who promotes moving from "social service" to "social change" work. In this shift our focus transforms from one of helping some people *get ahead* to one of helping more people *get together.*

BRIDGING THE INDIVIDUAL AND THE STRUCTURAL: SERVICE-LEARNING FOR CARING SOLIDARITY

Considering the enhancements to date regarding reflection on our work, inclusion of social theory as a way to frame the experience, and a posture of bringing people together, our fifth trip in 2002 provided the backdrop for my dissertation study on international service-learning. This involved coteaching a spring class at a college in the southeastern United States and helping lead the service-learning trip with our partners in Jamaica the summer that followed the semester. This trip was themed: "Sharing stories," and resulted in an even more critical service-learning framework of "caring solidarity" (Renner, 2002, 2005).

Work continued with the school and the orphanage, now spilling out into the local community. We outfitted the church/school with a new roof, taught lessons alongside Ms. Matthews, brought needed supplies to the orphanage and inaugurated our annual football match with our new community partner, the Reggae Lions. Preparation for this year's work was heavily influenced by important additions to the service-learning literature: Carolyn O'Grady's (2000) *Integrating Service-Learning and Multicultural Education in Colleges and Universities* and Alan Waterman's (1997) *Service-Learning: Applications From the Research.*

"In a service-learning program," O'Grady argues (2000), "individuals engage in community activities in a context of rigorous academic experience. service-learning allows teachers to employ a variety of teaching strategies that emphasize student-centered, interactive, experiential education" (p. 7). These would turn out to provide influential pedagogical possibilities. Further, clarifying the philosophy of a more critical service-learning, Cynthia Rosenberger (2000) cautions service-learning educators about focusing on an agenda for projects that is simply intended to "help other people" (p. 23). Rosenberger makes use of Freirean pedagogy to create a more progressive form of service-learning that moves "beyond empathy" and aims at uncovering imbalances of power. To that end, she endeavors to help bring about a more critical consciousness in the student server.

Likewise, Alan Waterman's edited research volume provided a helpful nuance to the service-learning literature. For example, Dale Blythe, Rebecca Saito, and Tom Berkas, provide some of the first and only evidence for the impact of service-learning programs that O'Grady (2000) laments is mostly lacking in the literature. They provide three findings that have implications for practitioners: (1) many of the students in service-learning classes saw the benefits of these type of classes and found them less boring and more related to real life; (2) absence of reflection in projects led to problems in understanding the significance of service work being done; and (3) service-learning activity as a strategy in regular classrooms seemed to help "at-risk" youth and prevent those who were already disengaged from school from falling further away. In another chapter, Novella Zett Keith (1997) offers evidence of the promise for activating service-learning projects in urban schools. She focuses her attention on how service-learning offers a tool "for promoting agency in students ... by opening the school door to activities that potentially can change the quality of relationships between students and teachers: leveling power differences" (p. 137). Thus, an intentional focus on pedagogy, a move beyond individual assistance, and an emphasis on consciousness, structural change, and student agency became influential in our preparations.

In fact, my intentions were drawn to these issues as I taught this 2002 service-learning class, interviewed my United States and Jamaican informants, and observed a growing relationship with our Jamaican partners. The dissertation (2002) would ultimately be entitled, "Butterflies, Boundaries, and Breadfruit," based on symbols and metaphors that emerged throughout the ethnographic research. One informant, Gabriel (a pseudonym), offered the symbol of a butterfly early in the experience. When prompted to describe what he thought Jamaica was going to be like, he responded, "I think of Jamaica as a butterfly. What you notice at first is its beauty, its wings, but, then, when you look a little deeper based on what we're reading, you see this ugly, hairy caterpillar at its center: violence and injustice." Providing the metaphor for the same theme, another informant, Nicholas (a pseudonym), suggested that this experience was constantly unfolding for him. "Everything is in flux," he noted. Thus, this was a process of becoming—from caterpillar to chrysalis to butterfly.

Similarly, the themes of boundaries and breadfruit emerged from the interviews and participant observation. Of note was the fact that (our mainly white) students struggled with race, being a numerical minority for the first time in their lives, as well as bridging the gap between theory (the universal) and practice (the individual). Both represented boundaries to be transgressed. Also, we came together differently with our Jamaican partners one damp afternoon as workers roasted breadfruit for us over an open fire. Here, we began to formulate the importance of breaking bread(fruit) and seeking some sort of solidarity which might begin with impromptu meals such as this. I would eventually particularize that earlier critical service-learning framework, forged with Masucci (2002), to be a process toward a "caring solidarity." Articulating social justice theorists such as Rawls (1971), Walzer (1983), and Miller (1999) with feminist theorists such as Noddings (1984), Benhabib (1992), and Thayer-Bacon (2000), I sought a constitutive theory that bridged the structural/universal with the individual/local and that, pedagogically: promoted transparent dialog, built trusting relations (as a class, with our partners), sought the long term (relationships beyond the auspices of the course, with our partners), overcame boundaries (on both sides), connected theory to practice, and resolved the contradiction in the "server" / "served" dialectic.

Sprinkling in Hope (Against the Backdrop of Neoliberalism)

Taking a break in 2003 to be married, and now a university instructor at Bellarmine University in Louisville, KY, my partner and I returned to Jamaica in 2004 and launched the trip in cooperation with the Center for Cooperative Study Abroad at Northern Kentucky University. This study abroad experience connected us with many of my partner's social work cohorts. As well, fulfilling O'Grady's definition for service-learning, we created the conditions in which rigorous theoretical study neatly wove itself into our service work as part of this 3 week "study abroad" experience. Over the three week study/service experience we connected our readings of *Pedagogy of the Oppressed* (Freire, 1970), *Jamaica Genesis* (Austin-Broos, 1997), and *RastafarI Women* (Lake, 1998) to our work with one of the children's homes and two schools (since Ms. Matthews had branched off to start her own school). While critical theory and analytical readings had informed previous trips to date, this was the first experience for which the entire service-learning class would take place over the course of the three weeks we worked in Jamaica (a function of the way these study abroad experiences were configured). Thus, each day's action was necessarily buttressed, immediately, by theory, making the readings seem all the more relevant and applicable in this compact course. This was clearly a benefit. The drawback, of course, was its compact nature, which eliminated any preparation phase and discouraged a long term conversation after the trip.

In 2005 we made a spring and summer trip, working with the orphanage and Ms. Matthews' school. In 2006 and 2007 we returned with a group of 10 to continue the work with these same partners, continuing to develop our relationship. On the theory side, we turned our attention more toward the structure of injustice, delving into a multiplicity of perspectives on neoliberal globalization: from Friedman's (2005) fantasy of a "flat world" to Cavanagh and Mander's (2004) "alternatives" to globalization to Klein's (2007) "disaster capitalism complex" to Black's (2002) "life and debt" to Solnit's (2004) politics of hope and "politics of prefiguration."

Needless to say, neoliberal globalization has become a rich archeological territory for us, mining the extent of our complicity with the system, witnessing its impact on our Jamaican partners and their country writ large, and analyzing the possibilities of moving beyond this (perhaps late) stage of capitalism. As I conclude this chapter, I will return to this issue of globalized capitalism as well as the importance of hope.

The Next 10 Years?

Given this 10 years of work, and the developing foundation we built with our partners, we expanded our basic service work in 2008 in an attempt to connect us more intentionally with our partners: amplifying these service efforts, staying in better contact throughout the year, and laying future plans. In 2008 we brought the front end of the annual work in Jamaica back into the classroom, reflecting a more service-learning approach to the experience once again. Noting the more specific needs of the orphanage, we recruited nine Doctor of Physical Therapy (DPT) candidates (a program relatively new to our university) to travel with us in order to work with the numerous children with physical disabilities. As well, we also developed a relationship with another group of medical professionals who were spread across the United States and who had recently begun to work with this same partner. Though support from the administrators of the DPT program waned, subsequent interest remains among students and graduates of this program. Therefore, work proceeds, however unevenly, as we try to make this a featured aspect of our work since it attempts to meet the stated needs of one of our partners.

In 2009, paralleling the strides we made with the children's home, we developed our work with the school (where Ms. Matthews now teaches) more fully, offering a spring course at our university, titled, "Education for Liberation or Domination?" to students who would complete the summer service experience. As well, we planned with our partners at the school to host a community dinner for the teachers and staff in order that we might begin to better and more critically map the future of our educational work together. Making use of Freire's (1987) "culture circles," we based our work in critical literacy and further explicated the generative themes of education, liberation, and domination with our Jamaican partners. 2010 has been an extension of that work. For instance, our lesson planning activities have proceeded much more deliberatively, since we have been given access to the school's curriculum. This way, we are able to treat our trips as co-professional development opportunities for which we share teaching strategies, reciprocally, "grasping the most valued things," as Ms. Matthews suggested earlier. (See www.bellarmine.edu/service/Jamaica) for more information on this critical literacy and community work.)

A final curriculum comment is worth noting. These last few years have been pedagogically informed by the "hopeful curriculum" (Renner, 2009; Renner & Brown, 2006), for which our work in the classroom and with our partners revolves around the vertices of community, consciousness, and courage. Taking seriously the dehumanizing and disconnecting trends that neoliberalism has wrought, we endeavor to resist this trajectory with a pedagogical project, built on ideas of that caring solidarity, for which our classroom work and work with our partners seeks to overcome alienation, deepen our consciousness, activate more democratic processes, and embolden us to speak truth to power. It is, indeed, a project of hope. Moreover, this hopeful evolution continues to inform my everyday classroom teaching and has provided the foundation for the next decade of our work in Jamaica (Stiens & Renner 2009). It will focus *on* issues of democracy and sustainability as a way to resist this alienation and dehumanization. We also consider to what extent, through the culture circles and professional developments, we might engage our Jamaican partners around the issues of neoliberal globalization, liberation/domination, power, and hope (Renner, Brown, Stiens, & Burton, 2010)

EXAMINING THE MECHANISM OF SERVICE-LEARNING

Does hope lead to false ideals, easy explanations,
or worse complacency with crumbs?
or does it give us something to strive for?
Something we can accomplish together
to create a more humane existence
for every human being.
I must stand
screaming at the top of my lungs
a sound that most will hear as silence
but a select few will understand.
(Community Poem excerpt from Jamaica team, 2009)

So far, I have examined the varied/multiple uses of service-learning in our effort to build a sustainable international partnership as well as how those uses have evolved informed by both theory and practice. What I intend to focus on now are particular service-learning issues/phenomena that might illuminate a path toward its transformational possibilities based on my experience. This illumination is, of course, tricky since I risk becoming prescriptive. In any event, laying out these possibilities however cautiously and tentatively, I suggest that service-learning should travel a particular arc in order for a revolutionary potential to reveal itself. It involves, at a minimum, constructing a recursive educational loop that trains particular kinds of educators in our schools of education prepared to unlock this potential. Once this possibility—with its attendant problematic—is articulated, I will return with a few final comments on the future of our partnership and offer some questions to guide service-learning projects/partnerships, generally.

A REVOLUTIONARY POTENTIAL?

Undoubtedly, service-learning, like most curricula has become increasingly co-opted by a narrowing, rigidifying, and reductionist trend. How can it help it, since it organizes itself within our nation's schools? Evidence abounds that schools have succumbed to the market-driven, alienating pressures of this late stage of capitalism—that is, capitalism gone global (Robbins & Bishop, 2009; Ross & Gibson, 2007; Sleeter, 2008). In this environment, service-learning easily loses its critical edge in most schools which become ever more constrained by a focus on high-stakes testing and reduced to reactive, scripted processes of regurgitation. Here, truth is something not to be sought after, discovered, or debated. Rather, it is a conclusion reached by someone else which merely requires our acquisition and submission. If service-learning is offered at all, it likely mirrors such an uncomplicated, top-down, and dominating approach: "server" as the provider, "served" as the one in need.

Even with attention to these matters, our success in our work in Jamaica in resisting these trends is mixed at best—though we hope our work and the ongoing relationship continues to offer the foundation for something more liberating in the future. Whatever that might be, though, will happen *beyond* the auspices of *a* course or *a* service-learning experience within that class. However, what is it about engaging in service-learning that does foster a liberating possibility? Answer: the extent to which it is activated with progressive social theory and a critical understanding of material reality, as well as that which conditions this reality—capitalism. That is, the prevailing hegemonic ideology and its accompanying apparatuses which structure lives across our globe in the twenty-first century must be named. That ideology of course is capitalism.

Our work has evolved into the following understanding of injustice: the unequal distribution of resources. According to Marx, of course, this is due to the lack of ownership of the means of production by the vast majority of society. In other words, production is socialized, while appropriation is privatized (into fewer and fewer hands). As a result, as workers, we become alienated from our labor—working under production conditions not of our creation and working in order to consume the commodities we and others produce (at a profit for the owners). As consumers, the social distance of the products we buy (i.e., the distance between producer and consumer) grows, particularly in global capitalism. Therefore, not only are we alienated from our own labor (working to buy, not in charge of the production process, etc.), but we are alienated from other workers who may be working in dehumanizing conditions. *Most times, these same workers play the "served" (worker—tomato picker, garment maker) to the relatively privileged "server" (consumer)—the same "server" who, in order to eat or to wear any clothing, is absolutely dependent upon the "served."* Capitalism creates this ironic and irrational situation. Yet, its ideology with its mutually confirming political, economic, and discursive apparatuses blinds us to this reality. It turns material reality on its head through socializing mechanisms like the media, school, and religion, providing mythological explanations of comfort for "servers" (one is privileged because they worked hard, God has blessed them, etc.) and mean-spirited explanations of the lowly station of the "served" (they are lazy, the poor will always be with us, etc.). Toward recognizing this trend, then, we name it. We acknowledge our struggle with it and the *systemic* inequality that pervades our society and history: form colonization to missionization to service (all serving capitalist ends).

To not name capitalism forever pushes to the horizon the possibility of "social change," opting instead for a more reformist agenda of social service, which will constantly yield more inequality until a more democratic ideology finds a foothold. Agreeing with Rich Gibson (2009), "The core issue of our time *is* the reality of booming [racialized and gendered] inequality and the promise of perpetual war met by the potential challenge of a rising mass class conscious movement prepared to act over time" (p. 57). Concomitantly, I argue with others that societal transformation requires a pedagogical component. Critical service-learning, then, in the pedagogical hands of an insurgent brand of instructor, makes a mass class conscious movement more feasible—able to connect oppression under the larger rubric of capitalism, and able to come to grips with material reality as it actually exists.

In a more recent review of the literature, searching "service-learning and democracy," one notes more critique from researchers, suggesting how service-learning has not lived up to its billing and/or how it has been complicated by various structures/roadblocks in schools/curricula. These are capital's schools, after all. For instance, Steven Hart (2006) illuminates how service-learning and critical pedagogy have been *disciplined*. He notes how, typically, service-learning *does not allow* one to dig into structural inequality and that critical pedagogy does not always give *instructors a* practical outlet. Educators must figure out, according to Hart, how to pair the two better in the service of those most marginalized and alienated in our schools. Providing a global lens, Alberto Arenas, Kris Bosworth, and Hardson Kwandayi (2006) provide a review of the international literature on civic service (an umbrella term that covers community service and service-learning). Noting a couple of the critical issues they raise, Arenas et al. discuss how the community should be inseparable from schooling and that too much attention is paid to the students and not the "served" in the service-learning literature. Cheryl Keen and Kelly Hall (2009) present a longitudinal study of student outcomes in service-learning. They suggest that the core experience of service is dialogue: with the "served," with peers/ "servers," and with staff. As well, they propose that for service-learning programs to have maximum impact, students need more than one experience/course and multiple opportunities at community service that engender dialogue.

On one take, when not acknowledging the prevailing ideology, the best service-learning may offer includes: (1) connecting your classroom with the world in authentic partnerships and making a more authentic curriculum; (2) providing an opportunity to research the needs of people in your community, helping some get ahead; and (3) creating students who are more aware and culturally "dexterous" (Warren, 1998), thereby building their agency, providing possible ongoing processes of reflection, and perhaps offering them opportunities to demonstrate their newfound sensitivities and knowledge.

The relatively one-way, hierarchical nature of how the service-learning work will unfold in the above list is noted. If the work ends with and is limited to this list, then service-learning *is* impotent against the prevailing power of the market and its alienating impact on our students. Isolated service experiences may cause students to question for a moment and glimpse the problematic structure of society. However, these more-than-likely unique experiences are overwhelmed in capital's schools by standardized curricula that foster high-stakes competition for scarce resources, specialized knowledge (tracked and meted out very particularly based on race and class), and alienation/disconnectedness helped along by a continued distancing of consumer/"server" and producer/"served."

Likely, executives at Enron, board members of Monsanto, and mercenaries at Xe have participated in service-learning projects in schools as students. Clearly, the transformational lessons we hope are learned from service-learning do not translate evenly across all participants as the recipients of the service provided by these "servers" may be the exact same "served" who are exploited by a corporate credo that values profits over people (even if it means their direct or indirect death through the augmentation of poverty; inclusion of pesticides in their food, water and/or air; and the prosecution of wars).

Therefore, while we are still able, we must train educators in our colleges and universities who are prepared to not only plant the seed of solidarity through service-learning experiences, but who are also committed to countenancing a more material view of reality as well as prepared to engage the longer term work of germinating and nurturing the solidaristic seeds for social change. These would be truly insurgent educators. Short of such a project, we run the risk of what the research suggests and what capitalists hope: feel-good projects that offer charity and reinforce the status quo.

As professors, we must continue to figure out ways to leverage our academic freedom toward an organic intellectualism that ultimately enjoins the struggle most face in the world. Ultimately, the ivory tower must become a rear-view mirror reflection. As well, and while it exists, we must continue to figure out ways to help advance other colleagues (ever more diverse) through the tenure process in our colleges and universities thereby creating an insurgency of organic intellectuals. Moreover, professors must figure out how to maintain continuing relationships with teachers graduating from their programs in order to help them through their own tenure processes in K–12 schools and provide them ongoing safe spaces of personal and professional development with other insurgent educators. Finally, these teachers, emboldened by their training as organic intellectuals, will need to find the courage to seek out and maintain these opportunities/relationships. The work in Jamaica has been one way for us to accomplish this as we draw teacher graduates back to this particular partnership.

So, let us bring this back to Jamaica with a final note on sustainability. Admittedly, work across borders such as these is precarious. We are dependent upon students, professional colleagues, and friends to continue with this work despite whatever life circumstances may arise. And, we are dependent upon the good-naturedness of our partners in Jamaica to continue to welcome us. The list of dependencies can obviously go on. Thus, one way we go about this work is to transcend the classic *service-learning* nature of the experience. While service-learning might be a tool that is relatively non-threatening to the status quo, our particular work has focused on making the initial 'sales' pitch as one of service-learning, since it is a palatable concept to administrators and since it is a somewhat understood concept by students. However, as the class begins and the classroom door closes, we quickly turn a traditionally understood form of service-learning into a more community-building, consciousness-raising, action-informed *lifestyle* that ultimately has no disciplinary bounds. It is a way of being that wrestles with the material reality noted above and seeks to decolonize our minds from the slick socialization of the prevailing ideology.

Students, colleagues and friends, of course, come and go relative to this experience. Our ultimate success, though, is bound up in the likely return of graduates/participants and the further connections they might make in *their* own work here in the United States or elsewhere abroad (into which they can draw us). Thus, it is important to reemphasize here the importance of that radical training which helps our teachers recognize the criticality of solidarity work (for which we have had a modicum of success). Conversely, it is also the work of our partners abroad who, likewise, want to sustain the partnership as they realize year after year that we intend to come back, that we are in the process of building something *with* them for which we do not want to run, administrate, or lead. We want, instead, to widen our community circle, reduce our alienation by closing our social distance, come to deeper understandings of the world through raising one another's consciousness, and creating the courage to live something closer to a discovered truth that embodies democracy and liberation.

The revolutionary potential of service-learning lies only in its capacity to imbue students, teachers, "servers," and "served" with a sense of the long term. As well, its revolutionary potential is enveloped in its ability to begin to resolve the dialectic between teacher and student, between "server" and "served," between the individual and the structure. Service-learning, as a *disciplined* aspect of one's schooling probably cannot do that. In the conservative trending of education, service-learning can easily reinforce hierarchies, privilege charity over social justice, and enact social service instead of social change. In the hands of insurgent educators, though, service-learning has the potential to blast open a liberating space of criticality and consciousness. While partnering with people in a long-term process built upon dialogue does not undo 500 years of oppression—nor does such a partnership start evenly given the hierarchical nature of a society which presupposes a minority of "servers" and an abundance of the "served"—we can take our point of contact and recognize our position relative to power and arc it toward something profoundly more democratic. In this way we might live lives that are more liberating and just. Armed with a deeper truth (that we decide upon), and an unusual courage to cut against the grain, we can translate service-learning into a revolutionary potential that pivots on community and consciousness and moves toward a pedagogy immersed in dialogue and participatory democracy.

Our work in Jamaica has been a process toward such a pedagogy and democratic practice. It has been an evolutionary progression moving between action and reflection/theory, and eventually better incorporating the voice of our Jamaican partners. It was launched from and often relaunches from the premise of a service-learning course. But, the argument has unfolded that this can only be the opening salvo in what must be longer term change projects *if service-learning is actually to have any revolutionary potential*. Disciplined and denuded of transformative possibility is the neoliberal education project for service-learning, particularly, and for all of schooling, generally. Capitalism confronts and complicates what might otherwise provide a resistive residual to our schooling processes. In the hands of insurgent educators, we can renew and energize a more hopeful curriculum poised to resolve the "server"/"served" dialectic, decolonize our minds, and enable courage. A more insurgent approach to education causes us to question everything—to demythologize our reality; to examine our complex histories; to interrogate ourselves in order to understand our *connection* to and interdependence with others; and to create a new world premised upon justice, democracy, and liberation. service-learning can be an educational tool to further these ends provided we are prepared to transcend the disciplinary boundaries, move from a language and philosophy of projects to *partnerships*, and are ready to leverage our relative privilege in order to live lives of solidarity—that is, humbling our individual selves for a more communal experience and recognizing the intimacy of giving our lives, our work, to others. This is our ongoing work in Jamaica. We have some ways to go.

QUESTIONS FOR REFLECTION

Remember, this is process. There is no clean, transferable, or downloadable model. This work is uneven. The work cannot fit under the umbrella of a one-size fits all rubric. And, we are not there yet. However, there are themes/questions that can make as critical an experience as possible.

1. In terms of a theme of *community* in the spirit of Freire's (1970) dialogical action, we might ask: How am I building community with my students? How am I allowing my students to build community among themselves? How am I allowing students to connect with members (professionals, those in need, etc.) of the surrounding community? *How are these relationships sustainable?*
2. In terms of *choice* and a problem-posing pedagogy, who has a decision/voice in how this partnership will unfold? Students? School? Community partners? What problems are there to be solved?
3. Regarding a theme of *consciousness* and more progressive mental conceptions of our world, we might ask: What needs to be learned about the issue? About the people with whom you are working? About ourselves? Why is it a problem? What is the history? How are the students' histories intertwined with theirs? What social constructions will need to make unraveled: racism, sexism, classism, nationalism, etc.? How can this connect to the curriculum?
4. And, finally, relative to *courage*, how might students work on their voice (speaking truth to power)? What can they learn about power and social hierarchies? What can they take with them for future experiences?

REFERENCES

Arenas, A., Bosworth, K., & Kwandayi. H. (2006). Civic service through schools: An international perspective. *Compare: A Journal of Comparative Education, 36*(1), 23–40.

Austin-Broos, D. (1997). *Jamaica Genesis: Religion and the politics of moral orders.* Chicago, IL: University of Chicago.

Benhabib, S. (1992). *Situating the self: Gender, community, and postmodernism.* New York, NY: Routledge.

Black, S. (2002). *Life and debt.* Tuff Gong Productions. Retrieved from www.lifeanddebt.org

Cavanagh, J., & Mander, J. (2004). *Alternatives to economic globalization: A better world is possible.* San Francisco, CA: Berrett-Koehler.

Fisher, S. (1997, June 5). Opening Remarks to The Service Learning for Social Justice Conference in Appalachia.

Freire, P. (1970). *Pedagogy of the oppressed.* NY: Continuum.

Freire, P. (1987). *Literacy: Reading the word and the world.* Westport, CT: Bergin & Garvey.

Friedman, T. (2005). *The world is flat: A brief history of the 21st century.* New York, NY: Farrar, Straus & Giroux.

Gibson, R. (2009). Rescue education from the elite. *The Rouge Forum News* #15. Retrieved from http://blogs.ubc.ca/ross/files/2009/12/Rouge-Forum-News-Issue-15.pdf

Hart, S. (2006). Breaking literacy boundaries through critical service?learning: Education for the silenced and marginalized. *Mentoring & Tutoring: Partnership in Learning, 14*(1), 17–32.

Keen, C., & Hall, K. (2009). Engaging with difference matters: Longitudinal student outcomes of co-curricular service-learning programs. *Journal of Higher Education, 80*(1), 59–79.

Keith, N. Z. (1997). Doing service projects in urban settings. In A. Watterman (Ed.), *Service learning: Applications from the research* (pp. 127–150). London: Erlbaum.

Kivel, P. (2000). *Social service or social change: Who benefits from your work?* Retrieved from www.paulkivel.com

Klein, N. (2007). *The shock doctrine.* New York, NY: Metropolitan Books.

Lake, O. (1998). *RastafarI women.* Durham, NC: Carolina Academic Press.

Masucci, M., & Renner, A. (2000). Reading the lives of others: The Winton Homes Library Project—A cultural studies analysis of critical service learning foreducation. *The High School Journal, 84*(1), 36–47.

Masucci, M., & Renner, A. (2001). The evolution of critical service learning for education: Four problematics. *Resources in Education: ERIC Clearinghouse,* ED456962.

Masucci, M., & Renner, A. (2002). The evolution of critical service-learning for education: Four problematics. *Resources in Education: Eric Clearinghouse,* ED456962.

Miller, D. (1999). *Principles of social justice.* Cambridge, MA: Harvard University Press.

National Association of Secondary School Principals and Quest International. (1997), *Service Learning: Raising service projects to the next level* [Brochure].

Noddings, N. (1984). *Caring: A feminine approach to ethics and moral education.* Berkeley, CA: University of California Press.

O'Grady, C. (Ed.). (2000). *Integrating service learning and multicultural education in colleges and education*. Mahwah, NJ: LEA.

Rawls, J. (1971). *A theory of justice*. Cambridge, MA: Harvard University Press.

Renner, A. (2002). Butterflies, boundaries, and breadfruit: The shared story of a service learning experience in Jamaica (Doctoral dissertation, The University of Tennessee).

Renner, A. (2005). Caring solidarity: Evolving a theoretical and practical agenda for service-learning and pedagogy. *Kentucky Journal of Excellence*, pp. 19–39.

Renner, A. & Brown, M. (2006). A hopeful curriculum: Community, praxis, and courage. *The Journal of Curriculum Theorizing, 22*(2), 101–122.

Renner, A. (2009). Teaching community, praxis, and courage: A foundations pedagogy of hope and humanization. *Educational Studies, 45*(1), 59–79.

Renner, A., Brown, M., Stiens, G., & Burton, S. (2010). A reciprocal global education? Working toward a more humanizing pedagogy and practice. *Intercultural Education, 21*(2), 41–54.

Robbins, C., & Bishop. J (2009). Accountability legerdemain and the intensification of inequality. *Dissident Voice*. Retrieved from http://dissidentvoice.org/2009/03/accountability-legerdemain-and-the-intensification-of-inequality/

Rosenberger, C. (2000). Beyond empathy: Developing critical consciousness through service learning. In C. O'Grady (Ed.), *Integrating service learning and multicultural education in colleges and education* (pp. 23–44). Mahwah, NJ: LEA.

Ross, E., & Gibson, R. (2007). *Neoliberalism and education reform*. Cresskill, NJ: Hampton Press.

Sleeter, C. (2008). Teaching for democracy in an age of corporatocracy. *Teachers College Record*. Retrieved from http://www.tcrecord.org/Content.asp?ContentId=14562

Solnit, R. (2004). *Hope in the dark*. New York, NY: Nation Books.

Stiens, G., & Renner, A. (2008). A decade of work in the Global South: Social service or social change? *The Rouge Forum*.

Thayer-Bacon, B. (2000). Caring reasoning. *Inquiry: Critical Thinking Across the Disciplines, 19*(4), 22–34.

Walzer, M. (1983). *Spheres of justice*. New York, NY: Basic Books.

Warren, K. (1998). Educating students for social justice in service learning. *The Journal of Experiential Education, 21*(3), 134–139.

Waterman, A. (Ed.). (1997). *Service learning: Applications from the research*. Mahwah, NJ: LEA.

CHAPTER 6

SERVICE-LEARNING, LIBERAL EDUCATION, AND THE PUBLIC SCHOOLS

D. G. Mulcahy, Wendy Doromal, Omaris Journet, and Donal E. Mulcahy

INTRODUCTION

The idea of a liberal or general education has long been associated with core academic studies. We believe there is much more than this to a good education, however, and it is often overlooked by policymakers, the public at large, and even well meaning educational theorists, practitioners, and institutions. Yet today those sometimes outspoken educational philosophers of the past, such as John Dewey and Paulo Freire, who proposed alternative and broader views have been joined by scholars in cognitive science, constructivist views of education, a new appreciation of the significance of practical knowledge, a heightened awareness of the potential of education for social progress, and the centrality of caring. New critiques and new conceptions of what makes for a good education are bringing into question the dominance of traditional thinking and structures, and

Critical Service Learning as a Revolutionary Pedagogy: A Project of Student Agency in Action, pp. 115–133

they are opening up new possibilities for transformative education. In this they give strong support to critical service-learning.

It is these cross currents that set our agenda in this chapter. This involves examining key features of traditional thinking on what makes for a good education, including the age old ideal of a liberal education. We will then look more closely at the new critiques and new conceptions just referred to. And we will conclude by examining some of the achievements, challenges, and promises of critical service-learning that emerge, matters that have been given a fresh and challenging analysis by Dan Butin (2010). We shall begin, however, by detailing salient features of two service-learning programs that embrace both critical service-learning and civic engagement in the public schools. The one is a large well established program, the other smaller and less well developed. Together, along with others to which reference will also be made, these will serve in their own unique ways as exemplars of what outstanding schools and teachers can accomplish in competing with existing power structures in schools and society and expanding the boundaries of schooling even in the face of these very structures. They will also serve as a point of reference in discussing new possibilities for reconceiving liberal education.

The focus in this book is upon critical service-learning and it is this form of service-learning in which we are mainly interested here. By critical service-learning we mean that element of service-learning in general in which the emphasis is upon critical reflection upon significant social, scientific, and political issues leading to or involving action for social betterment. It is precisely these kinds of issues that are highlighted in our treatment of the two public school programs that are discussed in this chapter. More specifically, attention is given to the manner in which critical service-learning is employed in teaching about issues of health, the environment, and social justice. Particular attention is given to the way in which critical service-learning may be promoted even within the constraints or barriers faced by the public schools. Along with assessment of student learning in various forms including state assessments and standardized tests, these include strict legislative, regulatory, and accountability mandates and controls.

TIMBER CREEK HIGH SCHOOL AND HARTFORD MAGNET MIDDLE SCHOOL

Timber Creek High School

The Timber Creek High School (TCHS) Service-Learning Academy in Orlando, Florida was established in 2005 under the leadership of

Wendy Doromal. It is composed of 14 teachers, an advisory council, and about 420 students. Academy students work on subject-related and interdisciplinary service-learning projects, and all students conduct an independent service-learning project with a community nonprofit agency of their choice. Students serve in tutoring and mentoring at-risk high school students, in reading buddy programs with elementary schools, and in raising awareness on issues such as bullying prevention, dangers of drug use, and driving safety. For 6 years, the Academy has planned and run a district-wide service-learning conference that attracts between 150 and 250 students, teachers, partners, parents, and community members. Students also trained 35 principals and assistant principals in service-learning and they regularly present workshops at school, district, state, and national conferences. In the 2008–2009, there were over 95 high quality service-learning projects funded through Academy grants (http://servicelearningacademy.blogspot.com/).

An early service-learning project designed by students involved partnering with area homeless agencies to raise awareness about homelessness and poverty in Central Florida. The issue has remained a prominent focus of the academy, and it exemplifies both the continuing service or civic engagement dimension of the program and, because of its attention to critical reflection, its critical service-learning dimension. Eric was a driving force behind the project as students organized walk-a-thons, sponsored food and clothing drives, and volunteered at a local soup kitchen. In all of this it was the critical dimension of service-learning that was most evident as students partnered with the Health Care Center for the Homeless HOPE Team in making a critically focused documentary video of the homeless living in the woods. Following a letter they published in the *Orlando Sentinel*, students were invited to speak at the Mayor's Forum on homelessness.

After graduating from TCHS, Eric continued his work with the homeless in a group called Food Not Bombs. When the city made a new ordinance prohibiting feeding the homeless in city parks, Eric, with the aid of legal support from the ACLU, successfully challenged the law. He continues to be a leading advocate and voice for the homeless today.

A substantial new critical service-learning project organized by students at TCHS was initiated last year on learning that Lake Apopka was seriously polluted from pesticides and fertilizers leaching into the lake from nearby fields causing serious illnesses to farm workers exposed to it. As a consequence, the service-learning council students voted to adopt issues relating to migrant farm workers and immigrants as the main theme for all of their major service-learning projects. Research was begun and partnerships were established this year with a focus upon the collection of scientific data on pollution and gaining information about workers whose health has been adversely affected by the pesticides. A number of these workers spoke at the Orange County Public Schools District Service-Learning Conference in February, 2010 showing the human cost in a manner that highlighted the critically-minded intent of the ongoing project. Next year students will begin taking oral histories of the farm workers with the goal of publishing a book to bring critical awareness to their plight.

True to the spirit of Freire and others, service-learning academy students at TCHS are agents for reflection and change on a range of issues of social concern as they arise throughout the school and community. This means that the TCHS program is very fluid enabling it to take on projects related to current local and international events such as hurricanes and the recent earthquake in Haiti. Because of their intense commitment, service-learning students have become very knowledgeable on such issues as immigration reform, human trafficking, homelessness, and issues affecting migrant farm workers. As a consequence, their capacity for bringing critical analysis to the discussion of social issues is heightened in a way that brings into view the special educational merits of critical service-learning.

The philosophy supporting service-learning at TCHS sees it providing a bridge from the classroom to the community by giving students opportunities to apply new knowledge and skills in a real-world setting. Academy teachers tell students that they can make a difference in their school, city, state, nation, and world *today*. And they do. They are critically engaged citizens intent on making the world a better place. Much of the teaching that takes place in academy classrooms is hands-on and involves group work. Critical reflection has long been considered a central element throughout the planning, action, and demonstration stages of all service-learning projects. At TCHS it is conducted through journaling, group discussion, and role play. Students use reflection to evaluate their progress, celebrate successes, discuss mistakes, make corrections, describe activities, come up with ideas, link their learning to their service, and provide feedback.

While the developing the capacity to engage in critical reflection on social issues is fundamental to the program, the TCHS service-learning academy also has broader goals. Students involved in service-learning are given opportunities to highlight their individual talents, interests and skills and to become effective team members and caring individuals. The academy has built up over 165 community partnerships with government offices, nonprofits, local businesses, and area colleges. The partners play an essential role by arranging venues for students to perform service, serving as guest speakers, and planning and participating in events and activities. At all times students have a major voice in selecting service-learning projects, identifying community needs, evaluation of projects, and assessing impact on communities. This encourages youth ownership of projects and empowers students to learn leadership and decision-making skills in community action.

Hartford Magnet Middle School

Hartford Magnet Middle School (HMMS) is designated as a Service-Learning School in Connecticut. Students serve their community throughout the school year taking on a leadership role in the Canned Food Drive, Coat Drive, and Fundraisers for Leukemia, Diabetes, and Cancer just to name a few. They set up activities, collect monies, deliver items, and promote for social causes. On a more developmental scale than at TCHS, middle school students at HMMS engage in service-learning by completing a total of thirty hours of service-learning by the time they complete the eighth grade. They are required to complete ten hours of service in each of Grades 6, 7, and 8. Students fill out a log/reflection sheet for each service-learning project which details the students' experience, how it made them feel to participate in a service-learning project, the hours completed, and the name of any organization participating. This is then submitted to the after-school program director and is reflected on each student's report card.

Currently HMMS students are engaged with organizations targeting hunger, poverty, homelessness, and cancer. The service-learning project introduced by Omaris Journet and reported on here was innovative for HMMS and aimed at extending existing boundaries by introducing a critical service-learning element into the existing program. As such it serves as a realistic model for initiating comparable projects in other settings. The project was supported by the school Principal and encouraged and influenced by the critical service-learning activities conducted by Wendy Doromal at TCHS. Revolving as it does around child labor practices in the United States as it relates to agriculture, in the HMMS project students became involved in an effort to change child labor law. This critical orientation can be seen in the steps taken in the implementation of the projects.

The first step was to engage the social studies teacher and the English teacher. The social studies teacher asked students to research information from a media database on three work groups that have been crucially involved in keeping America prosperous, namely, slaves, immigrant factory workers, and migrant farm workers. Students were required to find and research articles related to this proposition. Students then wrote an essay on how, and why, these three labor groups were important to the growth and prosperity of America and how they were treated. The final social studies project was to develop an info-graph that supported the essay.

In a second step, the English teacher presented a story to students taken from the regular class textbook. Following discussion of the story, students wrote a letter voicing their concerns about child labor law to Hilda L. Solis, Secretary of Labor and Representative Hector Robles of Connecticut among others. Students also reflected on this project by sharing their feelings and their contributions. A feature of this particular service-learning experience is the manner in which students talk about the increased caring, cooperation, teamwork, and motivation they experienced in their Service-Learning Log/Reflection sheets. It is also clear from the volume of letters written to politicians that the students were highly motivated and had a razor's edge focus on central issues.

The Child Labor Law project at HMMS is evidence of transformative work that could also be implemented elsewhere through programs of critical service-learning. Even at the middle school level, young students show themselves developing the capacity to be perceptive, critically minded, caring, and constructive in their attitudes. Such service-learning involves students in community engagements that they would never be exposed to through a conventional academic program, and it has led these middle-school students to become agents of change in school and community. In the process, it has taught them the importance of becoming both critically minded and civically engaged, how to oppose injustices, and how to communicate their thoughts and ideas to people in power. Authors of this chapter have yet to see such powerful objectives or intended outcomes laid out for so-called mastery tests of any kind.

THE STATUS QUO: CONSTRAINING STRUCTURES AND INFLUENCES

As will be elaborated upon at a later point, growth in the moral, intellectual, emotional, caring, action orientation, and community consciousness of students is increasingly supported by research and by programs in schools such as TCHS and HMMS. Yet this seems to matter little in tradition-bound hierarchies of what is considered worthwhile achievement of the kind paraded before the public in the form of results in standardized tests. A major constraint on critical service-learning programs and other innovative practices in public schools such as TCHS and HMMS are, of course, the requirements to abide by mandated assessments and various state and district regulations. Because established patterns of practice have right of way, irrespective of educational merit, critical service-learning programs have to seek out an existence by fitting into the few hours of credits allowed for elective courses, they are often considered to be of dubious merit, and they count for little in the comparative evaluation of school districts—and residential properties.

Not surprisingly, therefore, state-mandated standardized testing has limited the number of critical service-learning projects core academic teachers can carry out with their students in critical service-learning programs in TCHS. The school district has also mandated uniform curriculum, standards, schedules, and final exams for core classes. As a result, most of the academy's major critical service-learning projects originate from the critical service-learning council and volunteer public service classes which are considered academic electives. The district critical service-learning program also mandates that critical service-learning courses follow national standards, contain all the elements of high quality critical service-learning, are linked to Florida Sunshine State Standards, and contain a reading and writing element, although none of this may be undesirable in itself.

In Connecticut, as in Florida, because there are curriculum guidelines laid out for public schools, and teachers have to teach to the Connecticut Mastery Test, similar obstacles to critical service-learning exist at HMMS. These obstacles constrain practice from going outside of existing structured curriculum frameworks which, in several respects, are at odds with enlarging the boundaries of a liberal education as traditionally conceived. As will be argued, they are also at odds with forms of education that may be fundamental to the better all round formation of students. To exacerbate the situation, not only may critical service-learning be held in low esteem, but it may also increase teacher work load.

Constraints imposed on educational practice take many forms, including those just cited as well as various laws at the federal, state, and local levels, long established tradition, labor agreements, and bureaucratic structures of the kind indicated already. That said, however, these constraints are among the more obvious obstacles faced by critical service-learning programs. Additional obstacles that may be less visible and every bit if not more constraining include a variety of educational ideologies or philosophies, some having a longer lineage, a higher public profile, or otherwise exerting greater influence than others. Some of these are well reasoned and supported by respectable scholarship. Others are sometimes less so yet find their way into influential political discourse. A consideration of each kind will be helpful at this point in assessing the character of the status quo and the obstacles it poses, political, or otherwise.

THE FORDHAM FOUNDATION, ENGINEERING SOCIAL CHANGE, AND MANAGED SCHOOLING

Chester Finn, President of the Thomas B. Fordham Foundation, does not conceal his intentions. As the website of the Fordham Institute, a nonprofit organization affiliated with the Fordham Foundation, states, the Institute advances reform in education by disseminating information and ideas that that will "shape the debate" (Fordham Institute website: http://web.archive.org/web/20060206090258/http://www.edexcellence.net/institute/about/index.cfm). This is reminiscent of what Norman Fairclough (1995) calls the "technologization of discourse" in *Critical Discourse Analysis* (p. 3). This he describes as a "calculated intervention" for the purpose of "engineering social change" (p. 3). Foundations such as Fordham and the Broad Foundation engage in political spectacle and the technologization of discourse as ways of effecting the change they seek. With visions for school that are agreeable to the corporate community, such voices are well funded and have the ear of government at the highest levels.

His conservative associations notwithstanding, Finn has been a leading voice in standardization and federalization of schooling for almost 30 years (Mulcahy, 2010). In *What Do Our 17-Year-Olds Know?* coauthored with Diane Ravitch (1987), the authors point to a flimsy and failing school curriculum to explain an unacceptably uninformed populous in the United States. The curriculum, however, could be little more flimsy than portions of *What Do Our 17-Year-Olds Know?* itself. Although the title of the book, *What Do Our 17-Year Olds Know?*, almost implies it was commissioned by the government and overtly claims to be national in scope, neither is the case. Yet, it is a measure of the influence wielded by conservative foundations such as Fordham that, irrespective of their merits, they sway policy at the highest levels of government. Findings reported in *What Do Our 17-Year-Olds Know?* for example, found their way into both the address to the Education Summit in 1989 by President George H. W. Bush and into the national folklore.

The case in point is the answer to a test question pertaining to the Civil War on the assessment of 17-year olds on which the Ravitch and Finn (1987) book was based. The question is completely invalid because the correct answer to the question does not exist as an answer choice available to students taking the test. Here is the question in its entirety: "When was the Civil War?" The years 1860–1866 are not available to the students as the answer to the question. Rather, the answer choices read as follows: "Before 1750; 1750–1800; 1800–1850; 1850–1900; 1900–1950; After 1900" (p. 49). The answer to the question that is considered correct is "1850-1900," and *What Do Our 17-Year-Olds Know?* highlights that only 32.2% chose this answer. Needless to mention, 1850–1900 are not the war years. To improve this question from faulty and invalid to merely confusing, the question would have to either provide a correct answer choice, or be phrased: "within which half of which century did the 6-year Civil War occur?" The carefully crafted wording used by President Bush in referring to this was as follows: The National Assessment of National Progress estimates that "barely one in three can locate the Civil War in the correct half-century." (*Public Papers of the President of the United States, George Bush, 1989*, Book II, 1990, p. 1274).

Before leaving *What Do Our 17-Year-Olds Know?* it is worthwhile drawing attention to its evocation of fear as a tool of persuasion, a pattern of discourse attributed to neoconservative discourse in public policy matters outside of education. In the foreword to the book, Lynn Cheney writes, "where once grade school students had textbooks that contained Longfellow, Hawthorne, Shakespeare, and Dickens, now they have readers with essays about how to read maps and decide on careers" (Ravitch & Finn, 1987, p. viii). The implication here is clearly that the traditional literary canon has been lost and that bringing it back is in our interest or, more likely, as Jane Roland Martin (1994, pp. 212–227) once put it, in the interests of the restorationists. Although this claim goes unsubstantiated, its being said is reason enough for accepting the authors' jeremiad. This thematic use of fear is not only in keeping with *A Nation at Risk*, but also the title of the fourth and final chapter of *What Do Our 17-Year-Olds Know?* —"A Generation at Risk." This title appears on the top of each of the chapter's 54 pages (Ravitch & Finn, 1987, pp. 200–253).

THE INHERITED TRADITION IN LIBERAL EDUCATION

In a different example from the use of political discourse to shape the debate on education in the interests of powerful elites, strong allegiance to the much respected if traditional view of a liberal education also poses barriers to innovative practice. In this country one of the early statements influencing the idea is found in the report by Yale College (1828) commonly referred to as the *Yale Report of 1828*. A little later in England, comparable ideas were expressed by John Henry Cardinal Newman (1873/1947) in his classic work, *Idea of a University*. As Newman stated it, liberal education was simply "cultivation of the intellect" and its object was "nothing more or less than intellectual excellence" (p. 107). Although expressed in the context of higher education, both are landmark statements of the theory of a liberal education in modern times.

More recent expressions of this view include contemporary adaptations that hold on to core principles that outlaw practical forms of education and are insensitive to student experience. These are found, for example, in the writings of the English philosopher, Paul Hirst, and in this country in the popular little book, *The Paideia Proposal*, by Mortimer Adler (1982). According to Adler, there were three main components in a good basic schooling. It would provide students with core organized knowledge made up of the study of language and literature, mathematics and science, and the social studies. In addition, students would acquire the basic intellectual skills of learning. For Adler, these consisted first of reading, writing, speaking, and listening; second, calculating, problem solving, observing, estimating, and measuring; and third, exercising critical judgment. Finally, for Adler, a good education required students to gain an enlarged understanding of ideas and values through the study of great books and involvement in creative and artistic activities. In viewing schooling in this way, Adler was also adamant that students should follow the same 12-year course of study, that there should not be any electives, and that the course of study should be liberal and general, that is to say, nonvocational and nonspecialized. The influential book by E. D. Hirsch, *Cultural Literacy* (1988), advocated an even more prescriptive approach to the curriculum.

These treatments of what makes for a good or liberal education were extended into the political and policy spheres in the United States and abroad in the form of major policy statements emanating from state and federal governments during the past thirty years. In Connecticut, for example, the 1980s saw the creation of the Connecticut Common Core of Learning followed by the introduction of mastery testing; broadly similar developments occurred in Florida and other states dating back to curriculum reforms introduced in the early 1980s. But the most conspicuous and arguably the most influential developments took place at the federal level. These include the hugely influential report, *A Nation at Risk*, in 1983, the Goals 2000 Act in 1994, and the now almost infamous No Child Left Behind Act of 2002. Especially important from a curriculum perspective in these documents is their perception of a good education. In *A Nation at Risk*, this consisted of the new basics, namely, math, English, science, social studies, and computer studies. The definition contained in Goals 2000 was more wide ranging but once again emphasized the study of core academic subjects.

Last, these conceptions of a good education are reflected in popular thinking. They resonate with parents, they are the bedrock upon which applications for colleges and universities are designed, they are taken as predictive of future employee achievement, they are highlighted in the press, and they are pushed relentlessly by powerful and well funded conservative foundations. As a consequence, even if they are resisted by reform-minded educators, they are a constraint on innovative forms of education taking hold. This is especially prominent in programs such of critical service-learning that contain a service or action oriented component.

INNOVATIVE IDEAS AND PRACTICES

Successful challenges to the status quo whether in political ideology or educational structures and philosophies, will be led by innovative ideas and practices. Critique alone will not be sufficient. Fortunately, there is no shortage of such innovative ideas and practices. Even Newman, arguably the most prominent proponent of liberal education in modern times, expressed grave concerns that liberal education strictly interpreted as the study of academics constituted a full education (Mulcahy, 2008, pp. 35–69). The stance adopted by him where practical knowledge and practical reasoning are given an elevated status vis-à-vis theoretical knowledge is mirrored in a similar and more explicit way in later writings by Hirst. Long an advocate of a mandatory academic curriculum for schools grounded in seven forms of theoretical or academic knowledge (Hirst, 1974), in 1993 Hirst retracted his earlier position, proclaiming that "education may at many stages turn out to be best approached through practical concerns." He now considered "practical knowledge to be more fundamental than theoretical knowledge, the former being basic to any clear grasp of the proper significance of the latter" (Hirst, 1993, p. 197). At the same time, John White, another prominent English philosopher of education, highlighted what he called "the primacy of the practical." Expressing sentiments consistent with the critical service-learning programs at TCHS and HMMS, he argued that we ought to "begin our thinking about the curriculum with the human being as agent, not the human being as knower" (White, 2004, p. 184).

Writing in the early 1980s, Martin developed a powerful philosophical perspective that provides even stronger support for the principles evident in critical service-learning programs such as those at TCHS and HMMS. Martin (1994) argued that philosophical investigation of curriculum was stuck in a rut and "endorsed a theory of curriculum that is seriously deficient" (p. 171). Of particular concern to Martin was its exclusion of such values as practicality, feelings and emotions, and the 3Cs of care, concern, and connection. The traditional way of thinking about the school curriculum, she believed, ignored "feelings and emotions and other so-called 'non-cognitive' states and processes of mind." It also ignored "knowledge how," it excluded education for action (p. 173), and it relied on a conception of education that divorced mind from body (pp. 170–186). In addition, it may be added, it ignored the potential educational benefits of critical service-learning.

If there are serious shortcomings of liberal education—and by extension, of the idea of a good education—such as those now made explicit in Hirst and Martin, questions arise as to what alternatives might be considered. Here, too, Martin (1994) provides a starting point. She adds a new goal to the widely accepted goals of education, namely, preparing the young for family and for caring. Much like critical service-learning, this view does not overlook academic studies. It does see them as but one part of a person's broader education, however, one that "integrates thought and action, reason and emotion, education and life" (1994, p. 183). Notwithstanding the growing body of research that supports such forms of education, these are the very directions that innovative practice is fighting an uphill battle to have recognized. This research includes research by Eyler and Giles (1999) and Tonkin (2004) specifically in the areas of critical service-learning and that by Baxter Magolda (2004, 2006) and King and Baxter Magolda (2005) in the areas of self-authorship and intercultural learning. Research in learning theory and constructivist theory also support new directions in liberal education. This includes the work of Bransford, Brown, and Cocking (2008) as presented in *How People Learn: Brain, Mind, Experience and School,* which deals with what we know scientifically about learning, including the importance of prior learning. There is also an important literature on critical service-learning building on Ernest Boyer's early work (1984, 1987) at both the high school and college levels. The recent work of William Sullivan and Matthew Rosin (2008), in particular, brings a greater sense of urgency and possibility regarding the promise of practical knowledge, practical reason, and practical responsibility for liberal education, as it draws on case studies from a range of subjects and areas of professional study.

These theoretical advances have been accompanied in higher education by an impressive array of programs and methods of teaching, many of which are also found in schools. In addition to critical service-learning, examples include the case method, problem-based learning, simulations, studio classes, cooperative learning, interactive lecture demonstrations, science tutorials, peer instruction; and various other inquiry-guided, problem-focused, and collaborative teaching strategies. Especially pertinent here is the work of Joe DeVitis and his colleagues (1998), who brought their focus to bear directly on the potential value of critical service-learning in liberal education. They "envision a rich linkage between liberal and critical service-learning that will permit students to be critically reflective participants in whichever settings or callings they choose to enter" (p. 13). As is also true of the programs in TCHS and HMMS, it is a vision where students learn to critically examine service, helping, and intervention as they have the opportunity to investigate social institutions, power relations, and value commitment. In the opinion of DeVitis and his colleagues, the key values of autonomy and service to community are not taught through didactic methods alone. For this to occur, one must experience citizenship at a deep level of involvement and participation such as one finds in critical service-learning at TCHS and HMMS.

Even though it has traditionally been absent in liberal educ tis and his colleagues were clearly committed to the idea of engaging .. action in education. In this, they are following in the footsteps of Freire (1971), Ira Shor (1992), and Martin (1994). More recently, the related idea of knowledge production by students is elaborated in dramatic terms by Carl Bereiter. Drawing on cognitive science and the growth of knowledge-based organizations where everyone contributes to the creation of knowledge, Bereiter (2002) introduced other possibilities into the discussion as he explored the place and form of liberal education in a knowledge society. If liberal education is to survive, he suggested, it will require a careful synthesis of new ideas and enduring principles.

There are two distinct elements in liberal education as Bereiter (2002) understood it, namely, knowledge production and existing objective knowledge. His characterization of the place of knowledge production is rooted in his notion of a knowledge society organized around the production of knowledge in which "the school should be a productive part of that society, a workshop for the generation of knowledge" (p. 12). This idea, he suggested, sees schools such as TCHS and HMMS, like research laboratories, becoming knowledge-building organizations where the daily activities of the classroom undergo a cultural shift "from classroom life organized around activities to classroom life organized around the pursuit of knowledge" (p. 18). This broad orientation in which students take steps to add to what we know characterizes the critical service-learning projects addressing the plight of migrant farm workers in both TCHS and HMMS.

THE SPECIAL CASE OF TRINITY COLLEGE OF VERMONT

The foregoing discussion captures major points and new departures within the ongoing debate around what constitutes a good or liberal education, and it shows these ideas to be in flux. More specifically, it points to alternatives of a kind found in critical service-learning that reach well beyond a book-bound focus. The program of critical service-learning once offered at Trinity College of Vermont is a special illustrative case in point.

Oren W. Davis and Jennifer Dodge explain that in the program at Trinity College of Vermont, critical service-learning meant students learn by participating in "thoughtfully organized service experiences that meet actual community needs and that are coordinated in collaboration with the college and community" (Davis, with Dodge, 1998, p. 93). Here learning was "integrated into the student's academic curriculum" and structured time was provided for students "to engage in critical reflection about what they did and saw during the actual service activity." Critical service-learning was seen as providing students with opportunities "to use newly acquired skills and knowledge in real-life situations in the community." By enhancing what was taught by extending student learning beyond the classroom into the community, it was also seen as helping "to foster the development of a sense of caring for others" (pp. 93–94) and additional student outcomes including moral growth identified by Boland, Eyler, and others as important for civic engagement (Boland, 2009; Eyler, 2005; Eyler & Giles, 1999; and Tonkin, 2004, especially pp. 388–389).

A particular course that Davis (with Dodge, 1998) discusses deals with liberation theology. In that course, in order to enhance their theoretical understanding, students were engaged in community service in the belief that "the community service project helps students recognize that liberation involves more than theories—it also involves action, doing, praxis." Through an academic course in liberation theology, they conclude, "consciousness of oppression is raised; learning is enhanced by these practical, concrete experiences; and moral and civic values are reinforced" (p. 97).

To those who are skeptical that critical service-learning has any place in liberal education, what Davis and Dodge write, what the research suggests, and what is on display at TCHS and HMMS in varying degrees, gives reason to pause, for one may reasonably conclude otherwise. In these and other cases, critical service-learning may fairly be said to represent a serious and realistic approach to education for reflective action. When such learning is grounded in the personal experience and interests of students it also goes a long way to responding to the pedagogical imperative of building upon the existing experience of the learner. This is a point well captured by Myles Horton (1998) when he wrote, "you have to start where people [students] are, because their growth is going to be from there, not from some abstraction or where you are or someone else is" (p. 131).

Such learning may also contribute to the community in tangible ways and enable students to develop caring, interpersonal, and intercultural attitudes and skills not normally associated with liberal education. All of this may accomplish liberation while also serving the traditional intellectual ideals of liberal education. For as Dodge, then a student at Trinity College of Vermont, adds, it heightened her understanding in a way that "no book or lecture can elicit" (Davis, with Dodge, 1998, p. 98; See also King & Baxter Magolda, 2005; Baxter Magolda, 2006). In much the same context, in commenting on the approach taken by Barbara Stengel in the integration of philosophical and practical reasoning in the education of teachers, Sullivan and Rosin (2008) recognize this as an example of where theoretical reasoning and understanding are dependent upon prior practical experience. Stengel's students, they write, "form meaningful judgments about the normative significance of teaching only through growing participation in the unfolding drama of practice over time. They cannot be predetermined or derived deductively through theoretical reasoning alone" (p. 43).

CRITICAL SERVICE-LEARNING AND THE REDEFINITION OF A "GOOD EDUCATION"

Critical service-learning in a manner reflective of Freire's quest for praxis of the kind found in TCHS, HMMS, and Trinity College of Vermont presents practices suggestive of new possibilities for a reconceived idea of a liberal education. To sustain it, however, and thereby resolve the age old conflict between liberal education and practical knowledge, these practices need the support of a reformed theory of a good education of the kind hinted at by Sullivan and Rosin and a new image of the educated person.

If the ideal of the educated person is to embrace practical knowledge, attitudes, and skills not previously associated with liberal education, it will obviously differ considerably from the historical tradition of a liberal education. The ideal of the educated person as one of many-sided development articulated in *The Educated Person* (Lewis, 2009; Mulcahy, 2008, pp. 177–196) may hold promise in this regard. The justification and the content of an education fashioned to reflect this ideal would not be sought merely in the academic disciplines, but also in practical knowledge and lived experience. Both the curriculum and its accompanying pedagogy would be appropriately individualized for all students in accordance with their experience, interests, capacities, and needs. That is to say, its organizational principle would be shaped by two considerations: the imperative to engage in action as a duty vital to everyday living and personal fulfillment, and a respect for societal needs and the autonomy and experience of the individual student. Such a curriculum would be multifaceted and varied. It would, as a consequence, constitute an important shift toward incorporating education for praxis in how we view the scope and content of a good education.

CONCLUSION

The analysis presented here shows that the idea of a good education after the fashion of a liberal education is a rich and powerful one. Even though it has evolved over time it needs further redefinition if it is to realize more fully its historical aspiration to enable students to understand the complex natural and cultural environments in which they live today. Further redefinition is needed too if it is to fulfill the full promise elaborated in the historical American aspiration to education for democratic citizenship by encouraging students to welcome civic engagement. To achieve these noble goals, it needs to be recast in a way that retains its emphasis on what Newman called cultivation of the intellect; recognizes the importance of practical knowledge and education for action; accommodates the view that education of the whole person brings into play emotional, moral, and spiritual formation; and adopts a pedagogical stance that gives full recognition to the experience, capacities, and interests of the individual. Even though practice already reflects some such developments, the challenge to do so more fully and more consistently in schools and colleges is considerable. Despite the obstacles it has to deal with, critical service-learning holds out great promise in this endeavor.

QUESTIONS FOR REFLECTION

1. Consider the factors that pose the greater obstacles to programs of critical service-learning. Choose from these two examples: conventional school structures (such as the compartmentalized curriculum, tenure for teachers, and state or standardized testing) or powerful ideologies reflecting economic or political perspectives rooted in particular cultural traditions.
2. Consider the relative strengths of the traditional view of a liberal education as grounded exclusively in the academic subjects and the related values of intellectual excellence (as found in Hirst and Adler, for example) or more contemporary conceptions that favor supplementing such education with education of the emotions, education for caring, and education for action (as found in Martin).
3. How would you advise your principal to make the case for introducing a sophisticated program of critical service-learning such as that at run by Wendy Doromal at TCHS to the district school board or how would you yourself make the case to your principal for introducing a new project to the existing program such as that introduced by Omaris Journet at HMMS?
4. Courses taught in critical service-learning programs are frequently elective and not assessed on standardized tests of the kind associated with other subjects. President Obama raised controversy recently when he proposed factoring in student performance in the evaluation of teacher performance. Do you believe a teacher in

a critical service-learning program is at an advantage or disadvantage because he or she cannot be evaluated on the basis of student performance in such tests but on other forms of evaluation, such as student ratings of teachers, parental satisfaction, or some other such criteria? Would this question influence teachers to participate in critical service-learning or abandon it?

5. Writing of the benefits of critical service-learning as judged by its educational aspirations and outcomes (such as growth in community consciousness, caring for others, advocacy for social causes such as ending homelessness and seeking justice for immigrant farm workers) the authors of this chapter said that they "have yet to see such powerful objectives or intended outcomes laid out for so-called mastery tests of any kind." Consider this observation, and argue in support or against, providing evidence if available.

REFERENCES

Adler, M. J. (1982). *The paideia proposal: An educational manifesto.* New York: NY: Macmillan.

Baxter Magolda, M. B. (2004). Evolution of a constructivist conceptualization of epistemological reflection. *Educational Psychologist, 39*(1), 31–42.

Baxter Magolda, M. B. (with Crosby, P.). (2006). Self-authorship and identity in college: An interview with Marcia B. Baxter Magolda. *Journal of College & Character,* 7(1), 1–2.

Bereiter, C. (2002). Liberal education in a knowledge society. In B. Smith (Ed.) *Liberal education in a knowledge society* (pp. 11–33). Chicago, IL: Open Court.

Boland, J. (2009, March). *Agency and alignment: Insights from teaching and learning through civic engagement.* Paper presented at the Annual Conference of the Educational Studies Association of Ireland, Kilkenny.

Boyer, E. L. (1983). *High school high school: A report on secondary education in America.* New York, NY: Harper and Row.

Boyer, E. L. (1987). *College: The undergraduate experience in America.* New York, NY: Harper and Row.

Bransford, J. D., Brown, A. L., & Cocking, R. R. (Eds.). (1999). *How people learn: Brain, mind, experience and school.* Washington, DC: National Academies Press.

Butin, D. W. (2010). *Service-learning in theory and practice: The future of community engagement in higher education.* New York, NY: Palgrave Macmillan.

DeVitis, J. L., Johns, R. W., & Simpson, D. G. (1998). *To serve and learn: The spirit of community in liberal education.* New York, NY: Peter Lang.

Dewey, J. (1963). *Experience and education.* New York, NY: Collier. (Original work published 1938)

Davis, O. W. (with Dodge, J. (1998). Liberationist theology through community service-learning at Trinity College of Vermont. In J. L. DeVitis, R. W. Johns, &

D. J. Simpson (Eds.), *To serve and learn: The spirit of community in liberal education* (pp. 92–101). New York, NY: Peter Lang.

Eyler, J. (2005). Academic service-learning for effective civic engagement. *Diversity Digest, 9,* 16–17.

Eyler, J., & Giles D. E., Jr. (1999). *Where's the learning in service-learning?* San Francisco, CA: Jossey-Bass.

Fairclough, N. (1995). *Critical discourse analysis: The critical study of language*. New York, NY: Longman.

Freire, P. (1971). *Pedagogy of the oppressed* (Trans. New York, NY: Herder and Herder.

Hirsch, E. (1988). *Cultural literacy: What every American Needs to know.* New York, NY: Vintage Books.

Hirst, P. H. (1974). *Knowledge and the curriculum.* London, England: Routledge and Kegan Paul.

Hirst, P. H. (1993). Education, knowledge and practices. In R. Barrow & P. White (Eds.), *Beyond liberal education* (pp. 184–199). London, England: Routledge.

Horton, M. (1998). *The long haul: An autobiography.* New York, NY: Teachers College Press.

King, P. M., & Baxter Magolda, M. B. (2005). A developmental model of intercultural maturity. *Journal of College Student Development, 46*(6), 571–592.

Martin, J. R. (1992). *The schoolhome: Rethinking schools for changing families*. Cambridge, MA: Harvard University Press.

Martin, J. R. (1994). *Changing the educational landscape: Philosophy, women, and curriculum*. New York, NY: Routledge.

Mulcahy, D. E. (2010). Consolidating government oversight: How current reforms are undermining and overriding local voices. In N. S. Pope (Ed.), *Democracy in Schooling* (pp. 81-88).

Mulcahy, D. G. (2008). *The educated person: Toward a new paradigm for liberal education*. Lanham, MD: Rowman and Littlefield.

Newman, J. H. (1947). *The idea of a university defined and illustrated.* New York, NY: Longmans, Green and Co. (Original work published 1873)

Public Papers of the President of the United States, George Bush, 1989 (in two books). Book II July 1–December 31, 1989. (1990). Washington DC: United States Government Printing Office.

Ravitch, D., & Finn, C. E., Jr. (1987). *What do our 17-year-olds know? A report on the first national assessment of history and literature*. New York, NY: Fizhenry & Whiteside.

Shor, I. (1992). *Empowering education: Critical teaching for social change*. Chicago, IL: University of Chicago Press.

Sullivan, W.M. & Rosin, M.S. (2008). *A new agenda for higher education*. San Francisco, CA: Jossey-Bass.

The Thomas B. Fordham Institute. About Us. (n.d.). [Web log comment]. Retrieved from http://web.archive.org/web/20060206090258/http://www.edexcellence.net/institute/about/index.cfm

Timber Creek High School Service Academy. Service Learning Academy. (n.d.). [Web log comment]. Retrieved from http://servicelearningacademy.blogspot.com/

Tonkin, H. (Ed.). (2004). *Service-learning across cultures: Promise and achievement.* New York, NY: The International Partnership for Service-Learning and Leadership.

White, J. (Ed.). (2004). *Rethinking the school curriculum: Values, aims and purposes.* London, England: RoutledgeFalmer.

CHAPTER 7

EDUCATION, CRITICAL SERVICE-LEARNING, AND SOCIAL JUSTICE

The Australian Experience of Doing Thick Democracy in the Classroom

David Zyngier

INTRODUCTION

> No arbitrary obstacles should prevent people from achieving those positions for which their talents fit them and which their values lead them to seek. Not birth, nationality, colour, religion, sex, nor any other irrelevant characteristic should determine the opportunities that are open to a person—only his [or her] abilities. (Friedman & Friedman, 1980, p. 132)

It has been suggested that the success of public (government or state run) schools in Western democracies may well be part of the reason that (at least in Australia) they are faced with many seemingly overwhelming diffi-

Critical Service Learning as a Revolutionary Pedagogy:
A Project of Student Agency in Action, pp. 135–154

culties (Bonner & Caro, 2007). These schools, designed to create a "stable educated and prosperous economy and society" (p. 159), have been portrayed as the "zenith of democracy," but can we remain a functioning democracy without a strong public education system? A former director of education for the Organization of Economic Cooperation and Development (OECD) concluded that the school system in Australia does little to address inherited inequality. Instead, it reproduces existing social arrangements, "conferring privilege where it already exists and denying it where it does not" (p. 164). McGraw (2006) concludes:

> Educational inequity in the sense considered here involves a relatively strong relationship between educational outcomes and social background, with the implication that the education system is consistently conferring privilege on those who already have it and denying it to those who do not. (McGraw, 2006, p. 18)

Australia has witnessed a growing trend to mass secondary education in the past 50 years. In 1940 only 1 in 10 students completed 12 years of school. In the 1970s this rose to 1 in 3 and then 3 of 4 in the 1990s. There has been a corresponding flow on into higher education: 1 in 4 citizens are attending university in 2000s.

While this could be seen as a harmonic view of education and economy, it instead "represents a goal rather than an achievement" (Teese, 2007, p. 39). Comforting as these high rates might be, in the Australian context it rests not on higher aspirations conditioned on industrial change, but on a collapsing full-time labor market which effectively trapped people in schooling. Teese has argued that the expanding education system, driven by neoliberal choice policies, has resulted in an increase in social inequalities and economic segregation. This is due in large to parents with the economic and cultural capital removing their children from the local government funded high and elementary schools to the better resourced high fee paying private school system. This has resulted in what Teese has termed "residualized" or "sink schools" (p. 189), which holds students who are marginalized on the structural axes of race and class. The purpose of the chapter is twofold: It will highlight how the Austrian educational context has become further debilitating for minoritized students through neoliberal educational policies and practices as well as other pernicious policies to commodify social life, and it will capture how critical-service learning has the power to function as a pedagogy to challenge the commercialized educational social order in Australia and in other social contexts.

Major Public Policy Reforms in 30 years

The three major neoliberal economic reforms over the past thirty years—marketization, privatization, and rationalization—based on the so-called free-market ideology of Friedmanism, Thatcherism, and Reaganomics pushed for a reduction in government responsibility including education. The result of these three policies created a deregulated and heavily subsidized market of private schools, designed to shift enrolments away from the public sector. Talking up the language of choice and competition various federal and state minsters of education introduced reforms in response to what they described as observed deficiencies in the system

> The phrase failing public schools has a lot in common with the war on terror: get the media to parrot these phrases often enough so that you can't hear terrorism without thinking there's a need for a war, and you can't hear public schools without thinking they are failing and need to be fixed. This language works: ordinary people without an axe to grind, people who haven't set foot in a school for thirty years or more, will testify to failing public schools. Tis technique forestalls debate about what matters in public schools because the corporate and political elite have already defined both the problem and the solution. (Emery & Ohanian, 2004, p. 6)

This continues today with the calls for increased public private partnerships (PPPs) and corporate support of public schooling. The effects on education (and elsewhere) are profound. Marketization led to the reorganization of schools around market principles (Whitty, Power, & Halpin, 1998); privatization has seen increasing levels of public funding shift to private providers—public funding of private effort—the free market goal of ensuring diversity and choice; and rationalization resulted in the restructuring of schools through closures or amalgamations, particularly of smaller schools. This has made thousands of experienced teachers expendable.

During this same period of time, the federal conservative (Liberal-National Coalition) government led a campaign that was increasingly strident in its accusation that comprehensive public schooling was responsible for a perceived and claimed fall in teaching and learning standards (Leigh & Ryan, 2006, 2008). The result of these interventions has seen an increase in economic and social divisions in and between schools in Australia. Many schools started to lose their middle-class families and "accumulate the deficits created by this loss" (Bonner & Caro, 2007, p. 41). As a result, educators find it difficult to meet their students' intellectual, social, and emotional needs. Schools in poorer areas have become residualized repositories of failure or *sink schools*, denuded of numbers and cultural capital resources (Teese & Lamb, 2007).

> The question everyone in the political class is tiptoeing around is this. At what point do most public schools simply become sinks of disadvantage, places where the residue of kids with average or below average IQs and more than their fair share of other problems confound everyone's efforts to teach them life's basic skills? You could reformulate the question by asking: at what stage does the abandonment of public-sector education by what used to be called the lower middle-classes reach its tipping point? (Pearson, 2007)

While families with social power use education to "stake a claim" for their child's advantage, families without such cultural and social capital rely on governments to assert those claims. While the process of marginalization has been difficult to prevent, continuing to rely on market forces to improve students' social and intellectual growth has fostered "despair, racism, cover up, official avoidance [resulting in] a paralysis of public initiatives" (Bonner & Caro, 2007, p. 112). If competition drove school reform then the winners were schools serving wealthy suburbs. Students in these contexts were given additional resources and academic programs, which supported learning environments predicated on sparking students' intellectual interests and meeting their social needs (Lamb, 2007).

An Education Revolution—Or Is It Just More of The Same?

With the election of a new Labor government in November 2007 came a proposed "education revolution." The newly elected Prime Minister said that he

> cannot understand why public institutions such as schools should not be accountable to the community that funds their salaries and their running costs. Right now, we do not have accurate, comprehensive information to allow rigorous analysis of what schools and students are achieving.
>
> This must change. That is why today I announce that we will be making agreement on individual school performance reporting a condition of the new national education agreement to come into effect from 1 January 2009. (Kevin Rudd, Address to the National Press Club on August 27, 2008)

Once again the teachers who are responsible for the excellent achievements of Australian students (in comparison to other OECD countries) are being blamed for their supposed failures (Tomazin, 2008). Yet Prime Minister Rudd and his Deputy and Minister for Education, Gillard, together with their counterparts in Labor Victoria, are now proposing to copy the much critiqued (Boyd, Grossman, Lankford, Loeb, & Wyckoff, 2006; Darling-Hammond, Holtzman, Gatlin, & Heilig, 2005; Laczko-Kerr & Berliner, 2002) New York model of individual school performance. That is, reporting and public comparison of so-called *like schools* as determined by student's entry scores and scores on standardized tests, parental income, ethnic composition and other data as well as the educationally bankrupt policies of *Teach for America* (Decker, Mayer, & Glazerman, 2004).

And the solution proposed? Government leaders are encouraging so-called disengaged teachers to leave the profession (Pike, 2008), giving top education graduates and top teachers financial incentives to work in so-called failing schools, and publishing schools' standardized test scores. The solution will allegedly ensure that minoritized students will become as academically successful as their affluent counterparts in relation to how they score on high-stakes examinations (Dinham, Ingvarson, & Kleinhenz, 2008). It seems that government officials and business leaders in Australia want the public to believe that teachers are the cause for minoritized students' poor performance on standardized exams, rather than recognizing how the government's support of the neoliberal agenda makes it difficult for minoritized students to succeed in the circles of education.

Despite the neoliberal agenda taking a firm hold in schools across Australia, there are some schools that are finding cracks in and spaces amid the commercial status quo to do amazing things especially for children from culturally, linguistically and economically diverse (CLED) communities. Broadly speaking the strategies fall into the following three areas: new pedagogies and curricula; social support and well being; and community participation. It is the new pedagogies and curricula which I believe hold the greatest potential for what I have called the elegant subversion of the current dominant paradigm of division and disadvantage.

Key strategies adopted in programs emphasizing new pedagogies and curricula are:

- connectedness between subject areas, and between classroom activities and the real world, and
- intellectual challenge in key curriculum areas, valuing of diversity, building positive relationships and communication

The chosen strategies align well with the features of engaging schools (Murray, Mitchell, Gale, Edwards, & Zyngier, 2004). Most of the programs described have been initiated, developed or modified in context specific ways, and in so doing reflect the important point that there is no single recipe for program development (Smith et al., 2001a, 2001b). Those programs drawing on particular pedagogical frameworks have done so in order to meet the specific needs of groups of students. The pedagogical frameworks are invariably modified to suit particular classes, curriculum requirements and curriculum content. In those cases in which there is systemic funding, the emphasis is on using funds to sponsor cluster and school-based initiatives that are responsive to the needs of schools, their students and teachers, and the local community (Murray et al., 2004).

The rest of this chapter briefly reviews a school program that is *elegantly subversive* in that it is achieving the required results by doing school differently, especially for children from CLED communities. In doing so, I highlight the achievements of one particular critical service-learning project that has had enormous transformative impact on the participants and their communities.

RUMAD (ARE YOU MAKING A DIFFERENCE)

The ruMAD program (see http://www.rumad.org.au/) began as a pilot project of The Education Foundation in 2001 and currently in 2010 has over 230 schools throughout Australian participating. From its beginnings, the ruMAD Program recognized that

> In our current society, inequity exists, with people coming from places of privilege and disadvantage. Local community networks are where people first learn about inclusive and representative processes. Real and lasting improvement in many areas of social need can only be achieved through structural change. Band-aid or quick-fix solutions will not necessarily address the underlying issues. (Shor, 1992, p. 7)

It has the following aims:

- The active participation of young people in the community through action research projects
- To provide young people with opportunities for engaging, independent, student-centred learning
- To model engaging, student-centred learning for teachers
- To enable young people to make a difference in their school or community
- Supporting student leadership
- Creating the conditions for identifying core values
- Building social competencies such as self-esteem and confidence
- Building the skills and knowledge to solve real world problems. (Shor, 1992)

The ruMAD Program claims that "students who participate ... will be empowered to positively transform situations where they see disadvantage or unfairness in their own and others' lives" while involvement seeks to "empower students to inquire, act and reflect on the issues that are of real concern to them, and promote active citizenship" (Shor, 1992, p. 10). It is an inquiry-based pedagogical framework that (a) accords with state and federal policy emphasis on the incorporation of values education into school curricula; and (b) encourages, educates, and empowers young people to enact social change. Predicated on the belief that everyone is able to improve and help change the communities in which they live, the program provides participants with opportunities for experiential civic engagement in areas of their own interest and choice. Participants have dealt with environmental issues like recycling and land degradation, homelessness, poverty and bullying and harassment at school. Further, the program aims is based on

> a commitment to the values of **equity**—seeking a fair and just distribution of economic resources and political power; of **access**—providing fair and equal access to public services which is essential to achieving and maintaining a decent lifestyle; creating the opportunity for participation in social and political life and in the decisions which affect people's lives; and **equality**—ensuring opportunity and the capacity to achieve according to everyone's potential and to live without discrimination. (Shor, 1992, p. 10, emphasis in original)

Over 1000 Australian schools have participated in ruMAD since its inception. In 2008 some 35,000 students in 2008 alone were spoken to about ruMAD. This, however, does not reflect the actual number of students who then went on to participate in projects.

- ruMAD is underpinned by four main educational objectives:
- To engage young people in issues of social justice;
- To engage young people with a high level of authenticity;
- To promote student-led classrooms, thereby challenging teacher practice; and
- To create real community change. (Westheimer & Kahne, 2004)

It presents the concept of facilitated learning through Roger Hart's (1992) Ladder of Youth Participation[1] and explains it as a fluid continuum. A number of elements of the ruMAD program and philosophy were identified as holding particular attraction and relevance for schools, that is, for providing students and teachers with the following:

- Opportunities for real community engagement (both within and beyond school grounds)
- Opportunities for engagement with real issues
- Opportunities for transformative citizenship going (beyond responsible citizenship or thin democracy to participation in thick democracy) (Carr, 2008; Gandin & Apple, 2005)
- Opportunities for effecting and sustaining change
- Opportunities for independent learning
- Opportunities for changed teacher practice (Stokes & Turnbull, 2008)

WHAT DOES A TYPICAL MAD PROJECT LOOK LIKE?

"Jessie's Creek" School: Whitfield District Primary School

Whitfield is an agricultural township in the King River valley 170 km northeast of Melbourne. The primary (elementary) school has around 20 students from kindergarten to Grade 6 (ages 5–12).[2] Jessie's Creek runs through the town and behind the school and the river was cloaked in a blanket of weeds that had accumulated over the years aided by dumping of green garden waste (weeds, grass clippings, etc.) as well as miscellaneous rubbish. Despite the creek being the town's main water supply, there was also a lot of rubbish scattered about. Creepers, ivy, blackberry, and Lucerne covered the creek that looked like a botanical garden; however, nothing was indigenous (National Resource Management, 2008).

The adults in the town decided to have a meeting to clean up the creek, but after 3 hours, no decision could be reached. The students at the primary school took on an ruMAD project to carry out a biodiversity study of the creek and aimed to clean it up. The biodiversity study enabled the students to understand that invasive and often noxious plants, many of which were the result of inappropriate farming and land-management practices, had overwhelmed the creek's indigenous flora. From the outset the ruMAD students of Whitfield PS have been at the centre of the campaign to save Jessie's Creek, mustering community support by producing brochures, conducting surveys, and sending letters to government bodies linked with management of the creek.

After carrying out the biodiversity study, and after only one afternoon of attempting to clean up the creek, the students decided that there must be a better approach to making a difference to the creek. They also understood that the problem was greater than just a localized pollution issue. They looked at how they could influence other people and organizations to come on board and partner them in making a difference to Jessie's Creek. Thomas (Grade 6 boy, Whitfield District Primary) explains that "we quickly realized hand weeding wasn't going to do the trick, so we used an excavator to remove the big weeds." The students wrote to environmental organizations like the Wilderness Society, Greening Australia, and the Rural City of Wangaratta (the local shire) and shared their findings. They developed a survey for the local community, produced a brochure to publicize their ideas, and prepared presentations so they could speak to environmental groups like Landcare, the North East Catchment Management Authority, and the School Principals of the Goulburn North East Region of Education.

After the weeding and excavating, the locals could not believe the difference it made to the appearance of the entire town. They explained they had not seen the creek for 50 years (National Resource Management, 2008). A Grade 6 girl from Whitfield District Primary commented "You have to believe in what you are doing and make a fuss to get things moving. People were surprised that kids could do this stuff." With a greater awareness of what was required for long-lasting change, the students studied local native vegetation before planting hundreds of trees and shrubs along the creek together with a variety of grasses and sedges that were placed in flood-prone areas to prevent further erosion.

From their presentations, representation and letters, the students attracted funding and support from the Commonwealth Environmental Fund, from the activist environmental group Australian Geographic, and the Victorian Government as well as in-kind contributions from the North East Catchment Management Authority (CMA). Students were able to raise funds totalling more than Au$40,000, which they used to mobilize local action for the environment.

Students and teachers from surrounding areas were also affected by the project and pitched in with assistance with weeding and planting. Many of these schools have now started their own ruMAD Projects. A neighboring school, Myrhee Primary School in another rural township with around 30 students from Grades 1 to 6, started to research the problem of litter in the regional center of Wangaratta. Their survey found the most common form of litter was the plastic bag, but the community was ignorant of the size of the problem at that time. So the students set out to educate the community through a series of surveys and then worked steadfastly to eliminate the program. They found that 10,000 bags were used weekly. At first, the students made their own calico bags with environmental slogans, but could not keep up with demand. Therefore, they tried to source a manufacturer—only to find that all such items were imported from China, which they realized, was not an environmental solution. As a result of further research, they found a supplier prepared to manufacture onshore. The story ran in local papers and was picked up by national news. It raised widespread community awareness of the impact of the plastic bag pollution. By the end of that project Myhree Primary students had reduced the use of shopping bags in wider Wangaratta by 55% and began sending out information to other schools in the state. By moving beyond the symptoms and tackling the actual cause of the problem, the students had by the end of 2009 forced the Victorian government to legislate against the free distribution of plastic shopping bags. Today people throughout Australia have rejected the use of plastic bags and use recycled reusable "green bags" or pay for the privilege of plastic at their checkout. Federal legislation is currently being promoted in Parliament to ban completely the use of plastic bags.

Their focus for the children has moved now to understanding the impact of inappropriate farming practices that have disturbed the ecological balance in the fragile ecology of the area. They therefore have moved from mere moving weed regrowth to planting more native trees and shrubs along the creek. Work also began on a section of neglected public land between the school and town centre. The longer term focus will be on tackling weeds in the state forest and creating a wildlife habitat corridor to the state forest in the west to fully restore the flora and fauna indigenous to the area denuded by years of malpractice by farmers, developers and logging companies.

An evaluation of the ruMAD project (Bell, Shrimpton, & Leger, 2004) concluded as follows:

- Students developed organizational and leadership skills, greater community awareness and sense of responsibility, and self-confidence.
- Schools developed partnerships with the local community.
- The projects brought about real community change that students could see and feel a part.

Their evaluation noted that enabling factors associated with implantation of ruMAD in the school include a high degree of student ownership, congruence between school philosophy and ruMAD aims, broad-based participation by students and teachers, and key people in the school (teachers/leaders) being committed to the program. Future directions for the program include exploring ways in which ruMAD projects can be integrated into the school curriculum.

The two ruMAD critical service-learning projects described here inspired the young people to make real and lasting change in their world.

It assumes that young people have the power and potential to make a difference by working and learning together. They gave them the tools to shape their own destiny and take action on issues about which they care. Thus ruMAD enabled the students to lead change within their communities through becoming justice oriented citizens (Westheimer & Kahne, 2004). ruMAD is values-focused, student led, and at the very core starts from student identified values and visions.

Discussion: So What Are the Possibilities for Critical Service-Learning Through the Elegant Subversion of Educational Policy Beyond Compensation?

What this chapter has demonstrated is that the re-examination of education provision in so-called disadvantaged communities can foster the transformative engagement of students in empowering and collaborative experiences that link the three message systems of education (curriculum, pedagogy, and assessment) to identity, politics, and social justice. Teachers and schools can become elegantly subversive through a strong sense of collective effort that may initially be built on isolated individual projects as happened in the example of Jessie's Creek.

Programs like ruMAD are based on both redistributive and significantly recognitive social justice (Gale, 2000). They are school focussed, student centered, and antibureaucratic, giving prominence to teacher and student agency. Such discursive positioning of teachers and students together and reciprocally as solution makers not as problems highlights the importance of teacher and student agency (Hargreaves, 1994; Schlechty, 1997; Woods, Jeffrey, Troman, & Boyle, 1997).

The success of the program described here provides evidence that productive student outcomes for CLED children will be successful if nongovernment organizations (NGOs), teachers and academics work together, deconstructing the binary of hands-on versus heads-on learning and teaching. The programs described here have achieved this by redressing the lack of attention to family and neighborhood literacies and funds of knowledge (New London Group, 1995). At the same time they fully appreciate the need to reverse the debilitating and countereducative practices of high stakes academic testing, artificial streaming or setting of students and subject choice underpinning the competitive academic curriculum. Instead they reward professional development for teachers that includes learning about and promoting change (Thompson, 2007).

CONCLUSION CORE PEDAGOGY THROUGH PEDAGOGICAL RECIPROCITY

Important work is currently being undertaken in Australia (and elsewhere) on the kinds of pedagogies that improve outcomes for all students (Lingard et al., 2001a, 2001b), but in particular those variously labeled as "at-risk" of early school leaving, disadvantaged, or from low socioeconomic backgrounds.

Many students do not believe their school experience has much bearing on their future and do not feel that they are accepted by their classmates and teachers (Zyngier, 2007); they gradually feel disaffected and withdraw from school life. Some become disruptive and exert a negative influence on other students (Willms, 2003). As one former student noted, "when you are standing outside the classroom all day, it is very difficult to learn" (Brown et al., 2001, p. 105). Exemplary programs like ruMAD are further evidence that an engaging pedagogy should ensure that what teachers and students do is based on what I have termed CORE Pedagogy.

To create a more inclusive and empowering education system, one that engages with and responds to marginalized youth, we need to ensure that all students, not just the mainstream majority, feel that they belong and identify. In order to do this, schools "need to tap into the cultural knowledge of parents, guardians and community workers—this means that we value the different perspectives and knowledges that all people from all places have and can bring into the school system" (Dei, 2003, pp. 250–251).

Research with disadvantaged (McFadden & Munns, 2002) and marginalized (Slade & Trent, 2000) middle-years students (Brown et al., 2001) suggest that it is the students themselves who will be able to tell us that they are engaged, and will say whether their education is working for them in a culturally sensitive and relevant way (Education Foundation, 2002). It is the students who will say whether the offers that education purports to provide are real or illusionary. It is also at the messy point (McFadden & Munns, 2000) of teachers and students responding to each other in pedagogical reciprocity in relation to classroom pedagogical practices where we are truly going to see whether or not students feel that school is for them (Alexander, 2000). Rogoff, Turkanis, and Bartlett (2001) use the term community of learners to describe a pedagogy of adults and children engaging in learning activities together and collaboratively. It is within this space that education can provide a chance that is not illusionary (McFadden & Munns, 2000), and that can indeed be engaging and lead to purposeful, relevant and productive educational outcomes. This pedagogical reciprocity

> Disconfirms unilateral authority [and] by accepting student discipline, a power-sharing teacher then becomes *democratically* (not *institutionally*) authorised to make higher demands on the students because students have been authorised to make higher demands on the teacher. (Shor, 1996, p. 125)

My research (Zyngier, 2005, 2007a, 2007b, 2008) has suggested that the complexity of issues relating to student engagement (and early school leaving) cannot be fitted neatly into decontextualized accounts of youth experience, school interaction and socioenvironmental factors that in the first instance create student disempowerment and disengagement with school. A transformative student engagement was found to be an empowering one, developing a sense of entitlement, belonging and identification where teachers "create pedagogical practices that engage students providing them with ways of knowing that enhance their capacity to live fully and deeply" (hooks, 1994, p. 22).

Critically, if students are to successfully engage in doing thick democracy (Gandin & Apple, 2005) in school and their knowledge systems, then these systems must connect to and engage with the students' cultural knowledge while also "affirming the different strengths that knowledge forms bring to classroom pedagogy" (Dei, 2003, p. 252). This pedagogical reciprocity is critical if those most at risk are to find themselves in schools, so that their knowledges, histories and experiences are validated and accounted for. Such student engagement is an empowering one developing a sense of entitlement, belonging, and identification. Otherwise students are doing time, not doing education (p. 251). A critical perspective rejects an understanding that student engagement is something that is done *to* students by teachers. While "rapidly changing social, cultural, and technological conditions insist that [teachers] rethink" (Latham et al., 2006, p. 1) of themselves as teachers and learners, students too are subjectively different as a result of their relationship to new times (Green & Bigum, 1993). I refer to this new relationship between teachers and students as pedagogical reciprocity.

Through pedagogical reciprocity, what the teachers and students do together is termed CORE Pedagogy and involves the following:

- *Connecting* to and engaging with the students' cultural knowledge.
- *Ownership* by the students so that all students were able to see themselves as represented in the work as "ownership in their education reduces the conditions that produce their alienation" (Shor, 1992, p. 51).
- *Responding* to students' lived experiences and, actively and consciously, critically commenting on that experience; and finally

- *Empowering* students with a belief that what they do will make a difference to their lives and the opportunity to voice and discover their own authentic and authoritative life.

The teachers involved in the ruMAD program described here located their pedagogical practices in socioconstructivist and transformative pedagogies and were able to authentically engage their students moving from being personally responsible through participatory action to becoming justice oriented citizens (Westheimer & Kahne, 2004) involved in thick democratic (Carr, 2008; Gandin & Apple, 2005) work. This was also the view of both their students and their teaching colleagues.

My research (Zyngier, 2005, 2007a, 2007b, 2008) indicates that not all conceptions of engagement equally promote academic success for marginalized students. The instrumentalist and socioconstructivist conceptions of pedagogy portray engagement as "politically and educationally neutral" (McMahon & Portelli, 2004, p. 72). Where these conceptions dominate the field, these conceptions use engagement to advantage in the competition for legitimacy and authority in the pedagogical field (Bourdieu & Wacquant, 1992). Many programs designed to *re-engage students*, (un)wittingly reinforce the status quo, reproducing a pedagogy of poverty (Haberman, 1991) within their classrooms, even when this is not their aim. Transformative engagement, as employed by the ruMAD Program was not pedagogy *for* students or pedagogy *to* students, but pedagogy *with* the students, as an outcome of their pedagogical reciprocity. However, "participation is a means, not an end ... for empowering education" (Shor, 1992, p. 51). In the transformative classrooms, CORE pedagogical reciprocity made "students [feel] validated for the powers they possess, but have not been taught to use" (Shor, 1987, p. 107). In this situation, the students exhibited a "sense of power and the clarity" (p. 107) about themselves and show evidence of a restoration of self-confidence "eroded through years of depressant schooling" (p. 107).

This research indicates that, for students who do not come from 'mainstream' culture (the "gold" standard of school success), it is necessary (but not sufficient) to privilege student backgrounds in classroom pedagogy. Where this occurs under conditions of pedagogical reciprocity, the students have developed a strong sense of identity and begin to learn the "rules" of the dominator culture (hooks, 1994; Sarra & Australian College of Educators, 2003) empowering the students actively to contend with and resist the claims of the dominant stance (Bourdieu & Wacquant, 1992).

It is possible, through pedagogical reciprocity, for teachers to reconceive student engagement

> where difference is accorded respect and all voices are deemed worthy. [This] can make the classroom a place where students come out of shame ... to experience their vulnerability among a community of learners who will dare to hold them up should they falter or fail. (hooks, 2003, p. 103)

By making strange the familiar concepts of risk, connectedness, and engagement, this research highlights teachers' pedagogical practices that affect the extent to which they practise pedagogical reciprocity and CORE pedagogy. The extraordinary disruption of familiar order empowers students and converts them from manipulated objects into active and critical subjects with critical agency (Shor, 1987, p. 97). The role of teachers in this transformation is to become the "architect of the undoing and redoing" (p. 97). It is then not surprising that this is "an inspiring and awesome situation for teachers, who so often feel trapped in the slough of despond. So much gained or lost" (p. 97). My research confirms Haberman's (1991) hypothesis that

> The whole school faculty and school community—not the individual teacher —must be the unit of change: and there must be patience and persistence of application, since students can be expected to resist changes to a system they can predict and know how to control. (p. 292)

A CORE Pedagogy, founded on pedagogical reciprocity, is an opportunity "for activating individual enhancement as well as social critique, community and social change; school-parent-community collaboration will strengthen adolescents' commitment to schooling" (Fine, 1995, p. 86).

To solve such problems we need to be linking curriculum, pedagogy, assessment to identity, politics, and social justice where teachers take an historical and sociological perspective beyond the classroom and the school—becoming elegantly subversive through a strong sense of collective effort that may be built on what otherwise might be considered isolated individual projects. This research has highlighted the pedagogical possibilities for teachers to make a difference for their students' futures through CORE pedagogical reciprocity which conceives students' engagement as being generatively connected to students' lived experiences. Whether teachers will decide on the path of least resistance continue to try to change their students or try to change what they do, remains to be seen. Elegantly subversive critical service-learning like ruMAD challenge the dominant hegemonic retributive and redistributive (Gale, 2000) views that assert that, since school works for middle-class students, then working-class students "must deserve the blame" (Howe & Moses, 1999, p. 39).

QUESTIONS FOR REFLECTION

1. What is happening in your school or school system to promote greater student engagement and connectedness with the real world? What issues stand in the way or prevent such promotion?
2. Use the principals and philosophy of ruMAD to understand and critique a service learning school-community program that you are familiar with. Do the same analysis using Westheimer and Kahne's (2004) four principles. How might you alter this service learning to make it more closely aligned with these perspectives and principles?
3. If you are a teacher how does your teaching reflect CORE pedagogical reciprocity? What would you have to do to make it more so?
4. If you are (or were) a student does your experience of school reflect CORE pedagogical reciprocity? What would have made it more so?

NOTES

1. The Ladder of Youth Participation is a conceptual model created and developed by UNICEF sociologist Roger Hart. Based on a study of a youth involvement in a hundred international environmental organizations, the Ladder first featured in Hart's (1982) *Children's Participation: from Tokenism to Citizenship*. It comprises eight "rungs" or ways in which organizations involve young people, from "Manipulation," "Decoration" or "Tokenism" through "Assigned but Informed," "Consulted and Informed," "Adult-Initiated, shared decisions with young people' to 'Young people-initiated and directed" and "Young people-initiated, shared decisions with adults" (see Holdsworth, Stokes, Blanchard, & Mohamed, 2007).
2. See the website of the National Resource Management department of the Australian federal government for maps and more details at http://www.nrm.gov.au/projects/vic/nev/2006-02.html

REFERENCES

Alexander, R. J. (2000). *Culture and pedagogy: International comparisons in primary education*. Oxford, England: Blackwell.

Bell, C., Shrimpton, B., & Leger, P. S. (2004). Making a difference in schools and the community: Evaluation of ruMAD? (Are you making a difference?) Program in Victorian Schools. Melbourne, Australia: Centre for Program Evaluation The University of Melbourne.

Bonner, C., & Caro, J. (2007). *The stupid country: How Australia is dismantling its public education system*. Sydney, Australia: University of New South Wales Press.

Bourdieu, P., & Wacquant, L. J. D. (1992). *An invitation to reflexive sociology*. Chicago, IL: University of Chicago Press.

Boyd, D., Grossman, P., Lankford, H., Loeb, S., & Wyckoff, J. (2006). How changes in entry requirements alter the teacher workforce and affect student achievement. *Education Finance and Policy, 1*(2), 176–216.

Brown, J., Holdsworth, R., Mukherjee, D., Stokes, H., Tyler, D., Hebron, H., et al. (2001). *Building relationships—making education work: A report on the perspectives of young people*. Canberra, Australia: Australian Centre for Equity through Education, Australian Youth Research Centre (Melbourne University), Commonwealth Department of Education, Training and Youth Affairs.

Carr, P. (2008). Educators and education for democracy: Moving beyond "thin" democracy. *Interamerican Journal for Education for Democracy, 1*(2), 147–165.

Darling-Hammond, L., Holtzman, D., Gatlin, S. J., & Heilig, J. V. (2005). Does teacher preparation matter? Evidence about teacher certification, Teach for America, and teacher effectiveness *Education Policy Analysis Archives, 13*(42), 1–51.

Decker, P. T., Mayer, D. P., & Glazerman, S. (2004). *The effects of teach for America on students: Findings from a national evaluation*. Princeton, NJ: Mathematica.

Dei, G. J. (2003). Schooling and the dilemma of youth disengagement. *McGill Journal of Education, 38*(2), 241.

Dinham, S. E., Ingvarson, L., & Kleinhenz, E. (2008). *Teaching talent: The best teachers for Australia's classrooms: Investing in teacher quality: Doing what matters most*. Melbourne, Australia: Business Council of Australia.

Education Foundation (Writer). (2002). What school kids want [VHS]. Australia: Author.

Emery, K., & Ohanian, S. (2004). *Why is corporate america bashing our public schools?* Portsmith NH: Heinemann.

Fine, M. (1995). The politics of who's "at risk". In B. B. Swadener & S. Lubeck (Eds.), *Children and families "at promise": Deconstructing the discourse of risk* (pp. 76–97). Albany, NY: State University of New York Press.

Friedman, M., & Friedman, R. (1980). *Free to choose: A personal statement* (1st ed.). New York, NY: Harcourt Brace Jovanovich.

Gale, T. (2000). Rethinking social justice in schools: how will we recognize it when we see it? *International Journal of Inclusive Education, 4*(3), 253–269.

Gandin, L. A., & Apple, M. (2005). Thin versus thick democracy in education: Porto Alegre and the creation of alternatives to neo-liberalism. *International Studies in Sociology of Education, 12*(2), 99–1116.

Green, B., & Bigum, C. (1993). *Aliens in the classroom*. Sydney, Australia: Australian Council for Educational Research.

Haberman, M. (1991). The pedagogy of poverty versus good teaching. *Phi Delta Kappan, 73*(4), 290.

Hargreaves, A. (1994). *Changing teachers, changing times: Teachers' work and culture in the postmodern age*: London: Burns & Oates.

Hart, R. (1992). Children's participation: From tokenism to citizenship. Innocenti Essay No. 4. UNICEF, International Child Development Centre, Florence, Italy.

Holdsworth, R., Stokes, H., Blanchard, M., & Mohamed, N. (2007). Civic engagement and young people. Melbourne, Australia: Australian Youth Research Centre.

hooks, b. (1994). *Teaching to transgress: Education as the practice of freedom*. New York, NY: Routledge.

hooks, b. (2003). *Teaching community: A pedagogy of hope*. New York: Routledge.

Howe, K. R., & Moses, M. M. (1999). Ethics in educational research. *Review of Research in Education, 24*, 21–59.

Laczko-Kerr, I., & Berliner, D. (2002). The effectiveness of Teach for America and other under-certified teachers on student academic achievement: A case of harmful public policy. *Education Policy Analysis Archives, 10*(37). Retrieved from http://epaa.asu.edu/epaa/v10n37/

Lamb, S. (2007). School reform and inequality in urban Australia: a case of residualising the poor. In R. Teese, S. Lamb, M. Duru-Bellat, & S. Helme (Eds.), *International studies in educational inequality, theory and policy* (Vol. 3, pp. 1–38). Dordrecht, Australia: Springer.

Latham, G., Blaise, M., Dole, S., Faulkner, J., Lang, J., & Malone, K. (2006). *Learning to teach: New times, new practices*. South Melbourne, Australia: Oxford University Press.

Leigh, A., & Ryan, C. (2006). *How and why has teacher quality changed in Australia?* Canberra, Australia: Research School of Social Sciences Centre for Economic Policy Research Australian National University.

Leigh, A., & Ryan, C. (2008). *How has school productivity changed in Australia?* Canberra, Australia: Research School of Social Sciences Centre for Economic Policy Research Australian National University.

Lingard, R., Ladwig, J., Mills, M., Bahr, M., Chant, D., Warry, M., et al. (2001a). *Queensland school reform longitudinal study: Final report* (Vol. 1). Brisbane, Australia: Report prepared for Education Queensland by the School of Education, The University of Queensland.

Lingard, R., Ladwig, J., Mills, M., Bahr, M., Chant, D., Warry, M., et al. (2001b). *Queensland school reform longitudinal study: Supplementary materials* (Vol. 2). Brisbane, Australia: Report prepared for Education Queensland by the School of Education, The University of Queensland.

McFadden, M., & Munns, G. (2000, December). *Chance, illusion and engagement*. Paper presented at the Australian Association for Research in Education Annual Conference, Sydney.

McFadden, M., & Munns, G. (2002). Student engagement and the social relations of pedagogy. *British Journal of Sociology of Education, 23*(3), 357–366.

McGraw, B. (2006). *Achieving quality and equity education*. Paper presented at the VASSP annual leadership conference, Melbourne, Austalia. Retrieved from http://www.aspa.asn.au/images/conferences/state/vassp2006/mcgawppt.pdf

McMahon, B., & Portelli, J. P. (2004). Engagement for what? Beyond Popular discourses of student engagement. *Leadership and Policy in Schools, 3*(1), 59–76.

Murray, S., Mitchell, J., Gale, T., Edwards, J., & Zyngier, D. (2004). *Student disengagement from primary schooling: a review of research and practice*. Melbourne, Australia: CASS Foundation & Centre for Childhood Studies Faculty of Education Monash University.

National Resource Management. (2008). *Students save Whitfield waterway*. Retrieved from http://www.nrm.gov.au/projects/vic/nev/2006-02.html

New London Group (1995). *A pedagogy of multiliteracies: Designing social futures*. Haymarket, N.S.W.: NLLIA Centre for Workplace Communication and Culture.

Pearson, C. (2007, March 3–4). Our forsaken schools. *Weekend Australian*. Retrieved from http://www.theaustralian.com.au/news/opinion /christopher-pearson-our-forsaken-schools/story-e6frg6zo-1111113088523

Pike, B. (2008). *Blueprint for early childhood development and school reform: School reform discussion paper*. Melbourne, Australia: Victorian Government. Retrieved from http://www.education.vic.gov.au/about/directions /blueprint2008/papers.htm

Rogoff, B., Turkanis, C. G., & Bartlett, L. (2001). *Learning together: Children and adults in a school community*. New York, NY: Oxford University Press.

Rudd, K., & Gillard, J. (2008). *Quality education: The case for an education revolution in our schools*. Retrieved from http://www.deewr.gov.au/Schooling/Programs/ Pages/QualityEducation-ThecaseforanEducationRevolutioninourSchools.aspx

Sarra, C., & Australian College of Educators. (2003). *Young and Black and deadly: Strategies for improving outcomes for indigenous students*. Deakin West, Australia.: Australian College of Educators.

Schlechty, P. (1997). *Inventing better schools: An action plan for education reform*. The San Fransisco, CA: Jossey-Bass

Shor, I. (1987). *Critical teaching and everyday life* (Reprint ed.). Chicago, IL: University of Chicago Press.

Shor, I. (1992). *Empowering education: Critical teaching for social change*. Chicago, IL: University of Chicago Press.

Shor, I. (1996). *When students have power: Negotiating authority in a critical pedagogy*. Chicago, IL: University of Chicago Press.

Slade, M., & Trent, F. (2000). What the boys are saying. An examination of the views of boys about declining rates of achievement and retention. *International Education Journal, 11*(3), 221–227.

Smith, W., Butler-Kisber, L., LaRoque, L., Portelli, J., Shields, C., Sparkes, C., et al. (2001a). *Student engagement in learning and school life: Case reports from project schools* (Vol. 2). Montreal, Canada: Faculty of Education McGill University.

Smith, W., Butler-Kisber, L., LaRoque, L., Portelli, J., Shields, C., Sparkes, C., et al. (2001b). *Student engagement in learning and school life: National Project Report* (Vol. 1). Montreal, Canada: Faculty of Education McGill University.

Stokes, H., & Turnbull, M. (2008). *Real engagement with real issues: an evaluation of the ruMAD? Program. Final report*. Melbourne, Australia: Education Foundation Australia & Australian Youth Research Centre, University of Melbourne

Teese, R. (2007). Structural inequality in australian education: vertical and lateral stratification of opportunity. In Teese R., Lamb S., Duru-Bellat, M., & S. Helme (Eds.), *International studies in educational inequality, theory and policy* (Vol. 2, pp. 36–91). Dordrecht, The Netherlands: Springer.

Teese, R., & Lamb, S. (2007). School reform and inequality in urban Australia. A case of residualising the poor. In R. Teese, S. Lamb, M. Duru-Bellat, & S.

Helme (Eds.), *International studies in educational inequality, theory and policy* (Vol. 1). Dordrecht, The Netherlands: Springer.

Thompson, P. (2007). Making education more equitable what can policy makers learn from the Australian Disadvantaged Schools Programme? In R. Teese, S. Lamb, M. Duru-Bellat & S. Helme (Eds.), *International studies in educational inequality, theory and policy* (Vol. 3, pp. 239–256). Dordrecht, The Netherlands: Springer.

Tomazin, F. (2008, 7 April). Shake-up to hit bored teachers. *The Age*. Retrieved from http://www.theage.com.au/news/national/shakeup-targets-bored -teachers/2008/04/06/1207420202545.html

Westheimer, J., & Kahne, J. (2004). What kind of citizen? The politics of educating for democracy. *American Educational Research Journal., 41*(2), 237–269.

Whitty, G., Halpin, D., & Power, S. (1998). *Devolution and choice in education : the school, the state, and the market.* Buckingham, England; Bristol, PA, USA: Open University Press.

Willms, J. D. (2003). Student engagement at school. A sense of belonging and participation: Results from PISA 2000. Retrieved from http://www .sourceoecd.org/9264018921

Woods, P. (1997). *Restructuring schools, reconstructing teachers : responding to change in the primary school.* Buckingham England; Bristol, PA, USA: Open University Press.

Zyngier, D. (2005). Advancing student engagement through changed teaching practices. *The International Journal of Learning, 12*(1), 1–11.

Zyngier, D. (2007a). The challenge of student engagement—what the students say they want—putting young people at the centre of the conversation. *LEARNing Landscapes, 1*, 93–116

Zyngier, D. (2007b). Listening to teachers—Listening to students substantive conversations about resistance, empowerment and engagement. *Teachers and Teaching Theory and Practice Journal, 13*(4), 327–347.

Zyngier, D. (2008). (Re)conceptualising student engagement: doing education not doing time. *Teaching and Teacher Education, 24*(7), 1765–1776.

Zyngier, D., & Brunner, C. (2002). *The r.u.MAD? Program. Kids making a difference in the community with MAD projects* (Vol. 1). Melbourne, Australia: Education Foundation.

PART II

The objective of this section is to consider critical service-learning as a framework for social justice education. There is no one method of critical service-learning; it is not reductive in that sense. Rather, it uses understandings of critical theory and critical pedagogy to move service-learning beyond the service to an understanding of the structural inequities that feed the need for service. Bringing the critical perspective to service makes learning sustainable and systemic change more possible. Learners work in solidarity with those facing societal inequity rather than for them.

The chapters in this section consider critical service-learning in educational settings. One chapter looks at critical service-learning as it unfolded in three high school classrooms; teacher and student voices are represented. Two others look at it in the teacher preparation classroom as a tool for improving the preparation of social justice educators. Others consider the challenges of critical service-learning. One such chapter considers the difficulty of sustaining critical service-learning in the face of society and universities' need for "success" stories. Another discusses the structural barriers to critical services learning that students in a graduate program faced when trying to implement critical service-learning in PK–12 classrooms. The final chapters consider the lasting impact of critical service-learning and alternatives to critical service-learning when its full implementation is not possible—this chapter serves to demonstrate the path one can take toward a more critical perspective of learning.

As noted in the introduction, there are several scholarly texts on the topic of critical service-learning. However, this literature is centered on service-learning projects conducted in Western contexts and in university settings. The literature also does not account for how neoliberal policies and practices have impacted educators' abilities to implement their political projects or document the challenges they face from students, administrators, or community members during the scope of the initiatives. This section considers critical service-learning projects conducted by K–12 students and also the use of critical service-learning in teacher preparation.

Guiding Questions:

- How can teacher education programs be organized to present consistent messages about critical pedagogy regarding critical service-learning and other practices without lengthening programs or infringing on the academic freedom of faculty?
- How can teacher preparation programs make physical and conceptual space for critical service-learning?
- To what extent are teachers able to challenge dominance in school power structures to teach students critically?
- How can one move from a point of radical pragmatism toward a fully developed philosophy of critical service-learning?

CHAPTER 8

THE HUMANITY OF TEACHING AND LEARNING

Scenarios of a Pedagogy of Compassion, Community, and Change

Diana M. Feige, Maureen Connolly, and Michael Furey

> I am the survivor of a concentration camp. My eyes have seen what no man should witness—gas chambers built by learned engineers, children poisoned by educated physicians, infants killed by trained nurses, women and babies shot and burned by high school and college graduates. So I am suspicious of education. My request is to help your students become human. Your efforts must never produce learned monsters, skilled psychopaths, educated Eichmanns. Reading, writing and arithmetic are important only if they serve to make our children more humane.
>
> —Haim Ginott

INITIAL MUSINGS

Revolution is, perhaps, after all, an oxymoron; it is slow rather than immediate, gradual rather than instant. Or so it seems as we blow the dust

Critical Service Learning as a Revolutionary Pedagogy: A Project of Student Agency in Action, pp. 157–178

off an old standard published in 1969, a seminal work by both Neil Postman and Charles Weingartner (1969) titled *Teaching as a Subversive Activity.* It begins with a seventeenth century quote, setting the tone for Postman's and Weingartner's thesis; "Thank God there are no free schools or printing ... for learning has brought disobedience and heresy into the world, and printing has divulged them.... God keep us from both" (Berkeley as cited in Postman & Weingartner, 1969, opening page).

Change in schooling comes slowly. Change, large or small but particularly systemic change that endures over time and impacts student learning, moves at a petty pace. Some might argue (Postman & Weingartner, (1969) among them) that systemic change in schooling has yet to occur, and is still a hope, a dream of the revolution. Deborah Meier (2006), Cremin (1977), and the Sizer (1999) remind us that schools across the United States remain at their core relatively unchanged. Whether in Iowa or Vermont, California or Virginia, with minor (in terms of numbers) exceptions, one mirrors another. The paradigms of transmission or transaction rather than one of transformation remain the predominant models of supposedly effective schooling (Miller, Cassie, & Drake, 1990, pp. 102–114). Teacher as primary source of knowledge, students as beholden recipients of that knowledge, knowledge defined more quantitatively than qualitatively, and thinking and the imagination sacrificed for ingrained yet unexamined, fractured learning are preferred over integrated learning, self-assessment, and choice and ownership of the learning process. In Paolo Freire's (1970) vision (another advocate of revolutions), the "banking" passive system is eschewed for a more participatory, active system. However, the "banking" system is the ingrained tradition, and tradition, we all know, is buried deep in the national soul.

The following scenarios of three critical service-learning school experiences, propose a "shock therapy" (Postman & Weingartner, 1969, p. xv) to help revitalize and energize a tired system composed of far too many tired teachers, tired administrators, and exhausted students (Hatton, 2005; Meier, 2006; Palmer, 1998). As with many hopeless romantics, our assumption is that formal education is "improvable through intelligent innovation" (Postman & Weingartner, p. xiv). Revolutions are annoyingly slow; yet, they can occur. Paradigm shifts are possible (Kuhn, 1996); exceptions to the norm (a transaction or transmission norm) are growing and most definitely worth pursuing (or, more adamantly, must be pursued if we truly care about each other, the state of the world, and the hearts and minds of children and adolescents). The mustard seed travels and spreads; change can happen, does happen.

The assumption is that service-learning pushes educators towards a more critical pedagogical mode and is one of the noticeable exceptions to the norm that offers a taste of possibilities in a slow moving, thick and dense schooling paradigm shift. Critical service-learning offers a window into transformational schooling landscapes, an integral step in the road towards lasting change. It does so as it dramatically changes the very foundation of what schooling is and can be. It transforms the following rooted traditions of schooling as we know them: (1) the nature of teaching, (2) the role of the teacher and the student, (3) the quality of the teacher/student/community relationship, and perhaps most significantly 4) the underlying impetus of the classroom experience. In the best case scenarios, critical service-learning is an antidote to schools' "shielding children from reality," alienating, and "punishing creativity and independence" (Postman & Weingartner, 1969, p. xiv).

Critical service-learning is a possible antidote in that, as the three following scenarios share, its focus is on the humanity of teaching and learning. The human being in his/her wholeness is the core of the enterprise. The intent of the teaching and learning is the reciprocal dynamic between them, authentic connection among the teacher, student and larger community, and the redefined role of the teacher and student as cocreators of learning and change (personal, academic, and civic).

The three scenarios were born across the hall from each other on the second floor of Mineola High School. The seeds planted in rooms 254, 255, and 256 spread into the larger community, first the local Mineola community, then the New York neighborhood, then the national neighborhood (Washington, DC specifically), and finally the global neighborhood (Darfur, Afghanistan and Pakistan and Kenya specifically). They were born out of a vision of schooling that is passionate (rather than, as Deborah Meir [2006] bemoans, "impassioned" [p. 501]), meaningful and purposeful (rather than, as Postman & Weingartner [1969] bemoan, "obsolescent," "irrelevant" [p. xiv]), and grounded in the belief that compassion, curriculum and community are necessary teaching and learning collaborators. They see academics, advocacy and action, commitment and change as equally necessary and paramount collaborators.

The voices of the three scenarios vary. The first is Michael Furey's (veteran English Language Arts teacher) voice documenting the immersion of the school in what began as an English Language Arts (ELA) venture raising consciousness on the tragedy of Darfur refugees; the second is Maureen Connolly's voice (veteran English Language Arts teacher) documenting what began as another English Language Arts venture raising consciousness on children's rights to an education in Afghanistan and Pakistan; and the third is the story told to Diana M. Feige (university professor) by Mary Ann Beach (veteran English Language Arts teacher). This last vignette documents the roads traveled by Ms. Beach, university student teachers, and English Language Learners discovering that food is more than what we eat. Three voices tell one story of shifting pedagogical

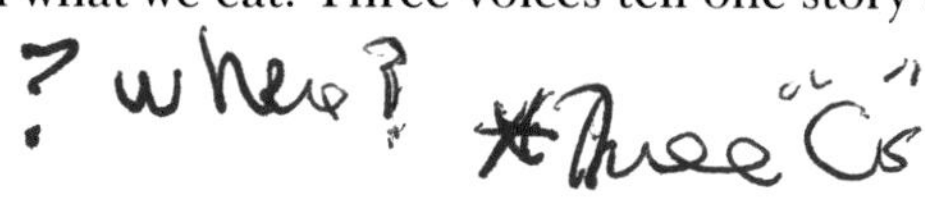

images in terms of (1) the point of entry for teaching and learning being extended to embrace students' personal interests (in this case their visceral connection to questions of fairness), (2) the boundaries of teaching and learning being extended to include the global landscape of painful struggle and injustice, and (3) the dynamics of the teaching and learning experience being deepened and authenticated, especially in terms of the redefined roles of the teacher and student (and by extension, the redefined content and products of schooling).

SCENARIO I: DARFUR AND THE TENTS OF HOPE

Overview

The power and impact of the Mineola High School students reached global levels when the school community joined together to address genocide in Darfur. As educators, many of us hope our lessons ring true in the world and that the content explored, skills and dispositions developed directly address current struggles and celebrations. As English teachers, for example, Shakespeare and Kerouac and Joyce offer us the keys to address real-world struggles; the litany of world inequities offer us the tragic template upon which to get to work, making these meaningful curriculum and community connections. At Mineola High School the connection made was with the refugees of genocide in Darfur. The Tents of Hope project (described below) embodied everything we thought a worthwhile pedagogical endeavor should as it reached far beyond the classroom walls. Tents of Hope asked students to consider their responsibility to the world around them, identifying, ultimately, how their humanity is connected to the humanity of others. This newly found connection to a global humanity helped them, in turn, to recognize (the first time for many) the remarkable power of their voices and the profound influence of their advocacy. The students took a stand for something and someone beyond their perceived boundaries of geography and culture. Eagerly they accepted the challenge, and as reflected in the Mineola Union Free School District's mission statement and mission statements nationwide, "contributed positively to a global society."

What follows is the story of the unfolding of the Tents of Hope project. Two faculty members began in the fall of 2007 pursuing an inquiry with 10th graders into the theme (captured in the often-heard phrase) "absolute power corrupts absolutely," as represented specifically in *The Chocolate War, Macbeth,* and *Antigone*. Genocide was addressed through *The Cage*, Ruth Minksy Sender's Holocaust memoir, and a viewing of the film *Hotel Rwanda*. When the sophomores realized that genocide was not just a problem of the past and existed tragically in their world and present day, they began to work together to demand change. They created informational posters about Darfur based on what they read on Amnesty International's website. Each poster included a powerful image, a brief description of the situation in Darfur, a compelling quote from a victim, and information on how to learn more and take action. These posters were displayed throughout the school.

In addition to educating their peers and school faculty and staff, students reached out to the community by organizing a day to disseminate information and make a public call for change. They joined a movement called Tents of Hope. According to the Tents of Hope website,

> The mission of the Tents of Hope project is to support a one-year process in which people respond as communities to the crisis in Darfur, Sudan by creating tents that are both unique works of art and ongoing focal points within communities for learning about, assisting and establishing relationships with the people of Sudan. The tents are not answers in themselves. Rather, they are points of entry for more concrete forms of Darfur advocacy. (Tents of Hope, About section, para. 2)

The 10th graders together with the Human Rights class organized a day of painting for Mineola's tent. The students created flyers to advertize the event in school. To encourage community members to take part, two students spoke at our town hall meeting, which was broadcast on local television. Their knowledge of this global issue and their passionate call for action made all who saw them proud.

When participants showed up for Tents of Hope at Mineola High School on a hot June day, not only did they paint, but they also viewed a video created by the Human Rights class that outlined a haunting timeline of genocide throughout the world. Community participants also had the opportunity to sign petitions and letters to The White House and to take part in a poetry walk in the school's expansive main lobby. The 70 published poems relating to Darfur and other current human rights violations poignantly and often dramatically demonstrated students' empathy, concern, and absolute outrage. It is interesting to note as further testimony to the authenticity of the human connections being made that many students chose to write their poems from a child's perspective.

This project did not end with the school year. Rather, students remained concerned and motivated to continue supporting Darfur when they returned to school in September of 2008. The first initiative of the year was to increase community awareness about Darfur. The students hosted an information night at the local library and arranged for the tent to be displayed at the library for the month of October. At the information night, students made presentations on the situation in Darfur as well as on their actions to call for change. One of the most moving components of the evening was the opportunity to hear from Hamza Ibrahim, a representative of the Darfur People's Association of New York, candidly sharing, as he said, his experiences "on the ground" fighting genocide in Darfur and thanking the students for their commitment and distinctive work for human rights.

In November, thanks to funding from a variety of sources (the school's Learn and Serve America grant, the site-based committee, The Long Island Regional Service-Learning Network, and Congresswoman Carolyn McCarthy) the two faculty members were able to escort 13 students to Washington, DC for "The Gathering of the Tents" on November 7 and 8. There, the students and teachers pitched the Mineola tent on The National Mall alongside 350 tents from 48 states. As part of "The Gathering of Tents," the students and teachers joined a group of 250 people at a rally on the steps of the Sudanese Embassy calling for a change in leadership in Sudan and an end to genocide.

While in Washington, students' attachment to this cause grew deeper. This weekend conference was held 3 days after the election of President Barack Obama. The city was buzzing with hope and opportunity for a brighter future, and the students were aware of that from the moment they got off the train at Union Station. Their experience at the conference's various events gave them the opportunity to share their thoughts and ideas about the horrors in Darfur with other high school and college students from around the country. Again, they made connections with other concerned citizens drawn together to struggle for human rights, equity and justice. They were able to not only recognize the magnitude of the cause, but to also understand the profound human aspect of the conflict.

On the second day of the conference, we (students and teachers) were returning from a late morning event to the National Mall and as we rounded the back of the Capitol Building we stopped at the overwhelming sight of over 300 tents dotting the mall against a brilliant blue November sky. In our collective silence, we saw the representation of a tent village for internally displaced peoples. The purpose of these elaborately painted tents decorated with images and messages of hope, love and compassion was clear; they would serve as classrooms and shelter for Darfur's countless refugees.

Upon return to the high school, the students initiated dialogue and began talking about next steps they wanted to take. We decided to spread the word to freshmen and sophomores in their social studies classes. The students met with the teachers and developed a 40-minute lesson involving student-generated video, PhotoStory, and PowerPoint presentations along with fact sheets and handouts.

This push-in teaching session informed students about Sudan. It also provided an opportunity to invite school and community members to the second community Darfur Information Night. This time, the information night was held in the school auditorium where the students screened *Darfur Now,* a film that traces the lives of six people who are connected with Darfur. The film was appreciated by the 100 people who attended this information night. A recent graduate of the high school who was student-teaching that semester, for example, spoke with our current students about their involvement and activism. She asked about what else could be done to help educate not only students in the schools but people within the community. Additionally, district administrators, community members, parents and university faculty and students who attended the forum remarked on how comfortable, articulate and knowledgeable the students were on the issues connected to the genocide in Darfur.

Students' Reflections

In discussing the students' reflections, we wanted their responses to be honest and to mirror the spirit and inspiration of the project. In short, we wanted their responses to challenge the status quo, just as they had done throughout their experience with this project. We were able to outline five questions we felt provided them with the framework to assess their involvement in the completion of the project and their lives afterward.

We first wanted to know how this opportunity to take action led them to continue to seek other means of taking action for this or other causes. Nick Gallina wrote,

> Tents of Hope, for me, opened up numerous and endless goals in my mind. The whole experience travelling to Washington, D.C. really motivated me to keep on taking action against injustices of the world. It cemented my mission to help people, to help others with no voice, to help every single person I possibly can that cries for safety and peace.

Nick has since joined STAND (Student Anti-Genocide Coalition) at his college to continue his support of the displaced people of Darfur. Another student, Alexandra Lisonek, took a direct academic approach with her experience. She wrote,

> Now, almost a year and a half after our trip to Washington, D.C., I am still eager to learn more about social issues and injustices. I am currently taking a class in school titled Violence and Justice. I love talking to people about these issues because I'd like to think that while talking about my experiences is a very miniscule contribution, it helps spread awareness, which is crucial.

Aside from their continued advocacy for social justice, we asked students to discuss how this experience impacted their own lives and changed how they view themselves and their responsibility to the world around them. The responses were varied but the impact profound. Caitlyn Taveira stated,

> When I became involved in this demonstration, I became more and more fascinated and concerned with worldwide issues. I've always been interested in social order, social justice and prejudice, and being a part of the Tents of Hope demonstration heightened this interest.

Jillian Wetzel recalled,

> This experience was a once in a lifetime journey that took me away from my little hometown and introduced me to a larger world, something different and out of the ordinary. I learned so much from this experience and look back at it with a true desire not only to help the people of Darfur, but people all over.

Mineola senior Jess Redondo reflected also on the personally meaningful impact of Tents of Hope. She said, "It made me feel like I meant something, or that I was actually making myself useful for once. This experience made me believe that there is still good in the world, that there are innocent people out there who care." Jess's classmate, Diana Ribeiro, who stood beside her at a town hall meeting two years earlier, had a similar recollection. Diana commented, "It all started off with one speech at village hall and in the course of a year that escalated to a whole new level. Every time I think about our experience, I start to tear up. It's amazing to know that just one person can bring hope to these victims in Darfur." Finally, Cristina Danielson had a revelation and broader understanding of her life and what it means in relation to others. She wrote,

> I saw that I needed to stop caring more about myself and care more about people who need it. I wish I had opened my eyes sooner to the world around me, but now that I have, I am not going to close my eyes to the issues in the world that need our help.

In addition to these questions we also asked students to recall a memory or an image from their experience. We knew that the trip to Washington, DC would be a popular response, but the specificity of one of the events we attended that weekend had an impact we had not expected. The rally on the steps of the Sudanese Embassy was as powerful an experience as these students had seen in their young lives, and their responses revealed the mixed emotions of sadness and pride that swelled through the gathered crowd on that Friday afternoon. Ashley Barnett revealed,

> At one point during the protest, the speaker said, "we all walk under the same moon." Then he began reading the names of men, women and children who had fallen victim to the genocide. In that moment, lying down on the ground, it finally hit me. We're all the same. Wherever or whoever you are, at the end of the day we are all people. The moon connected us all together and it was that moment when I realized I could make a difference in this world.

Lying right next to Ashley on the sidewalk and steps of the embassy was Alexandra Lisonek who had a similar revelation:

> I was lying on the concrete with my friends, and there were thousands of people, at that moment, lying in a cramped, boiling tents trying to keep from being killed. This combined feeling of tranquility and utter sadness was confusing. It was not until much later that I realized the significance of the moment of silence.

Teacher's Reflections: Fairness

As teachers, we can't help but be tempted to make assumptions about our students' knowledge, background and environment. We are human and just like our students, we are curious. So every September, teachers compare rosters to learn about the strange and unfamiliar individuals sitting at the classroom desks waiting to be inspired.

We first accept where the student is as a starting point. It is his/her starting point and it is our starting point as well. The beauty of that starting point is that it is not clouded by 20, 30 or even 40 years of life experience. It is a pure passion for life. Once we tune into those emotions, feelings, and urges, the work begins.

These adolescent hallmarks of passion are defined by fairness and justice. Adolescents want life to be fair and just, and they detest the violations perpetuated against fairness and justice. It is here where we must never underestimate an adolescent's will, thoughtfulness and compassion, especially when it comes to issues of social justice in their own lives and in the world of community. By entering the curriculum through the portal of justice, the students step from their personal domain into the shoes of the victim and feel the need for action. They empathize, become compassionate, and compassion then becomes the portal for inquiry, dedication, and purposeful action. Their response, while not initially visceral, reflects a direct, empathetic connection to the cause, their fellow advocates, and the cause's hopeful beneficiary. Heartfelt inquiry of the status quo becomes the entry point to awareness, action, and meaningful reciprocal learning.

Changing Surroundings and Roles

Teaching in western Nassau County, Long Island, New York affords us the unparalleled opportunity to experience the culture and wonder of New York City in just a 35 minute train ride. It is with some regret, however, that we have found our students live a relatively sheltered life. Their interests revolve more around the immediate social aspects of their day than in global, far less immediate events. Their world view can be a bit narrow even considering the multiethnic population of their community and school district. This richly diverse community, however, may be one of the reasons they are so compassionate and understanding when presented with inequities and unjust, unnecessary struggles (local, regional, or global).

New York City, let alone the Sudan, is a world far away for the students. As stated above, they seem to live more in the now and the immediate. Yet once educators accept that they can be taken out of this comfort zone, their compassion and world view is expanded. The apparent cultural, geographic and generational boundaries dissolve, and their engagement in local, regional, or global issues becomes inspirational.

Subsequently, as educators we do not necessarily have to change the students' physical surroundings, but we must and can eliminate the boundaries they see in their lives. That is our new and transformed role as educators, to invite students to expand comfort zones, dissolve apparent boundaries, and recognize and act on social issues often through unconventional means and strategies. In my fifteen years as an English Language Arts teacher at Mineola High School, the students have always shown sensitivity towards humanity (and inhumanity); yet, they generally won't seek out injustice in the larger world on their own. My role has been to be the provocateur; the students then powerfully, compassionately, and adamantly name the injustice and respond. By redefining and thus changing the students' surroundings and our own roles as educators in the classroom, we definitely can and do reach across oceans, continents and minds.

The Tents of Hope project, in other words, clearly has changed both the students' and the teachers' previously accepted boundaries. It has changed our surroundings and the definitions of our roles, relationships, and responsibilities. The connection made with these 13 students will last lifetimes. It has taken a conflict and tragedy 6 thousand miles from home to bring us together on a level deeper than the books we read and the essays we write. We have become equal contributors, advocates, and voices in the name of equality and fairness. What I may have provided for them in terms of guidance and support they have returned tenfold and will affect the students I teach for the rest of my career. As a result, my approach in the classroom has changed. My view of the content I teach as an ELA teacher has changed as well. In fact, my philosophy about the true purpose of secondary education has changed.

The student involvement in this project empowered me to believe that we can educate not only better readers, writers and thinkers, but also better people—people who take responsibility for the rights of others, people who care about injustice and take action to make change happen. A few months back I wrote to the students that our individual lives touch others in ways we might not even understand. Their lives have certainly touched me profoundly. Their work with Tents of Hope will always be a part of everything I am as a teacher.

As I reviewed the students' responses, it became apparent to me that I should also include a memory or image that I have taken from the experience. Their poignant and heartfelt descriptions of the rally inspired me to recall the hours we spent outside the Sudanese Embassy which helped me to understand that it impacted me as profoundly as it did our students. I remembered one point during the rally, as the rush hour traffic crawled past us on Embassy Row, our whole group of students, educators, advocates and Darfur refugees quietly singing "We Shall Overcome" (Tindley, 1947). I stood in awe of the moment as images of our own country's civil rights history that I had only seen in photos and film footage raced through my mind. If there was a moment when I realized what it truly meant to be an educator and what my responsibility as an educator was, it was on that day. What I did not realize at the time, but hoped, was that my students understood the weight and significance of our involvement. Their responses have revealed that my hopes had in fact become reality.

SCENARIO II: CHILDREN'S RIGHTS TO AN EDUCATION

Overview

Do we (teachers and students) have a responsibility to advocate for people in other countries? At first, our ninth graders at Mineola High School were not so sure. When asked to help students in the Middle East, they responded by asking, "Don't we have people in America who need help?" How can teachers help students who may never have left the state, let alone the country, see the connections between the improved quality of life of people halfway around the globe and that of people halfway across the classroom? Greg Mortenson's young readers' edition of *Three Cups of Tea* helped students to do just this, to recognize how the education of youth in Pakistan and Afghanistan makes for a better world here in the United States.

It is worth noting that this project began in September 2009, a fitting time since many students and teachers alike were begrudgingly returning to school. Rather than complaining about having to wake up early or turn in homework, we hoped that students might appreciate school if they read about other children who did not have a school of their own. In *Three Cups of Tea,* Mortenson tells the story of walking through Korphe, a village in Pakistan, and seeing children gathered together and writing in the dirt with sticks. When he asks where their teacher is, he is told that the village does not have enough money to pay a teacher to come every day. After reading this, we asked students whether they would attend school if there were no teacher present. A resounding chorus of no's filled the room. We also discussed what it would be like to try to learn without a proper building, supplies, or books. Students started to understand how children in the Middle East are drawn to *madrasas.*

We read the May 3, 2009 *New York Times* article "Pakistan's Islamic Schools Fill Void, but Fuel Militancy." The author, Sabrina Tavernise, describes *madrasas* as "Islamic schools, that feed and house the children while pushing a more militant brand of Islam than was traditional here" (para. 2). We discussed why children would be drawn to these schools (e.g., poverty, housing, hunger) and how such institutions may pose a threat to people in the United S. We also read Nicholas Kristof's July 13, 2008 op-ed column for *the New York Times*, "It Takes a School, Not Missiles." Kristof summarizes Mortenson's views regarding the importance of education in the Middle East, especially for girls; "The Taliban recruits the poor and illiterate ... when women are educated they are more likely to restrain their sons. Five of his [Mortenson's] teachers are former Taliban, and he says it was their mothers who persuaded them to leave the Taliban" (para. 11). Kristof notes that for the cost of one Tomahawk missile fired by the United States ($500,000), more than 20 schools could be built. He ends his column by stating, "Military force is essential in Afghanistan to combat the Taliban. But over time, in Pakistan and Afghanistan alike, the best tonic against militant fundamentalism will be education and economic opportunity" (Kristof, 2008, para. 17).

Reading these articles led students to ask, "How can we in the U.S. support education and economic opportunity for children in the Middle East?" They wanted eagerly to give children across the globe the right to a rich and equitable education not only because they recognized the unjust discrepancies between what they have in the United States and what children in the Middle East have and do not have, but also because they recognized that providing positive opportunities for children in the Middle East may have the potential to promote local and global peace.

Students agreed that Mortenson's actions made him a hero. An examination of the qualities that make a person a hero continued through the year when we read *Beowulf, Of Mice and Men, A Raisin in the Sun,* and *Romeo and Juliet*. Our students were eager to take their own heroic action like Mortenson. In the introduction to *Three Cups of Tea* Mortenson writes, "There are enough pennies in homes throughout the United States to be able to eliminate illiteracy completely throughout the world" (Mortenson & Relin, 2007, p. xxii). This statement made a profound impression on the students. They decided to work to collect money for Mortenson's organization, Pennies for Peace, which raises money for schools in Pakistan and Afghanistan. The students planned for a day of teaching third graders in our district about the needs of children in the Middle East. Their hope was that the third graders would join them in fundraising.

The planning for the third graders involved several steps. First, ninth graders brainstormed the types of skills needed for the group that would read *Listen to the Wind*, the children's version of *Three Cups of Tea,* and the group that would teach about Pennies for Peace and fundraising. Based on the skills students listed, they decided which group they should join. The students organized lesson plans including an aim, a motivating activity, a handout, and a summarizing activity. The ninth graders reviewed their lessons and a timeline for the day with the third grade teachers and revised the lessons based on the teachers' feedback.

The day of the third graders' visit included reading and learning about schools in the Middle East, teaching about Pennies for Peace, decorating containers to collect the change, and having an authentic tea party. The ninth graders were extremely proud of their efforts and the third graders left inspired.

Two weeks later, the third grade teachers called to say that their students had a surprise for us. Imagine how thrilled we were when the third graders presented us with a huge jar of change that totaled $514. One of the third grade boys was excited because this amount was so close to $600, enough to pay a teacher's salary for a year. Of course, this made the ninth graders eager to raise the additional money to get to $600—and they did.

Students' Reflections

Mortenson's Pennies for Peace program is about using change to create change. When asked to share a unique memory from the project, Paola Andrea Batres wrote, "Everyday we waste money on simple unnecessary things when children in Pakistan are suffering without necessary things a penny can buy—like a pencil." Shai'Ann Simpson stated, "I will definitely remember when I am screaming about how I hate going to school that people around the world don't even know what school is." In addition to increasing students' appreciation for what they have, Pedro Miranda showed how this project helped him to see a greater purpose for reading; "I will remember when we actually did something for the people of Pakistan because it made me feel like all the time we spent reading the book paid off." Julie Giamo and Brittany Gross commented on the experience of teaching. Julie wrote, "Even though the third graders didn't read the memoir, they got to see a picture book about other people's lives and how they can help, which they did!" Brittany wrote, "I feel that in their future, these kids will continue to want to make a difference." More than seeing themselves as agents of change, Julie and Brittany recognized the exponential power to help others see themselves as change agents.

The second question posed to students was whether this project led them to seek more opportunities regarding social justice. Maria Sepulveda shared, "It makes me think twice now and makes me realize we can help as individuals and as a community." Shai'Ann Simpson said, "It's become clear that people around the world don't have as many rights as I do....that makes me want to start a campaign on human rights." Catia Graca perfectly summarized the effect this project had on her, "This project has made me feel like I changed a small part of the world, and by taking a few steps at a time, I can change an even bigger part of the world."

When asked about how this project influenced students' views of themselves and their responsibility to the world, responses varied from focusing on helping others even if they are far away, to appreciating what they have, including the power they have to create change. Andres Zaldivar wrote, "I can help people even if they are in another part of the world." Pedro Miranda stated, "I know that we share the world with others who don't have as much as we do." Brittany Gross said, "Somebody so little (me), can do so much for a good cause, and I think everyone should know that." Julie Giamo wrote, "Even though I am only 14, I can still help and teach others how they can help people who maybe aren't so lucky." Catia Graca stated, "We can't just think about ourselves. We have to take time to think about how other people are suffering and how if we open our hearts wide enough, we can change the world." Finally, Paola Andrea Batres focused on the way this project affected her view of money. "I have to learn how to make my money last and use it wisely."

Teacher's Reflections: Fairness

Before reading *Three Cups of Tea*, we conducted a cookie experiment. Students were divided into groups based on the population of several countries around the world. For example, there were two people in the U.S. group, while there were 10 in the China group. The students were told to choose a group leader and then they were given a set number of cookies in proportion to the available food for their country. The two people in the U.S. received 9 cookies while the 10 people in China had to divide 3 cookies among themselves. This was interesting and at times sad to watch because most students did not look beyond their own group when dividing the cookies. They listened to what each of the other groups had. They complained if they were in a group that did not have enough for all, but they did not cross country lines. When asked why that was, the common response was "You didn't tell us that we could." Upon completion of *Three Cups of Tea*, students were not only told that they could help children in other countries, they were mentored in how to do so and raised the awareness of others about children's rights.

Changing Surroundings and Roles

The role of the teachers in this project was not that of the traditional instructor. Rather, teachers became guides and advocates. We guided the students through the lesson planning process, reminding them of the components they were expected to include. We cheered students on when they encountered obstacles and realized that the preparation for teaching involves some frustration along with those glorious moments of clarity and excitement. It was rewarding to see students begin to understand that, in fact, their teachers do not make up their lesson plans in the car on their way to work. This profession requires foresight and dedication; it requires people to make connections and take action building a more equitable world, in this case, advocating for the rights of children across the globe.

The role of the students also was not the traditional role. The students had to capitalize on their critical thinking skills, creativity, and energy. Critical thinking skills and creativity were needed for designing thoughtful, effective, and purposeful lesson plans that would be appropriate for their intended audience. To the ninth graders' surprise, they had to harness their energy as they interacted with third graders who looked up to them as role models. They had to work diligently to maintain the third graders' wonderfully high level of enthusiasm.

It was magical to watch a typically introverted ninth grader speaking excitedly to third graders about decorating a coin jar or putting together a puzzle with a picture of the first school Mortenson built. This young man had so much to teach these eager students in just one visit. Unlike the typical classroom setting, there was no opportunity for him to lay his head on his desk when 50 third graders were competing for his attention. This introverted student was involved in something that he saw as purposeful, and he could see the immediate effects of his actions upon the third graders. He responded enthusiastically to their excitement and respect for him.

The respect of a third grader may be, after all, more valuable to my ninth graders than the respect of their teachers. How can we fail to understand this? They believe that these younger children are going to play a powerful role in the future of our world and the ninth graders feel empowered by the fact that they can guide the third graders in doing so. As teachers and critical service-learning practitioners, this parallels our feelings about our students. We encourage our students to become more aware of unjust conditions in the world, such as the lack of proper equitable schooling in the Middle East, and to seek opportunities to take action regarding these injustices through advocacy (in this case, teaching third graders), action (raising funds), and perhaps most importantly, through being part of a classroom in which students are encouraged to think critically about the world, challenge the status quo, and be open to changing their minds regarding who needs help, how help is defined (to include advocacy for change), and who we have a responsibility to help. (It is important to remember that at the start of this unit of instruction students stated that there were plenty of people in the United States needing their attention. Only after reading articles and *Three Cups of Tea* and learning about Pennies for Peace were they motivated to take action and to realize that the needs of people on another continent (in this case, equitable education) can connect to their own needs (peace, safety, and also an equitable education for all).

SCENARIO III: *PUPUSAS* MATTER

Overview

Room 254 of Mineola High School is more bodega than market, more studio than classroom. It is the physical space that 15-, 16-, and 17-year old English Language Learners have arrived from El Salvador, Honduras, Portugal, and Korea. It is also the space that welcomes the English Language Learners to a foreign city and allows them to struggle through the sea of awkwardness, fear, confusion, trembling and excitement that is the tempo of their everyday.

The room belongs to Ms. Beach and her students. La Playa, as the students call Ms. Beach, is the the mentor and heart of this tiny microcosm of the much larger culturally diverse community in which these students live. Room 254's physical space is like any classroom we might see in the typical suburban United States high school; yet, in the context of teaching and learning, it is filled with the uncommon, unpredictable, and often the dramatic. It is Ms. Beach who purposefully nurtures the unpredictable and the dramatic. In her words,

> As an English Language Learner you often feel people don't want you here, [that] you don't belong. You can't share in all that the rest of us take for granted—going to the movies on a Friday night, choosing from a menu at any fine or ordinary restaurant, chatting with the cashier at the local Panera. You are a stranger in a stranger land. My job ... is to give them the way in ... to respect themselves, to be proud of their accomplishments, and in turn respect others, give back, build this country and world.

She adds, Academic Vocabulary (the name of this class)

> is not just a class—it's life, building the skills that allow them to live a good life, contribute, believe they are valued members of the community. Yes, that's what we do here. Together we become valued members of the world community.

And so, what began as Academic Vocabulary in Room 254 in fall 2009 transmuted itself into a classroom reflective of critical pedagogy that affirmed mutual respect, specifically individual and communal rights. The seminal event was as follows: It was 1:30 PM, a cool October afternoon. Samuel, a 16-year old reserved, tenaciously inquisitive and diligent young man, was sitting at the computer doing his best to complete a journal entry. He asked if he could go and bring a lunch to class. Across the room, Pedro yelled out, "Ah, he's so fat he don't think." La Playa stopped everything. Pens went down and computers went off. "I remember thinking," she reflects, "nothing will be the same in this room from this moment on. Respect [and] mores matter, and as much as they learn vocabulary, they are going to learn what it takes to treat each other [and] all people with kindness and reciprocity."

From that moment the curriculum pivoted. That one "fat" comment began a pilgrimage into the names we call each other, the reasons for those names, the ethics of name calling, and, amazingly, into a full year investigation of the uncomfortable "inconvenient truths" of mass food production, mass food marketing, and mass food consumption in the United States.

The revised curriculum included films (*Food Inc, Super Size Me, King Korn, The Botany of Desire, Food Revolution* and *To Market to Market to Buy a Fat Pig*), readings (*Chains, Soul Moon Soup, Eat Your Words, The Omnivore's Dilemma*, newspaper articles), participation in an Oxfam International Hunger (simulation) Banquet, interviews with a sociolinguistics class of future teachers, conversations with health studies professors, interactions with community organizers, and a culminating assessment of an advocacy service-learning project. The project began with an anthology of cultural narratives (artistic, expository, and poetic) exchanging students' food admonishments and celebrations with children of the Mungai Children's Home, Nairobi, Kenya. It also included a presentation to a few members of the school and university community based on these narratives advocating for a conscientious humanity that takes the steps towards building a world in which hunger is nonexistent and proper nutrition is available to all peoples. And in terms of immediate local contexts, the project lay the groundwork for school cafeteria menu proposals consisting of meals based on locally grown foods and balanced, more organic diets.

Teacher's Reflections: Fairness

The revised curriculum, in other words, became a collective dissection of accepted norms and the unexamined outcomes of mass food production and distribution. The students asked, Is it fair what is happening to cows, pigs and chickens so that I may have *empanadas* for dinner? Is it fair that I am eating food that makes me fat? Is it fair that the poor have less access to healthier foods? Is it fair that I don't know where my food comes from? Is it fair that special potatoes are grown for fast food chain restaurants? Is it fair that corn is in everything I eat? Is it fair that children in Kenya don't have much to eat when I have so much more than I can eat? These questions went on and on.

A revised curriculum based on students' questions rose from a very personal concern about the food on their plates. Suddenly, the conversations in the room were much more enthusiastic than in the past; discussions flowed about what was in their cafeteria lunch meals. They traveled down to the cafeteria together as a bonded team of burgeoning nutritionists choosing for each other what they should and should not eat, all eight students showing up in class with the same large salad. "But what is in the salad dressing?" they continued to dig. And Doritos were now hidden in Ms. Beach's desk drawer as they playfully cajoled her to eat them, "Ah, Ms. Beach, you know you want these. Go ahead. We won't tell." Lunch had become a core educational part of their day. Food was more than what they digested; it was the source of natural (not contrived) school conversations, brewing both friendships for students who were previously making fun of one another and place-based, action-based literacy development with thoughtful analysis.

The how and what suddenly evolved into the why. Why do the food companies allow this food to be made and sold? Who benefits from this mass production? Why am I told by TV to eat these foods? The "why" arose out genuine comprehension, and students began to unpack, for instance, the realities of world hunger and what to do about it. Hunger, as the local representative of Heifer International and Oliver, a young Kenya community organizer, told the students, exists not for lack of food resources but for lack of political will to distribute food equitably. World hunger is a man-made tragedy. And so, students began to explore what they could share with children in Kenya, how they could let others know of these inequities. The English language, the verbal and written literacy they were developing in Academic Vocabulary was embedded in a critical literacy. As they understood the meaning of the words they read, they understood and questioned the local and global contexts in which they lived. Academic Vocabulary had a new purpose; it was a response to current conditions, a means for personal and social change. And the revised curriculum that began with the comment thrown across the room, "Ay, he's so fat he don't think," culminated in the lunch-time complaint, "Ay, there is nothing I want to eat in the cafeteria." What, they asked, could they now do about that?

Changing Surroundings and Roles

"Sometimes the curriculum goes in a different direction than planned," Ms. Beach muses as we look back on the year's ventures in Academic Vocabulary. This is an understatement. And what it requires of the teacher is that she be utterly flexible, responsive to the students' needs and interests. Ms. Beach continues, "Their lives are my point of entry. We changed from the classroom being so formalized to focusing on background knowledge." "Background knowledge?" I ask. Ms. Beach responds by saying background knowledge is

> how to survive in the world, how to think about their world, how to ask questions and take nothing for granted. If they call each other "fat," [they] ask themselves, why are they fat? It's not really their fault. I have to teach them to look at what they say to each other, examine their habits (eating, shopping, buying), wake up to who they are and who they are becoming. Background knowledge ... they are going to be raising children, having families, working in a consumer society. I need them to know this world, know themselves, look behind the surface and see for themselves what is really happening.

The classroom has become a forum for discussing, analyzing, and acting upon daily routines and accepted norms, habits of mind, and deed. As they shop for produce, they examine the markets it has travelled, the processes it has survived, and the economies it has impacted. They advocate for the local farmer and nutritious school diets, support each other's more conscientious eating habits, question the sources of their daily meals. Academic Vocabulary students have extended themselves far beyond their light-green walls. The handful of eight English Language Learners have reached out locally and globally and through rather simple means to become voices in the school community acknowledging a shared humanity and asking for lasting change.

Final Musings

In many ways, the three scenarios of critical service-learning investigate the same implicit, provocative question: How do we (as teachers and students immersed in a dominant culture) respond to inequity? Whether it be authoritarian political rule that suffocates the rights of human beings or socioeconomic authoritarian norms that suffocate the rights of animals, the earth, and individuals, the inquiries are parallel; they search for more just, healthy, and sustainable worlds where invisible children are made visible (Books, 2003). The dynamic is parallel; there is mutual reciprocity of learning and courage to take risks, move beyond comfort zones, push boundaries, and be fluid enough to attend to controversial, provocative intellectual challenges. The transformations are parallel; the role of the teacher becomes that of "fellow learner" and "a moral and philosophical guide" (Coles, as cited in Hatton, 2005, p. 127). The voices of all students matter, and the students know this because their questions are at the core of inquiry. They know they are cared for, validated, partners in the learning process because they become decision makers in movements towards change. The "big desk" and "little desk" boundaries are flexible and fluid as teachers and students collaborate in "real world" exchanges. An authentic learning community develops with each member caring about something out there in the world that is real, uncomfortable, energizing, and profoundly human.

Was everything in these three critical service-learning experiences consistently and perfectly organized, implemented, completed? No. It was messy and unpredictable. Is the change in the students, teachers, larger community, and the schooling paradigm enduring? Maybe, time will tell. Lasting change comes slowly. Revolution is slow rather than immediate and gradual rather than instant, but it does happen. These scenarios demonstrate this astounding possibility.

QUESTIONS FOR REFLECTION

1. What do these three scenarios highlight about the processes and merits of moving from traditional service-learning to critical service-learning?

2. What does compassion have to do with activism? Is compassion the necessary seed for activism, the inevitable product of activism, or both or neither?
3. The three scenarios described in the chapter took place in classrooms located within the same second floor hallway. Ironically, although the students in the two general education classes address global issues explicitly, it is interesting to note that without some coaching, they typically do not, on their own, broaden their world view by interacting consistently with the English Language Learners.
4. What content knowledge, skills, and dispositions are developed in the three critical service-learning scenarios described in the chapter? How do these compare to the content knowledge, skills, and dispositions students will need to be successful in fostering an equitable world community, and, as much as we may wish we could ignore, also be successful with high stakes testing?
5. How can we continue to move the critical service-learning model beyond the classroom and into the community? How do educators, students, and parents reach out to include the larger community's input and involvement in the advocacy for human rights and social justice?

REFERENCES

Books, S. (Ed). (2003). *Invisible children in the society and its schools* (2nd ed.). Mahwah, NJ: Erlbaum.

Cremin, L. (1977). *Traditions of American education*. New York, NY: Basic Books.

Freire, P. (1970). *Pedagogy of the oppressed*. New York, NY: Continuum.

Hatton, S. D. (2005). *Teaching by heart: The Foxfire interviews*. New York, NY: Teachers College Press.

Kristoff, N. D. (2008, July 13). It takes a school, not missiles. *New York Times*. Retrieved from http://www.nytimes.com

Kuhn, T. S. (1996). *The structure of scientific revolutions* (3rd ed.). Chicago, IL: University of Chicago Press.

Meier, D. (2006). Reinventing teaching. In A. Sadovnick, P. Cookson, Jr., & S. Semel (Eds.), *Exploring education: An introduction to the foundations of education* (3rd ed.). New York, NY: Pearson Education.

Miller, J. P., Cassie, J. R. B., & Drake, S. (1990) *Holistic learning: A teacher's guide to integrated studies*. Ontario, Canada: the Ontario Institute for Studies in Education Press.

Mortenson, G., & Relin, D. O. (2007). *Three cups of tea: One man's mission to promote peace … one school at a time*. New York, NY: Penguin Paperbacks.

Palmer, P. (1998). *The courage to teach*. San Francisco, CA: Jossey-Bass.

Postman, N., & Weingartner, C. (1969). *Teaching as a subversive activity*. New York, NY: Dell Publishing.

Sizer, T., & Sizer, N. (1999). *The students are watching: Schools and the moral contract*. Boston, MA: Beacon Press.

Tavernise, S. (2009, May 3). Pakistan's Islamic schools fill void, but fuel militancy. *New York Times*. Retrieved from http://www.nytimes.com

Tents of Hope. (2007). *About the Tents of Hope Project*. Retrieved from www.tentsofhope.org

Tindley, C. A. (1947). We shall overcome. *People's Songs Bulletin*. New York, NY: People's Songs.

CHAPTER 9

THE EQUITY LEADERSHIP PROJECT

Preparing Socially Inclusive Educators

Christopher DeLuca, Meghan L. DeLagran, Eric Ferguson, and Stephanie Ho

I teach in a preservice teacher education program that maintains the following vision for its graduates:

> Graduates are expected to integrate theoretical, practical, and experiential knowledge in the understanding and resolution of professional issues. We see the beginning teacher as an active agent in the development of a socially inclusive pedagogy aimed at social justice. In our vision, the critically reflective teacher is the one who asks questions that go beyond immediate pressures of daily practice, and who has a disposition to work in collaboration with other members of the profession and with all those involved in the education and development of children. (Queen's University, 2009)

Further, the program aims to promote several critical teacher capacities including commitments to inclusivity and social justice education.

Critical Service Learning as a Revolutionary Pedagogy: A Project of Student Agency in Action, pp. 179–202

These program aims represent common themes across teacher education programs throughout Canada and the United States. In a recent survey of Canadian teacher education programs, Crocker and Dibbon (2008) noted that explicit commitments towards inclusivity, equity, social justice, and diversity were among the most widely cited in program mission statements. Moreover, although these commitments have only surfaced over the past 30 years within teacher discourse (Howard & Aleman, 2008), they continue to gain prominence as an international movement as they are fundamentally supported through human rights legislation (e.g., Canadian Charter of Rights and Freedoms in Canada), local education acts, and school district policies (Hutchinson, 2010; Retallick, Cocklin, & Coombe, 1999). However, despite this movement, Howard and Aleman (2008) contend that due to the historical emphasis on in-school teaching practice and discipline specific pedagogies, there has been notably little research on transdisciplinary practices and philosophies such as inclusivity and social justice. As such, there remains a need within contemporary research on teaching and teacher education that focuses on these transdisciplinary aspects of education.

The absence of research on developing teachers' capacity for inclusivity and addressing issues of social justice is particularly problematic given the increased recognition of diversity among student and teacher populations within public education systems (Blais & Ouedraogo, 2008; Gerin-Lajoie, 2008). In addition, practicing teachers are being explicitly asked to respond to equity initiatives through local educational policies and curriculum. For example, in Ontario, which is the jurisdiction for this research, the Ontario Ministry of Education (2009) recently released the *Ontario's Equity and Inclusive Education Strategy*. This new policy document outlines teacher responsibilities and school directives to achieving high levels of student success, reducing gaps in student achievement, and increasing confidence in publicly funded education through inclusive education strategies. Specifically, it is asserted that in order to "realize the promise of diversity, we must ensure that we respect and value the full range of our differences. Equitable, inclusive education is central to creating a cohesive society and a strong economy" (p. 5). Given this context of education, there is a need to examine how teachers are being prepared to engage a pedagogy for social justice. Specifically, Howard and Aleman (2008) emphasize the need for research that examines the capacity of teacher education programs to promote the "awareness of the social and political contexts of education and the development of critical consciousness about issues such as race, class, gender, culture, language, and educational equity" (p. 158).

While there is increased recognition that developing teacher capacity for inclusivity and social justice education is critically important at this point in education, there remains little guidance on the pedagogies and curriculum structures that promote these capacities in developing teachers (Darling-Hammond, 1999, 2006). In particular, there is a need to examine approaches that work within current conditions of teacher education programming. These conditions include relatively short programs with split coursework-practicum structures and high content demands. Further, within these contexts, issues of inclusivity, social justice and student diversity are typically treated as separate from core teacher education curriculum (Cochran-Smith & Fries, 2003; Hollins & Guzman, 2005; Ladson-Billings, 1995; Zeichner & Hoeft, 1996) with few opportunities for teacher candidates to engage in sustained learning in these areas (DeLuca, 2010).

In this chapter, we consider the viability of integrating a critical service-learning approach in current conditions of preservice education with the aim of preparing socially inclusive educators. In particular, we provide a detailed account of a specific pedagogical approach, The Equity Leadership Project, which has been used with one group of teacher candidates in Canada. Through analysis of three teacher candidates' work in diverse educational and service contexts, we present empirical evidence for this approach and consider the impact of this learning on teacher candidates' pedagogical philosophies and understandings of education. Hence this study contributes a concrete case of critical service-learning with the purpose of providing guidance on pedagogies and curriculum structures that work towards developing teacher candidate capacities of inclusivity and social justice. In this way, we respond to Cochran-Smith and Fries' (2005) call for practice-based research that addresses praxis in teacher education programs and that promotes critical values in the teaching profession.

THE CONTEXT OF TEACHER EDUCATION

Integrating inclusivity and promoting values of social justice, diversity, and equity with teacher candidates is a substantial and formidable task within teacher education programs. Solomon (2002) acknowledges, "one of the biggest challenges for teacher education in Western societies is to prepare practitioners for the growing diversity within their schools" (p. 261). Accordingly, in this section of the chapter, we explore the contextual features of teacher education programs that give rise to this challenge as well as consider literature that supports the education of inclusivity and social justice within preparatory programs.

In Canada, preservice education occurs through concurrent or consecutive university-based programs that lead to a bachelor of education (BEd) degree. Consecutive programs range from 8 months to 2 years depending upon the province and require teacher candidates to have completed another undergraduate degree (e.g., bachelor of science or bachelor of arts). Concurrent programs differ as teacher candidates complete both a BEd and a second undergraduate degree at the same time. The dominant structure for BEd programs involves a combination of on-campus coursework and field-based experiences (Crocker & Dibbon, 2008). Theoretically, both on-campus coursework and practice teaching experiences offer opportunities for teacher candidates to learn about inclusivity and social justice education (Solomon, 2002).

Despite these opportunities, a significant concern remains that issues of diversity, equity, and inclusion are neglected within preservice preparation programs (Gerin-Lajoie, 2008). Philpott and Beynon (2005) state concern that

> educators in various stages of their preparation are neither required nor encouraged to take courses in which they explore and articulate the sources of their ideas on social responsibility and the variety of issues of inclusion and exclusion it encompasses. (p. 35)

Crocker and Dibbon's (2008) research with 343 faculty members, 1,853 BEd graduates, and 865 principals across Canada echoes this concern. Based on survey results, topics in "dealing with diversity among children" and "teaching children with disabilities or other special needs" were perceived as very important for beginning teachers (principals' responses of 83% and 81%; faculty's responses of 82% and 61%, respectively). However, the perception of teacher candidate readiness in these areas by principals and faculty members was marginal (principals 7% and 3%; faculty 13% and 16%, respectively). Teacher candidates themselves also acknowledged a lack of emphasis on these issues with only 28% of them indicating "a great deal of emphasis" on dealing with diversity in their preservice program and 19% on teaching children with special needs. These statistics further point toward the need to find curricular and pedagogical approaches that better prepare teacher candidates to address diversity and promote inclusivity within their classrooms.

Inclusivity and social justice as fundamental principles of education can be promoted in preservice coursework through an infused approach, a separated approach, or through a combination of both approaches (Kosnik & Beck, 2009; Zeichner & Conklin, 2005; Zeichner & Hoeft, 1996). An infusion approach assumes that issues of inclusivity, diversity, and equity are embedded and addressed in all preservice courses and in practicum experiences (Darling-Hammond, 2002; Irvine, 2003; Nieto, 2000). In advocating for an infused approach, Beck and Kosnik (1998) assert that an infused approach has been found to be very effective in providing teacher candidates the opportunity to directly connect curriculum, policy, and pedagogy with social issues related to diversity and inclusion. They also assert that such an approach is viewed more positively by teacher candidates compared to a separated approach in which teacher candidates perceive the treatment of equity issues as tokenism or as a program "add-on."

As the most common structure, the separated approach promotes inclusivity through discrete courses that explicitly address issues of equity, diversity, social justice, and inclusion. For instance, it is not uncommon to have specific courses offered on special education, English as a Second Language (ESL), or multiculturalism in preservice programs. However, more often than not, these courses are electives that are taken only by certain students in addition to a required core program. Nieto (2000) acknowledges that although an infused approach is necessary for teacher candidates to understand the embedded nature of equity issues across educational contexts, specialized courses are also necessary and serve a critical function in the preparation of teachers. Separate courses on issues of equity and inclusivity enable teacher candidates to deeply explore the structures, policies, and pedagogies that promote inclusive learning communities. In their study of teacher candidates' experiences of preservice programming, Kosnik and Beck (2009) observed the benefits of these courses on teachers' practices. One participant in their study indicated that

> the most valuable course I had in pre-service ... was my multicultural education course.... It's an all-year course, and the value I gained from it was to be able to respond delicately, effectively, and critically when necessary, to issues in multicultural education. (p. 15)

As benefits exist for both infused and separated approaches, some programs elect to provide teacher candidates with both forms of learning. A combined approach ensures that all teacher candidates receive some teaching on issues of inclusion and enable those interested in pursuing topics further to do so through more specialized study.

Practica experiences also have the potential to promote issues of inclusivity and social justice; however, these experiences vary widely in duration and location between and even within preservice programs. Although all programs have a practicum component, some require less than 8 weeks of in-school experience while others require 21 or more weeks (Crocker & Dibbons, 2008). Most of these practica occur in teachable subject areas and are located in mainstream school settings (i.e., K–12 public, or separate schools) with assigned associate teachers. During their practicum experiences, teacher candidates most frequently reported engaging in the following activities: teaching within subject specialization (76%), reflecting on teaching (75%), observing teaching practices (74%), and receiving formative feedback (66%) (Crocker & Dibbon, 2008). In contrast, only 26% of teacher candidates reported that classroom work related to university coursework. Disconnects between university teaching and classroom practices have been identified as a central issue facing teacher education (Clift & Brady, 2005; Munby, Russell, & Martin, 2001; Webster-Wright, 2009) with particular disconnects identified in the area of social justice education (DeLuca, 2010). This disconnect is problematic because teacher candidates are being exposed to various contexts of education that promote diverse conceptions of inclusivity and social justice practice and required to independently bridge learning across these contexts and consolidate it with their university-based learning. While some teacher candidates may have the ability to negotiate their learning, others may not. Further, such an approach may contribute to fragmented, partial, or rudimentary understandings of inclusivity and social justice, not least an inconsistent and highly variable education for teacher candidates.

In addition to in-school practica, select programs also offer alternative field-based experiences that encourage teacher candidates to practice education in nontraditional settings. Several researchers (Darling-Hammond, 2002; Kosnik & Beck, 2009; Santoro, 2009; Solomon, 2002) have identified alternative placements as fostering teacher candidates' experiences and understandings of inclusivity in education. For example, in Santoro's (2009) qualitative study of teacher candidates working in culturally rich settings, teacher candidates' own construction of their ethnic identities and their understandings of the "ethnic other" expanded through guided activities that occurred during placement periods. In this case, onsite learning about students' and teachers' cultural backgrounds was found to promote more culturally inclusive pedagogies and teaching practices.

Solomon (2002) also describes a teacher education program and field-based learning opportunity that explicitly works towards promoting issues of social justice education. The Urban Diversity Teacher Education Program was designed to attract and admit culturally diverse teacher candidates with the intent to create an enriched cultural environment in which to learn about education. The program was composed of approximately half minoritzed students and half Caucasian students and sought to infuse equity and diversity into all aspects of the program's curriculum and pedagogy as well as teacher candidates' placement experiences. One of the most salient features of the placement component was its focus on intergroup collaboration and the intentional partnership of cross-race teaching dyads. The aim of these structures was to expand awareness and understanding of cultural similarities and differences within contexts of education. In addition to their in-school placements, teacher candidates of the Urban Diversity program were required to participate in a community involvement project. This project enabled teacher candidates to interact and collaborate with social service organizations, youth agencies, and after-school programs. The purpose of this program component was to help teacher candidates gain sensitivity as well as a cultural understanding of their local teaching communities. Cochran-Smith, Davis, and Fries (2004) support this approach, asserting that "a particularly promising teacher preparation program appears to be community-based experience, which offers teacher candidates new understandings about culture, families, and ways of life that are different from their own" (p. 964). Paired with teacher candidate-driven action research projects and on-site faculty learning about culture theory, these practicum experiences were shown not only to increase teacher candidates' cultural knowledge and understanding of equitable learning practices but also to promote teacher candidates' ability to practice inclusive pedagogies (Solomon, 2002).

This example points to the benefits of utilizing a critical-service orientation in teacher education. While traditional service-learning in teacher education is a fairly common approach with nearly one-fifth of programs in the United States offering some form of service opportunity (Root et al., 2000), critical service-learning maintains a reflective component that operates within a framework of social justice (Mitchell, 2007). In this way, critical service-learning in teacher education serves not only to engage teacher candidates in meaningful community work but more importantly aims to transform structures and perceptions that contribute towards social injustices and inequities. Often times, these projects involve deliberate education to promote skills and knowledge that lead to more socially just conditions (Mitchell, 2007). Research is beginning to demonstrate the impact of this educational approach on teacher candidate learning and on the communities in which they work (Bell, Horn, & Roxas, 2007; Brathwaite & Porfilio, 2004; Mitchell, 2007; Wade, 2000). For example, Brathwaite and Porfilio's (2004) study of 32 Ontario teacher candidates engaged in critical service-learning provided evidence of the benefits towards increased awareness of teacher candidates about urban school conditions and their communities. However, their study also pointed to the challenges of structuring useful partnerships within a cross-border teacher education program. Hence their work falls alongside others' with calls for more research on the pedagogical structures that guide critical service-learning and on the application of this approach across teacher education programs (Bell et al., 2007). In this chapter, we begin to respond to this call for research by providing a detailed description of the pedagogical approach used in one Canadian teacher education program.

THE EQUITY LEADERSHIP PROJECT

The critical service-learning project described in this chapter, The Equity Leadership Project, was part of a course on critical issues in education, equity and exceptionalities. The course was for third-year concurrent teacher candidates and occurred over two terms from September to April. While issues of inclusivity and social justice are infused through the teacher education program, this course is the only mandatory course (with the exception of an 8-hour module in social justice) that these teacher candidates are required to take in this area. However, teacher candidates may choose to enroll in an elective course that further addresses these issues in their final year of study.

The third-year critical issues course focused on systemic structures of inclusivity and social justice with specific topics related to policies, theories and practices that impact the role of teachers in contemporary school contexts. The pedagogical intention guiding this course was to connect personal experiences and philosophies to broader discourse on critical issues in education. Classes largely centered on critical discussions that integrated educational theory, practical teaching scenarios, and teacher candidates' personal beliefs. Following the practice of Alsup (2005), teacher candidates were asked to articulate a personal pedagogical statement during the first week of classes. Throughout the course, this statement served as a benchmark for their learning and as a source for critical reflection on their beliefs about education, inclusivity and social justice.

The substantive assignment for the course was the Equity Leadership Project. This project was introduced during the first class with teacher candidates invited to begin their project work as soon as possible to engage in sustained critical service-learning over the course of an academic year. Specifically, the project description was as follows:

> You are to engage in a leadership activity within the community that relates to an equity or social justice issue. Your project should involve education or advocacy for a cause with the aim of critically addressing an issue of inequity or injustice within education or the broader community. For example, you might hold a poetry reading night to bring awareness to issues of poverty or you may work with a local outreach group to offer workshops to students in schools. I encourage you to get creative and to make connections with local community groups. (Assignment description, course outline)

The project was scaffolded through a series of stages leading to a final round-table presentation and submission during the last class of the term. These stages also provided key opportunities for critical reflection on their work. First, teacher candidates were asked to complete a proposal for their intended project (see Appendix A for proposal template). Once their proposal was approved, teacher candidates could proceed with their critical service-work. Mid-way through the course, teacher candidates were invited to sit with the instructor and a group of their peers to discuss their emerging projects. During these discussions, teacher candidates articulated their projects by describing the central equity or social justice issue as well as the challenges and positive aspects of their work. The purposes of these discussions were to not only to check on the progress of projects (see progress template Appendix B) but to also support the teacher candidate by engaging in small group critical conversations about focused critical service-work. On the final day of class, teacher candidates shared their Equity Leadership Projects with one another through structured roundtable presentations. This presentation format allowed teacher candidates to learn from their peers about specific equity and social justice issues and educational approaches to critically addressing these issues. Teacher candidates also submitted a final report to the instructor that summarized their learning. Summaries included: (a) a description of the equity issue, (b) a description of the Equity Leadership Project and background information on the organization (if applicable), and (c) a critical reflection on how the experience has impacted both teacher candidates' pedagogical philosophies and issues of social inequity. The final reports were graded on a pass-fail scheme using a rubric approach (see Appendix C for grading rubric).

We contend that this pedagogical structure follows Mitchell's (2007) guidelines for critical service-learning. In particular, through the Equity Leadership Project, we aimed to (a) focus deliberately on issues of justice through reading, dialogue and community engagement, (b) create opportunities for critical reflection that bridge self, service, and broader social context, (c) engage in experiences of service that progressively move towards deeper action, (d) construct and cultivate relationships between students within and outside the classroom community, (e) support learning through sharing and teaching, (f) provide exposure to issues of social justice, and (g) support students' personal equity interests (Mitchell, 2007). As a further description of the Equity Leadership Project, three teacher candidates (co-authors of this chapter) articulate their projects in the following sections of this chapter. These three projects have been selected for analysis because each of them represents unique critical service work that aimed to shed light on social injustices or inequities and, through education, worked to transform structures and perceptions that contribute towards these issues. Specifically, the projects are: (a) The Poverty Challenge by Eric Ferguson, (b) Gender Treatment in the Elementary Classroom by Meghan DeLagran, and (c) Homelessness: A Personal Narrative by Stephanie Ho. Further, embedded within these project descriptions are teacher candidate reflections on the influence of this critical-service work on their personal philosophies of education.

THE POVERTY CHALLENGE

My Equity Leadership Project involved working with a local community committee to plan and deliver a 1-day experiential learning summit on poverty for students in Grades 9-12 from our community. The summit was called The Poverty Challenge. Part simulation game and part hard-hitting brainstorming session, The Poverty Challenge aimed both to educate students about the inefficiencies and inequalities that perpetuate poverty in our community and to empower students to become agents of social change.

The Challenge was divided into two parts. In the morning, 100 student participants took part in a simulation activity that cast them in the role of a community member living in poverty; each student was given a profile and a task to complete that involved interacting with local social services and community organizations. Using two floors of a large academic building and over 100 volunteers in role as agency employees, we created a microcosm of our community's poverty support network for the students to navigate as they tried to achieve the goals as outlined in their profile. The feedback from students was overwhelmingly a story of frustration; agencies were inefficient and unhelpful, but also staffed by workers frustrated by their own inability to escape insufficient budgets and sprawling bureaucracy.

The stories, objectives, and paperwork used during the simulations were all real and based on interviews with agency representatives and with local poverty experts—people who were experiencing or recovering from poverty in our community. Unknown to the students, all of the poverty experts were present at the conference. Once the morning simulation was finished, students split into groups by profile and met the real person whose role they had been playing. The building went silent as our participants learned first-hand that the stories played out earlier that morning corresponded to the real experiences of local people.

In the afternoon, The Challenge shifted its focus to a brainstorming activity that asked students to pitch a solution to one of the systemic problems they had encountered during the simulation. Our goal was not to rehash tired calls for volunteers or donations but to encourage students to understand the social and political problems that perpetuated poverty and come up with solutions. Adult involvement at this stage was kept to a minimum; we wanted fresh, original ideas unencumbered by concerns about politics or funding restrictions. At the end of the day, students presented their proposals to their peers and a copy of the proposals was then sent to the City Council.

The Poverty Challenge was planned in response to the need for poverty education that moved beyond a passive research-based model of student engagement with this social issue. Our goal was to show students first-hand the many systemic causes and experiences of poverty, to think through solutions, and then to immediately empower students to start affecting the political systems that contribute to issues around poverty. At the same time, it was also a chance for me and my fellow community members to affect the system by adding new voices to the call for reform and by giving our participants an early start in the leadership roles that they will someday assume in our community.

Undertaking this Equity Leadership Project gave me insight into the intersection between education and social justice in a way that no classroom-based activity could have done. As a teacher candidate, I have quickly learned that my personal pedagogy is most strongly influenced by experiences to which I feel personally connected, not by case studies or research encountered in the classroom. However, I have also learned that these experiences diminish in impact significantly if they are not followed-up by a structured opportunity for critical reflection. For me, the Equity Leadership Project was an opportunity to participate in an important social issue. While I might have undertaken this project on my own, participating in organizing The Poverty Challenge as part of critical-service work served to maximize its impact on my own professional practice as a teacher by consolidating my experience with other learning in the course and by articulating my experience and learning to my peers. Overall, the Equity Project provided a useful framework for pushing my learning forward in a way that turned my interest in poverty reduction into a fully-realized formative experience in my pre-service teacher education.

GENDER TREATMENT IN THE ELEMENTARY CLASSROOM

As a geography student, I have always been interested in the ways in which boys and girls contribute to and are influenced by socialized gender roles in classroom contexts. This interest has also been shaped by the work of scholars who challenge hegemonic ideas of childhood and who view children not as adults-in-the-making but instead as capable social actors who contribute towards establishing social constructs, such as gender (Thorne, 1993). In my Equity Leadership Project, I wanted to further explore children's conceptions of gender and their ideas about how this social structure affects students in the classroom. In order to do so, I set up a Voicethread on the Internet that posed a question about gender divisions in the classroom to students in a Grade 5 Ontario classroom. The question was simple: "Do you think boys and girls are treated differently at school? If so, how?" Using Voicethread technology enables students to record their thoughts through speech or text, while also providing the opportunity for them to listen and respond to their peers' ideas. The students then responded to the question and to each others' contributions. Data were then stored on the secure Voicethread website. Students were invited to discuss the Voicethread face-to-face during class time. I believe that this structure allowed students to not only articulate their own conceptions of gender equity but also to understand the perspectives of other students and teachers in order to better understand the social structures that give rise to differential gender treatment. In this way, I hoped that this Equity Leadership Project challenged and changed beliefs about gender for one class of Grade 5 students.

I situated this project in relation to gender and childhood research in order to better understand children's experiences at school through a gendered lens. According to Thorne (1993), the belief in innate gender differences continues to affect children today. In contrast, she argues that gender is a social construction, created and recreated by media, adult, social and cultural pressures. However, among these ideas of a gendered stereotype, children complicate and challenge gender hegemony by exercising their agency, which influences the power structures trying to force them to behave according to gender (Thorne, 1993). Most adults in North American society view children as "developing" or "socializing," yet children do not view themselves this way; "children's interactions are not preparation for life; they are life itself" (Thorne, 1993, p. 3). As an example, Valentine (1997) suggests that children's everyday experiences are ignored in academic discourse because they are thought to be "incapable of making rational judgments" (p. 67). Therefore, accessing and using children's opinions about gender equity became an important feature of my Equity Leadership Project.

In listening to the Voicethread, I found that while the children spoke about the ways in which gender affected their lives at school, they also challenged it. Both the boys and girls talked about the controlling power structures of teachers more than their friends. In fact, several students spoke with outrage about an incident during cross-country ski lessons where the boys were allowed to ski down the hill but the girls were asked to walk down. Interestingly, both girls and boys perceived this incident as unjust because it separated them from each other based on gender. Further, most of the children believed that the boys were not necessarily more capable in this physically demanding setting. Many of the students also stated that they believed boys more often got into trouble with adults because they were viewed as more aggressive than girls. Similarly, a number of the girls talked about the limitations they faced in gym class because of their gender. Across the students in the class, both boys and girls argued that gender division was not fair. What I found most interesting about the students' comments was the way in which children so readily recognize how the power structures of the classroom influence them, particularly the ways teachers unfairly reinforce gender differences. This sentiment is common among educational researchers since "stereotyped attitudes and values surrounding models of masculinity and femininity flourish [in classrooms] ... determining aspects of teacher and student behaviour" (Robinson, 1992, p. 274). These kinds of gender naturalizations can be extremely disadvantagous for students. For example, when girls are more aggressive, challenging the gender norm of gentle femininity, they are usually punished more severely by teachers because it is believed to be "unnatural" for girls to behave aggressively (Robinson, 1992). The kinds of moral judgments teachers make on girls who push their gendered boundaries can have profound and lasting effects on the reputation of the student, their self-esteem, and their ability to fulfill their academic needs. Therefore it is the responsibility of educators to begin to challenge the existence of gender hegemony within themselves as well as their classroom and students in order to move beyond its constraints.

After completing my Equity Leadership Project and reading more widely on the topic of gender equity in schools, I will be careful to think of my students as capable social actors, who view themselves as living now and not necessarily striving to "become" an adult. This means that from the position of a teacher, I have to work to understand students' perspective concerning their treatment in the classroom. Forums, such as the Voicethread, need to be created to access students' thoughts and give them an opportunity for active agency related to social issues. Unfortunately, ensuring that children are not separated by gender is difficult, especially in a world where ideas of masculinity and femininity have been so heavily normalized. Even calling our students "girls and boys" contributes to the creation and recreation of this dichotomous view of gender. Understanding the issues from student's perspective and working to create equitable learning environments from a student perspective has become critical to my pedagogy as a teacher.

HOMELESSNESS: A PERSONAL NARRATIVE

My project was a personal attempt to get involved with the homeless in my local community. I am concerned with both understanding and changing the cycle of poverty as it exists in my community and our response as students and future educators to the homeless. I decided that a good place to start was to assess my own response to homelessness. I did not want this project to simply be a charity donation of my time or money, as I believe that charity often only widens the gap between the upper and lower classes. My aim was to figure out if there is hope for empowerment in today's society and if developing empathetic responses to and solidarity with those in need presented the key to doing so. I was aware at the start that I probably would not be able to evoke large changes alone through the course of this project, but I wanted to at least begin to find answers to some of my questions regarding how we can provide help and what effective change would look like. Rather than speculate about a situation into which I have no real insight, I wanted to figure out answers by building relationships with homeless people and getting to a point where I felt comfortable asking them these questions.

I decided to do this by volunteering at a local soup kitchen and using this as an avenue to build relationships with the people that frequented it. The organization that I chose functions as a soup kitchen but is operated like a restaurant for "at risk" families and individuals. It is strictly volunteer and donation based, as various grocery stores or restaurants including Metro, Starbucks and Kentucky Fried Chicken donate either premade food or the raw ingredients needed to provide three course meals complete with desert, juice, coffee or tea. Customers pay either a dollar at the door or have prepaid meal cards and volunteers are required to plate food in the kitchen, serve customers in the dining rooms or to help with bussing and cleaning. Volunteering at the soup kitchen provided me with opportunities to converse with people, familiarize myself with some faces and ultimately build relationships. My project also consisted of a personal commitment to take increased initiative to stop and talk to homeless people on the streets and take the time to get to know some of them. This initiative was easier than I thought it would be. I found that many of the people who I met through the soup kitchen would frequently be sitting along street that I walk down everyday. Often times they would recognize or remember me and they would always be very willing to sit and talk.

To present my final project I decided to write a personal narrative about a conversation that I had with a man along Princess Street, Frank (pseudonym). It was difficult to find a way to represent learning that was primarily accomplished through spontaneous conversations, but I felt that the narrative form would best reflect my learning through these conversations while describing how they proceeded. I shared my narrative with peers in my teacher education class with the hope that it would open others' eyes to how willing people are to talk and inspire them to venture out into our community. The narrative begins with my thought process directly after I had asked a fairly personal question and the man's response to this question, which sparked an hour-long discussion on the inescapable cycle of poverty and how it has presented itself in his life. It recounts some of the struggles that he shared with me and describes the process by which my own preconceptions were challenged. It also describes Frank's response to some of my questions.

I learned a great deal through the various conversations I had about why poverty persists. There are several obvious factors that perpetuate the cycle of poverty such as addiction to drugs, alcohol and tobacco, trouble with the law, and dysfunctional relationships. One other predominant factor that appears to be driving the high rates of unemployment is a limited or lack of education. I found that education was very frequently brought up in conversation as something that people wished they had continued or at which they had a second chance. Frank shared that he had tried attending a couple classes at high school in hopes that studying English would help him to better develop his vocabulary and communication skills and enable him to succeed in the professional world. He said a few resources existed that provide writing aid, but very few that provide long-term literacy development for adults. I also learned that people, regardless of their wealth and social status, are very similar in their needs and wants, their desires for happiness and relationships. Ultimately, we all share the need to be validated as human beings. Some of us take this validation for granted because it comes easily to us. But there are vast numbers of people who do not get acknowledged or shown any compassion.

I would like to say that I was able to form a literacy program and change the lives of the people that I conversed with in a drastic way, but I can not. I can say, however, that I have made a start. I have built the foundation towards being able to provide help and compassion and I have found a cause about which I am passionate. I also learned to challenge my own preconceptions. My narrative describes my initial hesitation to approach Frank when I saw him on the street. I had seen him but because of his appearance I did not approach him, conveniently pretending not to see him. It was not until I had reached the end of the next block that I realized that the cycle of negative stereotypes could never be broken until I took the effort to break my own. I learned merely five minutes into our conversation that he felt uncomfortable sitting there and hated having to take money from people. I immediately felt an extremely heavy sense of remorse when I realized that my perception had been completely off.

The root of change is always concern. If we want to break the cycle of poverty, we need to start caring for those in need, and compassion can only be established through taking the time to understand others. My hope is that I have inspired both myself and others to take the time to notice the people that need to be noticed and to listen to what needs to be done.

DISCUSSION

The Equity Leadership Project reflects our initial attempt at engaging teacher candidates in critical service-learning within one Canadian teacher education program. The pedagogical delineation of the Equity Leadership Project offers a model for how critical service-learning can be integrated into preservice programs and courses that maintain competing content and time demands. Further, the three projects described in this chapter provide detailed accounts of initiatives that constitute critical-service work. Analysis of these experiences supports the finding that critical service-learning can contribute toward teacher candidates' growing awareness, understandings, and commitments to social justice and inclusivity in education. Moreover, there is emerging evidence to suggest that these experiences also impact candidates' broader philosophies and approaches to educating children and youth. While enduring learning was evident across teacher candidates' reflections in this study, we assert that there remain areas for continued development and research to refine this pedagogical approach within the context of teacher education programming.

While we acknowledge the critical importance of service work and its ties to systemic social issues of equity and justice, we also recognize that such work can seem like a large-scale undertaking for new teacher candidates. Positing critical-service projects as system-changing initiatives that confront "the larger inequities that impeded the creation of a just society" (Brathwaite & Porfilio, 2004) may seem overwhelming for some teacher candidates and result in disengagement from learning. As such, we suggest a reframing of critical-service work within teacher education contexts that positions this learning as an opportunity to further develop candidates' sense of social responsibility. In this way, the emphasis is placed on candidates' capacity to impact change based on their sphere of influence rather than on endeavoring to combat a system of injustice. This reframing falls alongside the notion that "every small change matters" and that teachers (and teacher candidates) have the ability to impact individuals within their local communities, whether that be in their classrooms, schools, or broader communities (Keiser, 2005, p. 54).

As evident through the projects described in this chapter, we assert that critical-service projects may operate at a range of scales that fall within teacher candidates' capacity to influence social issues. Hence we argue that critical-service work can involve initiatives that are broad reaching, such as the Poverty Challenge, or initiatives that are deeply personal and individual, such as a narrative account of homelessness. However, in all cases, the aim of critical-service work should be to transform perceptions and understandings of social issues and structures that give rise to inequities through education. We believe that personal motivation for engaging in critical-service work is a key factor in achieving this aim. As such, a central feature of the Equity Leadership Project was allowing teacher candidates to pursue their own compelling interests in issues of social justice and inclusivity within their sphere of influence. This feature aligns with Mitchell's (2007) assertion that critical service-learning needs to "support students where they are and affirm the commitments they are able and willing to make" (p. 110).

Based on our experience, we assert that the following three components are important motivating factors for engaging in critical service- learning within teacher education contexts: (a) exposure to critical service-learning, (b) connection between theory and practice, and (c) monitoring and scaffolding student learning. Exposing teacher candidates to critical service-learning requires spending time introducing teacher candidates to the significance and potential impact of critical service-work before they begin their projects. Part of this introduction should involve examining previous projects (such as those described in this chapter) as well as exposure to the gamut of social issues that provide opportunities for critical service work. Further, there is a need to reflect on aspects of social justice and inclusivity that have impacted teacher candidates' own lives in order to situate critical-service projects in personal experiences. Having candidates articulate the link between their personal interest in a social justice issue and their critical-service project provides a basis for designing a project that motivates candidates to engage in meaningful social justice learning.

Second, alongside project development, planning, and enactment, teacher candidates need to be exposed to general theoretical structures related to inclusivity and social justice as well as specific theoretical frameworks for examining issues directly relevant to their projects. For example, in exploring perceptions of gender treatment in the elementary classroom, it is necessary to consider broad theory on classroom inclusivity and theory on gender relationships within child development. However, one of the central challenges facing teacher educators in promoting theoretical frameworks that support diverse critical-service projects is that there is no unifying theory of inclusivity within current scholarship that bridges the treatment and education of diverse forms of difference (Trifonas, 2003). Rather, research in this area has been parsed into specific subdisciplines including (but not limited to) multicultural education, special education, anti-racist education, queer education, and the education of women (Trifonas, 2003). While theories of social justice education apply to diverse forms of difference, they tend to promote a specific treatment of diversity and do not necessarily demonstrate to teacher candidates the mechanisms and structures through which individuals are included and treated within educational contexts. Within relatively short teacher education courses and programs, teaching and learning across the multitude of theories becomes a tall order and often results in a patchwork of learning on discrete social justice issues (Villegas & Lucas, 2002). Hence what remains needed is a general framework through which teacher candidates can begin to understand the social structures that contribute toward diverse forms of social inclusivity. Such a framework would not only provide the structure and language for consolidating learning about social justice and inclusive education, but it would also help candidates to situate their critical-service projects within a common framework of understanding. Moreover, applying a unifying framework of inclusivity to practice-based projects would help to ameliorate the disconnect between theory and practice commonly identified in research on teacher education (Clift & Brady, 2005; Munby, Russell, & Martin, 2001; Webster-Wright, 2009).

Last, there is a need to monitor and scaffold learning so that teacher candidates continue to "move toward progressively deeper action" (Mitchell, 2007, p. 109). In order to support teacher candidate learning in the Equity Leaderhship Project, we used both a progress report and small-group conferencing to share and critically examine developing projects. Not only do these structures provoke deeper action but also serve to develop a "community of critical friends" (Nieto, 2000, p. 185) with whom to explore issues in educational equity, inclusivity, and social justice education. However, different from other instructor-based scaffolding approaches, this approach enables teacher candidates to maintain ownership over their learning and does not predetermine specific learning objectives; rather, learning emerges through joint critical inquiry and follows candidates' compelling interests related to social justice service (Nieto, 2000).

Preparing socially responsible educators who value principles of social justice and inclusivity is a required mandate for contemporary teacher education programs. As such, it is our responsibility as teacher educators and researchers to find and use effective pedagogies that promote this mandate (Darling-Hammond, 1999, 2006). Critical service-learning appears to be a promising and revolutionary pedagogy. However, we contend that in order for this pedagogy to be meaningful, it must be personally motivated, planned, and enacted within supportive structures of learning. Hence, we suggest continued research into the benefits and challenges of implementing critical service-learning within the complexities of different teacher education programs. Specifically, there is a need to explore structures that promote the linking of theory with practice and the development of communities of critical friends. Further, in validating this pedagogical approach for use in teacher education contexts, it would be useful to conduct longitudinal studies on the enduring impact of pre-service-learning on teachers' future projects of social justice.

QUESTIONS FOR REFLECTION

1. What aspects of inclusivity in education are personally compelling to you? Why?
2. How might you engage in critical-service work within your context of teaching and learning? What resources would you need? How would you construct a community of critical friends?
3. Where do you see a gap in research on teacher and student learning about (a) inclusivity in education, and (b) critical-service pedagogy.

Appendix A: Proposal Template

Student Name: Student Number:

1. Describe an equity issue you would like to pursue for the Equity Leadership Project.
2. Why are you personally interested in this equity issue?
3. What do you propose to do for your Equity Leadership Project?
4. What do you hope to learn/achieve through completing this Equity Leadership Project?
5. Will you be working with an organization?

☐ YES ☐ NO

If 'yes', please provide the contact information for this organization and identify:

Name of lead contact: ______________________________

Name of organization: ______________________________

Organization Address: ______________________________

____

Phone Number: ______________________________

E-mail Contact: ______________________________

Have you already been in contact with the organization? ☐ YES ☐ NO

6. Instructor Feedback/Proposal Assessment (filled-in by instructors)

Comments:

Approval: ☐ YES ☐ NO

Appendix B: Proposal Template

Progress Questions:
1. What were your Equity Leadership Project aims?
2. What have you completed to date?
3. What activities do you still need to complete?
4. What have you learned so far?
5. What challenged have you encountered?
6. What resource/supports do you need to complete your project?

Appendix C: Grading Rubric

Criteria and Component	*Incomplete/Fail*	*Pass*
Description of Equity Issue	• Description of equity issue is unsupported and does not reflect a critical social issue in education • No description provided	• Description of equity issue presents a critical social issue in education • Description is linked to a context of education • Description of equity issue is well supported by literature
Description of Equity Leadership Project	• Description of equity leadership project is vague and unclear • No description provided	• Identifies stages and activities of equity leadership project • Provides sufficient background information on organization to contextualize project
Statement of Impact	• Impact statement is disconnected from equity issue or personal teaching practice • No statement of impact provided	• Articulates impact of project on community/equity issue • Articulates impact of project on personal understanding of equity issue • Draws links between equity project and personal pedagogy • Suggests continued professional development
Writing Conventions	• Spelling and grammar impedes understanding • Lack of references/support materials for claims	• Spelling and grammar enables effective communication of ideas • Reference/support materials are used in description of equity issue

Comments and Grade:

REFERENCES

Alsup, J. (2006). *Teacher identity discourses: Negotiating personal and professional spaces.* Mahwah, NJ: Erlbaum.

Beck, C., & Kosnik, C. (1998). A Canadian perspective on values education: The Ontario experience. *Journal of Values Education, 2,* 32–43.

Bell, C., A., Horn, B. R., & Roxas, K. C. (2007). We know it's service, but what are they learning? Preservice teachers' understandings of diversity. *Equity & Excellence in Education, 40*(2), 123–133.

Blais, J. G., & Ouedraogo, D. M. (2008). A cross-sectional sketch of a few demographic characteristics of teachers in Canada. In D. Gerin-Lajoie (Ed.), *Educators' discourses on student diversity in Canada: Context, policy, and practice* (pp. 29–50). Toronto, ON: Canadian Scholars' Press.

Brathwaite, F., & Porfilio, B. (2004). A schoolbased project increasing Ontario pre service teacher candidate experiences with cultural diversity. *Networks: An Online Journal for Teacher Research, 7*(2).

Clift, R., & Brady, P. (2005). Research on methods, courses, and field experiences. In M. Cochran-Smith & K. Zeichner (Eds.), *Studying teacher education: The report of the AERA panel on research and teacher education* (pp. 309–424). Mahwah, NJ: American Educational Research Association and Lawrence Erlbaum.

Cochran-Smith, M., & Fries, M. K. (2003). Multicultural teacher education: Research, practice and policy. In J. Banks (Ed.), *Handbook of research on multicultural education* (2nd ed., pp. 931–975). San Francisco, CA: Jossey-Bass.

Cochran-Smith, M., & Fries, M. K. (2005). Paradigms and politics: Researching teacher education in changing times. In M. Cochran-Smith & K. Zeichner (Eds.), *Studying teacher education: The report of the AERA panel on research and teacher education* (pp. 69–110). Mahwah, NJ: Erlbaum.

Cochran-Smith, M., Davis, D., & Fries, K. (2004). Multicultural teacher education: Research, practice, and policy. In J. Banks, & C. McGee Banks (Eds.), *Handbook on research on multicultural education* (2nd ed., pp. 931–975). San Francisco, CA: Jossey-Bass.

Crocker, R., & Dibbon, D. (2008). *Teacher education in Canada: A baseline study.* Kelowna, BC: Society for the Advancement of Excellence in Education.

Darling-Hammond, L. (1999). *Teacher quality and student achievement: A review of state policy evidence.* Washington, DC: Center for the Study of Teaching and Policy.

Darling-Hammond, L. (2002). Learning to teach for social justice. In L. Darling-Hammond, J. French, & S. P. Garcia-Lopez (Eds.), *Learning to teach for social justice* (pp. 1–7). New York, NY: Teachers College Press.

Darling-Hammond, L. (2006). Assessing teacher education: The usefulness of multiple measures for assessing program outcomes. *Journal of Teacher Education, 57,* 120–138.

DeLuca, C. (2010). *Constructing a framework for the validation of complex program aims.* Unpublished doctoral dissertation, Kingston, ON, Queen's University.

Gerin-Lajoie, D. (2008). The issue of diversity in the Canadian educational context. In D. Gerin-Lajoie (Ed.), *Educators' discourses on student diversity in Can-*

ada: Context, policy, and practices (pp. 9–28). Toronto, Canada: Canadian Scholars' Press.

Hollins, E., & Torres-Guzman, M. E. (2005). Research on preparing teachers for diverse populations. In M. Cochran-Smith, & K. Zeichner (Eds.), *Studying teacher education: The report of the AERA panel on research and teacher education* (pp. 477–548). Mahwah, NJ: Erlbaum.

Howard, T. C., & Aleman, G. R. (2008). Teacher capacity for diverse learners: What do teachers need to know? In M. Cochran-Smith, S. Freiman-Nemser, D. J. McIntyre, & K. E. Demers (Eds.), *Handbook of research on teacher education: Enduring questions in changing contexts* (3rd ed., pp. 157–174). New York, NY: Routledge.

Hutchinson, N. L. (2010). *Inclusion of exceptional learners in Canadian schools: A practical handbook for teachers* (2nd ed.). Toronto, ON: Prentice-Hall.

Irvine, J. (2003). *Educating teachers for diversity: Seeing with a cultural eye.* New York, NY: Teachers College Press.

Keiser, D. L. (2005). Learners not widgets: Teacher education for social justice during transformational times. In N. M Michelli & D. L. Keiser (Eds.), *Teacher education for democracy and social justice* (pp. 31–56). New York, NY: Routledge.

Kosnik, C., & Beck, C. (2009). *Priorities in teacher education: The 7 key elements of pre-service preparation.* London: Routledge.

Ladson-Billings, G. J. (1995). Toward a theory of culturally relevant pedagogy. *American Education Research Journal, 35*, 465–491.

Mitchell, T. (2007). Critical service-learning as social justice education: A case study of the citizen scholars program. *Equity & Excellence in Education, 40*(2), 101–112.

Munby, H., Russell, T., Martin, A. K. (2001). Teachers' knowledge and how it develops. In V. Richardson (Ed.), *Handbook of research on teaching* (4th ed., pp. 877–904). Washington, DC: American Educational Research Association.

Nieto, S. (2000). Placing equity front and center: Some thoughts on transforming teacher education for a new century. *Journal of Teacher Education, 51*(3), 180–187.

Ontario Ministry of Education. (2009) *Ontario's equity and inclusive education strategy.* Toronto, ON: Author.

Philpott, R., & Beynon, J. (2005). Pause to reflect: Exploring teachers' notions of social responsibility. *Alberta Journal of Educational Research, 51*(1), 34–49.

Queen's University. (2009). *BEd/DipEd Program: Mission statement.* Retrieved from http://www.educ.queensu.ca/BEdDipEd.shtml

Retallick, J., Cocklin, B., & Coombe, K. (1999). Introduction. In J. Retallick, B. Cocklin, & K. Coombe (Eds.), *Learning communities in education: Issues, strategies and contexts* (pp. 1–6). London: Routledge.

Robinson, K. (1992). Class-room discipline: Power, resistance and gender: A look at teacher perspectives. *Gender and Education, 4*(3), 273–288.

Root, S., Anderson, J., Callahan, P., Duckenfield, M., Hill, D., Pickeral, T., & Wade, R. (2000). *Service-learning in teacher education: A handbook.* Retrieved from http://www2.alma.edu/academics/education/service/

Santoro, N. (2009). Teaching in culturally diverse contexts: What knowledge about "self" and "others" do teachers need? *Journal of Education for Teaching, 35*(1), 33–45.

Solomon, R. P. (2002). Reconstructing teacher education for education equity and diversity. In C. Reynolds & A. I. Griffith (Eds.), *Equity and globalization in education* (pp. 261–300). Calgary, AB: Detselig Enterprises.

Thorne, B. (1993). *Gender play: Girls and boys in school.* New Brunswick, NJ: Rutgers University Press.

Trifonas, P. (2003). Pedagogies of difference: Locating otherness. In P. Trifonas (Ed.), *Pedagogies of difference: Rethinking education for social change* (pp. 1–9). New York, NY: RoutledgeFalmer.

Valentine, G. (1997). "Oh yes I can" "oh no you can't": Children and parents' understandings of kids' competence to negotiate public space safely. *Antipode, 29*(1), 65–89.

Villegas, A. M., & Lucas, T. (2002). Preparing culturally responsive teachers. *Journal of Teacher Education, 53*(1), 20–32.

Wade, R. C. (2000). From a distance: Service-learning and social justice. In C. R. O'Grady (Ed.), *Integrating service learning and multicultural education in colleges and universities* (pp. 93–111). Mahwah, NJ: Erlbaum.

Webster-Wright, A. (2009). Reframing professional development through understanding authentic professional development. *Review of Educational Research, 79,* 702–739.

Zeichner, K. M., & Conklin, K. (2005). Teacher education programs. In M. Cochran-Smith & K. Zeichner (Eds.), *Studying teacher education: The report of the AERA panel on research and teacher education* (pp. 645–736). Mahwah, NJ: Erlbaum.

Zeichner, K. M., & Hoeft, K. (1996). Teacher socialization for cultural diversity. In J. Sikula, T. J. Buttery, & E. Guyton (Eds.), *Handbook of research on teacher education* (2nd ed., pp. 525–547). New York, NY: Macmillan.

CHAPTER 10

HELPING TEACHER CANDIDATES DEVELOP A CRITICAL PERSPECTIVE IN A FOUNDATIONS COURSE

A Freirian Look at How Teacher Candidates Interpret Their Service-Learning Experience

c. lynne hannah, Barri Tinkler, and Elizabeth Miller

> It is certain that men and women can change the world for the better, can make it less unjust, but they can do so only from the starting point of the concrete reality they "come upon" in their generation. They cannot do it on the basis of reveries, false dreams, or pure illusion. (Freire, 2004, p. 31)

Courses in the social, political, cultural, historical, and philosophical foundations of education in the United States are believed by many to help develop the critical thinking and problem solving skills of prospective teachers (Lukenchuk, 2009; Neumann, 2009; Pope & Stemhagen, 2008; Renner, Price, Keene, & Little, 2004). Despite overwhelming support for the importance of foundations of education courses, there are those who are calling for their removal from teacher education programs.

Critical Service Learning as a Revolutionary Pedagogy: A Project of Student Agency in Action, pp. 203–219

Neumann (2009) and Pope and Stemhagen (2008) discuss the current attacks on foundations of education courses as viable components of teacher education programs due in part to a renewed call for standardizing all aspects of education. In this "economic utility narrative" (Neumann, 2009, p. 82), the demand for increasingly pragmatic coursework is deemed important in order to prepare teachers who will implement a prepared curriculum that does not require teachers to question or reflect upon the goals of education or how to meet the needs of all students. We argue that a pragmatic stance to education de-intellectualizes what is essentially a highly intensive intellectual profession (Giroux, 1988). Critically reflective teachers do not blindly apply techniques in the classroom, instead they think carefully, examining the context of the learning situation, which includes the backgrounds of their students, as well as their skill level and content preparedness. In order to construct learning opportunities to meet the competing demands of the lesson at hand, critically reflective teachers do this both as they plan their lessons and while the lesson is in progress. Once the lesson is complete, critically reflective teachers examine the results of their teaching in terms of student feedback and achievement to determine how to proceed.

The knowledge that is part of foundations of education courses helps teacher candidates understand the many forces that affect education in schools including curriculum materials and their interplay with standards being tested by the school system in which teachers work. We want to ensure that these future teachers are prepared to make informed choices as they enact and help to develop policies in their classrooms and schools (Michie, 2009; Neumann, 2009). To that end, we developed a critical service-learning experience to incorporate in a Foundations of American Education course in order to promote an understanding of institutionalized racism, the "othering" of people based on socioeconomic status (SES), race, or ethnicity, and the unearned privilege systems from which teacher candidates may have benefited. We examine whether fostering reflection on these issues through an effective critical service-learning experience allows teacher candidates to understand the impact of unequal educational and economic opportunities and to critically examine their own learning experiences.

Paulo Freire (1971, 1998a, 1998b, 2004) calls on educators to acknowledge the political nature of education and the need to help students understand how institutions, including public schools, are designed to promote particular political ends. Students need tools to help them examine who profits from institutional structures that are in place and whose needs are not being met. Critical pedagogy provides some of the tools that citizens in a democracy need to actively participate in making informed decisions about the constantly changing nature of society. Because the nature of life constantly renews and changes, we need skills to move beyond the known; tools such as dialogue, problem posing, examining institutions for their underlying belief and benefit structures, unlearning, and dealing with ambiguity assist in this evolution (Freire, 1998a, 1971; Kellner, 2003; Kumashiro, 2000). Kellner also suggests that a "critical theory of education involves conceiving of what education could be" and Kumashiro argues that true learning only occurs through a crisis of unlearning past knowledge in order to move beyond what is already known.

Critical pedagogy as theorized by Paulo Freire (1971) also requires teachers to become students of their students. The issues, concerns, and understanding of the students we teach must infuse the curriculum. Through dialogue, students and teachers work to examine the students' world and to pose new problems to investigate. Students and teachers also develop transformational methods to interrupt oppression based upon their examination of existing power structures and the resulting institutionalized practices and values.

In a foundations course that examines the history of education, teacher candidates, the majority of whom are white, middle-class women, can hone their skills in becoming critical scholar-practitioners by examining the structures of sexual oppression that may have contributed to narrowing their career choices. This examination could provide a starting point for these teacher candidates to examine the unearned privileges they benefited from in terms of their education. Such an examination is difficult (Kumashiro, 2000); it requires an unlearning of the notion of meritocracy that is part of our country's ethos. Teacher candidates can learn skills for use in later life by discussing issues that are raised when looking at the history and foundations of education in the United States and posing problems that are illuminated by such a dialogue with others in their class.

In order to provide the lived experience that could enhance the conscientization of how institutionalized oppression, unearned privilege, and the "othering" of people based on race, ethnicity, and socioeconomic status affect schooling and learning, we added a critical service-learning component to our Foundations of American Education course. We believe that our teacher candidates need opportunities to examine not only their own educational experiences through historical and philosophical perspectives, but also to have a rare opportunity to learn about the educational experiences of students traditionally marginalized by institutionalized oppression. It is through this critical service-learning experience that some of the issues discussed in their foundations course can be codified (Freire, 1971) for deeper analysis. It is in field experiences, such as this one, when students with whom our teacher candidates work can tell their educational stories. These experiences may help our teacher candidates move from what Freire (as cited in Cammarota &

Romero, 2009) labels a naïve consciousness, a mindset where they assume that life situations are the result of family and cultural deficits to a critical consciousness where they "understand that living conditions derive from social and economic systems, structures, and institutions" (p. 468). The purpose of this study is to examine, through both qualitative and quantitative data analysis, whether the critical service-learning experience enhanced the conscientization of teacher candidates enrolled in the Foundations of American Education course and to determine whether the experience is appropriately labeled as critical service-learning.

Recent publications in service-learning reflect an emerging trend to differentiate types of service-learning based on intended outcomes. One strand that has emerged is critical service-learning. Critical service-learning refers to "academic service-learning experiences with a social justice orientation" (Mitchell, 2008, p. 51). From a review of selected works on critical service-learning, we identified five criteria for a basis of our analysis: (1) to examine, question, and transform alienating and oppressive aspects of schooling (Boyle-Baise & Langford, 2004; Daigre, 2000; Hart, 2006; Mitchell, 2008; Renner, Price, Keene, & Little, 2004); (2) to help students develop conscientization (Boyle-Baise & Langford, 2004; Daigre, 2000; Hart, 2006); (3) to develop skills in problem posing (Boyle-Baise & Langford, 2004; Hart, 2006); (4) to engage all the involved communities in determining goals, focus, and implementation of service (Boyle-Baise & Langford, 2004; Mitchell, 2008); (5) and to develop authentic long-term relationships among the members of all involved communities (Boyle-Baise & Langford, 2004; Daigre, 2000; Mitchell, 2008). Utilizing the literature on critical service-learning and Freire's construct of conscientization, the first and second authors developed specific goals for the service experience embedded in the Foundations of American Education course. These critical service-learning goals state that teacher candidates will: (a) critically reflect on how their backgrounds as people with unearned privileges (SES, ethnicity, first language) affected their success in schools, (b) participate in educational dialogues with students marginalized by their ethnicity, first language, or SES to help codify education issues raised in the course content, and (c) increase their experiences with students marginalized by their ethnicity, first language, or SES. This study examines whether we attained these goals.

METHODS AND PARTICIPANTS

Once again, there is no such thing as teaching without research and research without teaching. One inhabits the body of the other. As I teach, I continue to search and re-search. I teach because I search, because I ques-

> tion, and because I submit myself to questioning. I research because I notice things, take cognizance of them. And in so doing, I intervene. And intervening, I educate and educate myself. I do research so as to know what I do not yet know and to communicate and proclaim what I discover. (Freire, 1998a, p. 35)

In order to determine whether the critical service-learning experience met the goals we identified for the experience, the authors examined two data sets, one quantitative and one qualitative. The qualitative data set came from two sections of the Foundations of American Education course taught by the second author. There were 37 students, 9 male, 28 female, ranging in age from late teens to early 30s. In the instructor's absence, the first author introduced the research study to the class and handed out the consent to participate forms. The university students were assured that their decision about whether to participate or not was confidential and the instructor would not know who agreed to participate until after grades were submitted. Thus, lack of participation could not affect their grade. Out of 39 students, 37 agreed to participate. Data sources include an anonymous questionnaire with open-ended response items, and interviews with six teacher candidates who expressed their willingness to be interviewed on the consent form. These interviews took place in the summer following the class, after grades were submitted. The first and second authors coded the interview transcripts utilizing characteristics of critical service-learning. The second author also coded the anonymous questionnaire using these same characteristics.

The quantitative data set came from two sections of the Foundations of American Education course taught by the second author in a semester subsequent to the collection of the qualitative data set. There were 35 participants, 28 female and 7 male. Of the 35 participants, 33 self-identified as European American, one identified as Native American, and one identified as multiracial. Ages of the participants ranged from 18 to 44, but 30 of the 35 participants were 18–19 years of age. In the instructor's absence, the first author introduced the research study to the class and handed out the consent to participate forms. Once again, the university students were assured that the decision about whether to participate or not was confidential and the instructor would not know who participated and who did not. The third author assigned each participant a number, and this corresponding list of names and numbers was not provided to the second author.

The third author administered the Munroe Multicultural Attitude Scale Questionnaire (MASQUE) at the beginning and end of the semester. The questionnaire administered at the end also included an open-ended response item. The MASQUE (Munroe & Pearson, 2006) is designed to measure students' knowledge and understanding of various facets of diversity as well as their willingness to act on issues of injustice. All but one student out of 42 agreed to participate in the research; however, only 35 participants completed both surveys. The third author coded the surveys and completed statistical analyses. In addition, the second author coded the open-ended response items on the final survey.

THE COURSE

> Another kind of knowledge whose existence I cannot doubt for a moment in my critical educative practice is that education, as a specifically human experience, is a form of intervention in the world.... Education never was, is not, and never can be neutral or indifferent in regard to the reproduction of the dominant ideology or the interrogation of it. It is a fundamental error to state that education is simply an instrument for the reproduction of the dominant ideology, as it is an error to consider it no more than an instrument for unmasking that ideology as if such a task were something that could be accomplished simplistically, fundamentally without obstacles and difficult struggles. (Freire, 1998a, pp. 90–91)

Teacher candidates in this program complete only one course in social foundations. This course is titled the Foundations of American Education and addresses the historical, philosophical, sociological, and political foundations of schooling in the United States. This is the second course that candidates take in the program, the first being a general introduction to teaching and orientation to the program, and is usually taken during the freshman or sophomore year of course-work. After completion of this social foundations course, candidates complete a course in psychological foundations that also addresses how social contexts affect learning. Though the general goals of our Foundations of American Education course are to aid teacher candidates in their understanding of the historical, philosophical, and sociological foundations of the field of education, we also specify goals in relation to social justice and critical pedagogy. The course seeks to foster awareness of oppression based on color, culture, disability, ethnicity, gender, language, religion, sex, sexual orientation, and socioeconomic status. In addition to supporting teacher candidates in developing problem posing strategies, instructors seek to foster dispositions committed to interrupting oppression so that the needs of all students can be met.

In order to promote a context for rich and meaningful discussion, the teacher candidates read a variety of materials. There are three main texts for the course, *Experience and Education* (Dewey, 1938/1997), *Rethinking Our Classrooms: Teaching for Equity and Justice* (Au, Bigelow, & Karp, 2007;

Bigelow, Christensen, Karp, Miner, & Peterson, 1994; Bigelow, Harvey, Karp, & Miller, 2001), and *Educational Foundations: Diverse Histories, Diverse Perspectives* by Grace Huerta (2009). Dewey's work provides a theoretical basis to ground the critical perspective on learning (Hart, 2006; Kellner, 2003) while the *Rethinking Our Classrooms* readings present tangible experiences by teachers who reflect upon their attempts at social justice education. The text by Huerta (2009) works from Banks' (2004) transformative perspective and integrates diverse perspectives throughout the traditional topics covered in social foundations courses, such as the history of public schooling in America, philosophical origins of teaching, school governance and finance, sociological influences on schooling, and current educational issues and reforms. Besides these primary texts, teacher candidates also read various research articles and essays such as McIntosh's (1990) "Unpacking the Invisible Knapsack," and a chapter from Kozol's (1991) book, *Savage Inequalities*. Teacher candidates reflect upon these readings through guided discussions and reading reflections. Candidates write weekly reading reflections that require them to analyze the readings and make connections to their own experiences in schools.

Critical Service-Learning Experience

At the beginning of the 2002 academic year, the education director of the local Job Corps facility approached the first author, who was the chair of the Department of Education at that time. He wanted to place our teacher education candidates at the Job Corps facility to tutor his students from regional urban areas, such as Washington, DC, and Baltimore, Maryland, as well as those from the surrounding rural areas who were working on their high school diploma or their GED. Since we sought strategies to assist teacher candidates in developing a critical perspective, we decided to require our teacher candidates and other university students who enroll in our Foundations of American Education course (students with a minor in Education) to tutor the Job Corps students at their facility on five separate occasions totaling at least 10 hours. The goals of the critical service-learning component of the course stem from the overall course goals, but are directly linked to the service experience. The critical service-learning goals, developed by the first and second authors, state that teacher candidates will: (a) critically reflect on how their backgrounds as people with unearned privileges (SES, ethnicity, first language) affected their success in schools, (b) participate in educational dialogues with students marginalized by their ethnicity, first language, or SES to help codify education issues raised in the course content, and (c) increase their experiences with students marginalized by their ethnicity, first language, or SES.

With help from the Office of Community Service and Service-Learning on our campus, we institutionalized this experience as a critical service-learning opportunity, albeit a course requirement. While some argue that "forced volunteerism" changes the nature from service to coercion (Forbes, Garber, Kensinger, & Slagter, 1999), we believe the circumstances of this field experience mitigate against this. Our teacher candidates spend over 120 hours in different schools prior to their student teaching semester. Faculty tailor each field experience to flow from the content and goals of the corresponding course; therefore, in a class that examines educational foundations, we encourage our teacher candidates to learn from the Job Corps students why and how these institutional structures can be problematic.

As semesters went by, we heard more and more from our teacher candidates that while they initially were intimidated about venturing out to this facility to work with the students at Job Corps, at the end of the semester they were excited, energized, and expressed that they learned a great deal from the experience, particularly in terms of understanding how their experiences in schools were typically very different than the experiences of students at Job Corps. These positive anecdotal reports represented, by far, the majority of comments we received. Teacher candidates not only expressed these sentiments in their final course activities, such as in the writing and sharing of the critical service-learning reflection, but also in their anonymous critical service-learning evaluations which were administered like course evaluations and shared with instructors and the Office of Community Service and Service-Learning after the completion of the semester.

Anecdotal reports from the education director of the Job Corps facility and the Job Corps students involved indicated that this tutoring exercise was a positive experience for the students at Job Corps as well. In the spring semester of 2006, we started a "meet and greet" event at the Job Corps site to introduce the university tutors to the facility. In addition, in the fall semester of 2006, we decided to bring Job Corps students along with the education director to campus to introduce teacher candidates to the tutoring task. Based on the positive response of the teacher candidates, this visit became a routine part of the course. The young men and women from Job Corps who come to speak to the candidates realize that many of our teacher candidates are afraid of the task ahead of them, whether it is tutoring students so close in age to themselves (for many) or working with students of color, and they seek to dispel some of these fears by addressing them head on. The students from the Job Corps facility also emphasize how important this tutoring is to many of them as they strive to complete their high school diplomas, thus prompting the teacher candidates to take seriously their responsibility to their Job Corps tutees.

While these anecdotal reports were heartening, we wanted to know whether or not our program helped our teacher candidates understand the impact of the institutional structures they examined in their readings. We needed to know if we succeeded in developing a critical service-learning project, or if we had in fact developed a structure that maintained the status quo in terms of our teacher candidates believing that the problems faced by the Job Corps students stemmed from individual deficits. If we examine the five criteria of critical service-learning projects identified in the literature, we assert that this project already meets two of them. We have maintained this experience over the past 8 years, with all teacher candidates and other students (students with an education minor) in both regular semesters and summer sessions participating in this component of the course. This long-term relationship has evolved over those 8 years with different discernable milestones. In the first instance, the director's visits to our university to explain the nature of the experience developed into Job Corps students coming to introduce the experience; in the second, field trips for the entire group of university participants to tour the facilities and meet many of the participants progressed to the addition of Job Corps students coming to campus to debrief with the university classes on what was happening in the tutoring sessions and how the entire experience could be improved. Thus, the community into which we place our teacher candidates is actively involved in determining the goals, focus, and implementation of the critical service-learning component. However, since we also sought to examine whether or not the tutoring that our teacher candidates completed was meeting the critical service-learning goals we identified for the course, we conducted a study that asked the university students to report on their experiences.

FINDINGS

> The learning of those who teach ... is observed to the extent that, humble and open, teachers find themselves continually ready to rethink what has been thought and to revise their positions. (Freire, 1998b, p. 17)

Analysis of the qualitative data set demonstrates that the goals we identified for the critical service-learning experience were met to varying degrees. However, analysis of the quantitative data from the MASQUE survey yields inconclusive results. Though responses to the open-ended question included on the MASQUE postsurvey point to the impact of the critical service-learning experience, there were no statistically significant results between the items on the pre- and postsurvey. On the presurvey, many of the respondents rated themselves high on their knowledge of various aspects of diversity and their willingness to act in response to injustice leaving little room to demonstrate a statistically significant change in these areas. In fact, some respondents rated themselves lower on the postsurvey than they did on the presurvey. Since responses to the open-ended question demonstrate an increase in knowledge, we are left wondering whether the respondents' confidence in their knowledge and understanding of issues around diversity was challenged during the semester.

Critical Reflection on Unearned Privilege

The first goal for the critical service-learning experience requires our university students to critically reflect on how their backgrounds as people with unearned privileges (SES, ethnicity, first language) had an impact on their success in schools. Analysis of the qualitative data (both the interviews and the questionnaire) demonstrates that many of the participants developed an increased awareness of inequities in education. On the open-ended questionnaire, 28% of the students commented on these inequities in response to a question about what they learned from the course. One student wrote, "I see the results of inequalities in education." In addition, seven respondents made comments on the open-ended question on the MASQUE survey that demonstrate they were examining inequities in education and how these inequities impact achievement. One student wrote,

> At Job Corps, many aspects of our education system were changed in my mind. I began to understand that some students didn't just fail because they were stupid but because of other reasons. I really think this experience will help me better impact the education system.

Though the data demonstrate that students had an increase in awareness of inequities, only a few respondents articulated their recognition of their unearned privilege. Three students commented on their advantages in the qualitative questionnaire. One wrote, "I'm more grateful for my own education." However, all six of the interview participants verbalized impressions indicating they were critically reflecting on how their backgrounds had an impact on their success in schools. One participant stated,

> Even though I myself grew up in a somewhat impoverished situation, not as extreme as others I've seen, I still went to a good school district. And so I can't say that I felt that social impact ... whereas a child in inner-city D.C? I had no clue that the schools were that deplorable. I had no clue ... and it

> quite frankly really upset me to think about what daily message that's sending to them about their value in society.

Another interviewee stated,

> That really opens up my eyes to [the fact that] not everybody is like me ... not everybody has the same resources as I do.... It was a small school district, but like I said it was funded; we had support.... I definitely benefited.... It made me realize I'm very fortunate ... and it really made me appreciate the foundation I had, and it makes me kind of want to do that for students because I know that affected me positively.

Dialogue With Students Marginalized by Ethnicity, First Language, SES

In terms of the second goal for the critical service-learning project, that participating in educational dialogues with students marginalized by ethnicity, first language, SES helped codify education issues raised in their Foundations of American Education course, data from the qualitative questionnaire, interviews, and open-ended question on the MASQUE survey demonstrate that this goal was met. On the qualitative questionnaire, students were asked whether the service-learning experience helped them understand the issues that were studied in the course, and 97% of the participants responded yes. One student wrote, "By talking to students at Job Corps, I learned much more about the difficult issues in education."

All six of the interviewees indicated that participating in these educational dialogues helped codify topics examined in the Foundations of American Education course. Two of the students talked about the ideas in general terms. One student stated, "You can read about it all [you] wanted ... but really going out and doing it helped you understand." Another participant said, "Some of the topics in class ... weren't all registering until I witnessed them first hand in Job Corps.... The experience went hand in hand with what we were learning in the classroom." Other students were more specific about the topics that were codified for them,

> We talked a lot about funding, and I know several times you asked us to actually ask [the Job Corps students] about that ... the conversation [was] important because if I wouldn't have gotten to talk with the kids who went to inner-city Baltimore, inner-city D.C., and they said, "Oh yeah, we didn't have new textbooks, we didn't have all the resources," I don't think I would have really kind of comprehended that whole idea.

Five of the interviewees also made statements indicating that dialogue with their tutees at Job Corps had an impact on their thinking in relation to diversity and education. One participant stated,

> I met a really nice girl, she speaks Ethiopian and taught me to say, "hello." She told me a lot about her country and that whole experience ... really opened my eyes to students coming in from several different countries, different [language] backgrounds.

On the postsurvey administration of the MASQUE, respondents were asked to identify what portion of the semester's work had the biggest impact on their thoughts about diversity. Response options included: course readings, class discussion, tutoring at Job Corps, another college class in which you are currently enrolled, or other (participants were asked to explain this choice). Sixteen (46%) of the respondents selected tutoring at Job Corps, and three selected other and wrote in "all of the above." When asked to explain their choice, one student wrote, "Witnessing and listening to the students at Job Corps showed me how these things really do exist even though we don't want to believe it."

Increase Experiences With Students Marginalized by Ethnicity, First Language, SES

The final goal of the service-learning project was to increase our teacher candidates' experiences with students marginalized by ethnicity, first language, and SES. On the first administration of the MASQUE survey, respondents were asked to categorize their previous experience with diversity; 12% categorized themselves as having "extensive experience," 60% selected "some experience," and 22% chose "very little experience." On the postadministration of the MASQUE survey, 10 respondents (29%) commented on their limited experience with diversity. One respondent wrote, "It's one thing to talk or read about diversity but yet another to be submerged in it." Five of the respondents also commented on the fact that they were the minority at Job Corps. One respondent wrote, "Instead of fitting into the crowd, I stuck out, and it was a total role-reversal and culture shock."

The qualitative data set also provides evidence that the critical service-learning project was the first significant experience with diversity for many of the university students in that group. On the qualitative questionnaire, 33% of the participants described the experience as unique. One student wrote, "It was the first experience I had with a diverse group." All six of the students who were interviewed described having limited experiences with diversity during their K–12 education, though two of the students reported that they gained experiences with diversity in other life settings. One student stated, "I'll be completely honest with you, in my school district we had no African American students."

Not only did the critical service-learning experience provide many of the university students with their first significant experience with diversity, it also assisted them in their development as teachers. When participants were asked on the questionnaire if their experience at Job Corps provided them with a better understanding of how to work with students from diverse backgrounds, 82% responded yes. Of the students who responded no, three described having had previous experiences with diversity. Though most students felt the experience provided them with a stronger understanding of working with diverse students, there were some students who wrote statements that demonstrated that in some ways the experience may have been miseducative. One student wrote, "It made me realize how diverse the world is, and how that diversity leads to prejudice and racism. It's my job to help stop the diversity." Though it is difficult to discern what the student intended with this comment, since it seems odd to talk about stopping diversity, we read this to mean that the student felt that focusing attention on diversity leads to prejudice and racism. This raises questions as to what this student learned from this experience.

Raising a Critical Consciousness

We found evidence in the interviews that the experience of tutoring at the Job Corps facility during the course also helped to raise a more critical perspective in looking at educational situations. One interviewee stated, "[Foundations of American Education students] get to see the effects on children from communities that don't have the proper funding in their school system, that fall through all the cracks, and that it's not the teacher's fault, that there's more to it than [that]." Several students took a more critical look at themselves and their perspectives. One student noted, "It changed my ideas. It's sad for me to come to terms with it, but I guess I was close-minded and I followed or thought of the normal stereotypes of different diversities.... It just ... made me open-minded." And another student expressed a similar notion,

> It really did make me aware of preconceived notions that I had that I need to make sure I eliminate.... I was expecting lower income minorities.... I don't want to think that it's a prejudice that I have, but it was definitely a preconceived notion that I have. I now know that I need to rethink everything that I'm doing before I do it just to make sure.

One student articulated, what for us, is an essential component of critical pedagogy, being a student of your students (Freire, 1971, 1998a, 1998b). She stated,

> Our church youth group did a lot with that, but that was in small spurts and it was, "oh, we're here to visit and look at you and see how you're different," not "we're here to visit and learn how we can change each other."

WHAT DID WE LEARN?

> The best starting point for such reflections is the unfinishedness of our human condition. It is in this consciousness that the very possibility of learning, of being educated, resides. (Freire, 1998a, p. 66)

As we try to make sense out of what we have learned about our success or failure to incorporate a critical service-learning component in our Foundations of American Education course, we return to our service-learning goals and their intersection with the criteria for critical service-learning projects identified in the literature. As stated above, we believe we have already met the last two criteria for critical service-learning projects. Over the past eight years, a continuing dialogue among the Job Corps education director, the Job Corps students, the director of the Office of Community Service and Service-Learning, and the Department of Education faculty and administrators has strengthened the ties among these constituents and afforded more effective learning opportunities for the Job Corps students and the teacher education candidates.

We see a connection between the need to examine, question, and transform alienating and oppressive aspects of schooling and our goal to help teacher candidates codify education issues by participating in dialogues with students marginalized by ethnicity, first language and SES. If any transformation of oppressive structures is going to be possible, teachers who have not experienced oppression must recognize how unexamined schooling practices may alienate their students. The university students we surveyed and the teacher candidates we interviewed articulate the value in their Job Corps experience in helping them come to a better understanding of issues raised in their Foundations of American Education course. For many students in urban centers and rural areas, a lack of funding contributes to decreased educational resources. Many of the interviewees identified that the impact of funding inequities was made clearer by their conversations with their tutees. We suspect that education funding is one aspect of schooling that remains invisible to many students because they construct their understandings of what services school systems provide from their years in school. Learning about others' experiences in schools without similar resources moves the teacher candidates beyond their single story (Adichie, 2009) about educational opportunities and how they affect learning.

We believe that one way to help students develop conscientization is through critical reflection on their backgrounds as people with unearned privileges (SES, ethnicity, first language) and how that affected their success in schools. The responses to both the open-ended question on the survey and the interviews indicate that our participants were beginning to engage in this process. This is never an easy undertaking. Our own experiences become normalized through multiple exposures and lack of examples to the contrary, and thus, it takes a crisis of learning about alternatives to our own experiences to promote learning and unlearning (Kumashiro, 2000). As one of our interviewees stated in response to the question about the benefits of the critical service-learning project at Job Corps, "I think there are lots of benefits because … it makes you uncomfortable and when you're uncomfortable you're more likely to adapt." Once our understanding of schooling processes is expanded beyond our own experiences, we may then be able to conceive of new learning opportunities that engage, excite, and empower all students (Kellner, 2003).

It is through developing an awareness of inequitable education that teacher candidates are able to question why things are the way they are, instead of accepting the status quo. Requiring our teacher candidates to tutor students who are marginalized by their ethnicity, first language, or SES can promote problem-posing skills for future critical examination. For many of our university students, this was their first significant experience with students who are marginalized. We want our teacher candidates to learn how to talk *with* learners (Freire, 1998b). This starts the process of having teacher candidates look critically at issues of social justice. It also stresses the importance of understanding the background of their students as a dynamic and dialogic component of effective teaching, becoming a student of their students (Freire, 1971, 1998a, 1998b).

WHERE DO WE GO FROM HERE?

> There could be no creativity without the curiosity that moves us and sets us patiently impatient before a world that we did not make, to add to it something of our own making…. [O]ne of the essential tasks of progressive educational praxis is the promotion of a curiosity that is critical, bold, and adventurous. A type of curiosity that can defend us from the excess of a rationality that now inundates our highly technologized world. (Freire, 1998a, p. 38)

Despite the lack of significant results in the quantitative data, the intriguing change in some respondents actually rating themselves lower in their knowledge on the postsurvey than on the presurvey is suggestive of them becoming aware of, or grappling with, what they do not know. This requires further study in order to determine whether tutoring at Job Corps makes teacher candidates aware of their lack of knowledge. In this age of increasing exposure to computerized and media images from around the world that potentially perpetuate existing stereotypes, all of us can be lured into a false sense of our own cultural awareness. We would like to survey our teacher candidates in their very first professional education course, at the end of their Foundations of American Education course where the critical service-learning occurs, and several times later in their program to see if we discover any trends in their understanding of diversity. The actual experiences with their Job Corps students may help to dispel the stereotypes promoted by these media.

We remain convinced that foundations courses in teacher education programs are excellent sites for a field experience that promotes conscientization of oppression in education. Since these courses examine why schools are organized in particular formats and how curriculum is mandated for teachers to use and learners to be tested upon, they encourage an analysis of the impact of educational institutions on learners. Foundations courses can prepare teacher candidates to critically examine the mandates handed down from higher authorities and the impact these mandated structures have on all of their students. With this knowledge at hand, these new teachers may be able to resist the "undertow ... to abandon [their] belief that public schools can be transformed" (Michie, 2009, p. 709) and instead be able to articulate how their teaching choices interrupt and eliminate oppressive practices and thus promote effective learning for all of their students (Neumann, 2009).

Incorporating critical service-learning is just a start. To have teacher candidates develop a critical perspective, experiences such as this one at Job Corps must be available throughout their university experience. Due to credit hour constraints, our teacher education program has only one course in the social foundations of education. This course focuses on the history, philosophies, and sociopolitical aspects of education in the United States. Faculty are charged with infusing issues of diversity and social justice, students with exceptionalities, and technology throughout all of the professional education courses. The form these three strands take in each course depends upon the faculty member teaching the course. The professional education courses that follow the Foundations of American Education have required field components in public classrooms. While these field components can provide a laboratory for examining what is being taught and how the students' reactions to the curriculum can impact learning, again this requires the faculty member's attention to helping the teacher candidates go beyond observing to questioning what they see and how it relates to their own experiences with institutionalized structures. While some of the faculty infuse issues of social justice in their courses, other faculty focus more on issues of diversity without utilizing a critical perspective. Of the ten tenure track faculty who were at our institution during the year we started the service-learning project with Job Corps, only two remain. With at least a 40% turn over rate in our department and a commitment to academic freedom, it is not possible to mandate a social justice focus among our faculty, which then raises challenges in fostering a social justice perspective in our teacher candidates.

Challenging teacher candidates' views of the world and their place of privilege in it during one course may not, in most cases, lead to continued critical reflection or ongoing concerns about social justice in education. We want to make sure that teacher candidates develop dispositions for learning how to become effective problem posers alongside their students in order to challenge and interrupt oppression in education and society. As Donald Macedo writes in the "Forward" to Paulo Freire's (1998a) *Pedagogy of Freedom*,

> The real issue is to understand one's privileged position in the process of helping so as not to, on the one hand, turn help into a type of missionary paternalism and, on the other hand, limit the possibilities for the creation of structures that lead to real empowerment. (p. xxix)

QUESTIONS FOR REFLECTION

1. Is a project that takes place over one semester enough to initiate the process of conscientization?
2. In the realm of academic freedom, how do we develop a project that can be sustained over multiple instructors and years?
3. How can we expand the social justice outcomes of the critical service-learning project?
4. In what ways can we develop structures to facilitate the forging of authentic relationships that may last beyond the semester of work?
5. Do university students have an inflated sense of what they know about diversity?

ACKNOWLEDGMENTS

The authors express their sincere appreciation to Keith Leverett, Holly Frye, and the students at Job Corps for their guidance and support for our work in critical service-learning. We also wish to thank Melanie Goldsborough and Dr. Alan Tinkler for their assistance in the preparation of this chapter.

REFERENCES

Adichie, C. (2009). *The danger of a single story.* Retrieved from http://www.ted.com/talks/chimamanda_adichie_the_danger_of_a_single_story.html

Au, W., Bigelow, B., & Karp, S. (Eds.). (2007). *Rethinking our classrooms: Teaching for equity and justice* (Vol. 1, New ed.). Milwaukee, WI: Rethinking Schools.

Banks, J. A. (2004). Multicultural education: Historical development, dimensions, and practice. In J. A. Banks & C.A. M. Banks (Eds.), *Handbook of research on multicultural education* (2nd ed., pp. 3–29). San Francisco, CA: Jossey-Bass.

Bigelow, B., Christensen, L., Karp, S., Miner, B., & Peterson, B. (Eds.). (1994). *Rethinking our classrooms: Teaching for equity and justice.* Milwaukee, WI: Rethinking Schools.

Bigelow, B., Harvey, B., Karp, S., & Miller, L. (Eds.). (2001). *Rethinking our classrooms: Teaching for equity and justice* (Vol. 2). Milwaukee, WI: Rethinking Schools.

Boyle-Baise, M., & Langford, J. (2004). There are children here: Service learning for social justice. *Equity & Education, 37*, 55–66.

Cammarota, J., & Romero, A. F. (2009). The social justice education project: A critically compassionate intellectualism for Chicana/o students. In W. Ayers, T. Quinn, & D. Stovall (Eds.), *Handbook of social justice in education* (pp. 465–476). New York, NY: Routledge.

Daigre, E. (2000). Toward a critical service-learning pedagogy: A Freirean approach to civic literacy. *Academic Exchange Quarterly.* Retrieved from http://www.thefreelibrary.com/_/print/PrintArticle.aspx?id=68362994

Dewey, J. (1938/1997). *Experience and education.* New York, NY: Touchstone.

Forbes, K., Garger, L., Kensinger, L., & Slagter, J. T. (1999). Punishing pedagogy: The failings of forced volunteerism. *Women's Studies Quarterly, 27*(3 & 4), 158–168.

Freire, P. (1971). *Pedagogy of the oppressed.* New York, NY: Herder & Herder.

Freire, P. (1998a). *Pedagogy of freedom: Ethics, democracy, and civic courage.* New York, NY: Rowman & Littlefield.

Freire, P. (1998b). *Teachers as cultural workers: Letters to those who dare teach.* Boulder, CO: Westview.

Freire, P. (2004). *Pedagogy of indignation.* London: Paradigm.

Giroux, H. A. (1988). *Teachers as intellectuals: Toward a critical pedagogy of learning.* New York, NY: Bergin & Garvey.

Hart, S. (2006) Breaking literacy boundaries through critical service-learning: Education for the silenced and marginalized. *Mentoring & Tutoring, 14*(1), 17–32.

Huerta, G.C. (2009). *Educational foundations: Diverse histories, diverse perspectives.* Boston, MA: Houghton Mifflin.

Kellner, D. (2003). *Toward a critical theory of education.* Retrieved from http://www.gseis.ucla.edu/faculty/kellner/papers/dCT2003.htm#_edn1

Kozol, J. (1991). *Savage inequalities: Children in America's schools.* New York, NY: Crown.

Kumashiro, K. K. (2000). Teaching and learning through desire, crisis, and difference: Perverted reflections on anti-oppressive education. *Radical Teacher, 58,* 6–11.

Lukenchuk, A. (2009). Living the ethics of responsibility through university service and service-learning: Phronesis and praxis reconsidered. *Philosophical Studies in Education, 40,* 246–257

McIntosh, P. (1990). White privilege: Unpacking the invisible knapsack. *Independent School, 49*(2), 32–35.

Michie, G. (2009). Teaching in the undertow: Resisting the pull of schooling-as-usual. In W. Ayers, T. Quinn, & D. Stovall (Eds.), *Handbook of social justice in education* (pp. 705–710). New York, NY: Routledge.

Mitchell, T. D. (2008). Traditional vs. critical service-learning: Engaging the literature to differentiate two models. *Michigan Journal of Community Service Learning, 14*(2), 50–65.

Munroe, A., & Pearson, C. (2006). The Munroe multicultural attitude scale questionnaire: A new instrument for multicultural studies. *Educational and Psychological Measurement, 66*(5), 819–834.

Neumann, R. (2009). Highly qualified teachers and the social foundations of education. *Kappan, 91*(3), 81–85.

Pope, N. S., & Stemhagen, K. (2008). Social foundations educators of the world unite! An action plan for disciplinary advocacy. *Educational Studies, 44,* 247–255.

Renner, A., Price, L., Keene, K., & Little, S. (2004) Service learning, multicultural/antiracist education, and the social foundations of education: Weaving a cultural studies pedagogy and praxis in an accelerated teacher education program. *Educational Studies, 35,* 137–157.

CHAPTER 11

LIVING IN RIVERHILL

A Postcritical Challenge to the Production of a Neoliberal Success Story

Allison Daniel Anders and Jessica Nina Lester

BEGINNINGS

Since 2008, we have worked[1] in the afternoons as tutors with Burundian children in a small city in Appalachia[2] in the rural South of the United States. The families with whom we work have come from refugee camps in rural areas in Tanzania. Having fled first to the Congo and Rwanda from violence between Tutsi and Hutu identified people in 1972, and then to Tanzania in 1994 during the Rwandan genocide, these Burundians living in Riverhill[3] are transitioning to their third country of settlement. Burundians began arriving in the United States in 2007 after Tanzanian policies restricted opportunities for refugees to gain access to naturalization and property rights (UNHCR, 2008). Although the camps from which they left were located in rural areas of Tanzania, Riverhill, though situated in what we describe as the rural South and sometimes Appalachia, is radically different. Many of the Burundians live in apartments in public housing projects and all of them face a small, predominantly White,

Critical Service Learning as a Revolutionary Pedagogy: A Project of Student Agency in Action, pp. 223–249

monolingual, ethno-centric, industrialized city that provides limited resources, and limited public transportation. Our work with the children began with a social justice and education course through which we began English as a Second Language (ESL) tutoring.

This chapter is about the work of understanding our experiences of reading and living in Riverhill. As we reflect on what we tell here as our beginning and share our journeys with critical service-learning, we find that postcritical ethnography (Noblit, Flores, & Murillo, 2004) resonates most with us in the way we understand ourselves. A postcritical orientation moves with us across this chapter in many ways. Our commitments to postcritical work provide us with a way to frame our situatedness and our ethnographic research. Postcritical work requires an interrogation of power across structure, discourse, and practice, recursive reflexivity, and whenever possible, relationships of reciprocity in work with community and research. Additionally, postcritical orientations reflect moral preferences.

> Postcritical ethnographies in an important sense are not designed but enacted or produced as moral activity. Postcritical ethnographers then must assume they exist within a critical discourse that in part makes them responsible for the world they are producing when they interpret and critique. (Noblit et al., 2004, p. 24)

Acknowledging both the critical discourses in which we find ourselves situated and the responsibilities we must take up in the production of our work, reflects the "post" and the "critical" of "postcritical." The "critical" in postcritical ethnography reflects the idea that "social life is constructed in contexts of power" and the "post" in "postcritical" refers to postmodern and poststructural work, which explicitly "rejects a claim to objective knowledge" (Noblit et al., 2004, p. 18). Coupled together, "postcritical" frames work with implicit and explicit commitments to understanding power and to productions of knowledge that are always already contextualized through discourses (Habermas, 1988) and thus, fail to reflect an objective reality. If objective representations do not exist, then the work of representation ought to include the positionality of the researcher, the practice of reflexivity across the work, and transparency about choices regarding coding and analysis (Guba, 2981; Lather, 1986).

We endeavor to practice these things here as a postcritical orientation informs the way we spend time with the children and our reflections about that time. We introduce the resonance we feel with postcritical work here, so that you may engage with its shadows and frames as we represent this work.

We invite you to join us as we share some of our experiences as ESL tutors, as a doctoral candidate (Jessica) studying in applied educational psychology and as a faculty member working in cultural studies in education (Allison), from the elementary school classroom where we read and work with the children to their homes, from quiet seminar rooms at the university to performances (Warren, 2001) in meeting spaces about "service learning," "mental health," and "educational placement."[4] Recursively reflecting on our work as ESL tutors and these performances in informal and formal spaces has provided us with opportunities to recount our experiences (Bowers, 1986) with one another and deepen our understandings and practice with community. So, first, in this chapter, we will introduce ourselves, the way we frame whatever it is that we do. Second, we will tackle the messiness of what we do and how our experiences and the children's get lost in translation. Third, we ask how we might invite others to join us in what we do, and analyze the dominant response of decline and disinclination we receive when we extend the invitation.

We share three stories constructed from the NVivo and sociogically constructed coding and analysis of field notes (Coffey & Atkinson, 1996), field journals, and our own weekly communication about experiences in the public housing project, meetings, and e-mails. Our use of stories throughout the chapter reflects our argument that narrative works to complicate and deepen understandings and opens new spaces for new imaginings (Ferguson, 2000; Noblit, 1999; Noblit et al., 2004). As we represent what we do, we consider carefully lived experience (de Certeau, 1984), which for us is always already situated, the intersectionality of our own identities (Crenshaw, 1991), and the privileged mobility we have as we move across several spaces in multiple communities in Riverhill. In these ways, we share the positioning of our knowledges and our work by others, and ourselves, and signal with this text a defiance narrative with Derrick Bell's (1992) work on the permanence of racism.

Although a postcritical orientation remains powerful for us, as we do this layered work (Bochner, 2009) and as we share this work here, we resist constructing what we do as a success story (Bell, 1992). Racial realists, and in particular Derrick Bell, have taught us much about resisting success stories, which are most often produced and consumed by dominant Whites and people of privilege (Anders & Jay, 2010). We invite you, as the reader, to join us in what we have come to view as "the necessary if unglamorous world of organizing, of reframing debates and dialogues at every level, of challenging the insistent dogma of common sense, of beginning political education, of enacting self-change and taking a movement from the bottom up" (Ayers, 2009, p. 388); we invite you to question even here the way we frame these stories. Last, since our positions on the permanence of racism affect, in particular, what we do methodologically and how we respond emotionally, we take space here to share more about our positionalities (Aretxaga, 1997; Noblit et al., 2004), so that you may make more informed decisions about where you see us taking this telling of our experiences and where we do not.

A POSTCRITICAL ORIENTATION AND POSITIONALITY

> These days I live in three worlds: my dreams, and the experiences of my new life, which trigger memories from the past.
>
> —*A Long Way Gone,* Ishmael Beah, 2007

As we spend time with children, reflect, and write about that time with a postcritical orientation, we use an emic perspective. We actively seek "multiple perspectives" and "competing beliefs" as we try to understand "the way lives are lived and their implications for social relations" (Noblit & Engel, 1999, p. 54). As a part of recursive reflexive work, interrogating our positionalities is critical. As such, we share below some of the ways in which we have come to what we do and who we bring with us when we do it.

In the fall of 2008, I (Allison) taught a service-learning course on social justice and education, providing graduate students with an opportunity to study systemic inequities in education and tutor children and adults with refugee status. The winter before the course I had met with Greenland, the refugee sponsorship agency in the area and an ESL teacher who was worried about a small group of Burundian children who attended the elementary school where she taught. The children lived in a nearby public housing project where about fifty of the first 130 Burundians to resettle in the area had been placed. I worked with the ESL teacher and the ESL director from Greenland to match the children with course participants who would complete ESL training with the ESL director. For those students in the course who preferred to work with adults, I matched them with those whom the ESL director identified as most in need. The students paired with adults worked with Iraqi and Burmese women in the area.

For me, the matching was something familiar, as ten years before I had completed my own ESL training and had begun work with adults and children from Korea, and later young adults from China and Nepal. Instead, most salient to me was the way the experiences of the last 7 years as a qualitative researcher on an evaluation of a youthful offenders program affected me. Since 2001, I had been interviewing young men and women taking college courses while in prison. Amidst educational narratives I collected, in 2006–2007 I completed nine in-depth interviews for my dissertation research. In this group most of the participants self-identified as men of color, and one woman as African American. Over the course of 2 years, when we met, I asked them questions about school growing up and about school in prison. Not surprisingly, school experiences with teachers, principals, and other students discouraged many of them, some as early as the first grade. Listening to them, being with them, and remembering their voices and stories when I was not with them, changed me. It changed, too, the way I saw White dominance in the United States. Over time, memories of them and their stories became a part of memories of me and my stories (Krog, 1998; MacIntyre, 1984).

And when I pursued academic work professionally, I did so with explicit commitments to racial and social justice. Most of the students I interviewed in prison believed that there are ways to support and encourage children when they are young that can keep them from making choices the students I had interviewed had made. The students shared with me that they wanted their stories to be heard and that they wanted children in particular to hear them. Indeed, a charge from one of the students, Shoran, carried me to tutoring with Burundian children. Toward the end of our interviews, Shoran, asked me if, when I started my university job, would I sit in "a big office" or continue to work with "kids" (Anders, 2007). Ignoring this charge and escaping to the comfort that is institutionally and personally available and accessible to me through my race and class does not feel like an option. Though I am, indeed, saturated with racial and economic privileges as a White scholar at a university, I choose to respond to Shoran's charge and pursue equity in small and local ways even if the acts in that pursuit cannot change the structures of White dominance or dismantle institutionalized racism. This response to Shoran's charge does not disallow the accusation of "White savior" for me as a White individual doing work in targeted spaces with targeted children; at any time others may take up this charge. But Shoran is the one who keeps me company on the most difficult days in South Prarie (public housing project), never beliefs in an utopia. Alongside his company and his memory, I can call on others as well, what I know about postcritical work, defiance in the permanence of racism (Bell, 1992), and responsibility in community. Recursive reflexivity layers my understandings of my racism and my privileges as I live in Riverhill. For me the question of which stories do we find ourselves a part (MacIntyre, 1994) and apart reveals work in memory, communication, and action.

Shoran was with me on a cold winter day when I heard Spiderman,[6] one of the Burundian boys, say, "I hate school" for the first time half way through his third grade year. I was at school with him and other Burundian children on Thursdays, and Jessica on Tuesdays, to help with ESL and math. He used to love school, I thought. He hated being at home. He was eager to go to school last year. What happened? Shoran was there as I leaned forward and asked Spiderman to tell me how he felt. I heard him say, "I want to stay at home," and as I remember his second grade year, my heart broke a little as distant echoes from interviews in prison began to rise like a spring flood through the canyons of my memories. The struggle I feel in those moments is not just in memory, metaphor, in the question I asked Spiderman, or the charge I carry with me from Shoran, but in the weekly action inside and outside the classroom, in reading and in talking with the children and their families.

I (Jessica) initially came to this work as a graduate student in Allison's service-learning course. I first heard about the course from a fellow graduate student who described the course and Allison's work with community as having something to do with "systemic inequities," "individuals with refugee status," and the "political dimensions of education." At that particular time in my academic career, I was struggling to find a home, a space where systemic inequities were not evaded, privilege and power were not taken-for-granted, and community responsibility, normalized. In many implicit and explicit ways, the course opened a space for me, a home of sorts, captivating my attention, my energies, and my heart. Now, almost 2 years later, I continue to work alongside Allison and the Burundian families. As I do so, I remember and always carry with me the stories of many companions and teachers from my present and past.

Long before entering graduate school, I worked and learned alongside my mother in the barrios of Colombia, South America, as she worked with and advocated for the Colombian children whom many named "disposables." From her, I learned to question my privileged motives, to view community work as a social responsibility, and to feel deeply. I learned also the importance of staying and resisting my privileged ability to run away from loss, from pain, from the dread (Bell, 1992). Now, in my "professional" work as a certified and self-identified "critical" (Ferri & Connor, 2006) special educator, I am humbled to be invited daily to spend time learning from and with children and adults labeled dis/abled. Over the last 8 years, from this work with my students and friends, I have learned to listen carefully, acknowledge my abilist tendencies, and resist my desire to "fix" and render "docile" (Foucault, 1995) another's way of being. I know that I cannot escape my racial privilege, "ideological inheritance" (Kincheloe & Steinberg, 1993, p. 302), or the charge of White savior. I do not try. Yet, I choose to engage in local relations, daily learning that "when you understand people, when you have committed to them, and when you have learned from them, you advocate for them … where advocating means trying to promote their world view as reasonable" (Noblit, 1999, p. 8). Forever remaining a part of me, these students' and these friends' stories of exclusion, loss, and tenacity complicate my understanding of my own institutionalized knowledges and power. And I carry their stories with me in my work with the Burundian children, allowing them, at times, to slow my pace, quiet my being, and push me to recursively reflect upon my own situatedness and complicity.

Layers

Whenever we write or speak about our experiences, we face decisions about where to start, for there are many layers to our involvement in our communities and in our lives. For us, each moment we chose to represent in this chapter, and the feelings we selected to disclose, happened in layers, across many spaces and places, with many memories, people, and knowledges haunting the present. Daily, as we move across these spaces, we refuse to simplify and flatten our experiences as we speak back to the neoliberal[7] comfort of success stories (Bell, 1992) that so often become the White institution's story of service-learning.

So, as you move through this chapter, we ask you to think with us in layers, noting what we have learned and have yet to learn. We contend that it is through the telling and retelling of stories that we connect "the disconnections of human experience," producing meaning in the process (Livo & Rietz, 1986, p. 5). Narrative not only allows us to make sense of our lives, but also shows us that "many worlds are possible, that meaning and reality are created and not discovered, that negotiation is the art of constructing new meanings" (Bruner, 1986, p. 149). We intentionally call "for tension and differences to be acknowledged, celebrated, rather than buried alive" (Richardson, 1997, p. 168). And as we write to invent "disruptive images of what could be" (Fine, 1992, p. 221), our experiences and interpretations of our experiences are "always partial and positional" (Noblit et al., 2004, p. 24). Even here, there is always the story told and the story untold (Krog, 1998).

What follows are three representations that we generated from recountings of our experiences. Drawn from our field notes, field journals, electronic communication, and daily conversations with one another, we share these stories and invite you to note places where our language and our situatedness limits our tellings. Further, and for us, more importantly, as we share we think about the Burundian children and families we re-represent, acknowledging the performative in every exchange (Denzin, 2003), and work to question recursively how we represent those who do not write alongside us.

Working Against Success Stories

As we thought about our experiences with the children and the work of narratives that communicate what we do, we discussed at length the kinds of stories we tell ourselves about our work, others tell about this work, the myriad "success" stories that deans and chancellors (or rather their staffs) generate around it, and the genres upon which we call to decide what it is we think we are doing. Months ago in thinking about choices, I (Allison) imagined myself walking through a movie section of a store, reading the signs that categorize story by type: action, comedy, drama, horror. As I imagined my walk, I felt the way I resisted the sensationalism of "drama" and the exceptionalism found in so many dramatic stories, an element that I argue distances one from the everyday opportunities for change (Anders, 2007; Garrow, 1999). I resisted "comedy" in my inability yet to see a satirical critique of the stories from Burundians, though I know satirical power harnesses potential to rupture hegemonic narratives (Mbembe, 2001). I resisted the empty eruptions of unhinged "action" and the spectacle (Debord, 1967/1995) of "horror" as a way to elicit outrage.

Regardless of our own attempts to name our experiences, others continue to position us (Villenas, 1996). "Thank yous" for "ministering to community" and "helping" those who "do not have skills" to survive here and who have "learned helplessness" from "the camps" tear at our own unfolding postcolonial, postcritical critique of colonialism and our own positions of privilege. We are not suggesting here that our naming is a correct naming and other naming is not. We are suggesting that we must interrogate the differences in naming, who has the power to name, and who benefits from different kinds of naming. The witnessing of others' constructions of a "success story," and charges of "White saviors," allows us to engage actively through recursive reflection to complicate action and communication about it. We have found that tellings about the ways others position us and we position ourselves allows us to find new possibilities and complexities in the stories we narrate.

A Thursday Afternoon: Silence and Loss

Many afternoons we spend time with the Burundian children in the public housing project where they live. While there, we teach English, we read, we play, and we learn, always in layers, always within and alongside ambiguities. We listen to their stories and their interpretations of the world, we invite them to express their thoughts, however they so desire, and to share their own ways of being in the world. As we do so, we remind ourselves to listen, to feel deeply, and to be present. Here, we imagine community work as that which is in relationship to another. We push against the "institutionalized version of charity" that "inadvertently" acts to defend "the status quo, or ... consciously put certain intellectual enterprises at the service of the search for social justice and liberation" (Artz, 2001, p. 242). The longer we stay in relationship, in community, the more we learn to challenge our own and others' desires for whitestream comforts, for success stories that predictably end in rainbow skies far above the earth, miles from the ground upon which we sit and read with children. We have learned, too, to question the notion that the arc of history bends toward justice, as we learn to sit with loss and discomfort.

Situated within the messiness and conflicts of this work, we desire to share one recounting, drawn from my (Jessica's) research journal, as well as field notes from my early months of working with and learning from the Burundian children. We share poetically, hoping to represent the multidimensional nature of this work (Norum, 2000). As you read, we invite you to think again with us in layers, moving beyond the feelings of comfort and success that often accompany stories of "service."

> Our "tutoring" time was over or whatever it was we called this "thing" that we did every Thursday afternoon.
>
> "Community work," maybe?
> "Service learning"?
> "Research"?
> "Hanging out time"?
>
> Whatever this "thing" was
> that escaped words,
> it was over
> at least for today.
>
> So, I quietly whispered in each child's ear,
> "Ready, Happy Princess?"
> "Finished, Hulk?"
> "Coming with me, Spiderman?"
>
> With smiles,
> and sounds of Kirundi filling the room,
> the three children put their coats on,
> exiting the building with remarkable speed,
> at least compared to weeks past.
>
> I smiled,
> locked the door,
> and listened
> as the sounds of their voices filled the air.
>
> In an instant, their song-like voices were interrupted with,
>
> "AHH! NO! NO! HELP ME! NO! JESSICA, NO!"
> It was Spiderman.

I swiftly walked toward the children
Seeing Spiderman sprawled on the sidewalk adjacent to my car
crying
inconsolably so.

Happy Princess and Hulk hardly looked at me,
climbing into the backseat of my car
leaving me to "deal" with Spiderman's tears.
As I settled next to him on the sidewalk
I heard him say
"I lost my note from my teacher.
Where is it, Jessica?"

A note?
This was about a note?
His teacher can write him another note tomorrow
or
I can write him a note now.
I'm a teacher.

I didn't share my thoughts,
instead quietly saying
"Where did you leave the note? Can I help you find it?"
he muttered, "It was in your car. You lost it!"
"Oh, Spiderman," I said, "I never had it."

With that, he was up and off the sidewalk
running across the open field with great speed
leaving a trail
as the things within his backpack fell to the ground.

As I watched him run
I sat
yet could hear my mother's voice
echoing in my mind
"We run after those we are committed to
As you keep another, you are kept."

So, I ran
eventually reaching Spiderman
who upon seeing me
wrapped his arms around my waist
and folded his body into mine.

And then
for 20 minutes
we sat on the brown grass

and
he cried
and cried
and cried
and
I held him
as words escaped me.
and
silence prevailed.

As I waited
I had a tenuous, uncomfortable knowing
that this was not about losing a note.

It was about loss—
the kind with indescribable power
the kind I'd never known.
Loss far beyond my imaginings.

If only...
I could protect him from more loss,
from losing what he loved, be it
a note
a tutor
a friend

If only...
I could protect him from more loss,
from losing himself,
to a system capable of
labeling,
sorting, and
categorizing his black body.
If only...

What audacity! I knew!
I could not protect him
but perhaps
loss
didn't have to be a part of our relationship
perhaps.

As if reading my mind
Spiderman stood up with a smile
wiped his face
encircled his fingers with mine
and

guided us back toward the car.

As we walked, I whispered,
"I'll find your note."
he smiled and said, "Let's go find it."

We did.
Together
we found the note.

As we entered my car,
The laughing voices of
Spiderman, Happy Princess and Hulk quickly filled the space

And it was then,

My freedom is a function of freedom for everyone. Oppression of some is the direct corollary to slavery for others. I am only free myself when I recognize another's humanity and freedom.

words of Bakunin (1970) echoed in my mind

His words quieted me,
Slowing my being,
I wondered,
I wrestled
Yet
Still
I smelled
tasted
felt
LOSS.

Loss
It was waiting
Lurking

How do I respond?

I will sit
Tenuously
with silence,
with loss
with Spiderman.
We will sit
Together.

This retelling, written well over a year ago, has not stood still. Stories of loss, stories of sitting, stories of a system lurking—this story, sitting among many other stories, has only become more complicated, ambiguous, and at times even more profoundly discomforting. As we continue to learn to sit, we are ever-more aware of our own power to walk away from these moments of loss and discomfort. Our postcritical orientations demand that we take up a recursive stance with our stories. We must acknowledge our mobility, our ability to walk away from loss, and our desires at times to push fatigue far from the whited spaces in which we live. Indeed, since the retelling was constructed, the system has come many times and taken much, from Spiderman in particular—loss perhaps multiplied. And so we sit with the discomfort of unyielding loss, as this story becomes a "story less of success than of survival through the unremitting struggle that leaves no room for giving up. We are all part of that history, and it is still unfolding" (Bell, 1992, p. 200).

UNDERSTANDING SILENCES

> Not every day in South Prairie [public housing project] is full of roundoffs and giggles. There are disagreements, hurt feelings (among children and tutors now that I think about it), and occasionally a fight, sometimes with sticks, sometimes with kicking legs.
>
> —Anders' Fieldnotes, September 2009

Amidst the work we do as ESL tutors and advocates in the Burundian community, we are part of a larger "community-based research and service-learning initiative," which a group of graduate students from other disciplines and a faculty member in nutrition constitute. Beginning in winter 2009, the semester after the service-learning course in social justice and education, I (Allison) invited all the group members (at the time, twelve who studied across nine different disciplines) to consider completing the ESL training through the refugee sponsorship agency since so many families still needed assistance in learning English. Winter 2009 passed, as did Fall 2009, and then Spring 2010. No one "volunteered" or completed the training to become a tutor.

In the meantime, due to the lack of response and the need I (Jessica) saw each week with the families, I mentioned the work in each of the eight sections of a required course I and others taught for over 160 preservice teachers. Three students from these eight course sections went through training, two preferring to work with children but were told by an ESL director at Greenland that they had to be paired with an adult. The third student approached me after class one day and asked if she could come with me every week and read and play with the children. Eventually, she began to work alongside us on Thursday afternoons. She tutored every week until she moved to a different city after graduation for a job.

As Allison and I talked off and on about close friends and colleagues who wanted to know updates on the work but not involve themselves, or give money towards presents during the holiday season but not meet the children themselves, we reflected on the way that we framed what we did and how we talked about it. We realized that when asked about what we did, we described it as ongoing and often purposely avoided constructing success stories about resettlement. The following communication is representative of a number of conversations that we have both had with people of privilege "interested" in what we do. The excerpt is a response from Allison to an editor who handled reports for the chancellor and who wanted to write a glamorous success story about a small group of individuals from the University rescuing those less fortunate. Allison responded and tried to intervene (A. D. Anders, personal communication, winter, 2010):

> The research we do is a systemic analysis about the continued struggle these families face after 40 years of fleeing violence in three countries. Most of the (families) live in public housing projects in Riverhill where they are not free from struggle or violence. Many work as custodians on our campus making far below what is a living wage in this country.... If the resettlement process in (this region) was successful and without struggle, (we) would not have seen a need for any University involvement in community engagement. Our project is long term ... we are still in the early stages ... a "success story" ... does not exist now.

The irony that accompanies the framing of work with community as successful when the claim of success negates the need for work with community seems to sit outside the university. We witness and feel the irony, and yet seem to be alone in our conversations about it, except when we are with the Burundian families and children, and a local Burundian translator.

If it is, as we argue, that work with community occurs within moments of relationality and narratives of defiance against success stories, how do we invite others to join us? The invitations we offer to those around us are most often met with silence. When the social justice and education course ended at the close of the fall semester, three students from the eight working with Burundian children continued to tutor into the spring semester. Two finished the semester. We (Allison and Jessica) continued into summer and the next year and a second summer. As months passed our dynamics changed. We moved from the instrumental communication of faculty/student to expressive communication as colleagues and friends working and living in Riverhill. We brokered expressive communication first over e-mail in reflections we shared about afternoons learning with the children, and later in person in weekly meetings about our experiences.

For a year, I (Allison) truncated my communication with students, noting the pauses over my keyboard as I e-mailed about my feelings about the children and South Prairie. My experiences with the weight of the institutional structure and my own need to protect students from any additional challenges (I inferred—and was told explicitly by some students—that working alongside families with refugee status was challenging enough) affected me deeply, and I found myself leaning heavily on institutionalized knowledges rather than emotional and experiential knowledges. Spending time in South Prairie with Jessica and the children helped me redefine our relationship. And the day came when I said exactly what I thought, waited, and listened to what Jessica had to say. Over time the two of us exercised less reserve, revealed more of ourselves, and came to anticipate multiple positions we could take up and the navigation of them in supportive and collaborative ways (Smith, 2006). Both our communication and what we shared about our experiences expanded and deepened as we developed "rich" understandings (Barry & Crant, 2000) about each other and our respective commitments to racial and social justice.

Although we have experienced benefits from the richness of our communication, both of us wish we had cultivated expressive communication sooner. There were knowledges and actions that could have been taken up and were not because our communication began in an "hierarchical" relationship. Our exchanges have been more complicated than just those two elements, but breaking from an historic, modern relationship of faculty/student was conscious and difficult. As we produce meaningfulness from our work, we find ourselves interested in inviting others to work, too. In our reflections with one another, we noticed that we puzzled over the silences that met our invitations to research team members, friends, and colleagues to join us in tutoring children and families. We struggle still to make sense of these silences. Almost 2 years after beginning our work, on a Monday we wondered together why so few team members and friends respond. We know that we invite without glamour, seduction, or praise, but there is more in their silences than we can see in the absences within our invitations. In an attempt to represent these tensions, we share the following scene as performance ethnography (Denzin, 2003; Madison, 2005; Randolph & Weems, 2010).

Scene: A sunny afternoon during one of our weekly meetings at a local coffee shop.

Jessica: I'm thinking about invitations today and struggling to find answers as to why few individuals seem to join us in this work.

Allison: You mean, why with all the "talk" of "service" in community no one from the team makes a weekly commitment? (Pause). I don't understand it. How many times have we asked? How many times has it been on the agenda? I don't understand.

Jessica: Silences, so many silences, built in silences. (Pause). I felt deeply today. I pushed away a tear as I walked away from one of our Burundian friend's homes. I felt anger at the silences, the demands for success stories before agreeing to join, the whitestream "need" for comfort. This work, what we choose to do ... this is not exceptional. Today when I asked some people to consider spending one hour of their week tutoring children, they responded by asking me what changes I had seen thus far in the community. I felt that it was invitation to share a success story. I didn't. I don't have one. I fail at most invitations.

Allison: No, you don't fail. You just refuse to make this work exceptional, something to be sensationalized. You defy the success story and the invitation to tell one. Doing a "success story" performs something ..."the good White" (Thompson, 2003), and the comfort that goes with it. We don't comfort, because there is nothing exceptional here. It's not about serving community, it's not ... talking about ... it's living with.

Jessica: I feel, I need to resist, to push back against whitestream comforts, my own first and foremost. We refuse to invite, to lure with falsely constructed moments of "charity" and "success."

Allison: Right. Right. You know what it is? We don't, "please come and join us. We need your help." We don't beg. What if we did? What if we begged? I bet they would come. What if we seduced? ... Instead, we invite others to join in the—what does Ayers (2009) call it?—"unglamorous" work of looking for, creating ruptures in systemic inequities. Small, local change, that's it. And even that might not do any good. We don't know. Who wants to hear that? Come with us, tutor and be with the children even if we're not sure it does any good.

Jessica: **Yes,** believing in the local. Perhaps that's all there is. The local. Work that is small. Hmmm. And work that demands relationships, and learning. Work that does not tell, direct, fix, does not save community but that is about being with community and knowing that in the "being with" that the work is always partial, never complete (Clifford & Marcus, 1986).

Allison: because institutions deny such completeness.

Jessica: It's in that moment of acknowledgement, too, that perhaps we are creating more problems (Bell, 1992).

Allison: Ah. You know what it is? We invite them to the dread (Bell, 1992).

INVITATION TO THE DREAD

> I hope to emphasize the necessity of moving beyond the comforting belief that time and generosity of its people will eventually solve America's racial problem.
>
> Derrick Bell, *Faces at the Bottom of the Well,* 1992

For both of us, Derrick Bell's (1992) position on the permanence of racism in *Faces at the Bottom of the Well,* resonates with our own positions. Critical race theory houses a debate about and connections across racial realism and racial idealism (Delgado & Stefancic, 2001). In our work though, we find that both the "dread" and defiance narratives resonate with what we have experienced as the racist "reality" of the world. "Dread" has become code for narratives of defiance against neoliberal[7] success stories for us.

Conquering the "dread" presupposes an acknowledgment of "death" and a "deadening reality." Bell (1992) argues that defiance allows African Americans to conquer the dread. Facing the dread means relinquishing the comforts that racial idealism provides for many Whites. Bell critiques the "comfort" that "the goal of racial equality" has for Whites, for racial equality remains "more illusory than real for blacks" (p. 13). In order to "delegitimate" racism, we must, he argues, acknowledge that racist institutions, practices, and discourses structured the United States, literally and discursively, that slavery and systemic racial disenfranchisement and oppression were not aberrations in an historical arc that is produced too often in a teleology of progress, but that racist systems are "permanent, not fleeting; in the real lives of black and white people" (p. 198). For us, we do not see a history of progress, but instead we see a history of violence and oppression, and a teleology of progress that allows it to continue.

We contend that Bell's (1992) argument has consequences for ideas about commitment and outcomes when universities take up work with community and critical service-learning. As we experience Riverhill and as we study racial and social justice and critical race theory, we learn to "accept the dilemmas of committed confrontation with evils we cannot end. We go forth to serve, knowing that our failure to act will not change conditions and may very well worsen them" (p. 198). Knowing that the work that we do will not end "evils" signals to us that there is a choice to make. If our work with Burundian families will "slide into irrelevance as racial patterns adapt in ways that maintain white dominance" (p. 12), do we do the work anyway?

Although the Burundians are navigating systems of racialized hierarchies (Olsen, 1998) dominated by Whites in the United States for the first time, they bring with them analyses of economic and racial mobility. They demonstrate awareness of White dominance and White economic power in the United States. As one Burundian man shared, "I guess, we are here to work for the Whites;" and as a Burundian woman explained, "If [our children] get their education, they will be successful like White people. If they don't go to school, we are going to stay like the way we are now, begging and asking for help."

In addition to acknowledging White dominance in employment and social mobility, a Burundian man criticized the process of resettlement, what Riverhill as a community did not do for them, and specifically what Greenland failed to provide during their transition.

> They play us like a ball.... Why are the rules hard here? Like this old man has a son who left the refugee camp when he was in school. Now he doesn't go to school. When we left the camp we agreed that our kids would pursue their education. I am not scared to say that we came to live in a city that is not well prepared.... They said the case worker will help us for five years. This is not the case. Until now, we see that we are being played again; they let you go, even if you are not ready yet. They can't wait for us to spend a year in this country so that they have peace and they don't have to worry about us. Then they leave us alone. You are leaving us alone, and you know there are many who can't speak English.

The Burundians articulated both systemic unpreparedness in Riverhill and a violation of commitments by Greenland. The case worker's failure to facilitate the families' transition for 5 years contrasts with their own commitments to their children's transition. Some men, in particular, believed that the economic demands of an industrialized, capitalist country produced their exploitation and that the city housing codes limited their opportunity to grow food for their family. One man shared:

> You see, living in a refugee camp, we were given food, a tent, and then we had opportunity to build our own houses. But when we got here in the U.S.,

> we weren't given tents; they gave us houses. The only problem with these houses is we need to pay to live in them. You see, in Africa, we weren't paying for the tents. It is not because the U.S. provided us with tents that we are going to pay $560 per month now. You see, that's how we live now. You see, we have to pay every month. Then you wonder what we came to do here in the U.S. I came in this country to work for it; I am like his servant, and the only thing that I am working for at this time is to pay my rent.... Coming from Africa, I know we were living really bad, but at least we had a land where we could grow things.

As the men and women who participated in the focus groups shared their request for English classes and better communication from Greenland, they asked the larger "community-based research and service-learning initiative" team, too, what we would do to change things in Riverhill. We were aware, too, of limited resources, inconsistent support, and an absence of sponsors for many families. We knew that if sponsors and ESL tutors were not available when families arrived, families would go without support. We had interviewed Greenland's director and staff and knew they needed resources and training.

As racial realists we refuse the "belief" that "time" and generosity" will resolve racism in the United States. For some, the absence of hopefulness, in the acknowledgement Bell (1992) asks us to make, disorients and discourages work with community. For us, the defiance he offers in its place resonates and reinforces our commitments to what we do. The response for us was to continue to tutor children and adults, seek additional tutors at every opportunity, fill out free and reduced lunch forms, medical forms, and social service forms, assist in communicating with teachers and principals, doctors and nurses. We shared and learned, too, with each other what we could regarding the knowledge we had about Riverhill. Sometimes we co-constructed that knowledge on a front stoop over a book, on a field with a soccer ball, or in a living room over homework, other times in an ESL class, or a community forum, or an educational placement meeting, and sometimes in the embrace of a child after racial taunts or a fight at school.

Though we are committed to relational work and to analyzing relationships of power, including the ones we produce, neither our commitments nor our awareness, nor our education, nor our learning, yield panaceas for the resettlement process in Riverhill. The work is unending and it is unglamorous (Ayers, 2009). The system in which we find ourselves from the schools to area health providers is one of White dominance. As Bell (1992) notes, even in law, there are "no victories that do not slide back into irrelevance as racial patterns adapt in ways that maintain white dominance" (p. 12). With his analysis, we continue to work with the children and families, learning from them, and they from us. In this multidimensional space, recognizing the importance of "humility" is paramount. Important for us though, is the defiance we structure through the work we enact. In racial justice work, social justice work, in critical service-learning, we "remind the powers that be that out there are persons like us who are not only not on their side but determined to stand in their way" (p. 199). In this work, action may signal confrontation with "powers that be" but also may sputter in "futility." Yet, refusing to take up the work is not an option. The work is both, the "futility of action—where action is more civil rights strategies destined to fail—and the unalterable conviction that something must be done, that action must be taken (p. 199). For some in the "community-based research and service-learning initiative" the acknowledgements that racism is permanent and that actions may be futile, and even worse, may re-instantiate and re-entrench White dominance, "is too painful." The desire to live with narratives of hope and comfort, and protect one another from narratives of genocide and rejection sustains many of Whites with whom we work. Bell writes about the power of this yearning but calls on us to seek something else rather than the comforts of success. We "yearn," he writes, "that our civil rights work will be crowned with success, but what we really want—want even more than success—is meaning" (p. 198).

Although Bell (1992) avoids prescription for the production of meaning, he does suggest that listening to those "who have been most subordinated" and who have "survived as complete, defiant, though horribly scarred beings" (p. 198) is a way to meaning. We predicate the invitation we extend to others in our lives who may join in what we do in facing "the unbearable." This invitation holds the potential for the generation of meaning, too; yet we find ourselves asking, how do we share an invitation to dread and meaningfulness as a strategy? And how do we support work with community when the dread becomes for some "too painful" and meaningfulness too ephemeral? Although narratives of success may buoy work with community for some, for us, defiance drives what we do. Ultimately, we take up the defiance narrative Bell offers where the stories are "less of success than of survival through the unremitting struggle that leaves no room for giving up. We are all part of that history, and it is still unfolding" (p. 200).

QUESTIONS FOR REFLECTION

As we do what we do we question daily our own authority, privilege, and racism as we learn to coconstruct knowledge with those with whom we live. Like Freire (1999), we suggest that through being and dialogue with one another and recursive reflexivity we can create moments of solidarity and ruptures in dominant whitestream discourses. In this reflexive space, we do not seek "a comfortable, transcendent end-point," but instead learn to sit in "messy" and "uncomfortable realities" (Pillow, 2003, p. 193). Throughout the recountings we shared here we generated several questions, and ask you to generate more as you take up what you do where you are.

1. Where are knowledges located? Are knowledges bound up in lived experiences? Are knowledges bound up in institutions? What are the relationships across knowledges and who benefits when some knowledges are privileged over others?
2. How might stories function to direct work in a community toward solidarity? Who has the power to tell a story? or defy a story? What stories might you tell about your work? What stories may be told about your work?
3. If what we do, as we argued, occurs within moments of relationality and narratives of defiance against neoliberal comfort, how do we invite others to join us?
4. In what ways do those who chose to live in ways directed by critical service-learning make meaning of their experiences of their towns? of their institutions?
5. In the ongoing need for action to address systemic inequities, how do we work and represent work creatively and persuasively?

NOTES

1. As our journey of being and doing this work continues, so, too, does our naming of it. We resist the use of "service-learning," except in those situations and institutional spaces where we find ourselves communicating with people who have no idea what we study or what we do. We have found that using "service-learning" is a way to communicate what we do, while we use "critical service-learning" strategically whenever possible to deepen understandings about living with community. Although "community engagement" has been the way we have framed our work for months now, we have done so with reticence. In the deployment of "engagement" we feel the tug of "disengagement." Our postcritical orientations and commitments to our imaginings of equity caution us against using language that implies temporary work. There is always already so much work to be done that we prefer language that reflects ongoing "work;" yet this seems hard to find. "Community engagement" feels as though it fails us now, as only those who are privileged may move toward and away "from community work"—including ourselves. At one point, we moved to "community work," hoping to situate both the seriousness of commitment and to invite an understanding of

working in community that is complex. Indeed, there are days we want to "work" and days we do not. On days that we do not want to work, we are with the children anyway. Tutoring and being with children and families is not fun all the time. Children cry sometimes, siblings and neighbors argue with one another occasionally, projects fall apart in the rain, and academic activities are abandoned for tree climbing. Sometimes reading together fails to happen at all, and instead free and reduced lunch forms, medical forms, and social service forms need to be completed. Doing the work *anyway* has led us to consider the term "living with community" or even just "living in Riverhill." After 2 years of tutoring, movie nights, dinners, kite-flying, stoop-sitting, tear-wiping, hug-providing, and soccer playing afternoons, we call our original tutor matches, friends. But we do not live "in" the public housing project where families with refugee status live. "Living" remains still elusive and metaphoric even as it connects our deepest feelings to our work. Our friends are with us even when we are not with them. We know we experience our work as relational, and that we name this work with "community" as a part of that relationality. We know, too, that it has been in the doing of "living" that we have come to know and use the word "community." As you read, we invite you to problematize and reframe the words we use around "community," for as our journey continues to unfold so, too, does our naming. We would like to thank C. Amelia Davis, Karla Martin, and Amy Simpson Swain in particular for their insights and questions as we navigated these choices about discourse.

2. By some definitions Riverhill is an urban city located in an Appalachian county. We experience Riverhill as a rural town located in the South. We have struggled to describe the city where much of what we do occurs. Wanting to highlight the anti-immigrant sentiment felt in the words of county administrators, for example, "we don't want anymore [Burundians])," and the classist and White supremacist assumptions in congratulations offered for "our" work with that "population" (Anders, fieldnotes, 2010), we struggled to name and locate the city in which the Burundian children and families now live; for the White dominance and xenophobia that they now face and to which we have been witness is quite real (Huber & Espenshade, 1997).
3. We use pseudonyms throughout the chapter.
4. Some of the children with whom we work are considered for and eventually placed in alternative education and special education settings. We are concerned particularly with the historic trend that reflects disproportionate placement of children of African descent in special education (Bayton, 2001; Eitle, 2002; Esposito, 1973; Fossey, 1996) by administrators, teachers, and specialists. In some states, this disproportionate placement and classification of "intellectual disability" of African American children is 2.5 times more likely to occur compared to their White counterparts (Donovan & Cross, 2002). According to the Office of Special Education Programs (2003), Black students are 2.99 times more likely to be labeled with an intellectual impairment and 2.21 times more likely to be classified as having an emotional disorder than all other ethnic groups combined. Heward

and Cavanaugh (2001) reported that students of African American descent make up 16.3% of the school-age population, while representing 31% of students labeled with intellectual disabilities and 23.7% of the students labeled with emotional disturbances. Some literature suggests that this overrepresentation is a result of narrowly interpreting cognitive and affective schemas, drawing from culturally-biased frameworks (Artiles, Tren, & Kuan, 1997), something which we argue may have severe consequences for immigrant children of color alongside African American children.

5. "Targeted" refers to the active process of stigmatization and discrimination by people and institutions of privilege. We choose the term "targeted" in our work rather than a word like "marginalized" for two reasons. First, we want to call explicit attention to the ways in which people of privilege produce discriminatory discourses, institutions, and practices (e.g. homophobic, neoconservative, neoliberal, racist, sexist, xenophobic etc.). Often "marginalized" is used in a passive voice, making the subjects that discriminate—the actor(s) and institutions responsible for marginalization—invisible. People do not simply emerge on the margins. People of privilege situate them there. We argue that our language about stigmatization and discrimination needs to reflect this active process. Second, in naming the actors(s) in the process, we argue that using "targeted" generates the potential to situate oppression culturally, historically, politically, and socially.
6. Recognizing the power inherent in naming another, we invited all of the individuals included in this chapter to select their own pseudonyms. In this chapter, the three children we referenced by name requested that we use the names Hulk, Spiderman, and Happy Princess.
7. Advocates of neoliberal agendas actively ignore age, class, dis/abilities, education, gender, race, and so forth, typecasting individuals as skilled/unskilled, educated/uneducated, and successful/unsuccessful. Neoliberal discourses promise universal freedoms and serve to reproduce the illusion that individuals with the same talents and abilities will be equally productive, independent of the resources available to them (Anton, 2000; Gounari, 2006). This works to construct human suffering as an individual problem versus a community problem, leaving the existing inequality inherent within the system unchallenged and normalized. One of the "benefits" of a neoliberal state is found in the transference of responsibility for "failure" from the state to the individual. Through a discourse of meritocracy, the social position of the "other" is justified, as the privileged maintain a "purity of hands and consciences ... reached by the twin measure of the moral condemnation of the poor and the moral absolution of the rest" (Bauman, 2005, p. 78). Ultimately, this may create a cycle by which the targeted "other" is constructed as problematic, while the privileged are constructed as "normal" and "responsible" and seduce one another in participation of othering which "becomes normalized as natural and correct" (Francis, 2006, p. 195). Within this rhetoric, notions of community and solidarity are often supplanted with the discourse competitiveness and success. We appreciate the way Douthat (2005) describes the

importance of comfort for whom he names the "parlor liberal." For us, his description provides a way to understand progressive resistance to community work for racial and social justice:

> forming the mainstream at elite colleges. (Parlor liberals) sit comfortably on the left of the American political spectrum, believing in gun control and gay rights, in affirmative action and abortion, in a multilateral foreign policy and a significant social safety net and they will likely vote Democrat until they die. Yet there is something conservative about them. They are creatures of their class, not would-be traitors to it, and they are deeply uncomfortable with radicalism in any form. This discomfort ... extends easily to anyone who displays too much self-righteousness and zeal, too much anger at institutions and leaders and structures of powers.... Parlor liberals are ultimately well disposed to the world and to their privileged place in it, believing that what injustices there are can be righted without too much upheaval and unrest, and perhaps even without raising taxes. (pp. 203–204)

We contend that the gravitation toward and production of success stories in the fight for racial and social justice provide resonance of comfort for neoliberals and distance from community responsibility.

REFERENCES

Anders, A. D. (2007.) *Revisiting the panopticon: Educational narratives from incarcerated youth.*(Doctoral dissertation). Retrieved from Dissertations and Theses database. (UMI No. 3257541)

Anders, A. D., & Jay, M. (2010, May). *Derrick Bell and considerations in the naming of white allies.* Paper presented at the Sixth International Congress of Qualitative Inquiry at the University of Urbana-Champaign, Champaign, IL.

Anton, A. (2000). Public goods as commonstock: Notes on the receding commons. In A. Anton, M. Fisk, & N. Holmstrom (Eds.), *Not for sale: In defense of public goods* (pp. 3–4). Boulder, CO: Westview Press.

Aretxaga, B. (1997). *Shattering silence: Women, nationalism, and political subjectivity in Northern Ireland.* Princeton, NJ: Princeton University Press.

Artiles, A. J., Trent, S. C., & Kuan, L. A. (1997). Learning disabilities research on ethnic minority students: An analysis of 22 years of students published in selected refereed journals. *Learning Disabilities Research and Practice, 12*, 82–91.

Artz, L. (2001). Critical ethnography for communication studies: Dialogue and social justice in service-learning. *Southern Communication Journal, 66*(3), 239–250.

Ayers, W. (2009). Barack Obama and the fight for public education. *Harvard Educational Review, 79*(2), 385–395.

Bakunin, M. (1970). *God and the state*. Mineola, NY: Dover.

Bauman, Z. (2005) *Work, consumerism and the new poor.* Buckingham, England: Open University Press.

Barry, B., & Crant, J. M. (2000). Dyadic communication relationships in organizations: An attribution/expectancy approach. *Organization Science, 11*(6), 648–664.

Bayton, D. C. (2001). Disability and the justification of inequality in American history. In P. K. Longmore & L. Umansky, (Eds.), *The new disability history: American perspectives* (pp. 33–82). New York City, NY: New York University Press.

Beah, I. (2007). *A long way gone: Memoirs of a boy soldier.* New York, NY: Sarah Crichton.

Bell, D. (1992). *Face at the bottom of the well: The permanence of racism.* New York, NY: Basic Books.

Bochner, A. (2009). Warm ideas and chilling consequences. *International Review of Qualitative Research, 2*(3), 357–370.

Bowers, C.A. (1986). Promise of theory: Education and the politics of cultural change. New York, NY: Teachers College Press.

Bruner, J. (1986). *Actual minds, possible worlds.* Cambridge, MA: Harvard University Press.

Chomsky, N. (2002). *Understanding power: The indispensable Chomsky.* New York, NY: The New Press.

Clifford, J., & Marcus, G. E. (1986). (Eds.). *Writing culture: The poetics and politics of ethnography.* Los Angeles, CA: University of California Press, Ltd.

Coffey, A. & Atkinson, P. (1996). *Making sense of qualitative data: complementary research strategies.* Thousand Oaks, CA: SAGE.

Crenshaw, K. (1991). Mapping the margins: Intersectionality, identity politics, and violence against women of color. *Stanford Law Review, 43*(6), 1241–1299.

Debord, G. (1995). *The society of the spectacle.* (D. Nicholson-Smith, Trans.). New York, NY: Zone Books. (Original work published 1967).

de Certeau, M. (1984). *The practice of everyday life.* London, England: University of California Press.

Delgado, R., & Stefancic, J. (2001). *Critical race theory: an introduction.* New York, NY: New York University Press.

Denzin, N.K. (2003). Reading and writing performance. *Qualitative Research. 3*(2) 243–268.

Donovan, S., & Cross, C. (2002). *Minority students in special and gifted education.* Washington, DC: National Academy Press.

Douthat, R. G. (2005). *Privilege: Harvard and the education of the ruling class.* New York, NY: Hyperion.

Eitle, T. M. (2002). Special education or racial segregation: Understanding variation in the representation of black students in educable mentally handicapped programs. *The Sociological Quarterly, 43*(4), 575–605.

Esposito, D. (1973). Homogeneous and heterogeneous ability grouping: Principal findings and implications for evaluating and designing more effective educational environments. *Review of Educational Research, 43,* 163–179.

Ferguson, A. A. (2000). *Bad boys: Public schools in the making of black masculinity.* Ann Arbor, MI: The University of Michigan Press.

Ferri, B. A., & Connor, D. J. (2006). *Reading resistance: Discourses of exclusion in desegregation & inclusion debates*. New York, NY: Peter Lang.

Fine, M. (1992). *Disruptive voices: The possibilities of feminist research*. Ann Arbor, MI: The University of Michigan Press.

Fossey, R. (1996, January). *African American students in east Baton Rouge parish: How have they fared in desegregated school?* Paper presented at the annual meeting of the Southwest Educational Research Association, New Orleans, LA

Foucault, M. (1995). *Discipline and punish: The birth of the prison*. New York, NY: Vintage.

Francis, B. (2006). Heroes or zeroes? The discursive positioning of 'underachieving boys' in English neo liberal education policy. *Journal of Education Policy, 21*(2), 87–2000.

Freire, P. (1999). *Pedagogy of the oppressed*. (M. B. Ramos, Trans.). New York, NY: Continuum.

Garrow, D. (1999). *Bearing the cross: Martin Luther King, Jr. and the Southern Christian Leadership Conference*. New York, NY: Harper Perennial.

Gounari, P. (2006). Contesting the cynicism of neoliberal discourse: Moving towards a language of possibility. *Studies in Language & Capitalism, 1*, 77–96.

Guba, E. G. (1981). Criteria for assessing the trustworthiness of naturalistic inquiries. *Educational Communication and Technology Journal, 29*, 75–91.

Habermas, J. (1988). *Theory and practice*. (J. Viertel, Trans.). Boston, MA: Beacon Press.

Heward, W. L., & Cavanaugh, R. (2001). Educational equity for students with disabilities. In J. Banks & C. A. McGee Banks (Eds.), *Multicultural education: Issues and perspectives* (pp. 295–326). New York, NY: Wiley.

Huber, G. A., & Espenshade, T. J. (1997). Neo-isolationism, balanced-budget conservatism, and the fiscal impacts of immigrants. *International Migration Review, 31*(4), 1021–1054.

Kincheloe, J. L., & Steinberg, S. R. (1993). A tentative description of post-formal thinking: The critical confrontation with cognitive theory. *Harvard Educational Review, 63*(3), 296–320.

Krog, A. (1998). *Country of my skull: Guilt, sorrow, and the limits of forgiveness in the new South Africa*. New York, NY: Three Rivers.

Lather, P. (1986). Issues of validity in openly ideological research: Between a rock and a soft place. *Interchange 17*(4), 63–84.

Livo, N., & Rietz, S. (1986). *Storytelling: Process and practice*. Littleton, CO: Libraries Unlimited.

MacIntyre, A. (1984). *After virtue: A study in moral theory*. Notre Dame, IN: University of Notre Dame Press.

Madison, D. S. (2005). *Critical ethnography: Method, ethics and performance*. Thousand Oaks, CA: SAGE.

Mbembe, A. (2001). *On the postcolony*. Berkeley, CA: University of California Press.

Noblit, G. W. (1999). *Particularities: Collected essays on ethnography and education*. New York, NY: Peter Lang.

Noblit, G., & Engel, J. D. (1999). The holistic injunction: An ideal and a moral imperative for qualitative research, In G. W. Noblit (Ed.), *Particularities: Col-*

lected essays on ethnography and education (pp. 53–60). New York, NY: Peter Lang .

Noblit, G. W., Flores, S. Y., & Murillo, E. G. (Eds.). (2004). *Postcritical ethnography: Reinscribing critique.* Cresskill, NJ: Hampton Press.

Norum, K. E. (2000). School patterns: a sextet. *Qualitative Studies in Education, 13*(3) 239–250.

U.S. Department of Education, Office of Special Education Programs. (2003). Data Analysis System (DANS), Table AA15 in vol. 2. Data are for the 50 states, D.C., Puerto Rico, and the outlying areas. Population data are July 1 estimates for 2001, released October 2003. Washington, DC: Author.

Olsen, L. (1998). *Made in America: immigrant students in our public schools.* New York, NY: New Press.

Pillow, W. S. (2003). Confession, catharsis, or cure? Rethinking the uses of reflexivity as methodological power in qualitative research. *Qualitative Studies in Education, 16*(2), 175–196.

Randolph, A. W., & Weems, M. E. (2010). Speak truth and shame the devil: An ethnodrama in response to racism in the academy. *Qualitative Inquiry, 16*(3), 310–314.

Richardson, L. (1997). *Fields of play: Constructing an academic life.* New Brunswick, NJ: Rutgers University Press.

Smith, D. C. (2006). A universal perspective on communication: What every international business manager should know. *International Business & Economics Research Journal, 5*(12), 15–18.

Thompson, A. (2003). Tiffany, friend of people of color: White investments in antiracism. *Qualitative Studies in Education, 16*(1), 7–29.

United States Committee for Refugees and Immigrants, (2008, June 19). World Refugee Survey 2008—Tanzania. Retrieved from http://www.unhcr.org /cgi-bin/texis/vtx/refworld/ rwmain?page=search&docid=485f50d5c&skip=0&query =world refugee survey 2008&querysi =tanzania&searchin=title&display=10&sort=relevance

Villenas, S. (1996). The colonizer/colonized Chicana ethnographer: Identity, marginalization, and the co-optation in the field. *Harvard Educational Review, 66*(4), 711–731.

Warren, J. T. (2001). Doing whiteness: On the performative dimensions of race in the classroom. *Communication Education, 50*(2), 91–108.

CHAPTER 12

CRITICAL OPENINGS AND POSSIBILITIES

Navigating Challenges for Change

Steven Hart

In the current era of accountability, high-stakes testing-based policies have been designed and implemented in order to increase external control over schools and individual classrooms. Such polices have placed increasing pressures on teachers and administrators to increase their students' scores on high-stakes standardized tests, and a large body of research provides strong evidence that this pressure has worked to control *what* and *how* teachers teach (Amrein & Berliner, 2002; Au, 2007; Nichols & Berliner, 2007; Watanabe, 2007). These pressures have encouraged educators to narrow curricular content to focus only on tested concepts and restrict instructional techniques to those that mimic the structures of standardized tests. The climate resulting from these oppressive and restrictive conditions is one in which certain instructional practices are valued more than others (e.g., scripted instruction, rote memorization of isolated facts, skill and drill of discrete basic skills, low-level stimulus-response, test preparation worksheets).

Critical Service Learning as a Revolutionary Pedagogy: A Project of Student Agency in Action, pp. 251–271

Service-learning is one of the instructional strategies that has experienced this marginalization. Recent reports document that over the past decade the prevalence of service-learning in K–12 schools has continued to decline (Kielsmeier, Scales, Roehlkepartain, & Neal, 2004; Spring, Grimm, & Dietz, 2009). Much of this decline has been associated with the current restrictive federal and state policies driving educational practices. Spring et al. (2009) note that principals cited state curriculum requirements as a major obstacle to using service-learning. Some scholars have reported that the focus on teaching particular content standards has made it difficult for teachers to connect service-learning activities with their curriculum. This is in light of the fact that they are calling on teacher educators to guide future teachers to use service-learning as an instructional approach aligned with standards-based practices (Hill, 2009; Seitsinger, 2005; Wade, 2007).

Although these restrictive policies may be key factors for the decrease of service-learning in K–12 schools, another factor is likely related to educators' perceptions of service-learning. Skinner and Chapman (1999) found that most principals view service-learning as more beneficial to students' civic and social development than to their academic achievement. Such views position service-learning as a charitable activity, and might explain why schools might not use service-learning when faced with the pressure to increase student test scores.

Critical scholar-practitioners have argued that this perception of service-learning as "charity" could lead to its eradication from instructional contexts; therefore, they have called for service-learning practitioners to implement more critical service-learning experiences that attend to the causal forces influencing the need for the service (Butin, 2003; Daigre, 2000; Hart, 2006; Schensul, Berg, & Brase, 2002; Wade, 2007). Such a critical service-learning pedagogy unites democratic civic engagement with the processes of critique and questioning promoted by critical pedagogies. Through this transformation, civic responsibility and democratic participation become the means rather than the ends to addressing social issues. Service-learning is thus transformed into alignment with social change rather than social service or charity. Positioning critical service-learning in this way holds potential to increase the value and respect for it as a viable instructional approach.

Despite the oppressive polices and pressures associated with the commercialization and standardization of schooling in the United States, nearly a quarter (24%) (Spring et al., 2009) of all K–12 schools still integrate service activities into classroom curricula through service-learning. It is unclear how these schools and teachers are able to navigate through these challenging times to engage their students in service-learning experiences. This chapter adds to this dialogue through an examination of how classroom teachers enrolled in a graduate *Teaching for Equity and Justice* course navigated restrictive and oppressive educational systems to engage their students in critical service-learning experiences. The premise behind the course was to address the key factors associated with the low prevalence of service-learning and develop teachers' understanding of critical service-learning and how this approach could be aligned with curriculum standards.

First, I present the defining features of critical service-learning that framed the course and how these principles were enacted within the various projects. Next, I present key themes that illustrate the challenges these teachers faced and the various strategies used to navigate through them. Finally, I close with a discussion on how these processes of navigation and negotiation hold promise for transforming educational spaces to promote social justice education through critical service-learning.

TEACHING FOR EQUITY AND JUSTICE

As part of the Curriculum and Instruction graduate program, students typically enroll in a multicultural education course focused on theoretical and practical applications of multicultural curricula (see Grant & Sleeter, 2008). For the purpose of this project, this course was transformed and designed around a justice-oriented framework that viewed social justice education as a blend of content and process intended to enhance equity across social groups, foster critical perspectives, and promote social action (Bell, 1997; Cochran-Smith, 2004; Grant & Sleeter, 2008). Through this lens, the aim of the course was to develop teachers' understanding of multicultural education as more than one in which issues of diversity are examined. Such education also includes encouraging students to critically examine social inequalities and assisting them in locating opportunities for action to promote social change.

To address these social justice education goals, critical service-learning pedagogy was used to ground the theoretical and practical explorations of the course. Critical service-learning was presented as a philosophy and instructional method that engages students in critiquing and questioning social inequities and combines academic content and social action to address these inequities (Butin, 2007; Hart, 2006; Wade, 2007). As such, critical service-learning was distinguished from a more traditional form of service-learning because of its focus on developing a commitment to social justice more than individual civic responsibility. Emphasizing how critical service-learning moved beyond addressing individual needs to include inquiry into altering the root causes of societal issues provided the teachers with an understanding of how this approach could foster their students' development of "valuable skills, knowledge, and values that will contribute to their becoming active and informed citizens" (Wade, 2007, p. 26).

An action research assignment was developed, which required the teachers to design and implement a critical service-learning project with their students. Hackman's (2005) components for social justice education and Wade's (2007) principles of social justice-oriented service-learning served as tools to guide the development and implementation of these critical service-learning projects. The aim was to construct quality projects that included the following key structures: academic connections, critical thinking and analysis about social issues, social action, and personal reflection. Each of these elements will be highlighted throughout the project descriptions provided in the next section.

Critical Service-Learning Projects and Principles

The teachers' projects covered a range of social issues, academic areas, and social actions. Some of the projects involved the connection of curriculum to agencies beyond the school walls. The Quilt Project united Language Arts standards with issues of poverty and homelessness. Through this project, first and second grade students used their knowledge about syllables and poetry to construct "poem quilts" to contribute to mothers with young children in the nearby homeless shelter. Throughout the project students discussed the connection between homelessness and poverty. Similarly, the Plant-A-Row for the Hungry Project united multiple academic standards across Science, Social Studies, Math and Language Arts as they explored the connections between poverty and hunger. Through this project, students in Grades 1–5 designed, constructed, planted, and tended a garden and contributed the harvest to the local food bank.

Some projects engaged students as critical agents, conducting research in their surrounding communities in order to share this knowledge with others. The Citizenship Voter Project united Government Social Studies standards and English Language Development High School standards to address the low number of Latino voters in the town. Latino, English Learners, engaged in researching the democratic process within their community by attending city council meetings, school board meetings, and conducting voter registration drives within their community. Throughout the process, students reflected on their experiences in connection to the content in their Government class. As a culminating activity, the students presented their experiences to various classes, explaining the process and importance of voting.

The Water Issues Project also engaged students in active research in the community. Fifth grade students used Reading, Writing, and Science standards to critically explore the water conservation and access issues facing their community. Students visited local water treatment plants, conducted community surveys, and spoke with farm worker union leaders and university environmental scientists to collect information. This information was synthesized into a presentation for classes at the school and a brochure to distribute to community families.

The Discrimination Project engaged high school students to look at issues of discrimination within their local contexts, broader media contexts, and future workplace contexts. The group of English teachers that developed this project focused on using various Reading and Writing standards to explore these concepts. They used youth media resources as the springboard to engage in critique of various workplace practices, and eventually moved into school practices. This project culminated in the students designing and creating interactive presentations for other students to explore the same concepts and increase awareness about these issues.

OVERVIEW OF THE RESEARCH DESIGN

The findings presented in this chapter are from a larger study examining the impact of critical service-learning on teachers, students, and communities. While the various critical service-learning projects from this study ground the research in real-world applications, the focus is not on the projects, but rather the challenges faced during their implementation. Specifically, the question of what challenges do restrictive educational policies present for critical service-learning practitioners, and how do teachers navigate these challenges will be addressed.

Participants

The 28 teacher participants in this study were all graduate students enrolled in the Teaching for Equity and Justice course. Although all of the contexts for the teachers' projects were contained within five districts across California's Central Valley, the diversity of the group provided for a range of perspectives. There are 26 females and 2 males; over a third identified their ethnicity as other than White (1 Asian American, 9 Mexican American). Years of teaching experience range from 1 to 22 years, with roughly a third falling into each of three broad categories: novice (0–5 years), experienced (5–9 years), and veteran (10+ years). Likewise, the teachers also represent a broad range of contexts; 12 taught at the high school (9–12) level, 2 at the middle school (6–8) level, 6 at the intermediate (4–6) level, and 8 at the primary (K–3) level. Most of the teachers work in small town or rural school settings, with only 2 working in an urban context.

Data Collection

A triangulated approach was developed to cross-check for accuracy and address issues that might arise from a single data collection method (Denzin, 1989; Janesick, 1994). Multiple sources of data were collected throughout the semester as part of the course assignments. The teachers used individual electronic journals to postweekly reflections regarding their experiences using critical service-learning pedagogy to promote equity and social justice. Online threaded discussion assignments provided the teachers with a way to collaboratively reflect and share their experiences while making connections between course materials and their critical service-learning projects. Also, throughout the semester teachers participated in small focus groups. Following a semi-structured format, the teachers were asked to describe the progress of their projects and discuss any challenges they encountered and how they negotiated them. These tools were used to guide the process of the projects, facilitate the course seminars, and also provide a source of data to map the process teachers used to navigate points of challenge.

At the conclusion of the semester, the teachers completed an open-ended questionnaire and participated in focus group interviews. Using similar questions, these two tools served to gain insight into the teachers' perceptions of critical service-learning, the ways it impacted student achievement and dispositions toward social justice, and the potential transformations in their own perspectives. In addition, teachers were asked to reflect on the challenges they faced, the process they used to negotiate those challenges, and the outcomes of the various methods they used.

Several months after the course was completed, I conducted follow-up individual interviews. The interviews served as a way to provide verification of the findings from initial analysis. The interviews also provided for an update on the progress of the project, whether it had continued after the class, and to learn about further challenges and obstacles.

Data Analysis

A grounded theory approach (Glaser & Strauss, 1967; Strauss & Corbin, 1990) was used to analyze each set of qualitative data. The analysis began with repeated readings of the data, using memoing techniques to record initial perspectives. The analysis then focused on each teacher as a case, followed by each project group as a case. A series of cross-case analysis procedures compared teachers, project groups, and school levels. This process of case analysis focused on convergent views across cases as well as divergent views between cases. Open and axial coding procedures were used to identify emergent themes, group themes into coherent categories, and uncover the relationships between categories.

PROCESS OF NEGOTIATION

As the analysis of the data progressed, it became clear that there is no universal process for negotiating the challenges of engaging in critical service-learning in the current climate of restrictive and oppressive educational policies. Rather, as illustrated throughout the themes presented in this section, schools are unique contexts. Different perspectives of administrators and teachers and the intersection of these perspectives worked to shape the social and political context of each school, producing unique challenges that required equally diverse negotiation strategies. These challenges have been grouped into two main categories: *Initial Administrator Support and Curriculum and Instruction Mandates.* The following section organizes the themes in this way to highlight how the initial negotiation process set the foundation for future events and challenges. To conclude this section, a third theme is presented to describe how the negotiation process played a role in shaping teachers' perspectives about critical service-learning in particular and the potential for transforming oppressive educational policies in general.

Initial Administrator Support

At the beginning of the process, there was much concern over the possibility of implementing a critical service-learning project. The following journal responses illustrate how teachers across all grade levels doubted their administrators would permit the projects because of the pressures from high-stakes testing.

> A worry that comes to mind is getting my admin support. He'll be breathing down our necks if we can't prove that every minute of the project is standards-based and will help improve those almighty test scores. [Third Grade Teacher]

> The politics of our district define the focus of our instruction. Right now the focus is test prep for the [state tests]. I don't think we'll have their [administrators'] support. In order for us to use service-learning, we will need to see a shift in the mindset of our administrators. [High School English Teacher]

This initial challenge arose from the teachers' perceptions regarding the control administrators had over instructional decision making. This lack of agency existed throughout the teachers' comments in this study, and the statements above are clearly connected with the pressure to have their students perform well on the tests. In both instances, the dominant theme is preparing students for the test, and critical service-learning was not a test-prep activity.

While there was much concern over this potential challenge, teachers took different approaches to address the issue. Most of the teachers elected to discuss the projects directly with their administrators. However, several teachers avoided this obstacle and chose not to even mention it to their administrators. During a focus group discussing this issue, Louise explained, "We didn't think the administration would have been supportive of the project, but they didn't need to know what we were doing."

Those who chose the more direct route used a variety of strategies. Some teachers created a detailed description of the specific content standards that would be addressed through the critical service-learning project in preparation for meeting with the principal. For the voter registration project, this proved successful but not without some resistance. Stefan explained the events of the meeting during a focus group.

> You know, I went with a list of standards that I was going to address. I gave a lot of detail about how the different activities would match the standards. But, he still said, "No," at first. I was just emphatic about the connections to the standards and he gave the OK but reminded me to be sure and cover the standards.

For others, this strategy was not successful. Despite specific connections to the various content standards, administrators still denied the use of critical service-learning projects during regular class time. Teachers were forced to conduct their projects as "clubs" either before or after school. As Julia explained during a focus group, each of these options limited the potential of the project.

> It was a challenge convincing my school administration to allow for the service-learning project at our school. He seemed to like the fact that I was exposing more students to more science content, but did not like that the project would move away from the district's Explicit Direct Instruction

> approach to teaching. To get around this obstacle, I ensured my administration that even though I would not take an EDI approach, I would make sure the lessons were focused on specific science standards. He was still against the idea of using class time, so we [had] to do the project outside of school hours. It will be difficult for many students to stay after school, so we're going to do it in the morning, but in the morning there is much more limited amount of time.

The teachers who encountered the least resistance from administrators opted to transform established school activities or develop ideas that matched known administrator goals. This strategy required teachers to be familiar with their administrators' ideals as well as innovative in their project design. For example, Brenda felt her principal was "very supportive" of her project because it involved the anti-bullying curriculum that "was something already required and adopted" by her district. As she added in her journal, "I just thought we already had to do it, so how can I make it more toward social justice. Partnering with the Kinders [Kindergarten students] was a great way to get my fourth graders to take responsibility and teach others about respect." Similarly, the teachers working on the Plant-A-Row for the Hungry Project expanded on their school's garden club as a way to garner administrator support. As one member noted during a focus group,

> We felt like support would be tough, but taking one of our existing programs and making it real service-learning we knew he would like. Plus, showing how something that is a club could also connect with our standards was a big selling point.

These two examples provide some potential solutions to negotiating the challenge of obtaining support for engaging in critical service-learning projects. With this strategy, Brenda creatively worked from the inside out. Understanding her principal's focus on using mandated curriculum, she capitalized on this knowledge and expanded the mandated curriculum outside the classroom walls to engage her students in social action. In contrast, the Plant-A-Row group worked from the outside in. Recognizing their principal supported extracurricular activities, they started with his interest and brought the project across the threshold of an otherwise restrictive curriculum.

Appealing to administrators' objectives and building from established school structures appear to be two key characteristics of the negotiation process that may lead to initial support. Although this process could be viewed as compliance with oppressive educational policies and teachers yielding to the demands of administrators, it is through such negotiations that critical service-learning must create space to permeate current educational contexts. It is through such negotiations, or compromises, that issues of poverty, equity and social justice made their way into these classrooms.

Curriculum and Instruction Mandates

Curriculum pacing and curriculum mapping were mandated procedures that regulated the teachers' instructional practices. Pacing guides were used to delineate the sequence and timeframe of instructional content in order to ensure all tested concepts were taught prior to the administration of the state test, while curriculum maps served as recording tools to monitor what content was actually taught. Both of these practices dictated the content as well as the flow of instruction, and created several challenges for the teachers as they designed and implemented their critical service-learning projects.

One challenge involved determining where social justice issues and concepts fit within the prescribed curriculum. Many teachers saw strong potential for social justice issues to be connected with Science and Social Studies standards; however, the pacing guides neglected these subject areas. As a third grade teacher explained, "We are forced to focus on Reading and Math. We don't teach Science and Social Studies. It's not even on our plan." Karley also faced this challenge, and provided insight into how the pacing guides placed higher value on particular subject areas and marginalized others, particularly if they were not tested.

> I met with Mr. H [principal] to discuss the details of the recycling project. Initially, I wanted to do a whole environmental unit on natural, renewable, non-renewable resources to lead into the recycling project. This would give students the background needed to develop the project and raise the awareness of the other students. He liked my plan, and I had it connected to the standards. But [he] said I couldn't spare that much time because those standards weren't the "heavy-hitters" we needed to focus on. So we just discussed recycling."

As noted in Karley's comment, these tools created conditions that often preempted the potential of critical service-learning projects from being realized. In some cases, teachers yielded to the pressure to conform to these mandated processes. Projects were "put on hold" or ceased in an effort to try and "keep pace with curriculum calendars."

Many of the teachers found a way to navigate this challenge. Though they selected a variety of methods, these teachers viewed this process as one that began with a transformation in perspective. Some teachers viewed this transformation in relation to perspectives on curriculum. Sean shared his perspective in relation to the challenge of negotiating curricular mandates.

> I started to see how to use multicultural and social justice concepts as a way to build on the standards-based curriculum or look at the standards-based curriculum in a different light, rather than add to the already gigantic list of things we must accomplish. This made the process a lot more manageable.

From this perspective, the content of a particular class can be easily adapted and infused with social justice principles. The realization Sean makes is that this is merely a transformation in how a teacher approaches the presentation of content. Luz shared her struggles with this shift in her journal.

> I kept thinking to myself, "How can I fit this into my curriculum of Medieval History?" I was purposely staying away from that curricular area when choosing my service-learning project because it seemed so daunting. However, I began to see that I could choose an overarching theme that encompasses a broader sense of the standards. I knew my class and I could not change anything about the Crusades, Spanish Inquisition, or Fall of Rome. But, we could choose to view these events with a more critical eye, say, prejudice, gender inequality, oppression of minority and apply the learning to a present day situation. "How can we ensure these types of events do not happen again?" This is the real purpose of history, not spouting facts and dates, but learning from our past mistakes and ensuring a better world.

As with many teachers new to critical service-learning, the struggle to find space in mandated curriculum to address issues of justice and equity can seem daunting. However, as these comments illustrate, such mandated curriculum can be transformed through critical perspectives and engaged critique. Providing space for such questions allows for opportunities for social action to emerge, which eases teachers' anxiety and facilitates the process of designing a critical service-learning project.

Teachers also navigated this challenge to find space for social justice issues in the prescribed curriculum by integrating marginalized subjects, such as Science and Social Studies, with more valued subjects, such as Language Arts and Math. This approach was unique to elementary teachers in this study, most likely due to the fact that many of them teach multiple subject areas and are familiar with the various content standards. This method required the teachers to shift their perspective on the mandated curriculum and creatively construct connections across the different subjects. Deanna elaborated on this concept as she reported on her negotiation of this challenge.

> Well, it really got me to think about my teaching, well, what I teach in a different way. I was so used to thinking about a checklist of standards that had to be covered. In thinking about tying in social justice issues, I began seeing connections across the standards, and I just kept thinking, "Ok, oh, I could tie this social justice issue with this standard, or this with that." It helped to see those connections.

This shift challenged the dominant perspective of curriculum as fragmented and isolated concepts or knowledge codified as standards, opening up space for social justice issues to permeate the curriculum and also providing more opportunities for social action.

However, once teachers transformed their perspectives on curriculum, a new challenge arose regarding the lack of materials available to teach social justice concepts. Many of the teachers noted that their textbooks did not "address social justice or provide a variety of perspectives" on issues. Although frustrated by this time-consuming challenge, several teachers collaborated to resolve the issue. Working in groups allowed for teachers to share the workload, conducting Internet searches, visiting libraries and bookstores, and creating materials.

Across the grade levels, children's literature appeared to be a key resource for supplementing the standard curriculum. The use of children's literature was viewed as an engaging way to explore social justice issues while addressing Language Arts standards. As a high school English teacher commented,

> We needed to teach author's purpose, something that kids struggle to understand. This is an important component of social justice because you have to consider questions like: Who is marginalized? Whose story is being told? Is the argument valid? These are important for critical thinking. The children's stories made that easy for them.

Her colleague further elaborated on how the use of children's literature facilitated the students' grasp of complex critical concepts.

> I think it is interesting that we were able to use children's literature to teach such complex ideas. It seems like a great idea because it lowers the chance of confusion. We are simplifying one area of the equation. If we talked about a complex idea through a complex piece of text, students would have to work their way through both. Through children's literature, they were able to work their way through the reading more easily, and therefore be able to critically analyze the literature and get to the important discussion questions and ideas.

In addition, teachers supplemented the standard curriculum with other resources. For example, Alison integrated several Science standards into her Language Arts lessons, through her water conservation project. Newspaper articles, *Democracy Now!* Podcasts, and documentary films about water issues served as the instructional texts. Using these texts, she taught the students expository comprehension strategies and addressed science standards on "understanding local natural resources" while they uncovered and discussed the various perspectives regarding the cause of the water issues as presented in the materials. Similarly, Tanya, a second grade teacher, integrated Social Studies into her Language Arts lessons. Using websites about poverty and hunger, she taught students various reading standards and addressed Social Studies standards on "food production, consumption, and limited resources" while exploring the underlying factors associated with these social issues.

In addition to restrictive mandates dictating the content and pace of instruction, teachers also faced mandates requiring particular delivery methods. Several of the districts in this study required an explicit and direct method of instruction (EDI). This method is a systematic step-by-step structured format for delivering instruction, with specific pacing for each of the components of the lesson. This method provided an obstacle to the active engagement necessary for critical service-learning projects. "It is very difficult to do hands-on learning. Since we have to teach in the EDI format, this forces us to use worksheets." As noted by many of the teachers working under this model, worksheets served to provide the students independent practice and were required to document student participation and provide evidence of student work. The following journal entry from Meagan explains how this method interfered directly with the implementation of her critical service-learning project.

> Right now we are boxed in as far as what we can say and do each day in our classrooms. This really takes away the opportunity that we have to enact a true push toward social justice. I've been able to teach some aspects of social justice in the classroom through discussing marginalized characters in books or through some writing. However, I often feel that just when my students are starting to really reflect on their project and make connections to the issues I have to stop everything and make sure I'm CFU-ing (Checking for Understanding) or that I'm allowing for closure time, etc. along the EDI model in case my principal walks in.

Similar to Meagan, many of the challenges the teachers faced emanated from their worry about not adhering to school policy. The following comment from a focus group captures the dominant view of the group, which was that not following mandated pacing guides or structured lesson formats may lead to negative consequences.

> This type of learning veers from the direction of our district ... at our school, not doing the same thing as your team leads to a bad evaluation. Our district is strong-arming teachers to become models of conformity, who robotically create lessons and instruction that is uniform.

Despite these challenges created by mandated curricular and instructional policies, many of the teachers were able to overcome them and engage their students in critical service-learning projects. As with the teachers who struggled to navigate these challenges, their attitude toward these mandates influenced their decisions and actions. One teacher noted, "I just made service-learning the priority. I knew it was important, and I just focused on teaching the standards through the service-learning project." Another teacher also noted the importance she placed on the project and how this influenced her process of negotiation.

> Trying to find time to break out of the routines that are locked in by administrators to go deeper into the issues behind our project was challenging. I had to get creative and flexible to make the time and prioritize my teaching.

These teachers worked around the parameters established by the curricular mandates and placed precedence on the service-learning project over the adherence to policy. The question became, what fostered this attitude? Brenda explained how she found space to be flexible with her activities and instruction, "My administrators know that I get things done. I have good test scores, so they tend to leave me alone." Likewise, Alison shared a similar sense of freedom, "I don't have anyone breathing down my neck or watching my every move. I am a good teacher, and my test scores are always good." It appears that administrators did not enforce mandated procedures with these teachers because of their record of producing high student achievement. In essence, "good" test scores earned these teachers a higher status, which in turn earned them freedom and autonomy in their classrooms.

IMPACT OF NEGOTIATION

The teachers in this study experienced a variety of obstacles constructed by oppressive and restrictive educational policies. Lack of administrator support, curricular mandates, and pressures of testing are challenges faced by many teachers attempting to engage their students in a critical approach to service-learning (Wade, 2001, 2007). Like other social justice educators, these teachers selected a variety of strategies of subversion, resistance, and transformation to overcome or adapt to these challenges.

During this process of negotiation, these teachers found themselves "conflicted in this climate of standardized instruction and achievement centered around isolated subskills and tests, asking themselves how and where does such a pedagogy fit with the pedagogy mandated by state and local districts" (Hart, 2006, p. 29). The friction created by this dilemma prompted these teachers to examine their own educational contexts through a critical perspective. The following discussion explores how this critical perspective was developed and the ways it impacted the teachers' perceptions of the potential for transforming current restrictive and oppressive structures to open spaces for social justice education and critical service-learning.

The teachers recognized the dominant, oppressive, and authoritative structures embedded within their schools. They easily identified and critiqued the practices they believed created unfair and restrictive learning environments. However, they did not initially see themselves as having authority to disrupt these restrictions. During the final focus group, Alison reflected on her initial perspectives on the potential to use critical service-learning.

> You know, I've been teaching in the United States for seven years, and I didn't know teachers could do the things we did. Talking about issues of justice with the students and having them work on solving those issues. I thought we would have been fired.

Likewise, Mary's initial journal highlights this feeling of restricted autonomy. "I wish we had the freedom to do something like one of these projects. Maybe we do, and I just don't know it. I always feel like there is some parameter I have to maintain."

Through collaborative reflection with colleagues in the course, the teachers began to actively question and critique the oppressive structures dictating their teaching. The following discussion board sequence illustrates how this collaborative reflection guided teachers to recognize their compliance with the oppressive structures they critiqued.

Rhianna: I'm having an "ignorance is bliss" moment. I could go along like a horse with blinders on and pretend that I'm doing enough with my standards-based instruction. However, I'm glaringly aware that it isn't working; it isn't enough. My kids aren't motivated to learn; many of them don't see the value in it. They are bored, and they struggle to see ownership in their learning. I recognize there's a lot more to do, so now what?

Meagan: What we are required to do to our students is in direct opposition to what we know and believe to be "education." What are these "best practices" anyway? What are the results of these so-called '"best practices?" These questions have been on my mind recently. I feel so guilty and torn about how I'm expected to teach my students. I have become so angry about the current state of education. If we need to teach our students to question the status quo shouldn't we also be role models of that kind of thinking?

Alison: Most teachers avoid being political, but it is necessary if we want change and we want to teach from a social justice perspective. Obedience and conformity rule the schools.

Mary: You're right. I am learning a lot about myself through this course, realizing that I accept a lot of what I'm told to do, when I should be challenging or at least questioning it.

Louise: I, too, am learning a lot about myself. I need to challenge the status quo as I've been guilty of accepting the 'that's the way it is' line. Only then can I show my students how to discern and question things that don't seem right.

While emancipation from oppression begins with the type of critique illustrated above, it is only the first step. As the teachers developed and implemented their critical service-learning projects, they were actively engaged in taking action to transform the repressive structures they critiqued. It was through the negotiation process that the teachers engaged in a cyclical process of critique and social action. However, in reviewing the navigation methods and outcomes, some of the teachers found this process empowering, while others remained pessimistic.

For example, Meagan noted how this process altered her view on the authority of the pacing curriculum.

> Too often teachers get caught up in the daily grind and the requirements of a curriculum map. Doing this project helped me see that there is a way that I can remain a teacher dedicated to standards-based instruction, who also incorporates critical social action into my classroom.

Paola also highlighted how this process transformed her perspective on teaching and provided her the sense of power necessary to continue with this work.

> I think we should all find time to engage our students in these types of service-learning experiences, as we have seen its importance. We need to break out of the box, but [it] will definitely take some time to get used to changing our style of teaching that we are accustomed to. I feel like with our project

> we have taken the first steps, but we have a long way to go. This course has given me the confidence and knowledge to take on more issues I feel passionate about, something I would not have felt empowered to do before.

In contrast, some of the teachers did not hold such optimistic views. Although critique and awareness were raised for teachers in this category, they still felt powerless to change oppressive structures. Many teachers who maintained this perspective had very unsuccessful experiences during the negotiation process. For example, Deanna had her project relegated to an after-school club, and noted in our final focus group how she continued to struggle in the stage of critique.

> I agree with the concepts and realize the potential, but I want to keep my job. Some say this is the easy route, teaching traditionally, but I don't think it's that easy. I know changing how we teach is possible, and that would take a lot of time and effort. Right now I feel like I'm barely staying afloat.

Although Deanna continued to see potential and hope, Gianna viewed change as hopeless with her current administrator, "He still wasn't happy I was doing something out of the EDI box. I was able to do some things with it for the sake of this course, but I'm sure he wouldn't let me incorporate another one into the curriculum." Gianna faced initial resistance from her administrator, and her instruction was constantly monitored for adherence to mandated policies throughout the course of the study. Such close enforcement of restrictive policies worked to actively reinforce the powerlessness of teachers.

CONCLUDING THOUGHTS

These teachers' experiences illustrate the ways that schools operate as social hierarchies, where instructional practices are reified through curriculum and policy. Educators who wish to work in the realm of critical service-learning must be aware of the ways that these structures could potentially challenge and suppress their efforts. However, as the teachers in this study demonstrate, even in this era of accountability, space can be found and created to address social justice issues through critical service-learning. The external pressures that influenced their teaching were addressed in a number of ways. Whether the teachers chose to directly resist oppressive mandates, subvert the system, or compromise to work within the system, these choices were made to accomplish what they believed was right for their students.

To engage in such work requires teachers to be critically aware and reflective of the political and social context in which they teach. This critical awareness begins with recognizing the hegemonic practices of the school and how these established values and belief systems contribute to a legitimizing of the differential power structures. Embedded within this awareness is also recognition that power structures are constructed in social contexts, and therefore, open for reconstruction by those interacting within these contexts. Such reconstruction involves teachers recognizing themselves as agents who can wield power over their actions in order to influence educational practices.

To develop this critical awareness, teachers must engage in the difficult work of completely transforming their perspectives on the social, political, and organizational structures of the education system, their position within this system, and the agency that is available to them from this position. In essence, teachers must transform their view of teaching and their identities as teachers. This transformation is difficult because these subjective positions have been historically constructed, or as one teacher succinctly stated, "As teachers, we are taught to think these ways." Transforming one's worldview, way of thinking, seeing, and believing is not easily achieved.

The particular course that framed these teachers' engagement with critical service-learning may be viewed as an important contributor to this transformative process. Such a course may hold potential for teacher educators who wish to foster their students' understanding of educational inequities and take action through critical service-learning pedagogy. The course requirement to conduct a project could be seen as the catalyst that initiated the process. The collaborative design of the course could be the factor that supported the teachers' critical reflection on curriculum and instruction. Quite often it was through such peer dialogue and reflection that teachers came to see ways to transform mandated materials or to locate spaces where project activities could fit within mandated parameters. The professor could also be seen as a vital contributor, guiding the teachers to reflectively process through their challenges.

However, these same course structures could be viewed as another dominant system promoting a "correct" and "just" way of thinking. Forcing these teachers to engage in a process of self-transformation could be viewed as another way of oppressing their individual values and beliefs. In addition, teacher educators need to be aware of the potential for such a course to serve as a way to reinforce and perpetuate the dominance of current policies over teachers. Not all of the teachers in this study had empowering experiences that transformed their thinking. As evident in this teacher's final reflection, engaging in critique heightened their awareness of oppressive conditions but did nothing to change their sense of helplessness.

> The main challenge that continues to stand in the way of doing these kinds of projects is the focus of education itself. Education is currently focused on data that is produced from standardized tests. The people that make education demands and decisions want test results. The educational pendulum needs to shift back toward a more student-centered focus. This is an important factor that may have no other solution than time itself. (High School Teacher)

Rather than waiting for the tide to turn, the following teacher provides an alternative and productive view for transforming hopelessness into action aimed at change.

> The pressures and demands of the district are very demanding. The district is force-feeding specific instructional techniques, criticizing efforts and performance, and has created a system filled with hidden intentions, false statements, and miscommunications. This has left me with a bitter feeling of hopelessness. It seems like there is not much a teacher can do, but they need to make the most out of what they can do.

Any hegemonic system requires the compliance of those subjected to its dominance. As such, the current oppressive educational system only exists as long as educators comply with its dominant restrictive polices. Individual teachers may not be able to transform a whole system of restrictive and oppressive structures. However, in order to construct counterhegemonic practices, "teachers need to make the most of what they can do" and engage in dialogue to raise the awareness of their colleagues and administrators and work collaboratively to promote social justice in an effort to transform dominant and oppressive educational policies and practices.

QUESTIONS FOR REFLECTION

1. What are other ways to develop teachers' skills as critical service-learning educators?
2. What are the restrictive/oppressive structures influencing administrators' views and actions? How could these structures be critiqued, challenged and transformed?
3. What are potential structures or strategies that could ensure the transformative process these teachers started is sustained?
4. The course can be seen as a factor motivating the teachers to navigate through the challenges. What structures or supports could facilitate teachers continuing to challenge the system?

5. What structures or strategies could the teachers have utilized to more successfully navigate the challenges encountered?
6. Sean notes how "time" is the factor he's counting on for change. Is this a realistic perspective? What other actions are necessary to promote the use of critical service-learning?

REFERENCES

Amrein, A. L., & Berliner, D. C. (2002, March 28). High-stakes testing, uncertainty, and student learning. *Education Policy Analysis Archives, 10*(18). Retrieved from http://epaa.asu.edu/epaa/v10n18/

Au, W. (2007). High-stakes testing and curricular control: A qualitative metasynthesis. *Educational Researcher, 36*(5), 258–267.

Bell, L. (1997). Theoretical foundations for social justice education. In M. Adams, L. Bell, & P. Griffin (Eds.), *Teaching for diversity and social justice* (pp. 3–15). New York, NY: Routledge.

Butin, D. W. (2003). Of what use is it? Multiple conceptualizations of service learning within education. *Teacher College Record, 105*(9), 1674–1692.

Butin, D. W. (2007). Justice-learning: Service-learning as justice-oriented education. *Equity and Excellence in Education, 40*, 177–183.

Cochran-Smith, M. (2004). *Walking the road: Race, diversity, and social justice*. New York, NY: Teachers College Press.

Daigre, E. (2000). Toward a critical service-learning pedagogy: A Freirean approach to civic literacy. *Academic Exchange, 1*, 6–14.

Denzin, N. (1989). Strategies of multiple triangulation. In *The research act* (3rd ed., pp. 235–247). Englewood Cliffs, NJ: Prentice Hall.

Glaser, B. G. & Strauss, A. L. (1967). *The discovery of grounded theory: Strategies for qualitative research*. New York, NY: Aldine De Gruyter.

Grant, G. A., & Sleeter, C. A. (2008). *Turning on learning: Five approaches for multicultural teaching plans for race, class, gender, and disability*. Hoboken, NJ: Wiley.

Hackman, H. W. (2005). Five essential components for social justice education. *Equity and Excellence in Education, 38*, 103–109.

Hart, S. (2006). Breaking literacy boundaries through critical service-learning: Education for the silenced and marginalized. *Mentoring and Tutoring, 14*(1), 17–32.

Hill, D. (2009). Death of a dream: Revisited. In National Youth Leadership Council (2009). *Growing to Greatness: The State of Service-Learning Report*. St. Paul, MN: National Youth Leadership Council. Retrieved from http://www.nylc.org/objects/publications/ 8030548_Body.pdf

Janesick, V. J. (1994). The dance of qualitative research design: Metaphor, methodolatry, and meanig. In N. K. Denzin & Y.S. Lincoln (Eds.), *Handbook of qualitative research* (pp. 209–235). Thousand Oaks, CA: SAGE.

Kielsmeier, J. C., Scales, P. C., Roehlkepartain, E. C., & Neal, M. (2004). Community service and service-learning in public schools. In National Youth Leadership Council (2004). *Growing to Greatness: The State of Service-Learning Report.*

St. Paul, MN: National Youth Leadership Council. Retrieved from http://www.nylc.org/objects/inaction/initiatives/2004G2G/G2G04FULL3.pdf

Nichols, S. L., & Berliner, D. C. (2007). *Collateral damage: How high-stakes testing corrupts America's schools*. Cambridge, MA: Harvard Education Press.

Schensul, J., Berg, M., & Brase, M. (2002). Theories guiding outcomes for action research for service-learning. In A. Furco & S. H. Billig (Eds.), *Service-Learning: The essence of the pedagogy* (pp. 125–146). Greenwich, CT: Information Age.

Seitsinger, A. M. (2005). Service-learning and standards-based instruction in middle schools. *Journal of Educational Research, 99*(1), 19–30.

Skinner, R., & Chapman, C. (1999). *Service-learning and community service in K–12 public schools* (NCES Publication No. 1999043). Washington, DC: U.S. Government Printing Office.

Spring, K., Grimm, R., & Dietz, N. (2009). Community service and service-learning in public schools 2008. In National Youth Leadership Council (2009). *Growing to Greatness: The State of Service-Learning Report*. St. Paul, MN: National Youth Leadership Council. Retrieved from http://www.nylc.org/objects/publications/8030548_Body.pdf

Strauss, A. L., & Corbin, J. (1990). *Basics of qualitative research: Grounded theory procedures and techniques*. Newbury Park, CA: SAGE.

Wade, R. C. (2001). Social action in the Social Studies: From the ideal to the real. *Theory Into Practice, 40*(1), 23–28.

Wade, R. C. (2007). Service-learning for social justice in the elementary classroom: Can we get there from here? *Equity and Excellence in Education, 40*, 156–165.

Watanabe, M. (2007). Displaced teacher and state priorities in a high-stakes accountability context. *Educational Policy, 21*(2), 311–368.

CHAPTER 13

HOLDING ON TO TRANSFORMATION

Reflections on Global Service-Learning

Susan L. Herrmann

PRELUDE

This chapter will focus on the results of a modest qualitative study initially inspired by an archetypal story titled, "The Crescent Moon Bear," as told by Clarissa Pinkola Estes (1992), in *Women Who Run with the Wolves*. I came to her work during the 1990s, where her scholarship resonated with stories from my Indigenous heritage. Hundreds, perhaps a thousand years of sacred knowledge begged a larger audience. I began to wonder, "When a personal transformation occurs, when one reaches a pinnacle of wisdom, how does one hold on to that wisdom? Does personal transformation lead to social transformation?" Further, for those who do not have communities to support the transformed self, how do we create them? As a critical educator, I wondered if it is possible to "hold on" in an environment defined by advanced technology, the distractions of daily living, the alienation experienced from a capitalist economy, and a culture that

Critical Service Learning as a Revolutionary Pedagogy: A Project of Student Agency in Action, pp. 273–295

places greater value on the individual than recognizing the interconnectedness of all life.

The story of the "Crescent Moon Bear" suggests that it is just as difficult to maintain our wisdom as it was to obtain it. The story also speaks to the process of grieving that one goes through in order to reach a state of forgiveness. While this thread is beyond the scope of this study, I want to acknowledge that themes of reconciliation, forgiveness, grief, and patience were all powerfully present in page after page of student responses.

I dedicate this work to Phat, a 4-year old boy who is dying from complications related to Agent Orange, resulting from the spraying of dioxin during the (American) Vietnam War. He is one of an estimated three million Vietnamese currently affected by such exposure (York & Mick, 2008), and I hope this research inspires action towards alleviating the suffering we caused. As Americans, we represent those who unleashed dioxin onto innocents, we cannot move towards reconciliation and peace until we accept responsibility for the pain we perpetrated.

For the students who participated in this study, thank you for being the bearers of hope through your transformative experiences and subsequent commitment to social justice. To our in-country staff and governmental partners who move together as an orchestra, each playing a part, yet creating a symphony promoting effective social change to their fellow countrymen, meaningful educational experiences for our students, and guidance to their American counterparts, a depth of gratitude we extend.

Through the reaching inward that is required in the SUNY Brockport Vietnam Program, the students recreated themselves and reached out to their Vietnamese partners with sincerity, empathy, and friendship. Join me in bearing witness to their stories and in opening a space to learn what gems of wisdom they have to offer us on the path of transformative learning for social justice.

INTRODUCTION

As we engage the literatures on transformative learning, critical education, and critical global service-earning, we see common threads that have emerged over the last 100 years in discussions and debates about fostering democracy. As a social worker of Jane Addams' theoretical lineage, I situate myself within her radical pragmatism and honor her teachings on the importance of understanding context in the analysis of social ills. One of her many contributions to theory include her meditations on standpoint epistemology and the conclusions that she draws as a result. For example, she states,

> Formerly, when it was believed that poverty was synonymous with vice and laziness, and that the prosperous man was the righteous man, charity was administered harshly with a good conscience; for the charitable agent really blamed the individual for his poverty, and the very fact of his own superior prosperity gave him a certain consciousness of superior morality. (Addams, 1902, pp. 11–12)

To the radical social worker adopting the structural social work approach to theory and practice, the charity model is unacceptable. I depart from advocates of civic duty and democratic participation who suggest that the "goal for service-learning activities is to convey to students the importance of charity" because it is the "most broadly supported (and therefore most politically tenable)" (Kahne & Westheimer, 1996, p. 29). While it may be an easier approach to adopt, we cannot sell students (or anyone) short by promoting temporary good feelings over systemic, structural change towards the benefit of all.

Social work as a profession has struggled with numerous contradictions stemming from two differing assumptions about the vulnerable groups it serves. This struggle evidenced itself through the Charity Movement in the United States beginning in 1877 that viewed the poor as untrustworthy and deficient in character. Conventional social work methods worked to improve the lot of the poor through coordination of services and cooperation with the charity system.

> All decisions regarding this system were made by the 'right' people in the community (i.e., mainly white, middle-class businessmen) because the poor could not be trusted to make responsible decisions affecting their lives; their poverty, after all, was seen as evidence of this inability. (Mullaly, 2007, p. 45)

The Settlement House Movement is the other branch from which the social work profession has roots. This movement assumed that the poor "were victims of an unjust social order that discriminated against large numbers of people so that a few might benefit" (Mullaly, 2007, p. 45).

Ideology is a significant consideration when claiming to be a proponent of critical service-learning, and as a profession, social work has a history of wavering in its commitment to the professional mission to ameliorate oppression. An example of conventional social work methods in practice is the social worker who threatens court action against a juvenile probationer for drinking alcohol and participating in gang activity. By failing to take into account the environmental factors at play, the conventional social worker perpetuates the ideological hegemony of classism and racism while seeking the client's cooperation with the status quo. The radical social worker asks critical questions such as "Why is there a bar on every street corner of this neighborhood? How do I organize the neighborhood to reclaim its schools, streets, businesses to support the individuals living there? Is there a way to engage the gang through critical dialogue to constructively challenge the power structures that perpetuate poverty?" At the root of this discussion on critical service-learning, are the ideas of democracy, participation, and the transformative impact that education has on democratic participation from the radical social work perspective.

Known as the father of critical education John Dewey grounds his ideas on the importance of democratic participation from a bottom-up approach to theory. He views philosophy without attention to emancipation and action as a useless endeavor. Dewey and Addams share similar views in their pragmatism and guide us towards the lived experience of emancipation through a thorough examination of social historical context. Dewey (1969) claims

> Philosophy is criticism of the influential beliefs that underlie culture; a criticism, which traces the beliefs to their generating conditions as far as, may be, which tracks them to their results, which considers the mutual compatibility of the elements of the total structure of beliefs. Such an examination terminates, whether so intended or not, in a projection of them into a new perspective which leads to new surveys of possibilities. (p. 19)

It is important to recognize that most of the literature reviewed for the purpose of this conversation finds expression through humanistic philosophy. Humanism is the epistemological framework from which the literature springs; it entrenches the research, and it guides the analysis of this data. I echo Gil's (2010) assertion that while "destructive tendencies are, indeed, intrinsic to human nature, this does not mean that relating and interacting destructively is inevitable, rather than merely possible" (p. 138). Equally possible, is a world in which we acknowledge our differences, respect one another, behave towards humanity's highest potential, and manifest sustainable living in harmony with nature and the understanding that human beings are varying expressions of one human family.

METHOD

The initial method for obtaining data included in-person, qualitative interviews with the students, with the understanding that their responses would be audio recorded for later transcription. However, every participant requested time to reflect upon the questions and opted for their own written narratives, followed by telephone interviews in the event that I had additional questions for them. Participants responded to 12 questions titled, "Impact of Global Service-Learning" (see Appendix). As a serving member of the Fund's board for the last 3 years, I have traveled to Vietnam with some student cohorts and have firsthand experience of the families and communities that we collectively serve. I think this influences study participants to be forthcoming of their experiences in Vietnam as we share a common bond of service. There are certain individuals, families, and communities that leave "heart prints" on us. For example, 88-year old, Ba Coi, a resident at the Loving House Nursing home is "in love" with Ken. Particular family members become the driving force behind our service and bond us to one another and to them. As a result, I think these connections live in and through us. As such, I cannot remove myself from the research, the students, their experiences, or the Vietnamese we work with and serve. For me, the beauty of critical service-learning is in the genuine relationships created by our authentic selves.

Social Historical Context of Study Abroad, International Education, and Critical Service-Learning

The research on study abroad, international education, and critical service-learning are all rooted in American ideas promoting national security and national interests (Kiely, 2011). The focus of most study abroad and international education programs is to enhance students' ability to exhibit culturally appropriate behaviors and skills and to train students to be competitive in a global economy (Kiely, 2011). It is important to be mindful of the political, cultural, and historical currents involved in the sojourners' experiences and to make connections between those and the transformative processes that result from that dynamic.

There is agreement among researchers that service-learning pedagogy "varies greatly across educators and institutions" (Mitchell, 2008, p. 50). As such, it is difficult to pin down a consensual definition of what constitutes service-learning and critical service-learning. Similar to the tensions in the social work profession, are the differing ideologies between traditional and critical service-learning programs. Critics of traditional service-learning programs point to their charity orientation and the lack of potential for social transformation, while critical educators develop service-learning programs with a social justice orientation (Mitchell, 2008). I agree with the critical camp and argue that educators can both develop students and strengthen communities through critical service-learning programs.

Intercultural Learning, Study Abroad, and International Education

In this portion of the literature review, I rely heavily on Kiely's work as he is on the frontiers of critical service-learning and his forthcoming book chapter provides the most extensive review of the literature currently available.

Inquiry into intercultural and study abroad exchanges produced volumes of research on sojourner adjustment or culture shock. Such studies ground themselves in developmental models or problem approaches (Anderson, 1994; Kim, 2001). Both camps assume that culture shock is a temporary phase on the way to cultural competence. Kiely (2011) reveals that the problem approach to treating culture shock was limited to conquering the symptoms and understanding the personality structures of sojourners; whereas, developmental research resulted in "more sophisticated theory and model building." He credits Savicki, Cooley, and Donnelly (2008) and Ward and Kennedy (1994) for their research to this effect.

Earlier developmental research identified challenges that sojourners face upon return to their home culture. While some scholars asserted that re-entry is more difficult than the initial culture shock (Gaw, 2000; Martin, 1984; Ward & Kennedy, 1994), other scholars suggest that this assertion is too simplistic and not grounded in theory (Ward & Kennedy, 1994). This argument persists despite the accurate identification of sojourner challenges with re-entry including, "personal, psychological, political, social, cultural, physical, and interpersonal" (Gaw, 2000; Kiely, 2011; Martin, 1984; Ward & Kennedy, 1994).

Another line of research details the transformative impact of intercultural learning and study abroad. These include Peter Adler's (1975, 1987) theoretical model that describes developmental transitions that sojourners journey through on the way to multiculturalism. Janet Bennett's (1993) research takes Adler's research to another level in her ideas on cultural marginality and encapsulated marginality. Bennett's concepts suggest that those who are functionally adapted to numerous cultures live at the margins of each and are, therefore, "cultural marginals" who move among and between each culture with a fair amount of ease. "Encapsulated marginals," on the opposite pole, experience fragmented identities and are unable to adapt to their varied cultural experiences (p. 113).

Milton Bennett's (1986, 1993) research has gained much popularity as a theory in practice, resulting from his analysis of intercultural competence on a developmental continuum. He produced the DMIS, or developmental model of intercultural sensitivity. His model suggests that individuals engaged in culture learning can move from initial stages of ethnocentrism towards the highest level of integration, where the interloper is at home in no specific culture, but rather, finds solid ground within a holistic sense of self (M. Bennett, 1993).

Most of the theorists draw the same conclusions, despite the different lenses from which they conduct their research. For example, Kim (2001) suggests that the challenges to transformative development are in flux in accord with environmental changes. Kim's model also ends with the idea that fully adapted individuals are able to move among and between cultures with internal psychic harmony (p. 57).

Links Between Transformational and Intercultural Learning

There is tremendous agreement among researchers regarding Mezirow's description of individual transformation as a life-long journey through the developmental continuum. Mezirow (2000) explicates a fifth turn in cognitive meaning making, illuminating the importance of individuals questioning and monitoring their own epistemic assumptions (p. 4). To demonstrate,

> Transformative learning refers to the process by which we transform our taken-for-granted frames of reference (meaning making perspectives, habits of mind, mind-sets) to make them more inclusive, discriminating, open, emotionally capable of change, and reflective so that they may generate beliefs and opinions that will prove more true or justified to guide action. Transformative learning involves participation in constructive discourse to use the experience of others to assess reasons justifying these assumptions, and making an action decision based on the resulting insight. (pp. 7–8)

In his studies examining intercultural adaptation, Kiely (2011) credits Taylor (1993, 1994a, 1994b) with "identifying a strong link between Mezirow's (1991), transformational learning theory and intercultural learning models." Utilizing different terminology, the parallels between the developments of adaptive behaviors throughout the life cycle are evident in both Mezirow's conceptual framework and the research on intercultural adaptation (Taylor, 1994b, p. 159). In Taylor's (1993) research examining the links between transformational learning theory and intercultural competence, the prominent features consisted of the "disorienting dilemma" (Mezirow, 2000, p. 22) and "culture shock," to name two.

Kiely (2011), notices that while a review of the empirical literature by Lyon (2002) validates the "common patterns across studies" with regard to the domains of Mezirow's transformational learning theory, "none of the studies examined re-entry, nor did they study how structural and contextual factors shape the transformational learning process" (p. 261).

Kiely (2011), Belenky and Stanton (2000), and Mitchell (2008) suggest that there is a gap in research examining the link between how asymmetrical relations impact transformational learning. Further, there is an argument among theorists like Sparrow (2000), who suggest that constructivist epistemology driving cognitive developmental theories fail to explain how structural factors affect transformational learning. Kiely (2011) asserts, "There is very little empirical evidence to support the critical assumption that cognitive transformation leads to personal and/or social behavior change and/or action." Also missing from the research is

> theoretical guidance and empirical documentation of not only how individuals are transformed by study abroad but also how study abroad affects social transformation. The linkage between learning context, learning processes, and outcomes as well as the connections between individual and social transformation are missing pieces in the study abroad research. (Kiely, 2011, p. 263)

Critical International Service-Learning

There is growing debate within service-learning literature as to the inherent ability of service-learning approaches to achieve more than individual transformative experiences (Mitchell, 2008). Traditional service-learning research suggests that students participating in such programs experience transformations that encourage greater tolerance and strong leadership skills and develop strong critical thinking skills (Mitchell, 2008). As detailed above, however, most study abroad and intercultural learning programs do not consider asymmetrical relations in that discourse. Proponents of critical service-learning argue that without attention to structural and contextual issues, students engaged in service-learning activities are patronizing their hosts through a charity model that promotes their own sense of privilege and diminishes their hosts' who, it is assumed, would be helpless without service (Ginwright & Cammarota, 2002; Robinson, 2000).

Critical service-learning diverges from traditional service-learning in its mission towards social justice. Researchers such as Rice and Pollack (2000) and Rosenberger (2000) note that while traditional service-learning meets individual needs, it fails to direct action towards the alleviation of structural inequalities. Traditional service-learning programs do not promote the reflective practice that considers the social, political, historical, or cultural contexts in the areas served. As such, they are limited in their ability to contribute to individual transformation or social transformation.

Critical pedagogy is revolutionary in nature, as it seeks to both understand the nature of social problems and the forces that promote injustice and oppression. Critical service-learning supports student agency and community partnership in responding to structural inequalities (Marullo, 1999; Rice & Pollack 2000).

Research addressing the transformational impact of international service-learning is an emerging body of knowledge attempting to address the long-term issues associated with challenges to perspective transformation. Kiely's (2004) longitudinal study of international service-learning participants in Nicaragua found that students develop an "emerging global consciousness" that is challenged and results in a "Chameleon Complex" as they wrestle with American consumerism, lack of compassionate support for their experiences with dire poverty and social inequity, and disillusionment from how detached Americans are from global poverty and social inequalities (p. 9).

The chameleon complex "describes the struggle study participants experience in learning how to translate their emerging global consciousness into action upon reentry into the United States" (Kiely, 2004, p. 15). This study is also groundbreaking in that it "identifies three distinct learning dimensions of students' emerging global consciousness: (1) envisioning, (2) transforming forms, and (3) chameleon complex-expanding current conceptions of perspective transformation" (p. 9). Kiely's contribution to international service-learning cannot be understated. When study participants confront a society that fails to understand its role in global poverty and unjust wars, and is predominantly characterized by individualism, the chameleon complex results to assist them in blending in rather than utilizing their transformative experiences towards social action or social justice. What stands out from his study is that despite their desire for a socially just world, study participants lack the skills to manage the chameleon complex or the society that they confront upon their return. Kiely found that study participants feel misunderstood, that they have difficulty communicating their sojourner experiences, that they feel alienated from friends, family and their cultures, and that they experience tensions between their desires for a more just society while they live and participate in a consumer driven society (p. 15).

My curiosity of "how" students hold on to transformative experiences is the impetus for this study. It grew out of the desire to understand the conflicts and challenges to individuals who have such experiences and through a desire to question the assumption that critical pedagogy results in positive personal and social outcomes. While I believe that critical pedagogy is a useful approach for challenging hegemony, I wondered what happens to students when confronted with the human faces of suffering in global contexts and how they integrate and "hold on" to transformation given previous research results.

CRITICAL REFLECTIONS ON AMERICAN HISTORY

This brief detour from the literature to review American history is important in understanding that the assumptions underpinning international education, intercultural competency, and service-learning may be in conflict with commitments to social transformation. Are educators and students being manipulated to carry on the American legacy of imperialism in new and improved ways? I turn to history for guidance in the next phase of this inquiry.

America's attempts at world domination and fears of leftist regimes caused the unnecessary Vietnam/American War that lasted for over 2 decades and ended with the deaths of 58,000 American service-members and 5.2 million Vietnamese service connected and civilian deaths. America's foreign policy ended the lives of 1 million Vietnamese through Jimmy Carter's support of the Khmer Rouge following the Vietnam War (Kolko, 1994). Under Richard Nixon, the United States supported a military coup that replaced the first democratically elected president in Chile with Augusto Pinochet, the military dictator responsible for the torture of countless scientists, artists, musicians, and thinkers (Simon & Sater, 1996). The coup occurred on September 11, 1973, with the assistance of American CIA and supported financially (with one million dollars) by the American corporation International Telephone and Telegraph (Simon & Sater, 1996). All of these actions were manifestations of cold war politics and endeavors by the United States and the USSR to assert Western dominance on less developed nations.

Turning towards domestic issues that result from the quest for dominance, we see our history rooted in slavery, internment, indentured servitude, genocide of indigenous peoples, and more currently, clashes between those in power and those whose lives are defined by poverty, hunger, social violence, and lack of opportunity as evidenced in the eyes of every haunted American child. The tug of war between American political parties vying for power, the influence of corporations in policies that exploit the workforce and the environment, and the national security issues of the present day form a coalition that impacts education at every level.

Exposing the truth of our history, removing the veil of ignorance, and the ability to discern spin from reality are imperative if we desire social transformation. Called to be modern "fire-keepers," educators are the custodians of history charged with guarding wisdom and promoting humanity's promise into the future. Paying heed to the words we choose to communicate our messages and shedding light through the fog of deception, we are better prepared to participate in the dream of democracy through critical education. Freire (1970) articulates well the importance of words in their ability to transform. He says,

> But the word is more than just an instrument which makes dialogue possible; accordingly, we must seek its constitutive elements. Within the word we find two dimensions, reflection and action, in such radical interaction that if one is sacrificed-even in part-the other immediately suffers. There is no true word that is not at the same time praxis. Thus to speak a true word is to transform the world. (p. 87)

The recent and dramatic increase in focus on international education and study abroad are traceable to the murders resulting from the attacks on 9/11/01. The rhetoric in Washington that America must "win the hearts and minds" of citizens in Iraq and Afghanistan in the spread of "freedom and democracy" are merely attempts to placate those of us who question our reasons for killing innocent civilians whose nations we want to exploit with our bombs and corporations. Drawing from Brookfield, he asserts, "hegemony describes the way we learn to love our servitude" (Brookfield, 2005, p. 93). As critical social workers, critical educators, and change agents, we must constantly challenge hegemony, confront oppression, and peel back the layers of lies that shroud the best of humanity. Through reflection and action (Freire, 1970), theory and practice (Brookfield, 2005; hooks, 1994), our efforts to effect change are balanced and liberating.

What has this to do with international education, intercultural competence, and critical service-learning? If we fail to understand the conflicting motivations for these endeavors in our educational system, our ability to make meaning of research questions such as, "How do students who experienced a transformation during their sojourn hold on to their wisdom upon their return to the United States?" are limited to shallow analyses. Educators and supporters of international education and critical service-learning must be well versed in the historical, political, and cultural contexts of the host nations where students study abroad. While the implications of this research are limited in scope, I wonder how transformation is impacted when students learn how American foreign policy contributed to the poverty, tragedies, and consequences of wars waged (through explicit or complicit actions) from the hosts whose nations they visit. This is especially important when our hosts are fully aware of American hegemony and its implications on their history, culture, and current affairs.

THE SUNY BROCKPORT VIETNAM PROGRAM

The State University of New York Brockport Vietnam Program began sending students to the only study abroad program of its kind in 1999, nearly 25 years after the conclusion of the Vietnam War. Students earn 15 credits in general studies during their semester long sojourn. The program sends three cohorts of students per year to participate in a potentially life changing endeavor with a social justice mission embedded within the program.

The students engage in five courses led by Vietnamese instructors from Danang University (the public university), Duy Tan University (a private university), and The School of Politics (a state political education institute) in politics, history, culture, language, and community service. Students live in a program house within a thriving neighborhood in Danang, completely immersed in the community. Professors instruct students in an established classroom in the program house. In addition, full-time administrators act as community liaisons and teach the community service component of the program. Unique to this program is the year-round employment of six full-time staff, ensuring continuity for both the SUNY program and for the critical service projects that the students engage in as part of their volunteer status with the Danang/Quang Nam Fund, Inc. The "Fund" is a nongovernmental organization that finances community service efforts, including the provision of food, medicine, and school supplies to the Hoa Van Leper Colony, and cash assistance to families disabled by Agent Orange exposure for business initiatives, food, medicine and homebuilding efforts. The Fund also supports Agent Orange group homes for day treatment and vocational training of disabled youth and The Loving House Nursing Home for homeless elderly. Most donations come from private citizens, occasionally from corporate foundations, and are without controls that would thwart the mission of direct aid. Further, a group of uncompensated volunteers, ensuring that 100% of donations directly benefit recipients, comprises the Board of Directors.

The NGO operates in concert with Vietnamese governmental partners, including The Danang Union of Friendship Organizations, and interfaces with Vietnamese governmental officials (i.e., The People's Committee, Foreign Affairs, Ministry of Education) on a regular basis. The students benefit from participating in meetings with authorities, and this assists in deepening their understanding of Vietnamese politics and culture. During Vietnamese holidays, the staff brings students to their homes to enjoy the hospitality and join in family celebrations. The program house, where the students reside, rivals most college dormitory settings and is in stark contrast to the impoverished dwellings that make up the majority of the service sites that the students visit during their sojourn. While there is time built in to the program for social interaction, the students are exceptionally busy keeping up with the rigors of academics and service provision. In addition to their community service duties, students also provide language instruction to the English Club run by the Friendship Union for Vietnamese college students. The students take a weeklong trip to Hanoi and Ho Chi Minh City, where they have opportunities to integrate history with present day experiences. Students visit the Ho Chi Minh Mausoleum in Hanoi, and learn that despite his wishes to be cremated, "Uncle Ho's" remains are displayed Lenin style and attended by police guards. Many who walk the city streets feel haunted by the ghosts of war. In Ho Chi Minh City (formerly Saigon), students visit the War Remnants Museum and are confronted by pictures of American soldiers water boarding Viet Cong. How do students reconcile these pictures with the claims that water boarding is not torture and that Americans do not torture?

The historical backdrop upon which the Vietnam program was established is important to understand before moving on to the research. Kenneth J. Herrmann, Jr. is a professor of Social Work at The College at Brockport. For the past 30+ years, he has promoted various social causes, particularly, children's rights, advocacy for veterans, and recently, reconciliation efforts between the United States and Vietnam through the study abroad program. Asked to conduct a feasibility study in the late 1990s by the late Director of International Education, the professor embarked on a professional and personal odyssey that led to the establishment of this unique program. In so doing, he laid to rest the ghosts that haunted him from his combat experiences in Vietnam and began a love affair with 80 million people.

Recognizing that we are not separate from our personal histories and that at the intersection of social identities and creative potential, change processes emerge and bring forth new and different ways of being. How we become effective change agents and the forces that coalesce to trigger the "common fire" (Daloz, 1996 p. 241), are still under investigation by philosophers and researchers the world over. For Professor Herrmann (2003), his passionate commitment to social justice, advocacy, and the amelioration of human caused suffering occurred between the crossroads of his upbringing and through the crosshairs of the Vietnam War. In his words,

> The development of the SUNY Brockport Vietnam Program is a curious example of not only program development in Vietnam but also of fate and that which changes us. It has done that for students. It has done that for many others, including myself. It came unannounced and was certainly not a result of years of tedious academic planning. Some might say it happened by chance. Others might talk about destiny. (p. 146)

Herrmann (2003), like other change agents engaged in critical pedagogy, understands the necessity of interventions within the individual and society for sustainable social change. Daloz (1996) speaks to this in his interview with Carlyle (a study participant that resulted in the book *Common Fire*), after a speech delivered to prison inmates on the contributions of Martin Luther King, Jr. and Malcolm X;

> Malcolm was always trying to change individuals; Martin was trying to change society. You have to do both if you want real progress. It's important to change the individual who thinks there is no hope, and it's important to change the system that destroys hope. You have to do both. (p. 57)

Description of Participants

I sent an e-mail invitation to 10 potential research participants. Six individuals met the screening criteria and expressed a desire to participate in the study. I obtained informed consent from all participants and reported that I would furnish a copy of the manuscript upon request. All study participants are Caucasian Americans, four women and two men, of middle socioeconomic class, who attended the program within the last seven years. All participants entered the program during their undergraduate pursuits towards a bachelor's degree. Academic disciplines include History and Social Work.

Procedure

Institutional Review Board approval was obtained through Fielding Graduate University in January, 2010. This study entailed recruiting former students from the SUNY Brockport Vietnam Program through e-mail invitations that included research study materials (informed consent form, study description, confidentiality pledge, follow-up procedure), affording them the opportunity to determine their willingness to participate based on time commitment, interview questions, and follow-up necessary to complete data collection. Entry into the study occurred if former students indicated that a transformative experience took place during their sojourn.

When the students returned their Informed Consent Forms indicating their written understanding of the process, I contacted them via telephone to arrange a time to conduct an in-person interview. They each indicated a preference for furnishing written responses, as they wanted the opportunity to reflect upon the questions as a matter of respect for their Vietnam experience. I did not have to control for the alternative approach as they all opted to utilize narrative responses rather than in-person interviews.

Results

All participants reported that their sojourn in Vietnam was life altering in a number of ways. Most of the students agreed that they remain in a state of reflection about their experiences, that they did not go through "epiphanies," but, rather, the transformative process is alive and continues to visit them at varying times and to varying degrees. The students expressed that the domains most impacted by their sojourn were in the areas of interpersonal relationships, purpose and meaning, and their emerging global consciousness.

A student states,

> Vietnam opened my eyes to the importance of relationships. Prior to my experience abroad, I pushed through life focusing on my achievement of day to day goals, success in school and future career, rather than paying the most attention to my loved ones

This student and several others identified in themselves egocentric tendencies that manifested in behaviors that they later discarded in favor of embracing an "other-focused" stance in relationships. Many of them concluded that exposure to Vietnam, to the service populations, and the group-centered culture encouraged their compassion in new ways and reduced the drive towards goal achievement and consumerism. Where they previously admitted to participating in a continual acquisition of "stuff," this sojourn made them not only question their behaviors, but they abandoned them as meaningless and trivial. Another student points out that "these $40 blue jeans could feed a Vietnamese family of five for a month and a half." Many of the students suggested that they lost their personal veneer, and that their ability to identify a "more authentic self" became evident during their sojourn.

Another point of reflection for the students was confrontation with previously conceived beliefs about developing nations and, specifically, with what they had been taught about the Vietnam-American War. Confrontation with the devastating after-effects of Agent Orange exposure and the American role in the impoverishment of Vietnam gave several of the students reason to reflect on their privileged status as Americans and left them bewildered about an enemy who embraced them with hospitality, forgiveness, and humor. Many of the students were shocked that

Vietnamese people wished them good fortune and prosperity despite the fact that they represented the losses experienced during the war.

Several of the students reported that their "re-entry" experience and the related "reverse culture shock" were more difficult for them than the Vietnam experience. Especially notable are those students whose "emerging global consciousness" compelled them to question the underlying conditions that contribute to poverty, Agent Orange disabilities, and identifying the American role in the devastation of the environment and its people had the most difficulty with re-entry. For example, one student noted the following:

> When the weeks were drawing closer to leaving Vietnam and returning the U.S., I was, of course, excited to see my family and friends; however, I was also very nervous that the people at home would not understand the experiences I had when I was there. I was also nervous that they would not understand and accept the changes that I had undergone while I was away. Once I arrived back in the U.S., those concerns were only confirmed. It seemed that when people asked how my trip was, they only wanted to hear a nice, light-hearted, "Amazing! I saw many beautiful places!" When I began to talk about the suffering, poverty, the many misconceptions that the majority of Americans have about the Vietnamese, people became uncomfortable and no longer wanted to listen. The smile painted across their faces would slowly melt into an awkward expression of discomfort and excuses to leave could be seen anxiously running through their heads.

Emerging global consciousness was noted in 50% of the study participants, and these participants identified difficulty reflecting upon their Vietnam experience, as there was a sense of isolation upon re-entry. Reinforced by the lack of support from family and friends, it was not until the students reconnected with other Vietnam sojourners that they were able to make meaning of their experiences. There was a definitive absence of this sense of isolation for students reporting that they had received support from family and friends regarding the complexities of their sojourn. For the students whose reflections did not move beyond the personal domain, they reported the best sojourner readjustment upon the return to the United States.

Most of the students reported a physiological response to the questions posed for the purpose of this study. Revisiting their memories of Vietnam, particularly those memories containing the paradox of human suffering and Vietnamese warmth and compassion, contributed to an embodied expression bittersweet in nature. Tears arise, love enters in, and some experience bewilderment that the Vietnam experience resides in them still, after several years away from their 4-month sojourn.

All of the study participants reported that the challenge to "holding on to transformation" is egocentric and a result of becoming anesthetized by consumer-driven, individually oriented goal seeking and forgetting the human face of suffering. One hundred percent of the students report that their transformative experience led them to careers in the service to humanity and the alleviation of suffering either in the United States or abroad. Many of them serve as volunteers in community centers, most of them attempt to fundraiser for the work in Vietnam, and all of them struggle with the forces that distract and compel transformation. One student reported,

> When I was in Vietnam, I became accustomed to a simple life with few material possessions, including clothes. When I returned home, I was appalled by [the] excessive amounts of clothes that I had long forgotten about. I swore I was going to live a life similar to the life I lived abroad. That soon ended as I once again became accustomed to having lots of "clothes" and "things" [and] eventually becoming bored with them and desiring new things.

Another student comments,

> It is so easy to get sucked into the mundane, self-seeking, routines of everyday life, but it seems as though every time that happens, something pops into my life that reminds me of the bigger picture, usually those thoughts refer back to my time in Vietnam. Every time I think of Vietnam a sense of peace, tranquility, and humility comes over me and I am reminded of what life is all about; Having compassion for others.

DISCUSSION

The purpose of this study was to examine how students participating in the SUNY Brockport's Vietnam Program "hold on to transformation" upon their return to the United States. While these results cannot be generalized to other study abroad programs with a critical service-learning component, they suggest a mutual validation of previous research results regarding sojourner re-entry, the difficulty of integrating into their own culture without supports in place, and the overwhelming struggle between the competing forces of hegemony and humanism.

Confirmed in this study is Mezirow's explanation for how transformational learning occurs in critical service-learning settings. Students' responses are consistent with Mezirow's process-oriented model that identifies how students experience changes in the ways they perceive their personal identity, their culture, and their behaviors. He refers to this as "perspective transformation" (Mezirow, 2000, pp. 296–297).

Also congruent with previous research is the extension of Mezirow's work by Kiely in his transformational service-learning process model as it emerged from his integration of Mezirow's process-model on perspective transformation. Kiely identified five themes contributing to students' perspective shifts in the following domains. Contextual border crossing describes the varying factors that influence the experience of transformational learning. They include the intersections of the personal, structural, historical, and intercultural immersion students experience during their critical service-learning sojourn (Kiely, 2005). Dissonance refers to the "incongruence between participants' prior frame of reference and aspects of the contextual factors that shape the service-learning experience" (p. 8). The theme of personalizing refers to the individual emotional and visceral experiences that promote student ability to assess their own strengths and weaknesses. Processing describes engagement in individual reflection and social, dialogic learning. Here, students arrive at a problem-solving process resulting from their ability to question, analyze, and create interventions in their service-learning work. Finally, the theme of connection is the nonreflective process of sensing, empathizing, intuiting, sharing, feeling, and caring that develop from establishing relationships with community members (Kiely, 2005).

Contextual border crossing, dissonance, processing, personalizing, and connecting were equally evident in student responses regarding the steps they went through upon arrival in Vietnam to their reflective process upon their return. Perhaps there is a relationship between maintaining connection with programs engaged in critical pedagogy and assisting former students with the holding on process. This question remains unanswered without further inquiry.

Interesting to note are the long-term devastating effects of the Vietnam War on both the Vietnamese and Americans attempting to make sense of a senseless war. For example, both study participants and Vietnam veterans' experienced the same failure to find understanding and support from loved ones upon their return. Perhaps the human caused face of suffering is too much for most people to bear. While the Vietnamese victims of the war demonstrate remarkable resilience and psychological ability to move beyond the psychic assault of invasion, the invaders are at war with themselves and demonstrate difficulties reintegrating into society. It would be interesting to facilitate dialogue groups between Vietnam veterans and student sojourners to explore the similarities in difficulties with readjustment. Although the students receive exposure to American and Vietnamese veterans in Vietnam, the American veterans tend to be expatriates who now dedicate their lives to reconciliation efforts. The students' exposure to the children of veterans, the mothers who lost numerous family members during the 21-year war, and those disabled from postwar explosive devices, leave a different impression on them than the encounters they have with unhealed American veterans.

Although the small sample size of this study makes it difficult to generalize about perspective transformation or the holding on process, the findings appear consistent with Mezirow's concepts and with Kiely's critical service-learning model of transformational learning. This research could make a greater contribution to the established literature by utilizing a larger sample, extending the research to a more longitudinal focus, and by building interventions to aid former students in maintaining their connections to the programs engaged in critical pedagogy.

Resting on previous research, this study confirms the difficulties confronted by students upon reentry and validates the Chameleon Complex. As critical educators, we must be mindful of these issues in all phases of program development. Through careful attention to the "three distinct learning dimensions of students' emerging global consciousness" (Kiely, 2004, p. 15), critical educators can assist sojourners with "holding on to transformation" by creating communities of care for them, or through "debriefings" that explain the process they go through to normalize the perspective transformation they experience. These steps might compel actions steps for lifelong commitments to social justice.

QUESTIONS FOR REFLECTION

1. How might transformative learning be affected in a less hospitable host nation?
2. Study results suggest that critical pedagogy can have a negative impact on sojourners. What steps can educators engaged in critical service-learning programs do to critically support sojourners through the re-entry process and beyond?
3. How might critical educators assist students in moving from theory to action in addressing structural inequality?
4. What influence does globalization have on critical discussions about developing nations?
5. How do critical educators "hold on" to transformation?

APPENDIX

Impact of Global Service-Learning Questionnaire

1. Can you identify the ways in which your experience in Vietnam changed you, if at all? (This may include your worldview, your feelings, spirituality, and/or behavior).
2. When did you first notice the change occurring in you?
3. Was there a specific incident in Vietnam that triggered the change?
4. If so, what was the change "from and to"?
5. How did you feel upon your return to the United States?
6. As you reflect upon your experiences in Vietnam, what touches you most deeply today?
7. Has that changed from your initial reflections?
8. How does this impact your life (behavior, thoughts, feelings, spirituality)?
9. What forces in your life contribute to your ability to "hold on" to those experiences?
10. What forces in your life challenge your ability to "hold on" to those experiences?
11. Based upon your experiences with transformation, what would you offer others in the process of transformative learning? How would you recognize their process?
12. What would you most like to communicate with others about your experiences in Vietnam?

REFERENCES

Addams, J. (1902). *Democracy and social ethics*. Urbana, IL: University of Illinois Press.

Adler, P. (1975). The transitional experience: An alternative view of culture shock. *Journal of Humanistic Psychology, 15*, 13–23.

Adler, P. (1987). Culture shock and the cross-cultural learning experience. In L. Luce, & E. Smith (Eds.), *Readings in cross cultural communication: Toward internationalism* (pp. 24–35). Cambridge, MA: Newbury House.

Anderson, L. E. (1994). A new look at an old construct: Cross cultural adaptation. *International Journal of Intercultural Relations, 18*(3), 293–328.

Belenky, M. F., & Stanton, A. V. (2000). Inequality, development, and connected knowing. In J. Mezirow & Associates (Eds.), *Learning as transformation: Critical perspectives on a theory in progress* (pp. 71–102). San Francisco, CA: Jossey-Bass.

Bennett, J. (1993). Cultural marginality: identity issues in intercultural training. In R. M. Paige (Ed.), *Education for the intercultural experience* (pp. 109–135). Yarmouth, ME: Intercultural Press.

Bennett, M. (1986). Modes of cross-cultural training: conceptualizing cross-cultural training as education. *International journal of intercultural relations, 10,* 179–196.

Bennett, M. (1993). Towards ethnorelativism: A developmental model of intercultural sensitivity. In R. M. Paige (Ed.), *Education for the intercultural experience.* (pp. 21–71). Yarmouth, ME: Intercultural Press.

Brookfield, S. (2005). *The power of critical theory: Liberating adult learning and teaching.* San Francisco, Ca: Jossey-Bass.

Daloz, L. (1996). *Common fire: Leading lives of commitment in a complex world.* Boston, MA: Beacon Press.

Dewey, J. (1969). Context and thought. *University of California Publications in Philosophy, 12*(3). Berkeley, CA: University of California Press. Reprinted in LW 6: 3-21.

Estes, C. P. (1992). *Women who run with the wolves: Myths and stories of the wild woman archetype.* New York, NY: Ballantine Books.

Freire, P. (1970). *Pedagogy of the oppressed.* New York, NY: Continuum.

Gaw, K. F. (2000). Reverse culture shock in students returning from oversees. *International Journal of Intercultural Relations, 24*(1), 83–104.

Gil, D. (2010). From tribal consciousness and subjective rationality toward global consciousness and objective rationality. *Journal of Comparative Social Welfare, 26*(2), 137–144

Ginwright, S., & Cammarota, J. (2002). New terrain in youth development: The promise of a social justice approach. *Social Justice, 29*(4), 82–95.

Herrmann K. J., Jr. (2003). *Mot nguoi My o Viet Nam hom nay* [Lepers and lunacy: An American in Vietnam today]. Ho Chi Minh City: Phuong Nam.

hooks, b. (1994). *Teaching to transgress: Education as the practice of freedom.* New York, NY: Routledge.

Kahne, J., & Westheimer, J. (1996). In the service of what? The politics of service learning. *Phi Delta Kappan, 77*(9), 592.

Kiely, R. (2004). A chameleon with a complex: Searching for transformation in international service learning. *Michigan Journal of Community Service Learning, 3,* 5-20.

Kiely, R. (2005). A Transformative learning model for service-learning: A longitudinal case study. *Michigan Journal of Community Service Learning, 3,* 5–22.

Kiely, R. (2011). What international service learning research can learn from research on study abroad and intercultural learning. In R. G. Bringle, J. A. Hatcher, & S. G. Jones (Eds.), *Volume in International Service Learning Research* (pp. 243–273). Sterling, VA: Stylus.

Kim, Y. Y. (2001). *Becoming intercultural: An integrative theory of communication and cross-cultural adaptation.* Thousand Oaks, CA: SAGE.

Kolko, G. (1994). *Anatomy of a War: Vietnam, the United States, and the modern historical experience.* New York, NY: Pantheon.

Lyon, C. R. (2002). Trigger events meets culture shock: Linking the literature of transformational learning theory and cross-cultural adaptation. *In Proceedings of the 43rd Annual Adult Education Research Conference* (237-242). Raleigh, NC: North Carolina University.

Martin, J. N. (1984). Communication in the intercultural reentry: Student sojourners' perceptions of change in reentry relationships. *International Journal of Intercultural Relations, 8,* 115–134.

Marullo, S. (1999). Sociology's essential role: Promoting critical analysis in service learning. In J. Ostrow, G. Hesser, & S. Enos (Eds.), *Cultivating the sociological imagination: Concepts and models for service-learning in sociology* (pp. 11–27). Washington, DC: American Association of Higher Education.

Mezirow, J. (1991). *Transformative dimensions of adult learning.* San Francisco, CA: Jossey-Bass.

Mezirow, J., & Associates (2000). *Learning as transformation: Critical perspectives on a theory in progress.* San Francisco, CA: Jossey-Bass.

Mitchell, T. (2008). Traditional vs. critical service learning: Engaging the literature to differentiate two models. *Michigan Journal of Community Service Learning, 3*, 50–65.

Mullaly, B. (2007). *The new structural social work*. Canada: Oxford University Press.

Rice, K., & Pollack, S (2000). Developing a critical pedagogy of service learning: Preparing self-reflective, culturally aware, and responsible community participants. In C. O'Grady (Ed.), *Integrating service learning and multicultural education in colleges and universities* (pp. 115–134). Mahwah, NJ: Erlbaum.

Robinson, T. (2000a). Service learning as justice advocacy: Can political scientists do politics? *PS: Political Science and Politics, 33*(3), 605-612.

Robinson, T. (2000b). Dare the school build a new social order? *Michigan Journal of Community Service Learning,* 7, 142-157.

Roman, L. (2003). Education and the contested meanings of "global citizenship." *Journal of Educational Change, 4*, 269-293.

Rosenberger, C. (2000). Beyond empathy: Developing critical consciousness through service learning. In C. R. O'Grady (Ed.), *Integrating service learning and multicultural education in colleges and universities* (pp. 23–43). Mahwah, NJ: Erlbaum.

Savicki, V., Cooley, E., & Donnelly, R. (2008). Acculturative stress, appraisal, coping, and intercultural adjustment. In V. Savicki (Ed.), *Developing intercultural competence and transformation: Theory, research, and application in international education* (pp. 342–352). Sterling, VA: Stylus.

Simon C. & Sater, W. (1996). *A History of Chile: 1808–1994*. Cambridge, England: Cambridge University Press.

Sparrow, L. M. (2000). Beyond multicultural man: Complexities of identity. *International Journal of Intercultural Relations, 24*(2), 173–201.

Taylor, E. (1993). *A learning model of becoming culturally competent: A transformative process* (Unpublished doctoral dissertation, University of Georgia, 1993).

Taylor, E. (1994a). Intercultural competency: A transformative learning process. *Adult Education Quarterly, 44*(3), 154–174.

Taylor, E. (1994b). A learning model for becoming interculturally competent. *International Journal of Intercultural Relations 18*(3), 389–408.

Ward, C. & Kennedy, A. (1994). Acculturation strategies, psychological adjustment, and sociocultural competence during cross-cultural transitions. *International Journal of Intercultural Relations*, *18*(3), 329–343.

York, G., & Mick, H. (2008). Last ghost of the Vietnam War. *Globe and Mail.* Hanoi, Vietnam and Ontario, Canada. Retrieved from http://www.theglobeandmail.com/archives/article697346.ece

CHAPTER 14

TOWARD A THEORY AND PRACTICE OF RADICAL PRAGMATISM

Brian Charles Charest

Their fears of action drive them to a refuge in an ethics so divorced from the politics of life that it can apply only to angels, not to men. —Saul Alinsky

The one thing to be dreaded in the Settlement is that it lose its flexibility, its power of quick adaptation, its readiness to change its method as its environment may demand. —Jane Addams

INTRODUCTION

In this chapter I explore the connections that I see between community organizing strategies and service-learning pedagogy in order to identify what these ideas can teach us about the work we do in schools and communities. I introduce the term "radical pragmatism" in this chapter and work toward a broad definition of what the term might mean and how we might use it to describe service-learning practices that embrace an array of orientations to social action work that fall under its purview. I do so in order to describe my version of what it means to work and act in thought-

Critical Service Learning as a Revolutionary Pedagogy: A Project of Student Agency in Action, pp. 297–316

ful ways in our school communities—ways that might suggest practical approaches to service-learning that allow different practitioners to begin this work in different places. I borrow the term "radical pragmatism" from William James (1907/1981), philosopher and American pragmatist, and Saul Alinsky, a Chicago-based community organizer and founder of the Industrial Areas Foundation (IAF), both of whom used the term to describe ways of being and acting in the world particular to a certain set of circumstances. I see a useful marriage between the healthy skepticism of the taken-for-granted practices in school settings suggested by pragmatist like James, Dewey, and Addams and the community organizing strategies, such as relational meetings, accountability sessions, and collective organizing and action, developed by Alinsky and Ed Chambers that urge us toward action. It is my contention that pragmatists like James as well as his contemporaries like Dewey and Addams can help those of us interested in service-learning and social action to think in new ways—ways that include seeing school sites as legitimate spaces for public action. I use radical pragmatism here as an umbrella term that incorporates various ways of doing service-learning that practitioners and their students might find appropriate to their particular situations as they move toward more critical forms of engagement. The analysis that follows emerges from my experience as a service-learning coach and teacher at a Chicago public school on the far Southeast Side of Chicago as well as my work with Public Action for Change Today (PACT), a youth empowerment organization affiliated with the IAF in Chicago.

RADICAL PRAGMATISM AND THE SERVICE-LEARNING CONTINUUM

Service-learning practitioners are a diverse group, one that includes students, teachers, university instructors and professors as well as community partners, community organizers, and other allies, and because of the multiplicity of practices and practitioners there are important differences in orientation to public action and community-based work that are worth exploring. In other words, if we hope to have some idea of how to begin projects of our own, exploring some of these orientations toward social change can provide practitioners with various entry points along the service-learning continuum that might help us move toward the more critical forms of service-learning. Tania Mitchell (2007) in her important review of the literature puts the problem this way, "Because service-learning as a pedagogy and practice varies greatly across educators and institutions, it is difficult to create a definition that elicits consensus amongst practitioners" (p. 50). And, as Steven Hart (2006) tells us, "scholars have noted confusion of what service-learning represents and how it may be enacted" (p. 18). If scholars are confused about what it means to enact a service-learning pedagogy, it seems reasonable to conclude that practitioners may also be experiencing a sense of uncertainty about how to articulate a vision of what the practice is and can potentially be in different settings. The fact that service-learning evades easy definition, however, may actually be one of its greatest strengths, since by doing so, as Schutz and Gere (1998) note, service-learning can change and adapt to different needs and disciplines: "Unencumbered by a disciplinary identity, service-learning has, for a number of years, moved freely within the academy, sometimes attaching itself to sociology or psychology, sometimes to education or social work, and, in the past few years, to English" (p. 129). This ability to adjust to the needs of different situations, in my view, points to the potential for service-learning pedagogy to be used by teachers and students as a way to explore, critique, and challenge the policies and practices in schools that promote or reproduce inequalities and oppression. Such critiques are necessary because, as Kumashiro (2004) reminds us, "Many people in society do not acknowledge that everyday practices in schools often comply with or contribute to racism, sexism, classism, heterosexism, and other forms of oppression" (p. 1).

While I consider radical pragmatism to include critical, activist orientations to the work we do in schools and communities—this is, in fact, the orientation I prefer—I do not exclude what some might consider less activist orientations toward service-learning and civic engagement. Radical pragmatism, then, embraces the uncertainty inherent in teaching, learning and engaging in public life. I also want to make it clear, though, that I do not advocate uncritical forms of service that perpetuate inequalities or reproduce certain social hierarchies—for example, the paternalistic or neocolonial service models—us doing for them—that have already been widely critiqued elsewhere (Alinsky, 1971; Ball & Goodburn, 2000; Chambers, 2004; Feldman, Moss, Chin, Marie, Rai & Graham, 2006 Herzberg, 1994; Schutz & Gere, 1998). I do, however, want to support and encourage various activities and experiments that can benefit individuals and communities, even when they do not always result in easily identifiable successes or victories. In other words, while dismantling power structures and promoting systemic changes in the name of greater equality are important and laudable goals, it has been my experience that most service-learning projects fall short of this ideal. Participation in public actions, however, can still be transformative and educational for individuals and groups working together. For this reason, I believe that our emphasis in service-learning and civic engagement projects benefit from being attentive to the "situatedness" of any particular project or action. This, in my view, is what makes service-learning such a potential force for change in schools. In other words, a radically pragmatic conception of service-learning allows for the myriad ways in which practitioners engage in public projects and suggests taking the world as it is for our starting point as we move toward more systemic changes.

Radical pragmatism, broadly defined, is a way to go about making changes to the status quo or solving problems identified by a community of stakeholders in a specific situation. While putting the terms "radical" and "pragmatism" together may seem like a contradiction in terms, I hope to show that practitioners can act in radically pragmatic ways when they have a deep and thorough understanding of a particular context. Put simply, acting in radically pragmatic ways means acting in critical and thoughtful ways that question and challenge unjust and unproductive policies and practices, while still remaining open to the many possible ways of identifying and addressing such questions. Radical pragmatism frees us to synthesize a seemingly disparate set of orientations and models in order to capitalize on the productive tensions that emerge from particular situations in schools, communities, and universities. Aaron Schutz (2010), in his forthcoming book on social class and social action, reminds us that "this kind of practical integration is extremely difficult to do" (p. 288), and will require a large investment of time and energy by those involved. Despite these challenges, schools seem like an important and necessary place to begin our work, precisely because of the current pressures on educators to adhere to narrow definitions of teaching and learning.

I understand schools, urban schools in particular, as sites of multiple contradictions: contradictions that emerge from narratives of freedom, democracy, and equality that circulate in spaces that often lack the most basic resources and where access to opportunity may be systematically inhibited or denied. For this reason, I believe schools are uniquely positioned for educators to interrogate the confluence of political, economic, and cultural forces that limit educational and economic opportunity in certain areas while purporting to be solutions to those same problems. Such an understanding requires that educators look at current economic and education policy in order to examine the ways in which a combination of cultural forces reproduces inequities in metropolitan areas (Anyon, 2005).

I begin in the context of schools, first, because this is where I have spent a significant part of my professional life, and, second, because these public sites of resistance are places where we still might create space for valuing local knowledge, or what Schutz (2010) calls "different class-based practices" (p. 288) that can challenge traditional middle-class approaches to the work we do in schools. Such traditional practices include the current hierarchical organization of schools where such schools function as a means to control and regulate individuals and communities along narrow definitions of academic achievement and cultural competence. I suggest that appropriating community organizing strategies and connecting them to school-based actions might allow educators to successfully challenge policies and develop our own notions of accountability that can alter current conceptions of power and control in such schools.

In my experience as a high school teacher, service-learning coach, and university writing instructor in a civic engagement program, the work we do in these settings requires us to be flexible and to adapt to dynamic circumstances because there is "no way to set aside the histories, needs, abilities, and other particularities … and appeal merely to principles that are untroubled by reality" (DeStigter, 2008, p. 129). This is just to say that while I advocate challenging undemocratic policies and practices in schools, our students, colleagues, and allies should be given the chance to work out for themselves what it might mean to do critical or other kinds of service-learning in their particular contexts. Their actions, no matter how small, might be understood to be what Ellen Cushman (1996) describes as "the first steps to social change on micro-levels of interaction" (p. 13). This is a point that, in my view, is worth considering, since schools are places where what we can or want to do involves significant risks—losing our jobs, being expelled or arrested, facing other forms of retaliation—and is dependent on the support of our friends and colleagues. Such support for actions can and should be built around relationships and mutual risk taking toward collectively defined ends where participants understand the stakes and are willing to accept the risks.

It has been my experience with critical service-learning that teachers and students who take steps to act in thoughtful ways are our best allies in doing the work we hope to do that might point us toward a way to "deconstruct systems of power" in real situations. In other words, before we dismiss our colleagues who might want to organize a blood or food drive, a school-wide recycling program, teach a class in a local jail, start a community garden, volunteer at a local community theater, or tutor as part of a neighborhood arts program, we might consider the consequences of these acts of "service" to the community. Is "service" always something to be avoided? I would suggest that service can be a powerful learning and movement building tool. An important question to ask, might be: Who benefits from these actions (or services) and how might these forms of social action be seen as the initial moves toward new forms of collective action around new or different issues? Such a question compels us to examine how we might work together with groups and individuals to build stronger coalitions in our institutions and communities. In other words, radical pragmatism can help us take steps toward more critical and confrontational forms of social action by discouraging binary thinking and encouraging collective forms of public action, no matter how small.

Although community organizers are often the first to admit—and I am not immune to this kind of thinking either—that they have strong views about other organizations and orientations (e.g., they are too reactive, they do not do enough direct action, they do not have an offensive strategy, they are too education oriented, they are not building a movement, etc.), we need to do more to build partnerships across disciplines and organizations in order to make changes in our schools and communities. In other words, we need to form coalitions in order to build the necessary power to make broader, more lasting changes to policies and practices. The point that unites the work we do, after all, is the shared desire for a change in the status quo; a change that provides more choices and opportunities for ourselves and for those we work with in our schools and communities. In my view, service-learning can open up places in schools for students to develop the confidence to become relevant actors or agents of change in their communities and then make those important changes by organizing and working with others.

ORGANIZING ORIENTATIONS: THE SOCIAL ACTION CONTINUUM

Cathy Fleischer (2000) in her book, *Teachers Organizing for Change*, suggests five orientations for community organizing: education, planning/development, mobilization, advocacy, and social action. In Fleischer's reading of the community organizing landscape, these are the positions that most organizers take up in relation to the work they are attempting to do in communities (p. 84). In my reading, thinking, and participating in the work of service-learning and community organizing, as a teacher and service-learning coach, I have found this framework to be helpful in exploring the different ways we might enact change in our particular situations. Fleischer notes, too, that teachers are natural organizers—she used the term "teacher organizer" throughout—who organize students, parents, and colleagues all the time, in order to do their jobs. While I agree with Fleischer that teachers do "organize" bodies, often around shared goals or projects, many teachers I have known would not consider themselves "organizers" in the more activist sense of the word. I would suggest that Fleischer's description of teachers as organizers, as well as the different orientations that she outlines, could benefit from the additional analysis of how teachers, parents and students see themselves performing the role of both "teacher" and "citizen" in a democracy. In other words, how one understands these terms seems critical for understanding why our colleagues and friends take up the projects they do in their classrooms and communities.

In their article, "What Kind of Citizen?," Joel Westheimer and Joseph Kahne (2004) describe the different beliefs and assumptions that people bring with them to schools and other institutions about what it means to be and act in the community as a citizen. These beliefs about citizenship often translate into different forms of participation or different orientations toward social action (p. 27). Westheimer and Kahne suggest the following three types of citizens: personally responsible, participatory, and justice oriented. I want to suggest that while we might be able to think of more than three types of citizens, these different forms of civic participation, what Westheimer and Kahne call "the spectrum of ideas represented in education programs about what good citizenship is and what good citizens do" (p. 19), occupy different spaces along a continuum of social action. In other words, while Fleischer (2000) defines a social action orientation as being largely about the "long term change in the power relations among various groups" (p. 101), I would argue that change is generally at the heart—even if such change is only implicit in the work—of what we do in service-learning programs. However, how we come to think about ourselves as citizens, as Westheimer and Kahne (2004) point out, will play a crucial role in how and where we begin as well as how far we are willing to go with any activity that involves making changes in a community.

While I agree that most service-learning work is "inherently connected to concerns of social justice" (Mitchell, 2008, p. 50)—however we define a term like "social justice" in our communities—I also think that students who get involved in service-learning projects are more likely to take risks and get involved again when they are called upon by their peers, colleagues, or community to do so. My experience in schools and universities suggests that this initial involvement in civic or service projects—in whatever form it takes—helps students and teachers develop a stronger sense of shared responsibility to their community, because it involves them in shared work around a common interest or concern. In other words, even if the goal of a project is simply to educate peers or community members through a community journal or public service announcement, it is still a first, and I would argue, crucial, step toward further types of engaged work. Organizing communities through a process of critical inquiry can help students and teachers develop what Robinson (1998) describes as "civic literacy," in order to participate in "engaged acts of citizenship as they [seek] to learn about and take actions" in their communities (p. 12). In other words, teachers and other professionals interested in civic-engagement or meaningful participation in one's community might, as Cathy Fleischer and David Schaafsma (1998) tell us, be involved in,

> the creation of habitable spaces for all citizens which in turn allows for the development of human agency; the establishment of participatory communities in which students can move their private understandings into public settings, connecting their pasts with their presents, anticipating their futures. (p. xxv)

This type of social action or civic-engagement can take many forms—everything from organizing blood or food drives or recycling programs to more critical forms of social action such as school walk outs and accountability sessions. However, teachers might begin with the understanding that students and community members bring knowledge and language of their own about their communities, and it is this situated, contextual knowledge—sometimes called local knowledge—that we might take as our starting points for meaningful action in any school. All of this is just to say that radical pragmatism, as a form of critical service-learning, suggests that classrooms and schools can and should serve as public spaces where teachers and students might build relationships across differences in order to find ways of acting collectively to make changes or challenge unjust practices. Acting in radically pragmatic ways, then, means authorizing ourselves to act based on our situated knowledges and understandings, rather than waiting for authorization or instructions from "experts" or "authorities" that would tell us how to act and to what end.

OUR MUTUAL FRIENDS: FROM ADDAMS TO ALINSKY

Jane Addams worked for years at Hull House and stood with community members on issue after issue; she used her power and privilege to advocate for and with the people she worked with in the community. In her 1896 speech, titled, *A Modern Lear,* Addams, speaking about men like the paternalistic industrialist George Pullman, describes the situation this way:

> In so far as the philanthropists are cut off from the influence of the zeitgeist, from the code of ethics which rule the body of men, from the great moral life springing from our common experiences, so long as they are "good to people," rather than "with them," they are bound to accomplish a large amount of harm. They are outside of the influence of that great faith which perennially springs up in the hearts of the people, and re-creates the world. (as cited in Elshtain, 2001, p. 172)

Addams (1910/1981) understood what it meant to work with people rather than for them, and she was willing to test out her ideas—to pay her dues, so to speak—by advocating, challenging, collectivizing, and working alongside the people who came to Hull House. Through her work at Hull House she came to understand that she could not impose her ideas on others and that the work would need to be of a kind that came about through partnership and collaboration with others. She notes:

> The experience of the coffee house taught us not to hold preconceived ideas of what the neighborhood ought to have, but to keep ourselves in readiness to modify and adapt our undertaking as we discovered those things which the neighborhood was ready to accept. (p. 104)

The notion of working with others to solve issues that matter to them in ways that makes sense to them, is one of the most important lessons that the pragmatists have to teach those of us who see the potential in service-learning pedagogy. In other words, I advocate for a service-learning pedagogy that helps move practitioners along a spectrum to find entry points along the way that point to more critical forms of engagement. Such a pedagogy begins in conversation and collaboration with others as we examine our immediate surroundings and conditions.

While the idea of taking up residence in the neighborhoods where we work and teach—in the way that Addams did—may seem like a radical proposition to some of us today, the notion that we make efforts to become community stakeholders in the places we work and teach is still an important component of much current writing about teaching and learning. But, of course, writing about this kind of work from our offices, usually located at safe distances from underresourced communities, is often much easier to do than actually involving ourselves in the hard work of collectivizing, organizing, and implementing social action projects in communities. Thus, it seems, teachers and teacher educators need to ask, How can we—often, white middle-class educators—become community stakeholders in schools and communities that might seem far removed from the communities where we grew up or where we currently work and live? A partial answer to these questions might be to develop and adopt the kind of culturally relevant pedagogy advocated by Gloria Ladson-Billings (2006) where teachers begin to "see themselves as part of a community" (p. 41). But in order to see ourselves as community stakeholders, we will need to begin by taking concrete steps—joining with local community-based organizations, conducting listening campaigns, teaching courses at local public high schools, participating in the organization of community-based activities, helping to form coalitions around local issues, helping to create cooperative community-based businesses and green spaces—all in an effort to develop communities of interest that seek to challenge current understandings of equity, justice, and access to various opportunities.

One model that may help us develop or adapt ways of acting and engaging in communities, is the community organizing model developed by Saul Alinsky in the 1930s. This model, further developed by Ed Chambers and others, continues to be used in various forms by grassroots neo-Alinsky organizing groups today. And, while the Alinksy/Chambers model is not without its own limitations, I believe it does offer us some very practical ways of working in and with communities and schools to directly challenge current arrangements. Drawing on his early experiences as a sociology student at the University of Chicago and later as a community organizer in Chicago, Alinsky would come to a conclusion similar to the one Addams reached about working with communities for important changes (Horwitt, 1992), that we should not do for others what they can do for themselves. Alinsky's work in communities also suggests that we seize the opportunity in schools to organize what he calls a "community of interests" around specific questions in order to build power and take action on issues that matter to us (Alinsky, 1971, p. 120). Doing so might open up the possibility for people to work together, as Alinksy says, to "construct their own solutions" to the challenges we face as stakeholders in the community and education reform advocates. In his introduction to his primer for organizers, Alinsky declares, "Let us in the name of radical pragmatism not forget that in our system with all its repressions we can still speak out and denounce the administration, attack its policies, and work to build an opposition political base" (p. xxi). And, as Alinsky reminds us here, we must do more than just speak; we must act, too. According to Alinsky, then, "the most unethical of all means is the non-use of means" (p. 26). Or, to put this another way, there seems to be a consensus among these thinkers that thoughtful reflection needs to be coupled with collective action aimed toward specific goals in order to make meaningful changes in communities and schools.

Addams (1910/1981) was not unlike Alinsky in her understanding of the need for action. In her discussion of Tolstoy's "snare of preparation" she suggests the need to act in thoughtful and productive ways, lest we get mired in the intellectual work of finding the "right" way to do something. She writes:

> It is easy to become the dupe of a deferred purpose, of the promise the future can never keep, and I had fallen into the meanest type of self-deception in making myself believe that all this was in preparation for great things to come. (p. 73)

In other words, we can never be fully prepared to act, or teach, or speak on any particular issue or subject or for any particular cause, because our knowledge will always be partial, contingent, and incomplete. We cannot know beforehand how or what students will learn from these projects or what they will do as a consequence of their participation with us and our community partners. Of course, this is not to say that attempts at preparation are useless or ill-conceived, but rather that it seems crucial that we acknowledge the uncertainty— as well as the intangible and unquantifiable learning that takes place—inherent in the work we do; we should be prepared to move and act despite knowing that we could be wrong. Indeed, preparation, strategizing, and debating are all important parts of the process, just as uncertainty, doubt, fallibility, and revision will be as well. And, as Addams suggests, despite our uncertainty we still need to make space for students and colleagues to act in meaningful ways. Addams, writing about her own experience with young people, puts it this way,

> We have in America a fast-growing number of cultivated young people who have no recognized outlet for their active faculties. They hear constantly of the great social maladjustment, but no way is provided for them to change it, and their uselessness hangs about them heavily. (p. 92)

Alinsky and Chambers suggest organizing around a community of interest and using what's called relational meetings to get to know our students, colleagues, and community allies, as a way to find out what can and should be done in any particular context (Chambers, 2004, p.18). This is just one strategy that might help us remedy this sense of uselessness that Addams describes. Chambers (2009) portrays what he calls the "one-to-one" meeting this way, "Properly understood, the relational meeting is an art form in which one spirit goes after another spirit to create connection, confrontation, and exchange talent and energy" (p. 19). Such an approach—sitting down face-to-face with students, colleagues, parents, community members, and so forth—can help us develop the kinds of relationships necessary for meaningful action to take place. It is by taking such risks with others and working in and with the communities outside the borders of our universities or schools that we can begin this work.

The relational meeting is an important strategy that we might borrow or adapt to our own purposes (Alinsky, 1971; Anyon, 2005; Smith, 2009; Schutz, 2010). But the point of all of this is that we acknowledge the need to do more than simply talk with our colleagues and critique the problems we see in schools and other institutions. Alinsky (1971) writes: "I start from where the world is, as it is, not as I would like it to be" (p. xix), and he suggests that we move toward action from where we are and from what we see. In other words, rather than waiting for conditions to improve or for the "right" project to present itself, students, teachers, and local activists or community partners might begin where they are to address the concerns that matter most to them at any given time. Stephen Smith, a former PACT organizer, describing what he learned from working with Ed Chambers (2009), puts it this way, "Chambers taught me that real radicals exist *in between* the world-as-it-is and the world-as-it-could-be. In a group of ideologues and optimists, the radical is a pragmatist" (p. 21). In other words, this in between space—the place where we can acknowledge the materiality of where we are, but also see where we might go—can be the starting point for meaningful action in our different contexts if we are willing to seek it out and to see the possibilities that might exist there.

If we draw on the ideas, lessons, and examples of a pragmatist like Addams and organizers like Alinsky, Chambers, and Smith, then we might be able to define new ways of enacting forms of radical pragmatism. Fleischer (2000) describes community organizing as, simply, "people coming together to create change—whether it's getting the stop sign for the bad intersection ... or raising awareness about the hazards of the medical waste incinerator" (p. 77). In other words, acting in radically pragmatic ways involves work along the continuum of civic engagement and pushes us toward more critical forms of service-learning; it includes everything from volunteer work to more direct confrontations with power through collective actions. Alinsky (1971) tells us that radical pragmatism means "different people, in different places, in different situations and different times will construct their own solutions" (p. 4) to the challenges they face, by working and organizing in different ways. In fact, he insists this is the only way toward meaningful change. Addams (1910/1981), echoing these concerns, has this to say about her work,

> The Settlement, then, is an experimental effort to aid in the solution of the social and industrial problems which are engendered by the modern conditions of life in a great city.... It is an attempt to relieve, at the same time, the overaccumulation at one end of society and the destitution at the other; but it assumes that this overaccumulation and destitution is most sorely felt in the things that pertain to social and educational privilege. (p. 98)

All of these ideas point toward forms of engaged pedagogy in schools that in turn suggest ways we might act more critically in schools settings. Bell hooks (1994) summarizes it this way:

> Engaged pedagogy not only compels me to be constantly creative in the classroom, it also sanctions involvement with the students beyond that setting. I journey with students as they progress in their lives beyond our classroom experience. (p. 205)

In other words, our teaching does not stop at the classroom door and should not be confined to strict disciplinary ways of knowing and doing.

Or, as Smith (2009) suggests, "Learning what matters to us, and to each other, means taking risks over and over again" (p. 30).

MOVEMENT BUILDING: PRAGMATIC LESSONS FOR THE RADICAL PRAGMATIST

In my view, teachers acting as radical pragmatists will need to be willing to reflect, to revise, to change their minds, and to evaluate the value of any idea or belief in connection with its social consequences, or usefulness in lived situations. What the term "usefulness" means, as I understand pragmatists like James and Dewey to use it, is quite different from the way the term is used when linked to current notions of standardization, efficiency, and utility in schools today. That is, something considered "useful" to a pragmatist needs to be examined within the social context of those who will be most greatly impacted by the particular idea, belief, or policy. The difference, then, in my view, is that the radical pragmatist wants to evaluate the consequences of an idea or belief as it relates to a particular social context, while a more limited view of "usefulness" suggests a narrow definition of an idea's utility (e.g., the only "useful" knowledge is that which can be measured on a standardized test).

In a similar way, I want to differentiate between "being pragmatic" in the popularized sense of doing what is politically expedient and "being a pragmatist" in the way that I understand James and others to have thought about it. In other words, one might consider themselves "being pragmatic" to participate in the conventions of school standardized testing, tracking based on ability, zero tolerance policies, undemocratic decision making structures, etc. as they exist in a traditional school under a neoliberal policy agenda. Whereas, "being a pragmatist" would encourage an examination of the economic and political structures of schooling to evaluate the actual consequences of certain ideas and beliefs on students, faculty, and other community stakeholders. Therefore, "usefulness," in the sense that the pragmatists use it, would mean understanding our actions in broad social terms, as well as in particular, contextual terms. Furthermore, whereas "being pragmatic" has a direct connection with accepting a situation as given or fixed, the notion of "being a pragmatist" that I want to advance, suggests a direct engagement with and disruption of the "given" in schools or communities. Maxine Greene (1988) describes the climate we often find in schools this way:

> There is a general withdrawal from what ought to be public concerns. Messages and announcements fill the air; but there is, because of the withdrawal,

> a widespread speechlessness, a silence where there might be—where there ought to be—an impassioned and significant dialogue. (p. 2)

In other words, being radically pragmatic means acting in ways that might ignite the kind of "impassioned and significant dialogue" that Greene suggests here.

In my view, the radical pragmatist asks: What, then, does this idea (or these ideas or policies or set of values that are currently in place) mean for people when carried out in any particular situation? And, in terms of education and schools, this would mean answering, or attempting to answer, a series of questions related to any given activity that we propose for ourselves or our students. Does this particular activity help me develop a better understanding of what it means to be more fully human? Does pursuing this inquiry help me to better understand how the world works? What does this line of inquiry leave out or leave unexplored? Does participating in this activity help me learn to see myself as an active creator of something interesting or important (e.g., music, poetry, paintings, gardens, murals, short stories, political speech, social change in my community, etc.)? The pragmatist acknowledges the contingent, partial, and incomplete nature of knowledge, but also accepts a broad view of what might be termed "useful" for any group of people or individual to do in any context. And, the pragmatist attempts to find ways to respond to changing conditions and remain open to further experimentation, including being open to things that some might consider useless or unimportant.

As the literary critic Terry Eagleton (2003) reminds us, "The idea of doing something purely for the idea of it has always rattled the grey-bearded guardians of the state. Sheer pointlessness is a deeply subversive affair" (p. 39). In other words, what Eagleton seems to be suggesting here is that different ways of knowing and doing (as well as different forms of resistance) should not be jettisoned for the narrow top-down definitions that rely solely on what data can tells us about teaching and learning. That is, doing things in school (e.g., studying art, music, literature, critiquing school policies, or learning to paint with an airbrush), even when they do not easily translate into notions of "usefulness" for some people, should not be eliminated. Doing these things, particularly when they seem "pointless" to policy and standardized test makers, are precisely why, in some cases, we ought to be doing them.

It is important to acknowledge that whichever strategies we use, these strategies are open to interpretation and adaptation and may be used toward different goals or objectives. We might consider, too, that not all teachers, students, colleagues, or parents will want to take up the same positions as staring points for change. Therefore, in order to remain open to new possibilities, we might begin by honestly contextualizing our knowledge about different forms of civic engagement and examining how such knowledge is being used as well as how it has come to be understood as useful or otherwise by any community of practice.

The point, then, of a radically pragmatic approach to teaching and service-learning is that schools should be places where we challenge assumptions and question where our ideas and beliefs (or anyone else's) come from (Kumashiro, 2004, p. 25). Doing so, in my view, would help us call attention to the partial nature of our knowledge and its potentially damaging or empowering effects on ourselves and others. I believe the radically pragmatic teacher makes explicit the limits of our knowledge in order to discourage dogmatism or fanaticism. In other words, we want to discourage our students from the tendency to, as Maxine Greene (1988) describes it, "accede to the given" (p. 20) of any "truth" about the world. That is, however we choose to teach and whatever we decide to do with our students might be understood in radically pragmatic terms as always only one course of action based on a certain set of ideas or beliefs that will never take us to any final, perfect, or ideal conclusion; work will always remain to be done.

As Dewey (1939/1989) puts it, "No small part of the democratic problem is to achieve associations whose ordering of parts provides the strength that comes from stability, while they promote flexibility of response to change" (p. 127). Pragmatism, then, suggests a form of democracy and, in Dewey's view, it is a democracy based on shared inquiry that remains always open to dissenting views and to the potential for change (p. 87). As Robert Westbrook (2005) suggests, Dewey's pragmatism offers us a kind "epistemological justification for democracy" (p. 124) because it requires that we act in concert with others in ways that seem worthwhile to us and to them. That is, we always exist as part of some community, and in order to find out what we might do in any context, we begin by working cooperatively through shared inquiry to determine what steps to take next. This means, of course, as Westbrook tells us that we need to "radically reconceive the prevailing wisdom" (p. 142) that informs so much bureaucratic thinking in schools. Or, as William Ayers (2006) suggests, we might begin by challenging the prevailing orthodoxy in our schools and universities in order to invent new approaches to what we do and how we do it (p. 95). Such new approaches might allow us to form broad coalitions aimed at reconceptualizing what something like "school reform" should be about or look like in practice.

Thus, according to pragmatism as I understand it, we ought to submit our beliefs to a kind of shared judgment based on the practical consequences of our ideas in a given social context. While certainly not perfect—pragmatism rules out a perfect way to do things—a radically pragmatic approach does give teachers a way forward toward challenging and disrupting schooling as it is often practiced, in order to reinvent new ways of doing things that take into account local knowledges and concerns. As Schutz (2010) reminds us,

> community organizing as a model, even in its evolved neo-Alinsky form, is far from perfect. Nonetheless, currently it represents one of the most effective sets of pragmatic practices for generating power in impoverished and marginalized communities, something progressive visions of democracy have failed to provide. (p. 290)

I began this essay by suggesting that American pragmatism and community organizing strategies had something important to tell us about the *how* and the *why* of what we do in our schools. I hoped to examine what pragmatism could tell us about the kinds of habits of mind we might develop as teachers, teacher educators, and university professors. As Todd DeStigter (2008) notes, pragmatists like Dewey might help teachers develop "principled habits" that are, in fact, "a way of thinking and acting that leads them to explore what a principle like 'justice' or any other might mean amid all the variables of a given context" (p. 126). Echoing this idea, Schutz (2010) reminds us that community organizing is about trying to "create organizations within which participants' ways of thinking would be changed by their ongoing interactions, by how they were led to *act*" (p. 276).

In Chicago Public Schools, for example, where 40 hours of service-learning are now a mandated graduation requirement, teachers and students have a unique opportunity to work together, "to learn to become citizens—active participants of civic projects intended to improve and enrich collective lived lives" (Robinson, 1998, p. 16) and to have a hand in shaping current school reform efforts. This is an opportunity—officially sanctioned by school administrators—that students and teachers should make good on by beginning to organize around a community of interests in schools in order to take action on issues that matter to them. As longtime community organizer, Michael Gecan (2009), notes, good teachers are already "relational workers" who can, when given the chance, "create the educational and political conditions and institutions that enable most people to express fully their fundamentally affirmative natures" (p. 92). But this will not happen automatically or inevitably; it requires work, both individual and collective. Gecan notes that, "Relational work is essentially, almost radically, reciprocal; student and teacher, nurse and patient, cop and citizen—all need one another for long term success and real satisfaction" (p. 94). However, learning how to do the work of relating to our students, colleagues, and community allies in order to build a new social movement will require a radically pragmatic view of what "counts" as teaching and learning. As Jean Anyon (2005) reminds us, "Middle and high school teachers, in particular, can make a powerful contribution to movement-building by engaging students in civic activism" (p. 188). Building working relationships and identifying common projects will be an important step we will need to take toward building a larger social movement aimed at reforming education in ways that make sense to the teachers, students, and communities most affected by such changes.

Relational workers who seek a broader coalition might do well to develop the habits of mind described by DeStigter that can lead us to critically explore policies, standards, textbooks, access to curricular and extracurricular resources, and any other practices that are "given" in schools; we might also enact service-learning in ways that help us uncover and explore the cause and consequences of the processes of schooling as well as any community's access or lack of access to certain opportunities. This work moves in the direction of critical service-learning as teachers might draw from a wide range of experiences and resources to examine how different policies, knowledges, and disciplinary frameworks are produced and understood, in order to make explicit dominate ways of knowing and doing. Such critical examinations could be grounded in the lived experience of students, teachers, and other community stakeholders in order to bridge classroom discussions to what seems relevant and useful to any group of students and teachers in a particular community. We might, then, begin to revise what seems useful and worthwhile to teach and do in school, based on these inquiries. What I'm arguing for is my own version of what Arthur Applebee (1996) calls "knowledge-in-action" (p. 33). Such a view of knowledge-in-action suggests that what we do with students in our classrooms should have something to do with the world as they encounter it in and out of schools settings. Thus, our projects in and out of school should be reciprocal ones, projects that emerge from particular settings in particular ways.

The process of learning in any context should be recursive and have meaning for those who participate in the projects we develop together as community stakeholders. Exploring different kinds of questions and challenging current arrangements might allow students to research and examine various social movements, authors, texts, and current thinking on a particular issue, as well as create or enact a social action project based on their research. Why should not schools be places where students and teachers look carefully at the policies and procedures that shape our everyday lives as participants in these institutions? Linking what we do to current social concerns might also help us make the work we do more relevant and consequential for ourselves and our students. Teachers, then, might begin with a series of questions as they consider what to teach and how to connect it with service-learning and social action that is radically pragmatic and on its way to critical. How is "official" knowledge framed and understood in our disciplines? Our schools? Our communities? Who decides these questions? How are these decisions made? What kinds of things do we need to consider when developing a curriculum that makes room for action-oriented projects that take into account different ways of knowing and doing? What are the issues or concerns that matter most to students and their communities? Can these issues take center stage in our schools and in our classrooms? And, finally, if these questions and issues do become central to what we do, what, if anything, can or should we do about them?

QUESTIONS FOR REFLECTION

1. What issues seem the most pressing to you and your school community? Do others feel the same way? How can you find out whether others think about these issues?
2. Can you name the members of your local school board? Who makes the important decisions about schools in your area? How might these people help you address your questions or concerns about school policies?
3. What would you do if you were elected to the school board? Develop a plan and prepare suggestions for changes to your school community.
4. What can you do if your plans for reform are ignored or dismissed by those with decision making powers?
5. How might you organize your school community to effectively challenge those in positions of power?

REFERENCES

Addams, J. (1981). *Twenty years at Hull-House*. New York, NY: Signet Classics. (Original work published 1910)

Alinsky, S. D. (1971). *Rules for radicals: A pragmatic primer for realistic radicals*. New York, NY: Vintage Books.

Anyon, J. (2005). *Radical possibilities: Public policy, urban education, and a new social movement*. New York, NY: Routledge.

Applebee, A. (1996). *Curriculum as conversation*. Chicago, IL: University of Chicago Press.

Ayers, W. (2006). Trudge toward freedom: Educational research in the public interest. *In G. Ladson-Billings & W. F. Tate* (Eds.), *Education research in the public interest* (pp. 81–97). New York, NY: Teachers College Press.

Ball, K., & Goodburn, A. (2000). Composition studies and service learning: Appealing to communities? *Composition Studies, 28,* 79–94.

Chambers, E. (2009). *The Power of relational action*. Skokie, IL: ACTA.

Chambers, E. (2004). *Roots for radicals*. New York, NY: Continuum.

Cushman, E. (1996). The Rhetorician as an agent of social change. *College Composition and Communication, 47,* 7–28.

Dewey, J. (1989). *Freedom and culture.* Amherst, NY: Promethus Books. (Original work published in 1939).

DeStigter, T. (2008). Lifting the veil of ignorance: Thoughts on the future of social justice teaching. In S. Miller, L. Beliveau, T. DeStigter, D. Kirkland, & P. Rice (Eds.), *Narratives of social justice teaching: How English teachers negotiate theory and practice between preservice and inservice spaces* (pp. 121–144). New York, NY: Peter Lang.

Eagleton, T. (2003). *After theory.* New York, NY: Basic Books.

Elshtain, J. B. (2001). *The Jane Addams Reader.* New York, NY: Basic Books.

Fleischer, C. (2000). *Teachers organizing for change: Making literacy learning everybody's business*. Urbana, IL: NCTE.

Gecan, M. (2009). *After America's Midlife Crisis*. Cambridge, MA: MIT Press.

Greene, M. (1988). *The dialectic of freedom*. New York, NY: Teachers College Press.

Hart, S. (2006). Breaking literacy boundaries through critical service-learning: education for the silenced and marginalized. *Mentoring & Tutoring, 14,* 17–32.

Herzberg, B. (1994). Community service and critical teaching. *College Composition and Communication, 45,* 307–319.

hooks, b. (1994). *Teaching to transgress.* New York, NY: Routledge.

Horwitt, S. J. (1992). *Let them call me rebel: Saul Alinsky: His life and legacy.* New York, NY: Vintage.

James, W. (1981). *Pragmatism*. Sioux Falls, ND: NuVision. (Original work published 1907)

Knight, L.W. (2005). *Citizen: Jane Addams and the struggle for democracy.* Chicago, IL: University of Chicago Press.

Kumashiro, K. (2004). *Against common sense: Teaching and learning toward social justice*. New York, NY: RoutledgeFalmer.

Ladson-Billings, G., & Tate, W. F. (Eds.). (2006). *Education research in the public interest.* New York, NY: Teachers College Press.

Mitchell, T. (2008, Spring). Traditional vs. critical service-learning: Engaging the literature to differentiate two models. *Michigan Journal of Community Service Learning*, 50–65.

Robinson, J. (1998). Literacy and lived lives: Reflections on the responsibilities of teachers. In D. Schaafsma & C. Fleischer (Eds.), *Literacy and democracy* (pp. 1–27). New York, NY: Teachers College Press.

Schaafsma, D., & Fleischer, C. (1998). Introduction: Further conversations: Jay Robinson, his students, and the study of literacy. In D. Schaafsma & K. Fleischer (Eds.), *Literacy and democracy* (pp. xiii–xxxii). New York, NY: Teachers College Press.

Schutz, A. (2010). *Social class, social action, and education: The failures of progressive democracy.* New York, NY: Palgrave, Macmillan.

Schutz, A., & Gere, A. (1998). Service learning and English studies: Rethinking "public" service. *College English, 6,* 129–149.

Smith, S. (2009). *Stoking the fires of democracy: Our generation's introduction to grass-roots organizing*. Skokie, IL: ACTA.

Westbrook, R. (2005). *Democratic hope: Pragmatism and the politics of truth*. New York, NY: Cornell University Press.

Westheimer, J., & Kahne, J. (2004). What kind of citizen? The politics of educating for a democracy. *American Educational Research Journal, 41,* 237–269.

AFTERWORD

Christie Billups

Twenty years ago, I stood watching proudly as my eighth grade class presented what they had learned to journalists, the school students and administrators, and representatives of the wider community about the impact of gangs on their lives, their families and neighborhood and, ultimately, on their learning. I did not see it as critical service-learning at the time. I saw it as good pedagogy: taking students where they are at and helping them to explore the various realities that surround them. It was also a matter of confronting the oppressive realities in which they often found themselves. As Mexican Americans, the students at Providence of God School in Chicago faced many challenges, for example, crossing cultures and wielding two languages daily between their homes and their school, economic stress in their families, and high academic expectations but few resources since many of their parents had less than an eighth grade education themselves. These particular students faced the gang culture in their homes, on their way to school, when they went outside to play, and when they chose their friends and associates. They even had to consider gangs when they got dressed in the morning, because if they walked out of the house with the wrong colors on, they could get harassed, or worse, killed.

When I started the school year in 1990, I had no plan to explore gangs and their impact on the community. My students walked into the classroom with it regularly. If memory serves me right, the pivotal event that moved us toward this public presentation about gangs was the day that my student Victor came to school with his little sister who was in kindergarten at the time. Victor was panic-stricken because his little sister had discovered his older brother's gun and was found playing with it that morning. His older brother was on house arrest, but he was still drug dealing and "gang banging" from home, and the reality hit Victor hard that morning when he was terrified that his sister could harm herself. Up until that time, Victor was exploring gang life himself, but his love of and fear for his sister caused him to rethink his life's path.

Pedagogically, I could have stuck with my year's plan, remained wed to the curriculum and textbooks, but I listened to the voice inside me that said, quite loudly, that incredible learning could happen if the students had a chance to give voice to what they were living and how it was impacting them. They did research, they took photographs, they wrote letters to political figures and journalists trying to get their attention and raise awareness of what was happening to them, and then they presented what they'd learned in a public forum. If we revisit one of the definitions offered to us in this book's Introduction, we find critical service-learning in my eighth graders' learning and efforts: "a political project, embedded with a social-justice orientation with a commitment to guiding students to develop the skills, ideas, and attributes necessary to foster equity and freedom in K–12 schools and other contexts" (p. viii, this volume).

As one explores the insights and examples of this book, one is inspired to enhance the pedagogy and service-learning we are doing at our various educational institutions, from kindergarten through graduate school. While some distinctions are drawn between critical service-learning and traditional service-learning herein, from a wide angle, learning in general, and service-learning in particular should be relevant, meaningful, and transformative for students, community members and faculty involved. Much of service-learning is intended to address injustices and inequities in our human community. Critical service-learning highlights the importance of making this encounter with injustice a more conscious enterprise. All service-learning should confront, directly or indirectly, systems that keep oppression and imbalance in place and should empower students and community members to embrace their agency to change these systems.

Case studies are an immensely useful and powerful tool in elucidating ways to enhance and enrich pedagogy and service-learning. I hope to add a couple of examples of service-learning at other educational levels to humbly add to the strength of the case studies already provided in this text. Before further models, however, I would like to speak briefly of the intersection between the civic values of justice and equity in higher education so eloquently engaged in this book and the very clear directives in Catholic universities (of which Lewis University is one of the approximately 270 in the United States) to employ Catholic Social Teaching as a guide in our formation and teaching of young people. In my role as Coordinator of Service-Learning at Lewis University, questions are continuously raised about how we are approaching our teaching and learning and what's most effective for our students as well as the communities, both local and global, in which we live. How do the civic and religious injunctions to confront injustice and be good neighbors enrich our dialogue about service-learning?

At Lewis, our mission statement is clear that we are called to privilege values that reflect our traditions, both civic and religious. This is true of other faith-based institutions as well. Our own values at Lewis are named as Wisdom, Association, Justice, Knowledge, and Fidelity. To highlight the most pertinent for this discussion, Justice is described as "The affirmation of the equal dignity of every person and the promotion of personal and social responsibility." Further, the value of Association is defined as "The process of forming a community of mutual respect, collegiality, collaboration and service" (lewisu.edu/welcome/offices/mission.htm). The building blocks are in place, then, and the analysis starts to unfold. How do we form community? How do we teach respect? How do we model collegiality and collaboration? And most relevant here, how do we explore the call to service, again in both civic and religious contexts and institutions, in a way that honors the dignity of all persons? Further, how do we invite our students, community members and ourselves as faculty and staff to further commitment to walking in solidarity with each other by honoring voices and stories, gifts and assets? These questions are asked and answered most authentically by honoring mutuality between universities and community members and organizations, and by espousing true partnerships.

As a lover of pedagogy, I must start the analysis by being honest with my own successes and failures. As a White woman with three graduate degrees, it would be logical to see myself as knowledgeable, as the one with the "assets" to offer, as the giver more than the receiver. Busting through internalized white privilege and being willing to unravel the oppressive structures that hinder the wholeness of both privileged and oppressed persons alike is neither easy nor comfortable. Since a vast majority of our faculty at U.S. institutions continue to be from privileged realities as well, the promotion of critical service-learning, or even traditional service-learning, can be an uphill climb. But if I want to be a better instructor and to contribute to the enhancement of transformational education for our students, I need to be willing to be a perpetual learner.

As I look back at the gang project 20 years ago, I seek the lessons it taught me. The students with whom I was working at Providence of God were both students and community members in this undertaking, dual stakeholders if you will. They were an oppressed group in significant ways regarding race, age and economic status, but they became potential change agents from *within* the community. And I, as a White teacher who lived just outside their neighborhood, knew *about* gangs, but I could never fully understand what they experienced daily. It was my task to give them more tools to do their project effectively and to stand with them as they attempted to give voice to their circumstances. It was a balancing act between being a good resource and guide and staying out of their way.

What did we accomplish? If I could do it all over again, what would I do differently? I believe that we, as a class, managed to establish a community within a community, a place where students felt safe and able to be themselves. Given their walk home after school, a safe place was no small achievement. Also, my idealized memory of it suggests that I did let them take the lead on the project since they understood the realities better than I. (I hope my memory serves me well.)

However, beyond transforming the relationships in the room, and hopefully in the larger school community, what lasting impact did we make? I am not sure. The program was a solitary event with no thought of sustainability or ensuring that journalists and community leaders continued to carry the torch the students had so carefully lit. After the students graduated from eighth grade, they went to a number of different high schools. Some students fell back into gang related choices and even served some prison time. How could we have continued to empower and accompany those students? How might we have given them a deeper, more lasting sense of agency?

A HANDOUT MORE THAN A HAND UP: HIGH SCHOOL SERVICE PROJECT GONE AWRY

About 12 years later, I was campus minister in an all-girls' high school on the northwest side of Chicago. We had a "service requirement" for our students, but it was minimal and needed greater depth to be truly effective. But I remember one senior student who somehow caught fire after a presentation about poverty and homelessness. She decided to collect hats and scarves for people in shelters, and then she wanted to deliver the collections herself with some friends and meet some of the people her efforts would benefit. She was Latina herself and, like many of the students in the school, was from a family and neighborhood that experienced economic woes of their own. But still, the student was really motivated and very successful in the initial phase of her project. The school community rose to the occasion, and we had much to deliver when we went to an urban Salvation Army shelter and soup kitchen. However, I and my colleagues let this young woman down. We let her maintain the idea in her head that she was doing this great thing *for* other people, rather than teaching her the underbelly of the circumstances in which her gift recipients found themselves.

On the day of the delivery, about eight young women and I headed to the Salvation Army in our school van armed with future warmth in bags and boxes. We were met at the door by the director of the shelter who was aware that we were coming. We were shown where to drop off our donation in a room full of other items sent and dropped off by people with big hearts and good intentions. Then we went into the dining room to help serve the meal. Some helped in the kitchen, some served up the plates and other students went from table to table making sure the guests had what they needed, or what the students thought they needed. What I had failed to impart to the well-meaning students was that, more than anything, the people we would meet needed to be reminded of their dignity and their voice. Instead, I believe we dished up a hearty portion of lasagna and salad.

A handful of almost complete plates of food ended up in the garbage tossed there by disgruntled guests; the students' confusion and dismay were palpable. I was bothered by it myself. Of course, the waste was no different than privileged persons engage in all the time and it had nothing to do with the students. I think they may have taken it a bit personally. Again, this was a sure sign that we had done little to enhance understanding of the systemic injustices and economic imbalance that were two of the root causes of the circumstances in which the guests found themselves. They did not feel like guests. They were given a plate of food with no choice in the matter. They could not go "home" and fix what was more culturally or personally preferred. Some of them were angry with their circumstances, and I had done very little to prepare the students to respect and pose questions around these feelings and realities.

We talked on the way home in the van, reflected on the experience, but by then the damage was done. The student who had organized it was confined to thinking that doing good for other people wasn't worth the effort. She saw it as a slap in the face. Here she had done all of this hard work for "these people," and they did not appreciate it. Rather than turning a student on to life-long service and justice-making, I fear that the opposite happened that day. It was a transformative experience alright, but not at all the one we strive for as educators and service-learning guides.

What were the successes? Some students provided hats and scarves that would aid those on the streets to be a little warmer in the winter months. Hopefully, a handful of the students who went to the shelter had their minds opened to some of the challenges of poverty. What would I have done differently? I would have been sure that the students understood more about poverty and homelessness and the systems that perpetuate them before going. I would have encouraged them to go several times to the shelter, to build relationships with the people, to come to know their gifts and wisdom as well as their want, to understand why collecting warm clothing was a gift, but also how it was only the beginning of what the people served at the Salvation Army hoped for and needed.

INTERNATIONAL SERVICE-LEARNING

Live and learn is no trite cliché. Eight years later as I promote service-learning at Lewis University, the creative juices are flowing and the commitment to voice and justice are stronger than ever. The final example I'd like to share is a dream, an inspired idea. Given the challenges of international university travel, especially to the most impoverished countries wracked with political unrest and health concerns for residents and visitors, I am not sure when or if Lewis University will be able to bring this idea to fruition, but perhaps the idea will ignite some actualized variation of this dream at Lewis or elsewhere.

Since a dear friend from Togo, trained for priesthood in the United States, moved to northern Uganda to do missionary work, I have become more interested in the people of Uganda and their political and sociological realities. I have now visited my friend's mission parish twice and have subsequently been working with others to be part of the solution to the profound poverty of the region. We have started an organization named *Noté Karacel*, which means Unite Together in the local Lango language of Alenga. We started by sponsoring the education of a handful of girls, and it has taken off from there involving projects related to agriculture, water, and health care, among other things.

When I visited Alenga in June of 2010, I had international service-learning in mind. I asked my missionary friend to try to connect me with someone involved in higher education there in Uganda knowing that they would be able to shed valuable light on my goals. Fr. Simon Peter Olugu, a Ugandan priest charged with opening a second campus of Ugandan Martyrs University, and I met and talked about the hopes and challenges for both of our institutions. It was an engaging conversation seasoned with a lot of creativity and hope. Our dream slowly emerged and is still crystallizing.

Of course, I wanted to bring U.S. students to Uganda knowing that the encounter would be deeply transformative, as all travel has the potential to be. I stuck with realistic goals given the expense of a sojourn of this magnitude. What if five students and two faculty members traveled from

Chicago to Alenga for a total of 3 weeks? What could they offer to a culture and reality so very different from their own? Though the official language of Uganda is English, few in Alenga Catholic Parish are proficient in it. Needless to say, the U.S. students wouldn't know Lango, the local language of Alenga. The mission itself has running water and relatively consistent electricity, but most of the people in the area do not. And these huge issues only scratch the surface of the realities we would need to consider in our dreaming and planning.

Further, if we brought undergraduate students, what could they possibly offer from their own rather nascent toolbox of skills and knowledge? What areas would we focus on? What is concurrently most immediate and most realistic? Possible answers began to emerge as Fr. Simon Peter and I dialogued. Given that his own campus was just being formed, he was intrigued with the experiences I had had at Lewis. He was concerned about forming a curriculum for Ugandan students that would be relevant and useful to the people of the nearby villages and surrounding region. His concerns were also around empowerment and transformation.

As we discussed the various projects of Noté Karacel, we narrowed the disciplines that would be most pragmatic for such an undertaking. We honed in on health care, particularly education and public health, and microfinancing. Therefore, nursing and business students could lend practical ideas and skills to the problem solving of the local people.

As we continued the discussion, an idea surfaced that seemed unique, although some university may be approaching service-learning in this manner already. If U.S. students and Ugandan students worked in pairs or small teams to join with the people of Alenga to seek solutions to their most pressing challenges, what great possibilities could emerge? Ugandan students could be recruited who spoke both Lango and English thus forming a bridge between their U.S. counterparts and the local people. The Ugandan and U.S. students might have similar majors in their undergraduate studies and could exchange insights and skills. The pairs and teams could meet the community members and work with them to surface possible ways to address some of the more immediate concerns. All of the students would live, eat and learn at the mission in the evenings for the duration of the course.

The faculty from the respective institutions would be likewise fortified and enriched in their own areas. Courses could be taught in partnership. Local knowledge, advancements in the fields internationally, and varied pedagogies could make the encounters powerful. Lasting relationships could be forged at all levels, and the wisdom and assets of all persons would be necessary to frame realistic and sustainable solutions to some of the most pressing realties facing the people of Alenga.

Fr. Simon Peter and I took this dream, this idea, back to our respective learning communities and started to explore its practical possibilities. On the U.S. Side, expense for travel to Uganda postpones the likelihood of carrying this out in the near future. But I can do more to prepare the ground and plant the seeds for this project and others like it. Our College of Nursing is well on its way regarding commitment to service-learning and to addressing the injustices and imbalances they find in the community. They see "service" as built into their career paths. We are just beginning to explore what this means in the College of Business. More work, more consciousness-raising lies ahead.

To come 'round full circle, and to re-emphasize the idea of critical service-learning as "revolutionary," to remind ourselves of the significance of what we are trying to do, let me conclude with a quote by Václav Havel found in Parker Palmer's book, *Let Your Life Speak*:

> The salvation of this human world lies nowhere else than in the human heart, in the human power to reflect, in human modesty, and in human responsibility. Without a global revolution in the sphere of human consciousness, nothing will change for the better. (pp. 75–76)

ABOUT THE AUTHORS

Editors:

Brad J. Porfilio is assistant professor of education at Lewis University in Romeoville, IL. He teaches courses on critical pedagogy, qualitative research, globalization and education, multicultural education and curriculum theory in the Educational Leadership for Teaching and Learning Doctoral Program. The Educational Leadership Program at Lewis University is unique in its critical and transformative focus where students are prepared to become transformative educational leaders who are deeply discerning, knowledgeable and approach the educational system as a potential avenue for challenging and transforming the status quo. Dr. Porfilio received his PhD in sociology of education in 2005 at the University at Buffalo. During his doctoral studies, he served as an assistant professor of education at Medaille College and D'Youville College, where he taught courses across the teacher education spectrum and supervised preservice and in-service teachers from Canada and the United States. He has published numerous peer-reviewed articles, book chapters, edited volumes, and conference papers on the topics of urban education, neoliberalism and schooling, transformative education, teacher education, gender and technology, and cultural studies.

Heather Hickman is an adjunct instructor of education at Lewis University in Romeoville, IL and a full-time high school English teacher in a Chicago suburb. For the university, Heather teaches courses on reading instruction, curriculum, the history of American education, and introductory research. In her 11 years teaching high school, she has taught all levels of English language arts and literature. Dr. Hickman's teaching focus, whether at the university or high school level, takes a critical stance examining the status quo and addressing marginalization. This teaching lens was developed through her doctoral program at Lewis University in Educational Leadership for Teaching and Learning. Heather earned her EdD from Lewis in May of 2009. In addition to teaching, Heather has presented and published papers on the topics of heteronormativity and critical theory in education.

Foreword:

Mike Cole is research professor in education and equality, and director of the Centre for Education for Social Justice at Bishop Grosseteste University College Lincoln, United Kingdom. He is the author of *Marxism and Educational Theory: Origins and Issues* (Routledge, 2008); *Critical Race Theory and Education: a Marxist Response* (Palgrave Macmillan, 2009); *Racism and Education in the UK and the US: Toward a Socialist Alternative* (Palgrave Macmillan, 2011). He is the coauthor (with Sara C. Motta) of *Constructing Twenty-first Century Socialism in Latin America: The Role of Radical Education* (Palgrave Macmillan, forthcoming, 2012); and the editor of *Professional Attributes and Practice: Meeting the QTS Standards* (4th ed.) (Routledge, 2008); *Equality in the Secondary School: Promoting Good Practice Across the Curriculum* (Continuum, 2009); and *Education, Equality and Human Rights: Issues of Gender, "Race," Sexual Orientation, Disability and Social Class* (3rd Edition) (Routledge, forthcoming, 2011).

Chapter 1:

Andrea Yoder Clark works jointly with the California Department of Education and Excel Youth Zone to direct and support the work of California's Regional Service-Learning Leaders to further institutionalize service-learning within K-12 schools in California. Dr. Yoder Clark has also worked with the National Youth Leadership Council to produce a study documenting high quality case studies of urban service-learning programs throughout the country and has been a regular contributor to the National Youth Leadership Council's publication, *Growing to Greatness*. Dr. Yoder Clark enjoys keeping her work grounded in practice through her role supporting teachers to integrate science and global citizenship curriculum with critical service-learning as the SurfAid International Schools Program U.S. Coordinator.

Maura Nugent is an English teacher in Illinois. In 2004 she cofounded the Social Justice Academy, a program at Kelvyn Park High School in Chicago that integrates youth leadership, service learning projects, and themes of social justice with an academically rigorous curriculum. In the spring of 2008, she was honored by the Chicago Public Schools as the "Service Learning Teacher of the Year." Before becoming a teacher, Ms. Nugent worked for several years in community based organizations, and brings this perspective to her current commitment to urban education. She has facilitated numerous classroom-based service-learning projects including oral history, action research, and social documentary projects. Ms. Nugent has presented at multiple local conferences and several national conferences including the Ethnography in Education conference, the Breaking Ranks Secondary School Showcase, the National Service Learning Conference, and the Urban Service Learning Conference, at which she was a keynote speaker in 2008.

Chapter 2:

Kaylan C. Schwarz holds a bachelor of arts from the University of Guelph and a master of arts from the University of Toronto (OISE). She currently coordinates a global education program at an independent secondary school for girls in Toronto, Canada. Kaylan has participated in or facilitated international service excursions in a number of contexts, including Peru, Costa Rica, Dominican Republic, Russia and Azerbaijan. Locally, she is active on a number of boards of directors supporting youth-oriented community organizations. Kaylan's research springs from her personal interest in privilege and access to civic-related educational opportunities.

Chapter 3:

Kecia Hayes received her PhD in urban education from the Graduate Center of the City University of New York where she was a MAGNET Scholar. She is an assistant professor in the College of Education and Human Services at Montclair State University. Some of her publications include chapters in *19 Urban Questions* edited by Shirley Steinberg and Joe Kincheloe; *Metropedagogy: Power, Justice, and the Urban Classroom* edited by Joe Kincheloe and Kecia Hayes; *City Kids: Understanding, Appreciating, and Teaching Them* edited by Joe Kincheloe and Kecia Hayes; and *Key Works In Critical Pedagogy*: Joe Kincheloe edited by Kecia Hayes, Shirley Steinberg and Ken Tobin. She has presented her work at several conferences. Her research is focused on the education of court-involved youth, the impact of social policies and practices on the educational experiences of urban youth and families, and educational leadership in urban schools.

Chapter 4:

Elizabeth Doerr is the coordinator for Community Service-Learning, Immersion Experiences at the University of Maryland. She primarily oversees the Alternative Breaks program, which involves over 20 trips that travel locally, nationally, and internationally focusing on targeted social justice issues. Elizabeth served as a Peace Corps Volunteer in Malawi, Southeastern Africa where her primary focus was HIV/AIDS education. Later, she returned to the U.S. to work as a Peace Corps Recruiter in the Washington, DC recruitment office. Elizabeth is interested in alternative and experiential education practices with a focus on equity, equality and social justice. Interest areas include social justice education, critical pedagogy, sustainability education, and the impacts of volunteerism and service-learning on communities both domestic and abroad. Elizabeth is originally from Washington State and earned her MA in International Education Policy from the University of Maryland and her BA in Rhetoric/ Media Studies and Spanish at Willamette University in Salem, OR.

Chapter 5:

Adam Renner, "the Rouge Forum Community Coordinator and writer for *Substance*," was an educator, author, and friend. In each role, "Adam embodied the interaction of ethical theory and determined practice.... In the fall of 2010, Adam left a tenured position at Bellarmine University in Kentucky to move to California where he accepted a position as a math teacher at the June Jordan School for Equity in San Francisco. It was a good fit. While in San Francisco, Adam quickly became active in the student movement to defend education from the relentless attacks of the ruling classes.... Losing Adam was a terrible setback for the movement for equality and justice, in schools and out" (Gibson, R. & Goslee, A. (2010, December 24). Adam Renner, of Rouge Forum and Substance, dies at the age of 40. *Substance News.* Retrieved from http://www.substancenews.net/ articles.php?page=1862)

Chapter 6:

D. G. Mulcahy, is a faculty member in the Department of Teacher Education, Central Connecticut State University. He is the author of several books. In a recent review, his latest book, *The Educated Person: Toward a New Paradigm for Liberal Education*, was characterized as inspired and transitional. Journals in which his research is published include *Curriculum*

Inquiry, Educational Studies, Educational Theory, European Journal of Teacher Education, Journal of Philosophy of Education, and *Studies in Philosophy and Education*. He is contracted to write the chapter on "Liberal Education" in the *Routledge Companion to Education*.

Wendy Doromal is director of service-learning, Orange County Public Schools (OCPS) in Florida and teacher in Timber Creek High School (TCHS). She has vast experience in planning and operating a highly recognized service-learning academy accommodating 500 students in TCHS and in organizing the district service-learning program of OCPS. Awards at state and national levels have recognized her work.

Omaris Journet extends her work as physical education teacher in Hartford Magnet Middle School in Connecticut by overseeing the civic engagement of students. Their current project studies the schooling and living conditions of children of migrant farm workers. It culminates in students presenting letters to politicians such as Sen. Chris Dodd.

Donal E. Mulcahy is on the faculty of Wake Forest University, Department of Education. Drawing on critical pedagogy, his recent research has focused on the diversity and multilogicality of urban schools and the influence of private foundations, such as The Fordham Foundation, on public education policy. His research appears in such journals as *Educational Studies, The Educational Forum* and *Radical History Review.*

Chapter 7:

David Zyngier is a senior lecturer in the Faculty of Education at Monash University and a former school principal and state schoolteacher. His research focuses on culturally, linguistically and economically diverse (CLED) learning communities; social justice; democratic education; teacher knowledge and beliefs. He has published widely on teacher pedagogies that improve outcomes for students from communities of promise. He is a cofounder of the Global Doing Democracy Research Project an international project examining perspectives & perceptions of democracy. In 2010, the RUMAD program that he wrote received the prestigious Garth Boomer Award for its contribution to education in Australia. He developed the Enhanced Learning Improvement in Networked Communities program, which gained a Schools First Award of $25,000 in 2010 for its contribution to students experiencing learning difficulties and school engagement problems. He is also a member of the editorial board of *Teaching and Teacher Education* (Elsevier).

Chapter 8:

Diana M. Feige, born of Puerto Rican and English parents, spent her youth in Puerto Rico. New England became her home in her college years, graduating first from the University of New Hampshire (BA) and then Harvard Divinity School/Harvard University (MTS), Antioch/New England Graduate School (MeD.) and Teachers College/Columbia University (EdD). Her first professional venture was as a high school teacher; for the last 17 years she has been teaching Adelphi University teacher candidates, presently as a clinical associate professor. She was associate editor of the *Holistic Education Review* and a teaching fellow with Communities for Learning. Her most recent publications include *Mapping Slippery Transformative (Service Learning) Roads* (*Be the Change: Teacher, Activist, Global Citizen* (Ed. R. Verma, Peter Lang Publishing, Inc.) and *Confessions of a Reluctant Professor: In Gratitude to Service Learning* (*In the Spirit of Ubuntu: Stories of Teaching and Research* (Eds. D. Caracciolo & A. Mungai, Sense Publishers).

Maureen Connolly, EdD, is an English teacher at Mineola High School on Long Island, NY. She has also worked as a professor of education at Molloy College and Adelphi University. Dr. Connolly has served as a Learn and Serve America grant coordinator for Mineola High School and for the New York Metropolitan Area Service Learning Institute. She has developed many service learning projects that link community outreach, character education, and classroom content. In addition, she has been a part of the Learn to Serve with Character Research Project headed by New York State. Dr. Connolly has been honored by ASCD and by St. John's University for excellence in teaching. She was presented with the Long Island Teacher of the Month Award sponsored by News 12 and Hofstra University. She has also been recognized by Intergenerational Strategies for her commitment to linking youth and senior citizens. She has presented at regional and national service learning conferences.

Michael Furey is an English language arts teacher at Mineola High School, Long Island, NY. In addition to his 11th and 12th grade ELA courses, he teaches Human Rights and Peace Education electives. He also coadvises *Increase the Peace*; Mineola High School's human rights extracurricular club. The objective of the student-facilitated club is to provide a peaceful response to conflict resolution and to offer students an understanding of the different beliefs and lifestyles that are reflected in a diverse and global community. He earned his BA in literature from Marist College and his MS in secondary education from Hofstra University. He is a member and contributor to *Amnesty International, Human Rights Campaign, Save Darfur* and *ONE*.

Chapter 9:

Christopher DeLuca, PhD, Christopher is an assistant professor at College of Education, University of South Florida. His research interests are in the areas of teacher education, assessment, and inclusivity. Specifically, Christopher explores the pedagogical and curricular conditions that promote inclusivity as a fundamental principle of contemporary education. In addition, Christopher conducts research into how teachers learn to engage the complexities of educational assessment in relation to the evolving assessment culture in today's classrooms. Christopher's research has been published in various national and international journals.

Meghan DeLagran attained her undergraduate degree from Queen's University in Kingston, Canada and the University of Edinburgh in Scotland, majoring in geography and history. Her focus of study was on human geography, with particular interest in the way in which children move through and use different spaces. Meghan is currently completing her teacher's college degree at Queen's, finishing in 2011, and hopes to pursue graduate work in the field of children's geographies.

Eric Ferguson is an undergraduate student at Queen's University in Kingston, Canada. He is completing a bachelor of arts degree in English literature and film and media studies, as well a bachelor of education degree though the Queen's University Concurrent Teacher Education Program. Eric works with a variety of grassroots community groups in Ontario to extend social justice education beyond the classroom though experiential learning and online projects. He is interested in projects that challenge and overcome barriers to youth participation in local government, especially using new media. Eric is also an award winning filmmaker and photographer.

Stephanie Ho is a fourth year arts and science student at Queen's University. She is also part of the Concurrent Teacher Education Program and will complete her bachelor of education in Fall 2011. Her studies at Queen's have been concentrated in English literature and psychology but have also included biology and behavioral neuroscience. Her interests are in areas of literature and expressive art, particularly dance.

Chapter 10:

c. lynne hannah is an associate professor in the Department of Education at Shepherd University. Her research interests focus on social justice education and the impact of constructivist methods in foundational courses in teacher education.

Barri Tinkler is an assistant professor in the Department of Education at the University of Vermont. Her research interests focus on service-learning in teacher education with an emphasis on social justice.

Elizabeth Miller is an independent scholar. Her research interests focus on social justice education in elementary math and science teacher education.

Chapter 11:

Allison Daniel Anders, PhD, teaches graduate courses in critical race theory, social justice, sociology of education, and qualitative research methods in cultural studies in educational foundations and learning environments and educational studies at the University of Tennessee, Knoxville. She produces ethnographic work about targeted youth and systemic inequities in schools including educational narratives with Burundian children and families with refugee status.

Jessica Nina Lester, PhD, teaches educational psychology courses in the Department of Educational Leadership and Counseling Psychology at Washington State University. She is a former special education teacher, and currently works with children with autism labels. Her research focuses upon the social, cultural, and historical understandings of disabilities, inclusive pedagogies, and dynamic forms of assessment. She also engages in ethnographic work focused on the educational narratives of Burundian children and families with refugee status.

Chapter 12:

Steven Hart is assistant professor in the Literacy and Early Education Department at California State University-Fresno. He teaches courses on literacy foundations, literacy assessment, and multicultural education. Dr. Hart's passion for service-learning and educational equity and justice is grounded in his extensive experience working with diverse student populations as a teacher in urban elementary schools in Norfolk, Virginia and

South San Francisco, California. He maintains this passion and extensively uses service-learning pedagogy and social justice education in his courses to better prepare teachers to become agents of change. Dr. Hart's research stemming from these experiences has been published in international teacher education journals, several book chapters, and presented at national and international conferences. Dr. Hart continues to work for educational justice and social change through his research investigating how critical literacy, service-learning, and multicultural education can converge to impact literacy education for diverse student populations and their teachers.

Chapter 13:

Susan L Herrmann is a licensed clinical social worker in New York and Oregon; presently in private practice and with a wide-variety of professional experiences in several private and public social agencies, as a service provider, supervisor, and educator. Currently, Susan is a doctoral student with the Fielding Graduate University in the school of Human and Organization Development concentrating on transformative learning for social justice. Susan sits on the board of directors for the Danang/Quang Nam Fund, (www.agentorangchildren.org), a nongovernmental organization that provides direct aid to the poor in Vietnam. Academic interests include transformative learning for social justice, critical theory, archetypal stories, and structural social work. A spouse and mother of four, Susan is a singer-songwriter who also enjoys cooking, gardening, and raising critically conscious and environmentally responsible children.

Chapter 14:

Brian Charles Charest is a doctoral student in English education at the University of Illinois at Chicago. He is a former high school teacher and service-learning coach in the Chicago Public Schools. His current scholarly interests include exploring how the philosophy of American pragmatism and the strategies developed by community organizers can inform the work of teachers and teacher educators. His dissertation project involves examining the efficacy of community organizing strategies as a way to help teachers develop a stronger voice in school wide and classroom decision making. In particular, he hopes to help practicing and preservice teachers develop civic literacies, or strategies for acting in public life, that will allow them to engage more effectively with others to enact creative solutions to the problems they find in schools.

Afterword:

Christie Billups coordinates service-learning and teaches theology at Lewis University in Romeoville, Illinois. She has been an educator in Catholic schools since 1988 and higher education since 2006, a jail minister from 1992 through 2008, and a liturgical musician since 1976. She has a master of arts in teaching from National Louis University, a master of arts in pastoral studies and a doctor of ministry degree from Catholic Theological Union (CTU) in Chicago. Beyond her classroom learning, Dr. Billups has traveled several times to Central America and the continent of Africa. She currently leads the efforts of a non-profit organization called Noté Karacel (Unite Together) in northern Uganda. It is this project which has inspired her musings about international service-learning. (learn more at www.notekaracel.org.)

CPSIA information can be obtained at www.ICGtesting.com
227974LV00001B/17/P
9 781617 35432